D0108935

Also by William Greider

The Trouble with Money
Secrets of the Temple
The Education of David Stockman and Other Americans

William Greider

WHO WILL TELL THE PEOPLE

The Betrayal
of American
Democracy

SIMON & SCHUSTER
New York · London · Toronto · Sydney · Tokyo · Singapore

SIMON & SCHUSTER
Simon & Schuster Building
Rockefeller Center
1230 Avenue of the Americas
New York, New York 10020

Designed by Levavi & Levavi
Manufactured in the United States of America

9 10 8

Library of Congress Cataloging in Publication Data
Greider, William.
    Who will tell the people: The betrayal of American de-
mocracy/William Greider.
        p.   cm.
    Includes bibliographical references and index.
    1. Political participation—United States. 2. Democracy—
United States. 3. Representative government and representation—United States. 4. Pressure groups—United States.
5. Political corruption—United States. 6. United States—Politics and government—1989–   I. Title.
JK1764.G74 1992
323′.042′0973—dc20   92-3514
                                                       CIP

ISBN: 0-671-68891-X

For Cameron McClure Greider and Katharine Smith Greider,
with love and awe

Contents

PART FOUR
TRIUMPH AND LOSS

Introduction:
Mutual Contempt

The decayed condition of American democracy is difficult to grasp, not because the facts are secret, but because the facts are visible everywhere. Symptoms of distress are accumulating freely in the political system and citizens are demoralized by the lack of coherent remedies. Given the recurring, disturbing facts, a climate of stagnant doubt has enveloped contemporary politics, a generalized sense of disappointment that is too diffuse and intangible to be easily confronted. The things that Americans were taught and still wish to believe about self-government—the articles of civic faith we loosely call democracy—no longer seem to fit the present reality.

This dissonance between fact and faith is so discomforting that many naturally turn away from the implications. The visible dysfunctions in politics are dismissed as a temporary aberration or explained away, cynically, as the way things always were. The reluctance and evasion are understandable: Some unwanted truths are too painful to face.

The blunt message of this book is that American democracy is in much deeper trouble than most people wish to acknowledge. Behind the reassuring facade, the regular election contests and so forth, the substantive meaning of self-government has been hollowed out. What exists behind the formal shell is a systemic breakdown of the shared civic values we call democracy.

Citizens are cut out of the politics surrounding the most important governing questions. The representative system has undergone a grotesque distortion of its original purpose. The connective tissues that in different ways once linked ordinary people to governing—political parties, the media, the secondary mediating institutions—no longer function reliably.

At the highest levels of government, the power to decide things has instead gravitated from the many to the few, just as ordinary citizens suspect. Instead of popular will, the government now responds more often to narrow webs of power—the interests of major economic organizations and concentrated wealth and the influential elites surrounding them. These organizations and individuals manage to shape the largest outcomes to the extent anyone does, while they neutralize or deflect what ordinary people think and believe.

In place of a meaningful democracy, the political community has embraced a permissive culture of false appearances. Government responds to the public's desires with an artful dance of symbolic gestures—hollow laws that are emptied of serious content in the private bargaining of Washington. Promises are made and never kept. Laws are enacted and never enforced. When ordinary people organize themselves to confront the deception, they find themselves too marginalized to make much difference.

Governing elites, not surprisingly, tend to their own self-interest but, even when their intentions are broadly public-spirited, the result is generally the same: The people are missing from the processes of self-government and government itself suffers from the loss. Disconnected from larger public purposes, people can neither contribute their thinking to the government's decisions nor take any real responsibility for them. Elite decision makers are unable to advance coherent governing agendas for the nation, however, since they are too isolated from common values and experiences to be persuasive. The result is an enervating sense of stalemate.

In sum, the mutual understanding between citizens and government necessary for genuine democracy is now deformed or neglected. While democracy's decline has consequences for everyone, certain sectors of the citizenry suffer from the loss of political representation more severely and personally than everyone else. In general, they are the people who already lack the advantages of higher education or social status. Their political influence cannot depend upon private wealth since they have little or none. The atrophied political system has left them even more vulnerable to domination by others.

While none of these complaints can be regarded as exactly a secret, there is a deeper dimension underlying the democratic problem that is not so easy for ordinary citizens to see. Democratic expectations are now confined and debilitated by the new power relationships that surround government and are buried in the everyday context of the nation's politics—tacit understandings that determine who has political power and who doesn't. These power relationships are rooted in the complexities that have changed American politics so profoundly over the last few decades, either the deep tides of culture and economics or the conscious political action of interested parties.

Uncovering the patterns of these underlying power realities will be the principal task of this book. They are difficult to discern amid all the bewildering daily facts, but they represent the real source of the general discontent with American politics. They are, likewise, the unpleasant truths that people wish not to face.

Many citizens, especially those closest to power, will be reflexively inclined to resist this diagnosis. Partisans typically claim that the governing problems can be blamed on the people now in power—either Republicans in the White House or the Democrats who control Congress. Others will observe that, whatever obvious flaws now exist, American democracy has always been afflicted by large imperfections and contradictions. Both claims are narrowly correct, of course, but they are also ways to evade the present reality. The roots of democratic decay, as this inquiry will demonstrate, are deeper than personalities or parties and the familiar ideological arguments; the system will not be cured by an election or two that change the officers of government. Furthermore, the nature of the civic breakdown is peculiar to our own time, reflecting our contemporary conditions and failures; the questions cannot be answered by reciting the shortcomings of previous eras.

Another reason why the actual condition of democracy is difficult to grasp is that the form and facade of self-government remain elaborately in place and functioning. In fact, the mechanics of electoral democracy are now more highly developed (and more costly) than at any other time in history. Collectively American voters will select more than five hundred thousand people to represent them in the public's business, from local sewer commissions to the White House. The results, as everyone knows, are so unsatisfying that the active electorate has been steadily shrinking for a generation and ''reforming'' elections has become a major preoccupation of public-spirited debate.

The distinguishing premise of this book, however, is that the democratic problem originates from a different source—the politics of governing, not the politics of winning elections. Most political inquiries focus their analysis on campaigns and candidates, the techniques of persuasion and of assembling electoral majorities, the contest of slogans and ideology and so forth.

This book is centered on the complicated politics that lies beyond elections—the practical questions of how and why some interests are allowed to dominate the government's decision making while others are excluded. After all, this is the realm of politics that matters to people in their everyday lives. And this is the realm where we will find tangible explanations for their discontent.

Politics is not a game. It exists to resolve the largest questions of the society—the agreed-upon terms by which everyone can live peaceably with one another. At its best, politics creates and sustains social relationships—the human conversation and engagement that draw people together and allow them to discover their mutuality. Democracy promises to do this through an inclusive process of conflict and deliberation, debate and compromise. Not every citizen expects to speak personally in the governing dialogue, but every citizen is entitled to feel authentically represented.

The substance of governing politics is the stuff that election campaigns and standard political commentaries mostly ignore—the nettlesome facts of decision making behind the rhetoric and slogans. Typically, political reporters separate "politics" from substantive "issues" as though they were two different subjects. Yet, in government, even the dimmest member of Congress understands that the substance *is* the politics. No one can hope to understand what is driving political behavior without grasping the internal facts of governing issues and asking the kinds of gut-level questions that politicians ask themselves in private. Who are the winners in this matter and who are the losers? Who gets the money and who has to pay? Who must be heard on this question and who can be safely ignored?

Thus in order to examine the condition of democracy, this inquiry will explore the contours of a lengthy list of governing issues, some familiar and some obscure, asking the same kinds of questions. Economics, taxation, the environment, education, national defense, financial regulation, wages and working conditions, labor law and corporate citizenship—all these and some others will appear as the raw material. In every case, the overriding purpose is to plot out patterns of behavior that are general in governing politics. As the evidence accumulates from different examples, the central goal is to reveal the deformed power relationships that explain why this democracy regularly disappoints its citizens.

This critique does not rely upon any idealized notions of what democracy means, but on the elementary principles everyone recognizes. Accountability of the governors to the governed. Equal protection of the law, that is, laws that are free of political manipulation. A presumption of political equality among all citizens (though not equality of wealth or status). The guarantee of timely access to the public debate. A rough sense of honesty in the communication between the government and the people. These are not radical ideas, but basic tenets of the civic faith.

Nor does this analysis pretend that American democracy once existed in some perfected form that now is lost. On the contrary, Americans have never achieved the full reality in their own history or even agreed completely on democracy's meaning. The democratic idea has always been most powerful in America as an unfulfilled vision of what the country might someday become—a society advancing imperfectly toward self-realization. In that sense, democracy is not so much a particular arrangement of government, but a difficult search. It is the hopeful promise the nation has made to itself.[1]

The search itself is now at risk—the democratic promise of advancing toward higher ground. From the beginning of the Republic, the redeeming quality of American politics—and the central virtue of democracy—has been the capacity for self-correction. That capacity is now endangered too.

A democratic governance is able to adjust to new realities because it is compelled to listen to many voices and, sooner or later, react to what people see and express. In the American experience, the governing system has usually found a way to pull back eventually from extreme swings or social impasse and to start off in new directions. Not perfectly, perhaps not right away, but in time it did fitfully respond. This capacity was more than a matter of good luck or great leaders. As American democracy evolved, multiple balance wheels and self-correcting mechanisms were put in place that encourage this. They promote stability, but they also leave space for invention and new ideas, reform and change.

These self-correcting mechanisms are such familiar features of politics as the running competition for power between the two political parties, the scrutiny by the press and reform critics, the natural tension inherent in the coequal branches of government, the sober monitor imposed by law and the Constitution, the political energies that arise naturally from free people when they organize themselves for collective expression. People are counting on these corrective mechanisms to assert themselves again, as they usually have in the past.

The most troubling proposition in this book is that the self-correcting mechanisms of politics are no longer working. Most of them are still in place and functioning but, for the most part, do not produce the expected results. Some of the mechanisms have disappeared entirely. Some are atrophied or blocked by new circumstances. Some have become so warped and disfigured that they now concretely aggravate the imbalance of power between the many and the few.

That breakdown describes the democratic problem in its bleakest dimensions: Instead of a politics that leads the society sooner or later to confront its problems, American politics has developed new ways to hide from them.

The consequences of democratic failure are enormous for the country, not simply because important public matters are neglected, but because America won't work as a society if the civic faith is lost. Unlike most other nations, the United States has always overcome the vast differences among its people, the social and economic enmities and the storms of political disagreement, through the overarching bond of its democratic understandings. If these connections between the governed and the government are destroyed, if citizens can no

longer believe in the mutuality of the American experience, the country may
descend into a new kind of social chaos and political unraveling, unlike
anything we have experienced before. The early symptoms of such deterioration may already be visible.

Naturally enough, most people focus on narrower, less disturbing explanations of what is wrong. In the standard political dialogues, especially among
elites, the discussions generally settle on three familiar ways of explaining the
current political distress. The problem is diagnosed, for instance, as the failure
of ill-informed citizens and the exaltation of fickle public opinion. Or the
problem is attributed to the format of modern election campaigns and the
elaborate electioneering technologies surrounding candidates. Or it is defined,
more bluntly, as a problem of dirty money, the millions of dollars in campaign
contributions that flow to the politicians.

None of these is entirely wrong, but all are inadequate to the true scope of
the democratic problem. In order to proceed with an examination into deeper
causes, let us first take up these conventional ways that people think about the
troubled democracy and explain why each falls short. In doing so, I hope to
demonstrate that the only way out of the political distress is to address the
democratic problem in its fullest terms, whole and direct, as though the civic
principles still matter to us.

Many years ago, when I was a young reporter covering the Kentucky state
legislature, I witnessed for the first time a spectacle of democracy that is not
mentioned in the civics textbooks. In the midst of debate, the legislators
erupted in noisy chaos—shouting wildly at one another and throwing papers in
the air, charging randomly around the House chamber like angry children in
a group tantrum. As I later learned, any representative assembly may occasionally experience such moments of bedlam, from city councils to the Congress. They occur on especially divisive issues, when the emotional
frustrations boil up and overwhelm decorum.

At the time, I was quite shocked, a measure of my youthful innocence. A
jaded old statehouse reporter noticed my astonishment and offered some perspective on the unruly behavior of the elected representatives.

"If you think these guys are bad," he said, "you should see their constituents."

His wisecrack was wickedly funny but, as I came to understand in subsequent years, it also stated an inescapable truth about representative democracy. At its best moments and its worst, the democratic system is a kind of
two-way mirror between the people and those who are chosen to represent
them. It reflects the warts and virtues back and forth between them. Sometimes, as if in a funhouse mirror, the image of politics becomes grotesquely

distorted and mocks the public's virtuous sense of itself. At other moments, the mirror reflects political behavior that confirms and even exalts the public's self-esteem.

Either way, people cannot easily escape from the connection. If Washington is a city infested by fools and knaves, where did they come from and who sent them? If citizens do not like what they see in the mirror, what do they intend to do about it?

This tension is as old as the Republic, but a peculiar dimension has developed in modern politics. Politicians are held in contempt by the public. That is well known and not exactly new in American history. What is less well understood (and rarely talked about for the obvious reasons) is the deep contempt politicians have for the general public.

Politicians, rather like priests or police officers, are regularly exposed to the least attractive qualities of human nature—gaudy dimensions of greed and confusion and mindless fear. It requires strong character for a politician to resist cynicism and retain an idealistic sense of the democratic possibilities. The speeches invoking "the people" as the sacred source of political power have taken on a mocking ring for many.

A Washington lobbyist, a former congressional aide with close relations to influential Senate Democrats, described the perspective with more candor than is allowed to politicians. "This city is full of people who don't like themselves, don't like their jobs and don't like their constituents—and I mean actively don't like their constituents," the lobbyist told me not long ago. "I'm convinced one of the reasons they are in session so long is that members of Congress have gotten used to being here and they don't like going home where they have to talk to a bunch of Rotarians and play up to local leaders who are just dumb as stumps. They prefer to be here, to be around people they know and like and who understand them—lawyers, lobbyists, the press and so forth."

Alienation, in other words, runs both ways. The mutual contempt that divides the governed from the governing authorities is the attitude underlying everything else in modern politics, both a symptom of the decay and an active agent in furthering the deterioration. In many private quarters of Washington, Alexander Hamilton's derisive dictum—"The People! The People is a great beast!"—has become an operating maxim. Survival in office requires a political strategy for herding "the beast" in harmless directions or deflecting it from serious matters it may not understand. Now and then, to the general dismay of political elites, Hamilton's "beast" breaks loose and tramples the civility of the regular order, though this usually occurs on inflammatory marginal issues that have little to do with the real substance of governing.[2]

Political elites, nonetheless, complain constantly of their own powerlessness to govern. They depict the system as the hostage of random public opinion—a "plebiscite democracy" directly wired to every whim reflected in the polls and unable to lead in difficult directions. Among themselves, establishment leaders talk, somewhat nostalgically, about the old days when a handful of party leaders could dictate the terms of national legislation. They ponder structural reforms that might somehow restore centralized party control and insulate politicians further from the fickle voters so that "leadership" could flourish once again. Their anxieties, though sincere, would seem most bizarre to the millions of alienated voters who feel left out and ignored.[3]

Voters do sometimes resemble a leaderless mob—at least that is how they look through the lens of contemporary political events. They are ignorant on important matters and turn away from complexity. They do charge this way and that, spilling bile or temporary enthusiasms on the public arena, then moving quickly to something else. The jaded perspective shared privately among elected representatives is not altogether wrong. However, if the representative structure were someday altered to shield officeholders and distance citizens even further from power, the "people" would likely become even more disruptive.

Whatever frailty and infirmities dwell in the populace, Americans of today are not, on the whole, less capable than their forebears. But the political culture, the terms and conditions that now circumscribe democratic expression, certainly makes them look that way.

If citizens sometimes behave irresponsibly in politics, it is the role assigned to them. They have lost any other way to act, any means for influencing the governing process in positive and broad-minded terms. The subject of how ordinary people have been gradually cut out of a responsible place in the governing process (and how they still struggle to attain a share of power) will reappear in many forms throughout this book. It is one side of the two-way mirror and, in my thinking, the more important side.

Citizens have been pushed into two cramped roles in politics, neither of which can satisfy their own aspirations or the requirements for a functioning democracy. Both also tend to disturb the governing process that elites are concerned about. In one role, citizens are the mindless mass audience that looks so dumb—the faceless crowd that speaks in politics mainly through opinion polls. They are the spectators who react clumsily to only the most vivid events, a war or sex scandal or pretty TV commercials.

In this embodiment, the "people" are always present in the political debates, but mainly as scarecrows or totems invoked on behalf of someone else's argument. The rich and complicated diversity of the nation is reduced to a lumpish commodity called "public opinion" that is easily manipulated by the slogans and imagery of mass communications. While the spectators watch a political drama unfold, the media and polling companies instantly tote up their "responses" and feed the results back to the politicians.

The other narrow role open to citizens is as special pleaders, defending their own stuff against other aspirants. Millions of Americans are organized quite effectively for this kind of politics, whether as consumers or petitioners for special benefits or the victims of particular abuses. Some well-known citizen organizations—the American Association of Retired Persons, the National Rifle Association or the American Israel Public Affairs Committee, for instance—are formidable powers on their own terrain and they guard the subjects dear to their members like burly pickets. Self-interested pleas are the warp of democratic politics and always will be, of course, but the contours of modern government make it very difficult for citizens to accomplish anything else.

These two forms of political presence—the mindless mass audience and the churlish preoccupation with self-interest—are the familiar grist of political analysis and have been exhaustively examined. This book concentrates, instead, on the vast political space that is concealed by those two facile characterizations—the ground where citizens are allowed to connect with political issues larger than self, where their self-interest is harmonized with their broader expectations for the society. That political space is now empty on most important subjects—the vast middle ground where democracy has shrunk and citizens have lost their voice.

That observation does not presume that, a generation ago, there was a halcyon era when everyone felt represented on all the major matters in politics, but the politics that constructs such connections and keeps them in good repair has been severely stunted by modern conditions. This is the politics of building reliable mediating mechanisms that enable people to connect with the higher realms of decision making. It is the development of two-way channels of communication that both educate and listen. It is the many strands of connective tissue, both public and private, between the governed and those in power. Without these, most citizens will be rendered silent.

A central social irony is involved in this, one that elite critics seem to find difficult to grasp: The disorders of the governing process they worry about are rooted in this same territory of the debilitated citizens. If the government cannot govern effectively, it is not because the "people" are swarming over it with impossible demands, but because the bonds of dialogue and mutual understanding between citizens and government have become so weakened. The governing problem and the democratic problem are one and the same, created by the same circumstances.

Restoring a climate for responsible governing may thus require the opposite of what the elite analysis supposes. Instead of distancing people further from government decisions, it would entail bringing citizens back into the process in ways that seem genuine to them—that will allow citizens to feel responsible again for self-government.

Many in the mass audience, it has to be acknowledged, are uninterested in this prospect. Despite their grumblings, they have accepted the loss of status without complaint, neither knowing what political capabilities used to exist for them nor able to imagine what might be constructed in the future. Ernesto Cortes, Jr., a highly regarded community organizer from San Antonio, Texas, has observed that Lord Acton's oft-quoted aphorism—"power tends to corrupt . . ."—works both ways.

"Powerlessness also corrupts," Cortes said. "We've got a lot of people who've never developed an understanding of power. They've been institutionally trained to be passive. Power is nothing more than the ability to act in your own behalf. In Spanish, we call the word *poder*, to have capacity, to be able."[4]

The process by which the citizens of America lost the capacity to speak to power in their own behalf is long and complex (and began well before the present era of politics). Many different elements are involved, among them the institutional arrangements in politics, the rise of mass communications, the language of the expert policy dialogue that surrounds the machinery of modern government. While the complexity makes the loss difficult to visualize, most of the elements are not buried secrets, but familiar features of the everyday political landscape.

The transformation of these features was decisive, however. The most obvious one is the atrophied condition of the two-party political system. For all their flaws, the parties once provided a viable connection for citizens, even quite humble citizens, to the upper realms of politics. People who would never be present themselves in the debate, who lacked the resources or the sophistication to participate directly, had a place to go—a permanent organization where their views would be taken into account and perhaps mobilized to influence the government.

The parties atrophied as organizations for many reasons—social and political changes as well as their own undemocratic qualities. When they were stronger, the mechanics of party control were often closely held (and regularly abused) to favor certain citizens and interests while excluding others, especially racial minorities and the disorganized segments of society.

Nevertheless, the easiest way to visualize the empty space that now exists in American politics is to consider what party organizations used to do for people—and what none of the existing institutions of politics does for them now.

If democracy has lost any accountability to the governed, it is because there is no longer any reliable linkage between citizens and those who hold power. If the people sometimes seem dumb in public affairs, it is because no institution takes responsibility for teaching them or for listening to them. If communities now feel more distant from Washington, it is because they are.

Another familiar way of explaining the decline of politics focuses on the deterioration of elections and campaigns. The decline of electoral politics has been underway for at least a generation and is now so advanced that even political elites have become preoccupied with its implications. If the people no longer believe in elections, will they continue to believe in the power of the elected to govern their lives?

Every season, new discussions are convened around the subject, searching for the mechanical "reforms" that might restore faith in elections. A veritable fortune in foundation grants has been spent trying to devise solutions—educating inert voters or promoting old-style candidate debates or discouraging negative campaign tactics. Despite these good intentions, the active electorate continues to shrink and, as we will discuss at a later point, the shrinkage is almost certain to continue well into the future.

By focusing on the electoral process, these inquiries unconsciously define the meaning of citizenship in rather narrow and passive terms—citizens whose only role is to show up every couple of years and mark a ballot. Nevertheless, the steady decline in voting is the most visible evidence that something is wrong. Elections are the most direct link to governing power—the collective lever that is meant to make citizens sovereign and officeholders accountable to them. So why don't people use it, especially when they are so unhappy with government?

Since 1960, voting in presidential elections is down 20 percent (and down 30 percent outside the South where the newly enfranchised black citizens raised participation rates). Roughly half of adult America stays home, despite the hoopla and extraordinarily expensive campaigns for the presidency. Elected power in the representative branch rests on an even narrower base—a third or less of the electorate. In typical off-year elections, important senators and representatives are returned to office on the votes of small minorities, often as little as 15 percent or 20 percent of their constituents.

Nor are elections the satisfying public rituals they used to be—dramas that renew the popular faith in self-government. After the 1990 congressional contests, three in four Americans said they were not very satisfied with the outcomes, even when their candidates won.[5]

Paul Weyrich, a New Right conservative who heads the Free Congress Foundation, thinks the very legitimacy of government is at stake in those statistics, that people are sending a message the political system does not wish to hear. "We're perilously close to not having democracy," Weyrich said. "I worry about it night and day. Nonvoters are voting against the system and, if we get a bit more of that, the system won't work.''

What the disenchanted are saying, what I have heard them say in many different places, is that the politics of elections seem pointless to them—no longer connected to anything that really matters. Partisan attachments are still active, of course, but much weaker among Americans than they used to be. For most citizens, the point of holding elections is not simply to pick Republicans over Democrats (or vice versa) but to decide something real. Elections no longer seem like efficacious exercises for achieving that purpose.

The disconnection between electoral politics and governing was vividly illustrated in 1988 when a Washington polling firm posed a piquant question to voters a few days before the presidential election. Aside from what Bush and Dukakis are saying in their campaigns, what do you want the next president to pursue? The public responded with an unusual list of priorities:

Make sure the wealthy and big corporations pay their fair share of taxes (important to 77 percent; unimportant to 5 percent). Impose stricter environmental regulation on companies that produce toxic wastes (66 percent to 5 percent). Help the poor and homeless to find jobs and earn a decent living (66 percent to 5 percent). Protect American jobs from foreign competition by tougher trade laws (59 percent to 8 percent). Provide long-term health care and health insurance for everyone (55 percent to 5 percent).

The list seems jarring because, as everyone knows, these were not the mobilizing issues of George Bush's campaign nor did they remotely reflect his own priorities. Yet these are the same people who a few days later elected him president. It was only well down the list of the public's agenda that a significant minority could be found for some of Bush's principal goals—no new taxes (45 percent) or appointing antiabortion justices to the Supreme Court (35 percent). As opinion polls reported, however, most voters assumed that Bush's ''no new taxes'' pledge was a cynical campaign ploy. They expected him to break the promise once in power and were not especially surprised when he eventually did.[6]

The larger point is that these expressions of popular aspirations did not matter. No one would take them seriously, not the press or even rival politicians. The opinions were regarded as an idle ''wish list'' disconnected from the governing process. As president, George Bush would govern in a manner directly contrary to most of these particular public desires. Everyone understood this—including the voters. The disconnection is so commonplace that it now seems ''normal'' to almost everyone.

Indeed, the idea of accountability has actually been reversed in the logic of modern political analysis: Whatever the winning candidate wants and believes about government, it is conventionally inferred that the voters must want the same. Why else would they have voted for him? Thus, the voters become dependent on the politicians for their political positions rather than the other way around.

The common wisdom of politics has therefore settled on a much narrower idea of what elections are for—elections are a search for good character. Issues and ideas may provide the fodder of campaigns, but these are mainly useful in illuminating the temperament of the men and women who are running. Are they wise and honest people? Or do they have some hidden flaw? This definition allows conscientious observers to retain their faith in the electoral process and defend its efficacy.

Constructing campaigns around the character and celebrity of the candidates provides another convenient way to empty them of the substantive content of governing. If the search is mainly for good character, then the only "issues" that matter in electoral politics are ones that may help identify the candidate's personal qualities (or denigrate his opponent's). Thus, campaigns turn naturally to irrelevances that provide quick emotional attachments, but have no connection to the real sources of popular discontent.

Electoral politics in the age of mass communications serves as an elaborate mask—concealing what goes on in government from the untutored mass of voters. But, if the voters have only weak influence over those governing decisions, then who does influence them? That is the question neither political party will discuss with any candor, but citizens at large have inferred the answer. In the 1960s, surveys found that 28 percent of the public was convinced that "the government is pretty much run by a few big interests looking out for themselves." A generation later, this resigned view of politics was held by two thirds of the people.[7]

No amount of tinkering with the mechanics of electioneering is likely to reach the sources of that resignation because none of the people who are in power—neither Democrats nor Republicans nor their allied interests—have any incentive to remove the mask (and perhaps much to lose if they did). After all, it works for them. The elected officials of both parties, as well as their supporting interests, understand that their power relationships are sustained by the present arrangement of empty elections. They may occasionally lament the decline in voting, but incumbents are not threatened by this. The fewer citizens who are paying attention and actually voting, the easier it will be for the status quo to endure.

Against these bleak facts, there is a crucial contrary truth, one that is seldom acknowledged and, therefore, not widely understood. It is this: The nation is alive with irregular political energies, despite the failure of formal electoral politics. Citizens of every stripe and status do engage themselves one way or another in trying to move the public agenda, despite all the impediments. Though they may have given up on elections, ordinary citizens do still struggle for democratic meaning, and with imaginative diversity.

Americans have always organized themselves in the myriad "voluntary associations" that de Tocqueville observed in the young Republic, but if anything, the tradition has taken on a kind of manic quality in modern politics. There are literally millions of groups and associations pursuing politics in the broad sense of the word, everything from huge free-floating national organizations to neighborhood crime patrols. Some citizens are attached to so many public causes, they resemble a collage of bumper stickers.

Some of these activities, like the major environmental organizations, have developed real but limited political influence through their ability to define the outlines of the public problems and formulate goals that feed into the main political debate. More typically, citizen politics is detached from any formal structure of political power and, therefore, quite weak.

Even the environmental movement is not able to translate its general public support and potential power into real results since, as the evidence will show, its goals are regularly stalled and subverted by the governing system, even when it wins. The environmentalists' potential is enormous but largely unrealized, as their corporate adversaries recognize. Frank Mankiewicz, a liberal activist from the Kennedy era who is now an executive at Hill & Knowlton, the influential public-relations firm, provided a candid glimpse of their nervousness.

"The big corporations, our clients, are scared shitless of the environmental movement," Mankiewicz confided. "They sense that there's a majority out there and that the emotions are all on the other side—if they can be heard. They think the politicians are going to yield to the emotions. I think the corporations are wrong about that. I think the companies will have to give in only at insignificant levels. Because the companies are too strong, they're the establishment. The environmentalists are going to have to be like the mob in the square in Romania before they prevail."

The irregular politics underway in every corner of the nation provides an optimistic counterpoint for the story this book has to tell about Washington. The contrasting facts of people trying to be heard on large governing decisions, while the governing system responds evasively or not at all, confirm that the democratic impulse is alive. But their difficult experiences confirm also that the impulse is effectively blocked in modern politics.

Some citizens are reduced to flamboyant forms of street theater or even physical disruption in order to make their point. Many are obsessed with the news media because the press seems like their only chance of being noticed or accomplishing anything. Some citizens have become skillful political guerrillas, adept in the tactics of obstructing the government and negating the polit-ical agendas they could not otherwise influence.

Conscientious citizens, in other words, have also been stunted by the circumstances of the modern political system. They may blast away at power with telling critiques or try obstinately to block its path. But most cannot imagine the possibility of forming a continuing relationship with power—a political system that would enable them to share in the governing processes and trust in its outcomes. Even alert, active people have internalized a shriv-eled version of democratic possibility.

The scandalous question that hangs over modern government and excites perpetual outrage is about political money and what it buys. What exactly do these contributors get in return for the hundreds of thousands, even millions of dollars they funnel to the politicians? For many people, money explains almost everything about why democracy is in trouble, and exhaustive investigations are devoted to searching for hard evidence of bribery. The general pattern is more ambiguous than the cynics imagine, though still not very comforting to democracy.

What do major contributors get for their money? When I asked a lobbyist of long acquaintance who had served as the self-described "money guy" for selected Democratic senators, he responded with flavorful directness. "This was the period when we were shifting from black bags to accounting and disclosure," Charles Fishman explained, "and I knew how to shake the money tree. After the campaign-finance reforms were enacted, that's when the hor-rendous spigot was turned on. I phased out of fund raising and became a contributor myself.

"Different people wanted different things," Fishman recalled. "You han-dled 90 percent of them with a hand job. You played on their minds. It was dinner with the senator or serving on an advisory committee. You could take care of them socially. Ten percent were out to buy you, for whatever purpose, their industry or whatever. They weren't trying to buy you so much as to keep you where you were on their issue. The smart guys were the ones who came at you on something where you didn't have a position.

"The reaction to this depended on your guy. If you had a senator like Adlai Stevenson, he'd throw you out of the office. He reamed my ass one day because I brought in a guy who was too aggressive in what he was saying. He kept saying: 'I expect . . . I expect . . . Let's understand what we're doing here. . . .' Then there were other senators who said to me: 'Get out of the room. I want to talk to this guy alone.' That's when it happens—when they're talking one on one."

Enterprising reporters and reformers who keep the seamy subject of campaign money on the front pages are encouraged to do so by a time-honored syllogism of democracy: Dig out the sordid facts, expose them to the people and public outrage will lead to reforms. The trouble is, this logic doesn't seem to be working anymore. One money scandal after another has been offered to the public in recent years, lurid tales of senators and others trying to fix things in government for their big-bucks contributors. But reform does not follow. The system does not get repaired. The parade of scandals simply continues— "rituals of purification," as Lewis Lapham called them.[8]

The deleterious effects of money are real enough, but the argument of this book is that money scandals reflect not just simple bribery, but much larger and more systemic disorders in governance. As the modern system has evolved, the complexity and diffusion of decision-making points in the federal government have multiplied the opportunities for irregular intervention and bargaining on behalf of interested parties. Nothing in law ever seems finally settled now because there is always one more stop in the process where both losers and winners may try to negotiate different terms.

The federal government has thus become a vast arena for bargaining and deal making on every conceivable question. This reality, in turn, has fostered a permissive culture in Washington politics that tolerates loose legal standards and extracurricular actions far beyond the view of citizens or formal accountability. The campaign money lubricates the deal making, to be sure, but the debilitating impact on democracy would endure, even if money were magically eliminated from politics.

Everyone lives in this political environment and adapts to it, whether he or she is clean or dirty in the handling of campaign money. A newly elected representative quickly discovers that his job in government—aside from making new laws—is to act as a broker, middleman, special pleader and finagler. In casual conversation, a senator spoke unself-consciously about "my client," meaning a defense contractor in his home state who was quarreling with the Pentagon over contract bids. The senator worried aloud about whether to go to bat for the firm since its campaign donations to him might smell bad, if his intervention were ever exposed.

"Client" has a different meaning from "constituent" or "citizen," but the word accurately describes the common relationships that define contemporary politics. The representative structure has been transformed into something quite offensive to its original intent—a system in which it is nearly impossible to distinguish the relatively honest, hard-working politicians from the old-fashioned crooks, since they both do the same chores for clients. One must examine motives or eavesdrop on private conversations to establish if a political transaction was bribery or the normal daily business of Washington.

In fact, while Congress is most visible in this arena, the legislators are often only peripheral players. The well-placed officers of the Executive Branch, as the facts will show, do the same sort of work every day on behalf of their clients but with more influence over the outcomes and much less risk of exposure.

Politicians, in other words, are trapped in their own debilitating circumstances, as much as citizens are trapped in theirs. This is why the money scandals do not lead to meaningful reforms—because even the most honorable lawmakers know that they too are implicated in the moral ambiguities created by the governing system.

Evidence for this conclusion is abundant and appeared most vividly in the celebrated Keating Five scandal of 1990, in which five senators were accused of fixing things for an important contributor from the savings and loan industry. Despite sensational facts, the Senate ethics investigation ended limply and without meaningful disciplinary action. Fellow senators likewise balked at punishing Senator Alfonse D'Amato of New York though he was caught in a series of transactions that earned him the label "Senator Sleaze." D'Amato explained their reluctance as he defended his own behavior. "There but for the grace of God go most of my colleagues," he said. Even colleagues who despised D'Amato's flagrant deals recognized his point.[9]

If this analysis is correct, if the recurring money scandals are really symptoms of deeper pathologies in the way the government is organized and functions, then it opens up propositions that are even more difficult and disturbing than reformers imagine. Among other things, it suggests there are no easy "villains" to be indicted in the search for a restored democracy but a much heavier burden. It points toward terrain that many will find threatening—reexamining the very modes and methodologies embedded in the common politics of Washington, confronting the permissiveness about law that has become the shared standard for Republicans and Democrats alike.

This search may be especially painful to those who think of themselves as liberals or progressives because part of what we are talking about is actually the inheritance from the New Deal era—one of the great moments for democratic reform in the nation's history. The New Deal created many new corrective mechanisms in government designed to redress the imbalances of power—programs and operating features intended to protect the weak from the strong and give many excluded sectors of the population a seat at the table in politics. On the whole, these innovations worked effectively for a generation or longer and some of them still work.

But the New Deal legacy rests upon an idea of interest-group bargaining that has gradually been transformed into the random deal making and permissiveness of the present. The alterations in the system are decisive and, given everything else that has changed in politics, the ultimate effects are antidemocratic. People with limited resources, with no real representation in the higher levels of politics, are bound to lose in this environment.

The painful irony this book explores in different quarters is how the reforms of an earlier generation have become encrusted as new barriers to democratic meaning. The burden of the present is to find new ways around those obstacles.

The contest of American politics has always been a dynamic drama of "organized money and organized people," as Ernie Cortes put it. Nothing is ever likely to change that. What is missing in contemporary politics, however, is a clear understanding of how this conflict has been changed and why power has accumulated steadily in the direction of "organized money."

Americans find it awkward to examine power directly. The democratic ethos discourages frank discussion, and everyone in politics, including the most powerful, understands that it is unwise to boast about having more influence than others. Important economic interests are sensitive to democratic attitudes and typically seek out allies that do not themselves seem so powerful. Community bankers are recruited to speak for banking. Small-town insurance agents lobby for mammoth insurance companies; independent drillers and gas-station operators defend big oil.

Given the wonderful fluidity and diversity of American life, power is also difficult to pin down in concrete terms. The confusing features of the social reality have frustrated critics and led some to make elaborate road maps of the powerful, lists of the people and institutions said to be running America—the two hundred largest corporations, the fifty biggest banks and so forth. The lists prove what most people already understand: Money is power in American politics. It always has been.[10]

This book approaches the subject of power from a different angle—not to make road maps, but to explore the functional realities of government that will illuminate why some powerful interests manage to prevail with some consistency, while the broad public is assigned to a lesser rank. It is these warped power relationships between people and monied interests and government that tangibly define the democratic problem.

As the evidence accumulates, it should be clear that the mystery of how these new power relationships developed is much too complex to be explained by simple moralisms. On one level, powerful economic interests—corporations and private wealth—actively set out to seize the high ground of politics by deploying their superior resources and they largely succeeded. In another dimension, however, these powerful interests were merely reacting to the same destabilizing political changes that confronted everyone else. Out of practical necessity, defending their own well-being, they adapted better than others. "Organized money" is ascendant and "organized people" are inert because money has learned how to do modern politics more effectively than anyone else.

The fundamentals of how and why this condition occurred are set out in the six chapters that form Part I of this book, "Realities of Power." From Congress to the complex chambers of the Executive Branch, a series of invisible fences have been erected around important public issues—operating practices and assumptions that both exclude people from the action and subvert such elementary principles as equal protection of the law. The result is government decisions on matters people care about intensely, from taxation to environmental protection, that are cloaked in reassuring rhetoric but driven by favoritism and manipulation on behalf of monied interests.

The fences include the very language and texture of the contemporary political debate, a mystique of rationality that gives natural advantage to educated elites and corporate interests while shunning the values expressed by ordinary citizens. This common barrier is the focus of Chapter One, illustrated by issues ranging from clean air to junk bonds.

Chapter Two, "Who Will Tell the People?," examines the breakdown of the representative system itself and another barrier—the culture of political clientism. It will answer an intriguing political question about the now-familiar savings and loan disaster: How exactly did the politicians from both parties manage to keep this from the people for so many years and then dump a huge liability on the taxpayers? It turns out that self-correcting mechanisms in both government and the media are nonfunctional.

Chapter Three, "Bait and Switch," moves to a deeper and more sophisticated plane of political control—the artful illusions and bipartisan collusion by which monied interests succeeded in steadily reducing their federal tax burdens over fifteen years while everyone else was compelled to pay more. Taxation, after all, is not an obscure subject that citizens don't much care about. How were the few able to win, year after year, at the expense of the many?

Chapter Four, "The Grand Bazaar," confronts territory that is less familiar to people—the permissive culture of deal making and regulatory bargaining that permeates Washington and underlies virtually every aspect of governing decisions, both in Congress and in the Executive Branch. The result is random law enforcement, so subject to political manipulation that it creates a kind of lawless government in which the weakest players, like injured industrial workers, are left to defend themselves against the more powerful violators.

Chapter Five, "Hollow Laws," reveals the operating methodologies that enable Congress and the Executive Branch to enact hollow laws—grand pronouncements on toxic wastes and other problems designed to sound responsive to the public, but also designed to be neutered or neglected later in the dense details of the regulatory government. In this realm, meaningless laws exist, not just for years, but for decades, and the political action never ends. In this realm of politics, most citizens cannot play.

Finally, the capstone of this system is the White House, and Chapter Six, "The Fixers," describes how irregular political intervention on behalf of powerful clients is now institutionalized there—out of public sight and beyond democratic accountability. In sum, from Congress to the White House to the federal courts, there is no protected ground for citizens—no corner of the political system that faithfully defends their interests or even tells them the truth about what is happening.

Part II, "How May the People Speak to Power?," turns from the deformed governing system to the people themselves—the irregular politics of active citizens who are struggling to overcome these disadvantages. Their experiences confirm the bleak analysis of the power realities in Washington. But their struggles also demonstrate their own weaknesses. Citizens have largely confined themselves to the margins of politics, distant from formal power—using "rude and crude" tactics that reflect how disconnected they are, when there are no mediating institutions to speak for them.

Part III, "Mediating Voices," confronts the core political institutions that have failed the people—the two major political parties, the press and the mass-media culture. Each in different ways has lost the ability to mediate for the people at large, but each has also converged with the powerful elite interests that dominate politics. Ironically, the only viable mediating institution in contemporary politics—the dynamic player that has filled the vacuum—is the corporate political organization. Corporations speak for their own interests, but they also claim to speak for others. In their own way, they have taken the place of political parties.

Finally, the deterioration of American democracy is now enveloped by larger forces—the politics of the world—and this reality is addressed in Part IV, "Triumph and Loss." The end of the Cold War offers a historic opening for Americans to rehabilitate the democratic principles that were corrupted by the long struggle with Soviet communism. Yet the global economy is confronting American democracy with the prospect of great loss—the steady erosion of national sovereignty, the power to enforce laws, and the widely shared prosperity that supports social amity. The democratic challenge now requires new democratic sensibilities—larger than the nation's borders.

All these burdensome facts need not lead to despair, however, and the conclusion, "The American Moment," describes why it is possible to imagine a regenerating politics that restores democratic meaning. People have it within their power to overcome all of these obstacles and restore a general sense of mutual respect to public life.

That is the hard work of democracy, but it is not more daunting than what

people faced and overcame at different times in America's past. The politics
of restoration will start, not in Washington, but in many other places, separately and together, when people decide to close the gap between what they
believe and what is. People may begin this work by understanding what they
are up against.

REALITIES
OF
POWER

PART ONE

REALITIES
OF
POWER

1

MOCK DEMOCRACY

In a democracy, everyone is free to join the argument, or so it is said in civic mythology. In the modern democracy that has evolved, that claim is nearly meaningless. During the last generation, a "new politics" has enveloped government that guarantees the exclusion of most Americans from the debate—the expensive politics of facts and information.

A major industry has grown up in Washington around what might be called "democracy for hire"—business firms and outposts of sponsored scholars devoted to concocting facts and opinions and expert analysis, then aiming them at the government. That is the principal function of all those enterprises along Washington's main boulevards like K Street—the public-relations agencies, the direct-mail companies and opinion-polling firms. All these work in concert with the infrastructure of think tanks, tax-exempt foundations and other centers that churn out reams of policy ideas for the political debate. Most are financed by corporate interests and wealthy benefactors. The work of lobbyists and lawyers involves delivering the material to the appropriate legislators and administrators.

Only those who have accumulated lots of money are free to play in this version of democracy. Only those with a strong, immediate financial stake in the political outcomes can afford to invest this kind of money in manipulating the governing decisions. Most Americans have neither the personal ability nor the wherewithal to compete on this field.

The contours of this barrier are embedded in the very texture of everyday political debate itself. Citizens have been incapacitated, quite literally, because they do not speak the language. Modern methodologies of persuasion have created a new hierarchy of influence over government decisions—a new way in which organized money dominates the action while the unorganized voices of citizens are inhibited from speaking. A lonely congressman, trying to represent the larger public interest, finds himself arrayed against an army of authorities—working for the other side.

Beyond the fact of unequal resources, however, lies a more troubling proposition: that democracy is now held captive by the mystique of "rational" policymaking, narrow assumptions about what constitutes legitimate political evidence. It is a barrier of privilege because it effectively discounts authentic political expressions from citizens and elevates the biases and opinions of the elites.

This mystique, not surprisingly, is embraced and exalted by well-educated citizens of most every persuasion, the people who are equipped with professional skills and expertise, including the dedicated reformers who attempt to speak for the larger public. After all, it is the basis for their own primacy in political action. Yet the premise of rationality, as the evidence demonstrates, is deeply flawed and routinely biased in its applications.

For those who are active every day in the conventional politics of governing, this proposition may not be so easy to grasp. Indeed, it will seem quite threatening to some of them, for it challenges their own deeply held beliefs about how politics is supposed to work and puts in question the meaning of their own political labors. Ordinary citizens, those who are distant from power, will have much less difficulty seeing the truth of the argument—that information-driven politics has become a convenient reason to ignore them.

Jack Bonner, an intense young denizen of K Street, has the squirrelly enthusiasm of a salesman who can't stop talking about his product because he truly believes in it. What Bonner's firm sells is democracy, not the abstract version found in textbooks, but the living, breathing kind that occurs when people call up a senator and tell him how to vote. Bonner & Associates packages democratic expression and sells it to corporate clients—drug manufacturers and the cosmetic industry, insurance companies and cigarette makers and the major banks.

Jack Bonner's firm is an exotic but relatively small example of the vast information industry that now surrounds the legislative debate and government in general. You want facts to support the industry's lobbying claims? It pumps out facts. You want expert opinions from scholars? It has those in abundance from the think tanks corporate contributors underwrite. You want opinion polls? It hires polling firms to produce them. You want people—live voters who support the industry position? Jack Bonner delivers them.

When the Senate was debating the new clean-air legislation in 1990, certain wavering senators received pleas from the grassroots on the question of controlling automobile pollution. The Big Brothers and Big Sisters of the Mahoning Valley wrote to Senator John Glenn of Ohio. Sam Nunn of Georgia heard from the Georgia Baptist Convention and its 1.2 million members. The Easter Seal Society of South Dakota lobbied Senator Thomas A. Daschle. The Delaware Paralyzed Veterans Association contacted Senator William V. Roth, Jr.

These groups and some others declared their opposition to the pending clean-air amendment that would compel the auto industry to improve the average fuel efficiency of its cars substantially. The measure would both conserve energy and reduce the carbon-dioxide pollution that is the main source of global warming. These citizen organizations were persuaded to take a stand by Bonner & Associates, which informed them, consistent with the auto industry's political propaganda, that tougher fuel standards would make it impossible to manufacture any vehicles larger than a Ford Escort or a Honda Civic.

Vans and station wagons, small trucks and high-speed police cruisers, they were told, would cease to exist. The National Sheriffs Association was aroused by the thought of chasing criminals in a Honda Civic. The Nebraska Farm Bureau said rural America would be "devastated" if farmers tried to pull a trailer loaded with livestock or hay with a Ford Escort.

For twenty years, whenever the government has attempted to improve auto safety or environmental protection through new regulation, the auto industry has always made similar groans—satisfying tougher standards would be impossible without dire social and economic consequences. The industry warnings have always proved to be false, but the innocent citizens recruited to speak for Detroit probably didn't know this history.

Jack Bonner was thrilled by their expressions of alarm and so was the auto industry that paid him for them. Bonner's fee, which he coyly described as somewhere between $500,000 and $1 million, was for scouring six states for potential grassroots voices, coaching them on the "facts" of the issue, paying for the phone calls and plane fares to Washington and hiring the hall for a joint press conference.

"On the clean-air bill, we bring to the table a third party—'white hat' groups who have no financial interest," Bonner explained. "It's not the auto industry trying to protect its financial stake. Now it's senior citizens worried about getting out of small cars with walkers. Easter Seal, Multiple Sclerosis—a lot of these people have braces, wheelchairs, walkers. It's farm groups worrying about small trucks. It's people who need station wagons to drive kids to Little League games. These are groups with political juice and they're white hot.''

In the textbook version of democracy, this activity is indistinguishable from any other form of democratic expression. In actuality, earnest citizens are being skillfully manipulated by powerful interests—using "facts" that are debatable at best—in a context designed to serve narrow corporate lobbying strategies, not free debate. Bonner & Associates does not start by looking for citizens whose self-interest might put them on the auto industry's side. It starts with a list of the senators whose votes the auto industry needs. Then the firm forages among those senators' constituents for willing bodies.

"We sit down with the lobbyists and ask: How much heat do you want on these guys?" Bonner explained. "Do you want ten local groups or two hundred groups? Do you want one hundred phone calls from constituents or a thousand phone calls?"

Bonner's K Street office has a "boiler room" with three hundred phone lines and a sophisticated computer system, resembling the phone banks employed in election campaigns. Articulate young people sit in little booths every day, dialing around America on a variety of public issues, searching for "white hat" citizens who can be persuaded to endorse the political objectives of Mobil Oil, Dow Chemical, Citicorp, Ohio Bell, Miller Brewing, U.S. Tobacco, the Chemical Manufacturers Association, the Pharmaceutical Manufacturers Association and dozens of other clients.

This kind of political recruiting is expensive but not difficult. Many of the citizens are no doubt flattered to be asked, since ordinary Americans are seldom invited to participate in a personal way in the larger debates, even by the national civic organizations that presumably represent them. In a twisted sense, Jack Bonner does what political parties used to do for citizens—he educates and agitates and mobilizes.

Since members of Congress are not naive, they understand the artificiality well enough. They know that many of the 400 million pieces of mail they receive each year are contrived by interested parties of one kind or another. Hearing authentic voices from the grassroots, however, provides them with a valuable defense on controversial votes, especially when a senator intends to vote with the auto-industry lobbyists and against cleaner air. Public opinion, as every senator knows, is with the air.

"Obviously," Bonner said, "you target senators inclined to go your way but who need some additional cover. They need to be able to say they've heard from people back home on this issue. Or we target people who are genuinely undecided. It's not a good use of money to target senators who are flat opposed or who are already for you."

Corporate grassroots politics, as Bonner likes to emphasize, is really borrowed from the opposition—the citizen "public interest" organizations, especially in the environmental movement, who first perfected the technique of generating emotional public responses with factual accusations. "Politics turns on emotion," Bonner said. "That's why industry has lost in the past and that's why we win. We bring emotion to the table."

The democratic discourse is now dominated by such transactions—information and opinion and scholarly expertise produced by and for the self-interested sponsors. Imagine Bonner's technique multiplied and elaborated in different ways across hundreds of public issues and you may begin to envision the girth of this industry. Some firms produce artfully designed opinion polls, more or less guaranteed to yield results that suggest public support for the industry's position. Some firms specialize in coalition building—assembling dozens or hundreds of civic organizations and interest groups in behalf of lobbying goals.

This is democracy and it costs a fortune. Democracy-for-hire smothers the contemporary political debates and, while it does not always prevail, relatively few Americans have the resources to hire a voice for themselves. David Cohen of the Advocacy Institute, which trains citizens in how to lobby for their causes, recognizes a kind of class system emerging in the political process itself. "We are moving to a system," he said, "where there are two different realms of citizens—a society in which those with the resources are going to have the ability to dominate the debate and outcomes while others are not going to be able to draw on the tools of persuasion." If democratic expression is reduced to a question of money, then those with money will always have more.

In previous times, reformers wrote devastating critiques about the "capture" of government regulatory agencies by the industries they were supposed to regulate. The Civil Aeronautics Board became the puppet of the airlines. The Bureau of Mines was owned by the coal industry. The Federal Communications Commission belonged to the broadcasters. The occasional exposés sometimes produced reforms though the basic problem endured.

Now, however, it is not an exaggeration to say that democracy itself has been "captured." The forms of expression, the premises and very language of debate, not to mention the rotating cadres of experts and managers, are now owned in large measure by relatively few interests, much the way that powerful industries came to own regulatory agencies. Democracy is held captive, not just by money, but by ideas—the ideas that money buys.

Some citizens have discovered that the best way to avoid being overwhelmed by the "shadow government" of K Street is to proceed stealthfully in the legislative arena—to launch sneak attacks before the information industry notices.

Year after year through the 1980s, Representative Byron Dorgan of North

Dakota pursued this lonely strategy, as he tried to get Congress to curb the profligate buildup of junk bonds and corporate debt. As a former state tax commissioner, Dorgan understood that the Wall Street takeover deals were cannibalizing productive companies and leaving U.S. corporations dangerously overleveraged. Junk bonds didn't become a visible political issue until they started collapsing in the late 1980s, threatening the solvency of S&Ls, banks and insurance companies. But Dorgan could have explained it to people years before.

"I've been giving Wall Street fits," he said, "and they're furious with me and my constituents don't quite understand why I care because we're not exposed to hostile takeovers and stuff like that in North Dakota. But, starting in 1982 when I saw what was happening on Wall Street, I just got much more interested in junk bonds and mergers."

Dorgan set out to eliminate the federal tax deductions for the interest paid on junk bonds—the implicit federal subsidy for the deals that made the explosive buildup of corporate debt possible. If these tax breaks could be removed or scaled back, Wall Street would find fewer opportunities for raiding companies and breaking them up or leaving them mired in debt.

But the congressman did not launch a noisy campaign to alert the public to the threat posed by junk bonds. Nor did he push the Ways and Means Committee on which he serves to take up the matter directly. He did not make speeches or call press conferences. Dorgan knew all those would be futile—and would simply alert the opposition to his intentions.

Instead, Representative Dorgan practiced the kind of guerrilla politics that is sometimes possible in the parliamentary confusions of Congress. He literally tried to sneak his amendments into tax measures before the other side found out about them. These were like midnight forays against the opposing army of lobbyists and financial experts (and sometimes even occurred late at night when legislators were weary and the army was asleep). Sometimes, he even succeeded.

Byron Dorgan's personal campaign against junk bonds illustrates how much the legislative process has been distorted by the presence of the K Street industry. Indeed, though he was representing a potentially popular cause, Dorgan's approach was the reverse image of Bonner & Associates, which, though representing industrial clients, went to the "grassroots" in search of popular support. Dorgan's effort is public-spirited but secretive. Bonner's is flamboyantly "democratic" but driven by narrow special-interest objectives.

The flourishing of junk bonds posed an issue of government tax policy with profound economic implications and ought to have aroused a great political debate during the 1980s. Yet there was no debate. Dorgan understood there was nothing to be gained by provoking a democratic dialogue on the subject.

"If you have a controversial idea in this town," Dorgan explained, "the last thing you want to do is raise it up the flagpole where everybody can see it. It's not difficult now for a business to launch thousands of pieces of mail on Capitol Hill and that scares off everyone."

Dorgan chose as his point of attack the gargantuan budget reconciliation measures that move through Congress each year late in the session and are loaded down with hundreds, even thousands of legislative riders. The confusion and complexity of these measures gives an alert legislator the chance to sneak all kinds of things into law without arousing the enemy.

"In reconciliation," he explains, "you have a bill that's ninety-six pages long and with 140 different tax changes which are all little pockmarks on the tax code. If my provision is number eighty-nine on the list and it's not very clearly described, it's likely you can get it passed with about seven and a half seconds of discussion."

In 1987, Dorgan scored in this manner by attaching an amendment that created a 50 percent excise tax on the so-called "greenmail" deals in which a corporate raider is bought off by the corporation under attack. The tax would take the profit out of "greenmail" and save millions for stockholders and targeted companies. Dorgan's amendment was accepted without debate—before the lawyers and lobbyists from Wall Street brokerages awoke to the threat.

If they had known, the lobbyists could have buried Dorgan in elaborate, authoritative argumentation ostensibly proving that his amendment would unhinge the financial system and destroy jobs. Members would have been buried in mail from protesting clients and constituents. Nor would any lobbyist need remind the politicians that both political parties depended heavily upon the generosity of the corporate raiders for campaign money. During the 1988 election cycle, 240 of the leading dealmakers in leveraged buyouts contributed $3.5 million to Republican and Democratic candidates.[1]

Congressman Dorgan struck again in the 1989 reconciliation bill with an amendment restricting the so-called "payment-in-kind" junk bonds—a form of discounted debt paper in which the lenders are not paid any actual interest yet the borrowing corporations can still claim a federal tax deduction for making interest payments. The massive takeover deal engineered for RJR Nabisco involved $9 billion in these so-called PIK bonds and might not have gone forward without the hidden and illogical federal tax subsidy.

Salomon Brothers, Morgan Stanley and Drexel Burnham (before it became defunct) all came after Dorgan, but since it was too late to stop the measure, they turned their attention on the Treasury Department where the new tax law would be interpreted in new regulations. "They're trying to screw me at the Office of Tax Policy," Dorgan said.

That same year, Dorgan staged another successful ambush, this time on the House floor in the savings and loan bailout legislation. His amendment prohibited the troubled S&Ls from investing in junk bonds. "Had I proposed that in committee a year and a half earlier, I'd never have gotten anywhere," he said. "The committee would never have scheduled hearings, never would have reported it. It would have been swatted away like an annoying fly. On the House floor, it carried by thirty votes—just because by now it's impossible to say you're voting for junk bonds."

In broad daylight, Dorgan's argument was a winner, but that is not where most matters get settled. The complex and necessarily drawn-out processes of legislative decision making are dominated by what Dorgan calls "the shadow government"—the elaborate mechanisms of persuasion that surround most issues.

"All of us who work here are frustrated by the shadow government," the congressman said. "The way attorneys do business in this town is by finding an issue and then going out and recruiting a coalition for it so maybe forty businesses will feed his resources. They write op-ed pieces, they lobby Congress, they write to stockholders and generate a blizzard of computer mail."

Byron Dorgan draws a grim summary of the consequences: "Ideas are the enemy of progress here. At least to some extent, that's true."

While industry and finance generally had their way in the politics of the 1980s, on one important issue they were devastated—the Superfund legislation enacted in 1986. Among the outrages of the Reagan years, nothing aroused public opinion more effectively than the scary stories of these man-made toxic swamps and their threat to human life and the environment. Popular anger was aggravated further by the revelations of scandalous industry fixes at the Environmental Protection Agency. With citizens fully aroused, Congress was enabled to pass a very tough measure that assigns the cleanup costs where they rightfully belong, not to the general taxpayers, but to the specific companies that created the mess. The discredited Reagan White House was in no position to resist. Popular opinion clearly won the day.

In the months after its defeat, industry did not sulk aimlessly but instead began to plan for the long-term counterattack. By mid-1987, it had created a Coalition on Superfund, a group that would sponsor authoritative analyses on how the Superfund law was working and perhaps recommend "improvements." Major environmental organizations would be invited to join the project, but the founding members were the leading culprits in hazardous-waste pollution—General Electric, Dow, Du Pont, Union Carbide, Monsanto, AT&T and others. They were joined by major insurance companies that were also potentially liable for huge losses—Aetna, Cigna, Crum & Forster, Hartford and others.

The Superfund Coalition illustrates a sophisticated form of political planning that might be called deep lobbying. It is another dimension of mock democracy—a system that has all the trappings of free and open political discourse but is shaped and guided at a very deep level by the resources of the most powerful interests. The Superfund Coalition is more representative because it demonstrates the strategic skills of the corporate interests and the depth of their sophistication and patience as well as the depth of their wallets.

Other participants come and go in the political debate, especially unorganized citizens, who cannot always afford continuous involvement. They are temporarily aroused by an issue, see reforms enacted and then move on to other concerns. But the corporations do not go away from the legislative debate, even in the off-seasons. By their nature, the people and institutions with large amounts of money at stake are always at the table, fighting over the same points year after year. It is their business to be there. Their profits depend on the outcomes.

If they lose in 1986, the companies begin immediately to prepare the ground for the next fight in 1991 or 1992. The purpose of the Superfund Coalition was to target public opinion in the distant future—five or six years hence when the Superfund legislation would be up for renewal.

The companies' shared objective, according to an organizing memo prepared by Charls E. Walker Associates, the corporate lobbying firm, was to create "an equitable system of allocating costs" for the cleanup. In simple English, they wanted to escape the onerous financial burdens that Superfund imposed. To achieve this, the coalition members understood that they would have to convince the uninformed that the law was not working. "The nature of changes will depend on the emotional climate at the time of reauthorization and public perception of problems with the existing law."[2]

Given the public's skepticism of industry claims, this could not be accomplished by public-relations hacks. The corporations would have to finance high-quality research and concentrate on "the building of key allies in industry, Congress, the administration, academia, think tanks, the media and select environmentalists." The initial budget was set at $840,000 a year—a lot of money for political "research" but a pittance compared to the billions the companies might save by changing the law.

To develop the Superfund Coalition, Charls Walker's firm, which specializes in tax issues, formed a joint venture with another consulting firm whose specialty is environmental issues, William D. Ruckelshaus Associates. Ruckelshaus had served twice as EPA administrator, first under Richard Nixon and again when President Reagan called him back in 1983 to restore EPA's tarnished reputation following scandals of nonenforcement. Recently returned to private life, Ruckelshaus assigned the Superfund project to F. Henry Habicht II, who himself had recently resigned as assistant attorney general in the Justice Department for environmental enforcement.

The corporate coalition sought out participation by "select environmentalists" (the planning memos called this "outreach") and chose the Conservation Foundation headed by William K. Reilly to undertake the large research project that the companies wished to fund. Other groups were invited to take part too—the Sierra Club, the Natural Resources Defense Council, the Environmental Defense Fund, the Audubon Society—but they didn't like the smell of what was unfolding. They denounced the coalition as a scheme to undo the new Superfund law even before it had a chance to work.

Once the industry coalition became controversial, its sponsors decided to retreat a bit from such high visibility. "I thought what we ought to do was shift management of the study to the Conservation Foundation and let them run it and throw in some EPA money," Ruckelshaus said. "If the study was funded by industry, the results would be suspect."

EPA cooperated in this strategy, despite some congressional complaints, and in 1988 EPA Administrator Lee Thomas contracted with Reilly's organization for a $2.5 million study of the Superfund law. The taxpayers were now picking up the tab for research the polluters had originally envisioned as their political counterattack. The Conservation Foundation said it would deputize a "policy dialogue panel," including the interested industries and environmentalists, to help steer the project to the right questions.

The Superfund law, it is true, wasn't working—partly because the affected corporations were stubbornly resisting their financial liabilities and partly because EPA was itself quite slothful, cleaning up only a handful of hazardous sites each year from the backlog of thousands. Now, the two main delinquents—EPA and the corporations—were teaming up to ask what the problem was.

The larger point is that an informal alliance was being formed by two important players—government and business—to massage a subject several years before it would become a visible political debate. There was nothing illegitimate about this. After all, it was only research. But the process that defines the scope of the public problem is often where the terms of the solution are predetermined. That is the purpose of deep lobbying—to draw boundaries around the public argument.

The political alignments first established by the Superfund Coalition proved to be quite productive for the corporate sponsors, regardless of what happened in Congress. William K. Reilly left the Conservation Foundation before the research was completed because in 1989 he became the new EPA administrator himself. He was appointed by George Bush on the strong personal recommendation of William Ruckelshaus, who by then had become CEO of Browning-Ferris Industries, one of the largest companies in the waste-disposal sector.

Henry Habicht, who had managed the industry's Superfund Coalition for the Ruckelshaus firm, also went to EPA, as the deputy administrator, Reilly's second-in-command and, by many accounts, the man who managed the agency day by day. Lee Thomas retired to private life in Atlanta where his consulting firm was awarded a research contract on Superfund questions from—guess who—the Superfund Coalition.

None of this influential back scratching guaranteed, of course, that General Electric, Dow Chemical and the other corporations would ultimately get their way, but it prepared the ground for political battle on their terms. As an exercise in deep lobbying, their craftsmanship was to be admired as a nifty feat of triangulation. Three EPA administrators, past and present, as well as important environmental groups were recruited to hold hands with corporate America in the high-minded task of making Superfund into a better law.

By the fall of 1991, the polluters were beginning to get the kind of headlines they had hoped for when they created the Superfund Coalition four years earlier. Various authorities were being quoted on how flawed and wasteful the Superfund law was. And some of these experts worked for the very same companies lobbying to escape their financial obligations. At the top of the front page of *The New York Times*, there was this news:

EXPERTS QUESTION
STAGGERING COSTS
OF TOXIC CLEANUPS

A NEW VIEW OF THE PERILS

Most Health Dangers Could Be
Eliminated for a Fraction of
Billions Now Estimated[3]

If anyone is an authority on how modern democracy works, it is Tommy Boggs, the son of a former Democratic majority leader, a good friend and fundraiser for many members of Congress and one of Washington's premier corporate lobbyists. In an interview with the *National Journal*, Boggs explained how the system has changed:

"In the old days, if you wanted a levee in Louisiana, you voted for a price support program for potatoes in Maine. Nobody knew what was going on. Now, all of a sudden, there's this tremendous need for a public rationale for every action these guys take."[4]

As lobbyists will tirelessly explain, their basic function in politics is to provide information, fact-filled arguments that provide what Boggs called a "public rationale" for the governing decisions. Many cynical citizens automatically reject that bland explanation as evasion, a self-serving cover for the black bags stuffed with cash. Tommy Boggs and his peers, it is true, do handle lots of money for election campaigns and they perform other ingratiating tasks for politicians unrelated to information gathering. Nevertheless, what the lobbyists say about their role is essentially correct.

Information, not dirty money, is the vital core of the contemporary governing process. This simple truth about the system is difficult for many people to accept, especially middle-class reformers, because it raises an unsettling paradox about the nature of democracy and what exactly has gone wrong with it. "Information" that leads to "rational" choices is supposed to be a virtuous commodity in the political culture. Democracy, it is presumed, can never get too much of it. After all, the lobbyists who inundate politicians with facts are only doing what ordinary citizens, including the reformers, can do themselves.

The reality is that information-driven politics, by its nature, cannot produce a satisfying democracy because it inevitably fosters its own hierarchy of influence, based on class and money. Lawyers or economists or others who are highly trained become, in a sense, supracitizens whose voices are louder because they speak the expert language of debate. Ordinary citizens who lack the resources or a strong personal financial incentive are priced out of the argument—and that means most citizens. The playing field of democracy tips toward those few who have the money to acquire the information and a compelling economic motivation to purchase influence over political decisions.

Many Americans perhaps think this is how the governing system is supposed to work—directed and dominated by an elite few. Many have come to accept the imbalance as inevitable and normal. But it is a political system of privilege and inequality, a rank ordering that assigns most citizens to inferior status. If fact-filled arguments and expensive expertise are the only route to influencing government decisions, then by definition most citizens will have no access. This is the functional reality. It cannot fairly be called democracy.

The origins of information-driven politics are, ironically, traceable to progressive reform as much as to large corporations or wealth. Middle-class and liberal-minded reformers, trying to free government decisions from the crude embrace of the powerful, emphasized a politics based on facts and analysis as their goal. They assumed that forcing "substance" into the political debate, supported by disinterested policy analysis, would help overcome the natural advantages of wealth and entrenched power. But information is never neutral and, in time, every interest recognized the usefulness of buying or producing its own facts.

The modern starting point was World War II and the economic planning that developed under Franklin Roosevelt. But the faith in rational, supposedly objective public policy really originated with the good-government reformers in the Progressive movement early in the century, middle-class professionals and managers themselves. In a complex modern society, they believed, government was corrupt and wasteful because it did not employ the unsentimental decision-making techniques of business—rigorous economic and scientific analysis done by professionals. In many respects, the Progressives tried to shield the governing decisions from what they regarded as the raw and ignorant passions of the public at large.

The liberal intellectuals who came of age in the New Deal institutionalized the idea more substantially. The Full Employment Act of 1946, a milestone for its liberal political goals, also codified the technical methodologies on which the government would manage the economy. The Council of Economic Advisors was created to assist the president with scholarly advice, an approach copied subsequently across many other fields of public policy.

The energetic reform movements launched by Ralph Nader and others in the 1960s—and new information technologies like computers—gave new relevance and momentum to the idea of rational policy analysis. Why should an issue be decided by a few old bulls in the back room when, in the media age, everyone could have facts and opinions on the matter? The internal democratization of Congress—and the ventilation of Executive Branch agencies—created new markets for factual argument to justify decisions, augmented by the news media's unquenchable thirst for information. Instead of following the leader, members of Congress would be free to make up their own minds, and they needed their own facts.

Greed, malice and other crass motives did not exactly disappear from politics, but the spirit of reform now demanded more respectable "public rationales" for agency decisions or how a politician would cast his vote. Chuck Fishman, a Democratic lobbyist, described the new world that faced agents of political influence: "It used to be, if you had access, that was enough. Then there came a time when you had to have substance too. You couldn't just say: 'Do me a favor, blow these guys away.' The change came because publicity was too much of a threat, the risk of exposure by the media or public-interest groups. But the substance doesn't do diddly-squat if you don't also have access."

The risks facing politicians and interests were raised significantly by the public-interest critiques of reformers like Ralph Nader and the environmental organizations. Their exposés repeatedly stung the political system by revealing the irrational basis for many government policies—decisions that had been driven by raw power and secretive influence.

The rise of "public-interest" groups, organized by Nader and others, promised to provide permanent watchdogs for citizens at large. Further, their legislative lobbying spawned a long list of democratizing reforms—opening up closed meetings and private files, requiring public hearings at various stages of the decision process, forcing federal agencies to explain in detail why they had made certain decisions and what the economic or environmental consequences would likely be. Facts, not influence, would be the new talisman of politics.

The democratic illusion did not last. For a brief moment in the early 1970s, the reformers held the field, but they were swept away as soon as the monied interests figured out the new language of politics and learned to play by the new rules. In 1970, only a handful of the Fortune 500 companies had public-affairs offices in Washington. Ten years later, more than 80 percent did. In the same period, not coincidentally, business political-action committees displaced labor as the largest source of campaign money. In 1974, labor unions accounted for half of the PAC money; by 1980, they accounted for less than one fourth.

Business simultaneously proceeded to finance a counterrevolution of ideas that would overwhelm the voices of vigilant citizens. The American Enterprise Institute, once a cranky little conservative backwater, became a primary source of Washington opinion—the intellectual fodder that shapes the thoughts and reflexes of both politicians and the media. By 1980, AEI's budget had multiplied tenfold and it acquired the patina of disinterested scholarship.

Meanwhile, AEI's sponsoring patrons include the largest banks and corporations in America: AT&T, $125,000; Chase Manhattan Bank, $171,000; Chevron, $95,000; Citicorp, $100,000; Exxon, $130,000; General Electric, $65,000; General Motors, $100,000; Procter & Gamble, $165,000, and so on. What do these companies get each year for their money? One need not infer that AEI scholars have been corrupted in their thinking by this corporate money. But a reasonable inference is that major business enterprises will not pay large sums of money, year after year, to people whose "ideas" cannot be useful to corporate political interests.[5]

The money was spread around widely. Murray Weidenbaum, a conservative economist at Washington University in St. Louis, founded the Center for the Study of American Business in 1973 and was given a $750,000 annual budget to crank up the intellectual attack against government regulation. Eight years later, Weidenbaum was chairman of Ronald Reagan's Council of Economic Advisors and deregulation was in the saddle.

The Brookings Institution, once labeled the home of liberal intellectuals, moved steadily rightward, both in its personnel and in its ideological preferences, as corporate contributors financed new rivals that challenged Brookings's status. Right-wing millionaires like Joseph Coors, a beer magnate from Colorado, plunked down small fortunes on conservative scholars, most notably at the Heritage Foundation, an aggressive new think tank that was more willing than AEI to pitch the narrow objectives of particular investors.[6]

The corporate counterattack also had a profound social effect on government: Over the last generation, big money came to Washington, a rush of affluence unprecedented in the city's history. The general political vision was inevitably warped by the gilded prosperity that politicians see all around them. The federal government is now situated in the best-educated and best-paid metropolitan area of the nation. The capital of democracy is seated in a city where citizens of average means cannot afford to live.

"Everyone's here now—private America," said Richard Moe, formerly the chief of staff for Vice-President Walter Mondale and now a lawyer-lobbyist in the Washington office of an important Wall Street firm. "That's what has changed so dramatically in the last quarter century. Because of regulation and so forth, everybody feels the need to be here—and they brought a lot of money with them."

That statement provides a crucial framework for understanding every aspect of the democratic problem that will follow in this book: They brought a lot of money with them. The Commerce Department's annual list of the ten richest counties in America, measured by per capita income, is now led and dominated by the Washington metropolitan area. Five of its suburban jurisdictions rank in the top ten. Places like Marin County, California, and Fairfield County, Connecticut, that were once the favorite symbols for the "good life" in America now rank below Arlington County, Virginia, or Montgomery County, Maryland, where so many of Washington's lawyers and lobbyists live.[7]

While Wall Street's new wealth was more spectacular at its pinnacle, Washington's new wealth has a broader base. Between 1980 and 1986, for instance, the number of Washington households earning more than $75,000 a year increased more than fivefold. Meanwhile, the median household income for America at large hovered around $30,000. That is, half of American households earn less. Families of such modest means are actually disappearing from the capital's metropolitan area—compelled to move elsewhere by luxury home prices and rising rents. Their numbers shrank by 18 percent during the 1980s.[8]

Commerce naturally gravitates to where the high incomes are concentrated and the once sleepy town has become a cornucopia of luxurious shops, prestige department stores and gourmet dining, both the ostentatious and the tasteful. While many other American cities look worn and shabby at the center, Washington's commercial core has taken on an elegant newness.

The capital's rarefied culture of new money, inevitably, did something to the social sensibilities of government, even among those in politics who are concerned about the less fortunate. The general affluence makes it harder for the people in power to see the contradictory social facts beyond their own everyday experience.

Public-interest reforms did indeed open up the processes of government decision making to alert citizens, but these changes had another consequence for democracy as well. As an economist would put it, the reforms raised the cost of entry and participation. Democratic expression became much more expensive—too expensive for most Americans to afford.

Who can afford to show up at all of these public hearings? Who will be able to deploy their own lawyers or scientists or economists to testify expertly on behalf of their agenda? Who is going to hire the lobbyists to track the legislative debate at every laborious stage? Most citizens do not qualify. Unless they wish to give their lives over to politics, they cannot possibly keep up with the demands on their time and attention or afford the expanding costs. Indeed, unless they have an intense moral commitment to political activism, very few citizens will be able to identify any governing decisions in which their personal stake is so large as to justify the daunting cost of protracted involvement.

The Jeffersonian ideal of engaged citizens, splendidly articulated by Ralph Nader and others, did motivate hundreds of thousands, perhaps millions to participate and it created a vast new network of activist organizations. But it presumes qualities of citizenship that are not inherent in all people and, indeed, the assets of leisure and money are distributed mainly to the best-educated and most affluent.

In any case, even this expansion of citizen involvement was swiftly outflanked by the increased political investments from business. By the 1980s, there were seven thousand interest organizations active in Washington politics, and business's share of this pressure system was overwhelming—actually greater than it had been a generation earlier, before the public-interest reformers came on the scene.

Public-interest groups, according to a Senate study, were stretched so thin that they were absent at more than half of the formal proceedings on regulatory issues and, when they appeared, were typically outnumbered ten-to-one by industry interests. On some important matters, industry would invest fifty to one hundred times more resources than the public-interest advocates could muster.[9]

This paradox—democratizing reforms that actually deepen the disadvantages of ordinary citizens—is rooted, of course, in a much older dilemma of American democracy, the political inequality generated by inequalities of wealth. The fundamental dimensions were starkly outlined nearly thirty years ago by Anthony Downs in his landmark essay, *An Economic Theory of Democracy*, a book that devastated political scientists' smug faith in pluralist democracy.

"In an uncertain world," Downs wrote, "it is irrational for a democratic government to treat all men as though they were politically equal."[10]

If democracy is analyzed in the economist's terms of costs and benefits, Downs explained, then political action for most citizens will logically be an "irrational" expenditure of their resources, including time, since they cannot possibly derive personal returns sufficient to compensate for their output. In the economist's perspective, he observed, "Only a few citizens can rationally attempt to influence the formation of each government policy."

Downs's analysis provides a plausible explanation for why voter participation has declined steadily in the modern American electorate. As citizens have become better educated and less bound by the "irrational" political habits of family and party tradition, perhaps they perceive more clearly the economic logic that Downs described—that political participation, even just going to the polls and voting, offers such a diffuse and uncertain return that a "rational" economic man will decide: Why bother?

But Downs's description of "economic democracy" applies with equal force to the governing processes that lie beyond elections—where the cost of collecting information and acting on it is even higher than for voting. If cost is a permanent barrier to democratic expression, as it obviously is, then democracy becomes a contest merely for the organized economic interests, not for citizens. If there are no strong mediators equipped to speak for them, then most citizens will never be heard. If public desires and aspirations cannot be easily reduced to definable economic outcomes, then they will be treated as secondary—wishful spectators to the real action. In fact, those conditions form a fair description of the contemporary system—a shrunken version of "economic democracy" that mocks the original idea.

Democracy, one would think, should at least be permanently committed to the goal of nurturing and defending equality in political expression, even if everyone concedes that private wealth and power will always be unequal and that individuals thus will always be unequal in their ability to exert influence. The reform ideal, one might suppose, would be to create in politics what business people like to call a "level playing field."

The existing political system is prejudiced in the opposite direction. It actually subsidizes the political expression of those who already enjoy the advantage in resources. This subsidy is embedded in the federal tax code in the form of allowable tax deductions for activities that are really self-interested political expression—tax breaks that, practically speaking, are only available to corporations and people with substantial surplus wealth.

In terms of business tax accounting, this may seem plausible. In terms of everyday democracy, however, it means that all other taxpayers are picking up part of the tab for the political exertion of the vast corporate apparatus that surrounds government. The "white hat" citizens Jack Bonner recruited to lobby against the clean-air bill are a deductible expense for Ford, Chrysler and General Motors. Likewise, both corporations and wealthy individuals are given tax deductions for their "charitable contributions" to tax-exempt foundations, including all the think tanks that produce the sponsored research for them.

In fact, think tanks and foundations perform the research and advocacy functions that in many other industrial nations would be undertaken by the organized political parties. The economic function of political parties and secondary mediating institutions is that, by performing expensive tasks for others, they spread the cost of political participation among many, many people. In other words, only collective action—organized citizens with common interests—can reduce the entry costs that are political barriers for all of them.

In an elaborate fiction, the tax code pretends that tax-exempt foundations are not political since they are prohibited from participating in campaign politics. Everyone knows this is a sham. Tax-exempt money, it is true, cannot play directly in partisan elections, but that is not where most things get decided anyway. The tax-exempt foundation is such a congenial mechanism for political influence that politicians have started using it directly for their own purposes.

Representative Les Aspin of Wisconsin, chairman of the House Armed Services Committee, founded his own think tank, named after himself and financed by "charitable" contributions from defense manufacturers. Senator Jake Garn of Utah, ranking Republican on the Senate Banking Committee, did the same, though the Garn Institute is financed by tax-deductible donations from banks and other financial institutions. A survey by the *National Journal* found 51 senators and 146 House members who are founders or officers and directors of tax-exempt organizations that produce research and propaganda.[11]

Any American, of course, is free to start his or her own tax-exempt foundation. All one needs is the money. Aside from the insult of helping pay for this hidden political subsidy, most ordinary citizens cannot themselves enjoy it. Most Americans do not itemize deductions on their income-tax returns and they will receive no tax benefit even if they contribute twenty-five dollars to a tax-exempt organization working for their favorite cause. An auto company deducts the cost of flying its executives into Washington to lobby senators on the clean-air bill. An ordinary citizen has to pay his own way.

To begin to redress these inequities, the Congress would have to rethink the political favoritism fostered by the tax code and try to correct the balance in favor of ordinary citizens. At the very least, this requires defining the tax code in more honest terms and eliminating the fictions about what is "educational" and what is really self-interested political activity. Government would either withdraw tax concessions for all lobbying and other political actions or make the tax breaks truly available to all citizens.

If government were truly interested in fostering political equality, it would go much further. If tax deductions were curtailed for corporate politics and the assets of foundations were modestly taxed, the revenue could be devoted to the noble purpose of reinvigorating democracy. The tax code might offer an annual tax credit of one hundred or two hundred dollars to every citizen who wished to engage in political expression.

Any citizen would be free to contribute the money to any political activity—parties, candidates, issue organizations, local political clubs, whatever—and then be reimbursed for the contribution at tax time. This modest subsidy would not come close to overcoming the advantages of wealth, but it would certainly widen the field of democratic energies. If the reform were to cost the Treasury $10 billion or $20 billion in lost revenue, that does not seem too much to spend on restoring the national legacy.

A new broad-based source of potential funds would create a powerful incentive for political organizations of every kind to redirect their attention to the neglected citizens—all those people who lack major resources or status. Citizens themselves would have an independent resource base for inventing their own politics—defining political goals and strategies in their own terms—without the need to beg for funds from beneficent patrons.

Political reforms such as this speak to real questions of who has power. They would thus be deeply threatening to nearly all elements of the status quo, including some of the virtuous citizen organizations that claim to speak for the public at large. Whether they are left or right or nonpartisan, if groups depend upon foundation grants and tax-exempt donations for their own budgets, they do not have much incentive to experiment with citizen choice. Likewise, universities and academic scholars at think tanks would doubtless resist any effort to remove the political sham from the tax code since they are major beneficiaries of the present system.

Giving individual citizens the capacity to deploy political money—however modestly—would inevitably shift power away from existing structures and disperse it among the ordinary millions who now feel excluded. Could ordinary Americans be trusted with this power, the ability to decide where and how vast political resources should be directed? How one answers that question will say a lot about whether one believes in a real democracy.

The inequality of resources, however, is not the only barrier erected by information-driven politics and not the most important one. In practical terms, the most dreadful consequence is the way in which ordinary citizens are silenced and demoralized—made to feel dumb—by the content of information politics. The very language of the debate and the value-laden ideas that now dominate political decisions have created their own set of privileges.

Political values are mostly derived from personal experience—commonsense ideas about what constitutes a just relationship, the things one learned in early childhood from parents or the Bible or other children. Those values are what most citizens bring to the table when they engage in political activity. In a democracy, those expressions would be greeted as a valuable contribution.

In the modern political culture, they are disparaged. The public's broad political values have been preempted by other materials—arcane rules drawn from economics, law and science—that provide the main grist of information politics. On issue after issue, the public is belittled as self-indulgent or mis-informed, incapable of grasping the larger complexities known to the policy-makers and the circles of experts surrounding them. That complaint, though sometimes correct in the narrow sense, masks the nature of the conflict.

The real political contest, on issue after issue, is a struggle between competing value systems—the confident scientific rationalism of the govern-ing elites versus the deeply felt human values expressed by people who are not equipped to talk like experts and who, in fact, do not necessarily share the experts' conception of public morality. Outcomes that economics describes as efficient (and therefore just) will not necessarily satisfy the public's thirst for justice. Aroused citizens, who resist the economist's version and enter the debate not fully understanding its terms, are often puzzled about why no one will listen to them seriously.

If one listens carefully to the language of political decision making, the raw outlines of this struggle can frequently be heard. The public's side of the argument is described as "emotional" whereas those who govern are said to be making "rational" or "responsible" choices. In the masculine culture of management, "emotion" is assigned a position of weakness whereas "facts" are hard and potent. The reality, of course, is that the ability to define what is or isn't "rational" is itself laden with political self-interest, whether the def-inition comes from a corporate lobbyist or from a federal agency. One way or another, information is loaded.

For elites, the politics of governing is seen as a continuing struggle to manage public "emotions" so that they do not overwhelm sound public pol-icy. The corporate sponsors of the Superfund Coalition worried in their plan-ning memos about how to shape the "emotional climate" that would surround the next Superfund debate. Frank Mankiewicz of Hill & Knowlton described his industrial clients' fear that "the politicians are going to yield to the emo-tions" on environmental issues. Jack Bonner boasted that his recruitment of grassroots citizens "brings emotion to the table" in behalf of the business position. These expressions are commonplace among governing elites. The theme of unstable public emotions is a staple of newspaper editorials and learned conferences.

The rise of information politics enhanced the elite side of this argument, equipped it with precision and authority and daunting complexity. A favorite put-down of the unreasoning public, for instance, is the accusation that Amer-icans wish to live in a "risk-free society"—a desire that is obviously utopian, too costly to achieve and ignorant of scientific uncertainty. The complaint is usually expressed by business leaders or conservative scholars who do not themselves live next door to a hazardous-waste dump or downwind from a factory spewing dangerous chemicals into the air. Their economic status and political power protect them from such risks, though they think others ought to be willing to accept them.

In any case, their economic analysis has determined that, dollar for dollar, the cost of eliminating the pollution risk will exceed the potential benefits and is, therefore, an inefficient use of economic resources. The application of this standard is itself fraught with uncertainties and debatable assumptions that the sponsors usually neglect to mention, but essentially they are making an argument about social values, dressed up as a sophisticated claim about economic science.

Angry parents, worried about their children's health or their own, would skip over the economic logic altogether. They are not talking about cost-benefit economics or a utopian "risk-free society." They are talking about the possibility of cancer in their own family. What makes them so angry is the blind injustice—their well-being threatened by third parties who seem not to care.

Furthermore, the uncredentialed public sometimes "knows" things before science does. Starting in the 1960s, for instance, a popular folklore developed in America concerning a "cancer epidemic" stemming from dangerous industrial chemicals freely distributed in the air, land and water. Science—and public-policy officials and, of course, chemical companies—dismissed this talk as stemming from irrational fears, utterly without a factual foundation.

Twenty years later, science began to see the facts that were arousing the public's fears. The National Cancer Institute reported in 1989 that cancer incidence among children under fourteen increased 21.5 percent from 1950 to 1986. Cancer cases among adults (excluding lung cancer) were up by 22.6 percent over the same period. The authors of a similar study by the New York Academy of Sciences did not claim to know the exact causes, but suggested "environmental factors" as the explanation because cancer death rates increased fastest in industrialized regions and among men rather than women, suggesting occupational exposure to cancer-causing chemicals. This does not establish, of course, that widely held popular opinions are always rational or always right, but simply that popular perceptions are entitled to much more respect than the political elites give them.[12]

Many citizens, given these experiences, have come to distrust scientists almost as much as they distrust lawyers, if the scientists are employed by a polluting industry or even by the government. Their skepticism is not altogether irrational. Scientists, like lawyers or economists, may well reflect the institutional biases of their employers. A survey of scientists' attitudes on environmental risk found this bias to be strong and clear. Among industry scientists working for corporations, 80 percent said they believe there is a "threshold exposure" to cancer-causing materials and thus below certain levels there is no health risk. Among government scientists, only 63 percent agreed. However, a majority of academic scientists, 60 percent, believed the opposite—that there is no safe level of exposure to carcinogens. If the experts' opinions on such a basic question can be defined by where they work, who can say what is rational or irrational?[13]

In any case, the deeper argument is not about science or economics, but about moral law, though most citizens would perhaps not put it that way. Lois Gibbs, national leader of Citizen's Clearinghouse for Hazardous Wastes, a national grassroots movement, explained how the moral issue is obscured by political debate on toxic pollution.

"Would you let me shoot into a crowd of one hundred thousand people and kill one of them?" Gibbs asked. "No? Well, how come Dow Chemical can do it? It's okay for the corporations to do it, but the little guy with a gun goes to jail. . . . What they throw at me is that I am a single-issue person. Yeah, I am a single-issue person. I look at the issue of people being poisoned and it makes me mad and I wonder why it doesn't make everybody mad. It's a moral issue and that's why we won't go away. This is a movement for justice and, if people have their morals and ethics intact, regardless of what issue they face, they'll be okay."

By Gibbs's political measure, for instance, the new Clean Air Act enacted in 1990 was a moral travesty. It permits oil, chemical and steel companies dispensing toxic air pollution to kill as many as ten people in one hundred thousand in the neighborhoods surrounding their factories, refineries and mills (and gives companies twenty years to achieve this standard). The new law abandoned the moral standard enacted in the first Clean Air Act in 1970—that protecting human life and health would be the overriding purpose of clean-air regulation.

As a practical matter, the federal government had already abandoned the human standard long before, for it now subjects policy decisions of almost every kind to a crazy quilt game of elaborate rationales, economic analyses designed to justify doing—or often not doing—what the law seems to require. These calculations, formally known as "cost-benefit analysis" or "regulatory impact analysis," attempt to measure the dollars that will be expended versus the dollars to be saved as a result of particular government decisions, from the Department of Housing and Urban Development to Agriculture to EPA.

While the use of cost-benefit formulas originated in the Executive Branch, every legislative debate is now fought out on this murky technical ground. Cost-benefit calculation is the highest art form in the realm of persuasion by information—and the most deceitful. Its purpose is to construct ostensibly scientific benchmarks to justify what are really political judgments. The results are anything but scientific.

To construct cost-benefit equations, for instance, economists must first decide how much a human life is worth—since the supposed economic benefit of saving a life will be measured against how much it costs to do so. The government has produced many godlike answers to that question. The Federal Aviation Administration put a value of $650,000 on a human life lost in an airplane crash. The Occupational Safety and Health Administration in the Labor Department decided a dead construction worker would be valued at $3.5 million. The Office of Management and Budget countered that a dead construction worker was worth no more than $1 million. Across the government, nearly every federal agency and department has played Solomon, coming up with wildly different judgments.

The use of these technical tools—aside from the ludicrous biases and inconsistencies—leads to conclusions that offend public morality as well as law. In essence, property rights (and profit) are being assigned a higher value than human rights. Human lives are discounted, quite literally, by government economists, as they decide whether it is worth the cost of saving them. Not surprisingly, their supposedly scientific methods are usually biased in favor of not doing anything.

When agencies concoct statistical life values, for instance, they typically include the economic benefit of preventing a death caused by industrial hazards or pollution, but not the benefit of preventing long-term illness and injury, since that is more difficult to quantify. The omission automatically skews the equation in favor of the industrial polluters by reducing the potential benefits of action. "We all know it's much cheaper to bury someone than it is to treat them on a long-term basis," David Vladeck, a lawyer with Public Citizen, observed.[14]

The cost-benefit approach, more fundamentally, obscures the elemental questions of justice that are present in much of what Congress debates—who must pay and who will suffer if they aren't made to pay? Cost-benefit theory pretends that everyone in the society will share the economic cost of protecting the environment or eliminating occupational dangers, but that is only true in some distant economic sense. In the here and now, the bill has to be paid by particular parties, usually the offending business enterprises, their owners and customers.

That is why businesses lobby so strenuously to escape the costs—it's their money. Victims, on the other hand, are mostly unknown and in the future, unable to write their congressman because they don't yet know they will be the victims.

The triumph of the cost-benefit logic is perhaps the starkest example of how professional expertise has overwhelmed the public's sense of political values, in the name of economic efficiency. If American lives are only worth what they produce, then some lives should logically be treated as more valuable than others, since obviously some people will produce "more" economic return measured by dollars. Naturally no one would articulate that premise directly, but it is often reflected in which life-threatening problems the government decides to take seriously and which ones it chooses to ignore.

When all the technical complications are stripped away, these economic calculations assume that citizens exist, not as free-standing creatures leading their own lives, but merely as agents of the overall economy. The implicit premise has a faint odor of fascist thinking: that people belong to the state and its larger purposes, not the other way around.

In legislative debate, the economic argument regularly prevails over the human values, not solely because politicians are enthralled by economists, but because the economist's dry statistics are often accompanied by a powerful threat—the company will close the factory if it doesn't get its way. If the standards are set too high, if the taxes are too onerous, the business enterprise will be shut down, destroying jobs and livelihoods. The threat is often bluff and artful exaggeration. In an earlier era, American industrialists warned that there would be economic chaos if children were prohibited from working in coal mines and garment factories. But the economic threat can also be actualized.[15]

Information politics crystallizes the threat with "facts" and a nervous politician, confronted with elaborate studies, may not be able to tell which is bluff and which is real. During the clean-air debate, the National Association of Manufacturers distributed a "Jobs at Risk" map purporting to show the job losses in every legislator's home state if Congress enacted a tough measure. The data was extrapolated from EPA technological studies in a most dubious manner, but it had a wilting effect on congressional enthusiasm for a tough clean-air measure.

Politicians dwell in the middle of this contest—caught between public "emotions" and uncompromising "economics"—or at least that is how most politicians see themselves. But elected officials, unless they are very sophisticated, are not much better equipped than average citizens to judge between business threats and the popular sense of the right thing to do.

Unless one imagines a society in which everyone goes to law school or gets a Ph.D. in economics, the average citizen cannot be present in the contemporary debate, often cannot even understand what it is about. The various public-interest organizations that field lawyers and other experts in their behalf help to compensate for the absent citizens, but that is not the same as democratic representation.

Democracy is about aggregating the collective power of citizens to speak in their behalf. That process requires strong mediating institutions that are loyal to their adherents, that will listen to them and translate their values into technically plausible language, that will defend their claims and not forfeit them because the other side has hired better economists or more lawyers. That linkage is a large part of what's missing in contemporary politics.

The underlying contest is not just the tension between values and facts, but also that between personal loyalty and disinterested rationalism. Loyalty is another word that has fallen into disuse in politics—the other side of trust. Trusted representatives are rare because the public senses that too few of the people they send to Washington will remain loyal to their untutored opinions, when confronted with the information army. Loyalty and trust are not easily established in politics and certainly not by the manipulative techniques that invent artificial public opinions. The familiar routines of modern government only sow more popular distrust because these are the methods that disparage and dismiss the deeply felt expressions from citizens at large.

The better-educated classes perhaps find it difficult to understand that there are real limits to "rational" information politics. But this is not a mystery to those who lack professional credentials or privileged status. At any neighborhood bar or lunch counter, when citizens talk about politics, they do not talk about the governing process as a rational search for "responsible" policies. They see it, plain and simple, as a contest ruled by power and they know that they do not have much.

2

WELL-KEPT SECRETS

———

Because of its shocking size, the savings and loan disaster that unfolded in the late 1980s with massive losses for the taxpayers was widely portrayed as a unique failure of government. In fact, the patterns of political behavior that produced the savings and loan disaster are fairly typical of contemporary government and routinely replicated across many other issues, albeit with less costly results. Leaving aside the financial and economic complexities, the savings and loan bailout is most disturbing as a story of politics—a grotesque case study of how representative democracy has been deformed.

The political question is simple: How could they have let this happen? The answer involves a tangled drama of governing politics that played out for nearly a decade without the public's ever catching on to the implications. Indeed, the real politics of the savings and loan crisis involved bipartisan management to keep this scandal from public view, even through the glare of a presidential election. Republicans and Democrats cooperated in this objective, and the taxpayers remained ignorant until 1989, when it was abruptly announced that they must put up hundreds of billions of dollars to clean up the mess.

Even the public's huge bill fails to describe the entire loss. In their manipulation of the government's financial regulation, politicians of both parties effectively destroyed a system of financial institutions that was explicitly created to serve citizens with the least resources. The original objective of savings and loan regulation was one of liberalism's noblest legacies—broadened home ownership among all Americans, even families of modest means. In the end, the goal of housing was thrown over the side and the government's regulatory system was perversely diverted to a different purpose—"socializing" the losses accumulated by freewheeling bankers and developers by making every taxpayer pay for them.

The obvious explanation for how this happened is the domination of government decisions by special interests. That is true enough, but too simple to be very helpful. Pushy lobbyists and interest-group parochialism are as old as the Republic, and it is impossible to imagine a robust democracy without them. Reformers who dream of "good government" without special interests and lobbyists are trying to imagine politics without the normal human appetites.

The more challenging question about the savings and loan fiasco is: What happened to the public voice in all this? Why was no one looking out for the rest of us? As the story demonstrates, democracy has been deformed by the breakdown of different self-correcting mechanisms, and by the operating climate of government itself. Modern representation has assumed a different purpose—taking care of clients, not the larger public interest. Since most everyone is engaged in this enterprise, both legislators and the Executive Branch agencies, a mutual interest arises among them—how to manage things so that all of them will be able to elude public accountability.

In that sense, the savings and loan disaster was actually a success story for the politicians. They managed the crisis year after year to protect their clients from loss, then they abruptly informed the voters of their obligation to pay— right after the 1988 election. Yet no one in government was made to answer for the enormous injury they inflicted on taxpayers. The same political officers continued in power—still managing things in much the same manner.

The story begins, however, with a revealing complication: A handful of conscientious representatives did try to warn the public. A few representatives did prod their colleagues, year after year, to face the problem before it was too late. These honorable politicians were ignored, along with the public.

One of the honest voices was Representative Henry B. Gonzalez of Texas, who has represented his San Antonio district for more than thirty years, accumulating seniority but little prestige. In 1989, despite the doubts and grumbles from some younger colleagues, he succeeded to the chairmanship of the House Banking Committee.

Gonzalez saw the outlines of financial disaster forming quite early and for more than five years made lonely speeches, trying to get someone to listen and act. Nobody in authority would do either. As early as 1982, he testified before his House colleagues, explaining the long-term consequences for the taxpayers if they further liberalized the regulatory rules for the S&L industry. They ignored his warnings.

"It was very difficult," Gonzalez recalled. "The only avenue I had for speaking out was special orders [when the House floor is open to random speeches on any subject]. Going back to 1984, I was making speeches and warning. None of the other members wanted to look at them or apparently anyone else. I made speeches and they were all printed in the *Congressional Record*. Ah, nobody read them. Nobody cared."

At seventy-four, Henry Gonzalez is an interesting exception to the political norm—a solitary figure who never bought into the clubby arrangements of Congress, an inner-directed man who regularly upsets colleagues by plunging into discomforting subjects. His character deserves brief examination because the differences reveal many of the qualities that are now missing from the representative system.

"One good thing about not having any clout," Gonzalez confided, "is that all this money didn't come around and try to buy me. It didn't seem worth it to them. So I could say what was on my mind and not worry about losing contributors or anything like that."

To most of his colleagues, Gonzalez seems merely peculiar. He has the demeanor of an agreeable old uncle who insists on telling lengthy stories that will bore the children. He has a large nose and emphatic black eyebrows and a wincing expression when he talks. Listening to Gonzalez requires patience, for he is the type of politician who recounts historic moments with excruciating literalness. His account of counseling Lyndon Johnson back in 1964 on the war in Vietnam begins by describing the highway route the congressman drove from San Antonio to the LBJ ranch and where he stopped for breakfast.

His discourses on government loop loosely back and forth across fifty years of political memory—from the San Antonio City Council in the 1950s to Reagan's unprovoked invasion of Grenada, back to the Texas legislature where Gonzalez filibustered for civil rights, then over to Richard Nixon's abandonment of the Bretton Woods monetary system in 1971. His elliptical sequences may bewilder even those who are old enough to remember the history.

Only with great patience does one discern that, indeed, these scattered recollections do form a coherent message. The story Uncle Henry is trying to tell is about the slow death of constitutional democracy in our time, as he himself has witnessed it. The American republic, Gonzalez laments, now resembles Rome in the time of the Caesars.

"The Caesars," he explains, "weren't tyrannical. They were guys who wanted to be loved, like the president. But they exercised power unrestrained by a Constitution, just like the president.

"When the president can bomb a foreign leader who's unpopular, we no longer have a constitutional democracy. If a president can do what Reagan did in Lebanon and Grenada and Nicaragua and Libya and what Bush did in Panama, we don't have a constitutional democracy. I'm still in kind of a daze. We have learned nothing. It demoralizes me. Makes me, not sad, but sick of heart. It's too great a country to go by default.

"We have so traduced democracy, cut off the participatory side, that the people don't see any point," he lamented. "I find that the people can see through things. The people are there. But what can they do? When they have no choice between the two parties, no real choice between the overwhelming preponderance of candidates?"

In Washington, these qualities have earned Gonzalez an unfavorable reputation—he is regarded as an eccentric and dismissed, sometimes quite cruelly, despite his sophisticated grasp of the financial system. "I think all along their concept of me was that I was somewhat limited or inferior," the congressman said. "I've gone through the agony of being pictured or labeled with very little opportunity to give the real picture."

Gonzalez's ancestors came to North America nearly one hundred years before the *Mayflower* landed in New England, but his family settled in Durango, Mexico. His father was the first generation to live in the United States, where for forty years he was editor and manager of *La Prensa* in San Antonio, at that time the nation's only Spanish-language daily. The congressman is from a very old American family, yet feels the intense patriotism of the new immigrant who has found his home.

"I am completely indebted to this system," he said. "Without any particular resource, money, position and so forth, I've been given the privilege to serve. My gosh, I'm not going to do anything to ruin it for those who come along next."

Gonzalez is combative in politics and stubbornly so. He filed an impeachment resolution against Ronald Reagan after the Iran-Contra scandal, accusing him of betraying law and Constitution. He introduced another one against Paul Volcker, chairman of the Federal Reserve, during the deep recession in the early 1980s.

"You have to fight a fight," Gonzalez explained. "The trouble with these younger guys is they think you can talk a fight and the people won't know what happened."

If Gonzalez seems eccentric to modern Washington, it is because he is a living remnant from an earlier style of representation—a politician who tries to do his own thinking. Rather than rely on sponsored policy studies or interest-group propaganda, Gonzalez mostly reads books and, compared to most of his congressional colleagues, is a man of wide-ranging erudition. His idea of a big night out in Washington is browsing in a secondhand bookstore.

Gonzalez is a kind of Jeffersonian fundamentalist living in an age of easy compromises—a small-r republican who still believes, quite literally, in the restraints and responsibilities set forth by the Constitution. Liberal by political persuasion, he is populist in his skepticism of concentrated power—including governing power. Naturally, this makes him seem eccentric.

His type is ill-adapted for survival in modern politics and is gradually disappearing. This constitutes a loss for democracy that, though intangible, explains much about the irresponsibility of government. In addition to his own strong character, a congressman like Henry Gonzalez has been empowered by his own constituents to function independently, to be free of the interest-group pressures that confine other politicians. The people back home know him. They trust him. Gonzalez has thus acquired a license to speak on behalf of the larger public interest, regardless of small-minded political currents. His constituents protect him against the retaliation from special interests.

The enduring question for democracy is how to revive and encourage the trusted representative—how to create political conditions that would permit such relationships to develop and survive. Among other things, trust requires time and patience and sustained human engagement. In the quickness of mass-media politics, it is extremely difficult for either politicians or constituents to develop any sense of personal loyalty to one another. Local party organizations that once lent confidence to such relationships are now mostly defunct. Imposing term limits on elected representatives would, of course, have the opposite effect. It amounts to a permanent declaration of distrust between the voters and their representatives.

Democracy does not require a representative system peopled with philosopher kings or saints, but it does need circumstances that encourage politicians to represent their constituents while also, now and then, speaking for the national interest. Not every politician will rise to the opportunity, even when conditions are favorable. But this much is certain: If the Congress were amply populated with men and women of Henry Gonzalez's nettlesome independence, the savings and loan scandal would never have occurred.

The fact that no one listened to Henry Gonzalez might be interpreted as cultural bias or attributed to the congressman's independent qualities, except for this: The same warnings were also sounded year after year by Representative Jim Leach of Iowa, the second-ranking Republican on the banking committee.

Jim Leach is from the other end of America's cultural spectrum—an Episcopalian businessman, a blond graduate of Princeton, Johns Hopkins and the London School of Economics. He is a forty-nine-year-old moderate conservative whose Davenport district lies in the heart of middle American tradition. Leach also understands finance and banking on a most sophisticated level and, like Gonzalez, tries to be a representative in the larger sense of the word.

Leach saw the savings and loan crisis approaching for approximately the same reasons as Gonzalez and, year after year, he too spoke out. He called press conferences and issued dramatic warnings. He produced financial analyses that described the prospective losses mounting for the taxpayers. Nobody would listen to Jim Leach either.

"It's a wonderful story about the nature of modern politics," Leach said ruefully in 1989. "Why is it so hard for the Congress to do something for the public?"

The savings and loan industry originated on the wrong side of the tracks—as mortgage associations in working-class neighborhoods. So, despite the industry's subsequent growth and power, the S&Ls were naturally aligned socially with Democrats, the party of labor. Commercial banks, the much larger and richer establishment institutions, are Republican. Investment banks and the securities industry have long-standing ties to both parties. The old blueblood investment money tends to be Republican but, since New Deal days, some of the largest Wall Street brokerages have been close to the Democrats.

The basic sociology of these rival financial interests that encircle legislators and banking legislation is important to grasp because it gets mixed up in complicated ways with the other source of their political influence—campaign contributions. What often frustrates critics of modern politics is that, while political money is always present and always at work, it doesn't always neatly explain why things come out the way they do. The campaign money flows back and forth across these social divisions and sectoral interests in dizzying ways that defy a simpleminded analysis of who bought whose votes.

For instance, Democrats who take care of commercial banking interests, as many of them do, may or may not get bundles of campaign money in return. Some do it because it provides both self-protection and social enhancement —an entree with the Republican establishment on the other side of town. Many Republican members have played a similar game with S&Ls, going in the other direction. Political service on behalf of finance is like a price of admission to respectability.

"We've had a lot of liberals who were good on housing and would take care of the banks on the other side," said Jake Lewis, a longtime committee staff aide. "As long as they took care of the banks, they could be as liberal as they wanted."[1]

Some legislators are for sale, no question. But most legislators will take money from several or all of the contending forces in finance and so cannot possibly keep all of them happy at the same time. The Banking Committee, like Appropriations or Ways and Means or Finance, is known as one of the "money committees" because it is always so easy for its members to raise campaign funds from everyone. "If you're on Banking or the Finance Committee," said Senator Dale Bumpers, "you don't even have to open your mouth. They'll throw money at you over the transom."

The larger point, however, is that the setting for nearly all legislation in Congress assumes these client-representative relationships, however tangled. One can go down the dais in the Banking Committee chamber and label most of the members—though not all—by simply naming the financial sector or sectors for which they speak, whether it is hometown S&Ls or securities firms, the super-regional banks or the money-center behemoths.

One could draw similar seating charts for most committees of Congress and, for that matter, most regulatory agencies and officials in the Executive Branch. Nearly everyone in government has "clients" to protect or advance, sponsors who often helped put them there.

But this is a crucial point that many miss: Aside from the need to raise campaign money, most politicians *want* clients. The results of working for a client are visible and concrete, unlike so much of the sprawling legislative process, and client work is often more personally satisfying. Most members of Congress, after all, are relatively anonymous themselves in the larger dramas of Washington. Despite flourishes of grandeur, representatives and even many senators are generally unremarkable people who, without their titles, would be indistinguishable at a Kiwanis dinner anywhere in America.

Their work is unglamorous too—the exhausting attention to small details of language that is the essence of legislating, the tedium of waiting and listening through endless amendments and arguments. Democracy, at its core, is plodding work and requires a heroic sense of patience.

Clients make them feel important. Who cares about what they do or think at the daily level of their existence? Lobbyists care. They are always available to discuss the fine-print problems of government. A few assorted civic groups might care and, on rare occasions, the C-Span audience might be watching the action. Otherwise, on most complicated and obscure matters, lawmakers are alone with their colleagues and the community of lobbyists. Absent a strong signal from their political parties, they are distant from any larger public and may feel only a distant responsibility to it.

Thus, the utterly normal thing about the savings and loan scandal, as it developed over a decade, is that it was never really treated as a "public issue." It was an intense, complicated political struggle between contending sectors of finance, but not something other citizens were expected to understand or care about. Restoring a public voice on such issues, amid the normal clamor of interests, is the difficult problem that faces democracy.

With some validity, the S&Ls always saw themselves as the historic

underdogs on this political battlefield, fending off the superior political influence of the commercial banks while serving a "public purpose" larger than
their own profit, namely, providing the easy mortgage terms that fostered
broader home ownership. This was the Democratic party's great postwar
domestic policy, a marriage of private enterprise and social policy created
through the federal ceilings imposed on interest rates. The system provided a
discreet subsidy for home buyers, regardless of their economic status, and, for
forty years, the system worked: Home ownership steadily increased among
American families. It was stopped in 1980 with the deregulation of interest
rates—and home ownership has decreased among Americans every year since.

For competitive reasons, commercial banks had waged a twenty-year
campaign against the federal regulatory controls. Starting in the 1960s, banks
lobbied to strip the thrifts of their protected position, and they finally succeeded in 1980, amid double-digit inflation, with the deregulation of interest
rates. Financial deregulation was done by Democrats in the Carter administration, not by Ronald Reagan and the Republicans as so many assume.[2]

It left Democrats (and many Republicans) feeling vaguely guilty. Their
favored clients, the S&Ls, were left in a gravely exposed condition, perhaps
doomed by the head-to-head competition with banks. Everything that happened subsequently was influenced by a general feeling that Congress should
do what it could to help the S&Ls survive the trauma of deregulation.

In 1982, the thrifts were given more liberal accounting rules and new
lending powers that allowed them to plunge into the unfamiliar terrain of
commercial real estate. Henry Gonzalez appeared alone before the House
Rules Committee, pleading futilely against the measure and explaining the
likely consequences if it passed. By 1990, the consequences were fully visible
in all the defaulted shopping centers and office buildings owned by the federal
government. This same measure, incidentally, also expanded commercial
banks' ability to do real-estate lending and, thus, set the stage for another large
financial crisis in banking that would also require a huge taxpayer bailout.

As for the public, its visible stake in this sectoral battle was virtually
eliminated by the 1980 deregulation legislation. The implicit interest-rate subsidy for savings and loans that for forty years had stimulated housing and the
gradual spread of home ownership was abolished. In the ensuing decade,
mortgage interest rates were the highest of this century in real terms and home
ownership declined for the first time since the 1930s.

Campaign money undoubtedly drove many of those congressional votes
and framed the attitudes of legislators. Reforming campaign finance might
well weaken the client linkages and thus create more space for a larger public
perspective in the debate. Genuine reform could strike at the heart of the
matter by enacting this rule: Senators or representatives can serve on the
Banking Committee or they can take the bankers' money, but they can't do

both. A strict prohibition on campaign contributions from any interest-group organizations directly affected by the committee's legislative jurisdiction—bankers, stockbrokers, home builders and developers, all of them—would help liberate the lawmakers.

But such a general rule, applied to all relevant committees, would produce fierce resistance since it would also sever the political-money linkages for interest groups of every sort—organized labor, the elderly, the pro-Israel lobby, farm groups, the doctors and insurance agents and teachers.

Furthermore, for those who believe campaign money is the core of the democratic problem, there is the disturbing case of Senator William Proxmire. The Wisconsin Democrat, until his retirement in 1988, was chairman of the Senate Banking Committee and a figure of unquestioned rectitude. During thirty years in the Senate, Proxmire made himself famous as a pinch-penny watchdog of public spending, lampooning dubious federal projects with his "Golden Fleece" awards. More important, Proxmire accepted no contributions for his low-budget campaigns, not from bankers or any other interests that came before his committee. If anyone was untainted by money, it was Proxmire.

Yet, on the savings and loan question, Senator Proxmire behaved more or less like everyone else in authority. He ignored the same facts, made the same misjudgments and took the same evasions. In retirement, he offered the same lame excuses as everyone else. "We were kept in the dark," the former senator claimed. "If we'd known, if we'd had the facts, it would have been a simple decision."

When he was faced with the crucial moment of decision in 1987, what Senator Proxmire did was no different from what so many members of Congress typically do. He called a friend in the industry for advice, someone whose judgment he trusted, the executive of a well-managed savings and loan back in Milwaukee. And the senator followed the friend's advice—which was to postpone the day of reckoning for another year or two and see what happened.

In May 1985, four economists at the Home Loan Bank Board, the federal agency that regulated the savings and loan industry, prepared a study that made matters plain. At least one sixth of these federally insured institutions were broke—insolvent. Liquidating all of them and promptly paying off their depositors would cost $15.8 billion. But the federally guaranteed insurance fund had only $6 billion and was, therefore, effectively insolvent itself. In other words, it was a $10 billion problem. If public officials had acted on that estimate in the spring of 1985, that would have been the approximate cost, whoever had to pay it.

Instead, when the report became public two months later, Senator Jake

Garn of Utah, then the Republican chairman of the Senate Banking Committee, dismissed the likelihood of a busted insurance fund as "very, very remote." Senator Proxmire agreed, though he acknowledged that the problem was clearly "getting worse, not better." Treasury Secretary James A. Baker III assured senators they were right not to be alarmed.

"Obviously, it's no secret that thrifts continue to be in a fragile transition period," Baker testified. "I think we are encouraged, however, with respect to the earnings trend for thrifts. . . . So we are optimistic with respect to thrifts. . . . I don't think there is any cause for undue concern and I would reject any suggestion that we are in the midst of some sort of a major systemic problem with respect to any element of our financial services industry."[3]

Six months later, as declining oil prices collapsed the economies of Texas and other southwestern states, the size of the problem became much worse. By the end of 1985, economist R. Dan Brumbaugh, a principal author of the original study, concluded that it was now a $30 billion or $40 billion problem and growing ferociously every day. When he tried to explain the economic fundamentals driving the financial crisis, Brumbaugh was brushed off—both in Congress and at Treasury.

"These people were profoundly anti-intellectual," he said. "They did not engage in the ideas of this crisis. They were engaged in the politics of the crisis. They never really attempted to understand, on their own, how bad it was." Brumbaugh, incidentally, began sounding similar warnings in 1988 about impending insolvency for the Federal Deposit Insurance Corporation, the fund that protects depositors at commercial banks. He was again dismissed by bankers, the Treasury secretary, banking regulators and some congressional leaders as an irresponsible alarmist. Three years later, his dismal forecast was confirmed and taxpayers were required to provide $70 billion for the banks too.

The first substantive response to the ballooning S&L crisis did not occur until July 1986—a bit more than a year after the economists' initial warning—when the Reagan administration sent a proposal to Congress for a $15 billion refinancing of the S&L insurance fund. Congress responded by stalling for another fifteen months in wicked back-and-forth between House and Senate. Finally, in the fall of 1987, two and a half years late, Congress approved special federal borrowing of $10.8 billion to replenish the broke insurance fund. Everyone in authority knew this amount was too little. By then, it was no longer a $10 billion problem but more like a $40 billion or $50 billion problem.

Staff economists at the Office of Management and Budget in the White House, the FDIC, the Federal Reserve, the General Accounting Office, and the Senate and House banking committees were all tracking the same problem, making their own calculations of the true cost and coming out, more or less, where Brumbaugh had. "There was a general feeling that it was going to be too low," said William Seidman, chairman of the FDIC. "We certainly knew it was too low." Then why didn't his agency say anything? It was not done. "We have been tarred before for speaking ill of our fellow regulators," Seidman explained.

The august Federal Reserve was, likewise, monitoring the S&L losses and designed a special lending program by which it could provide temporary liquidity loans to the embattled insurance fund, in the event of crisis. As it turned out, one of the first endangered S&Ls that would receive substantial lending from the Federal Reserve in early 1989 (about $100 million) was the infamous Lincoln Savings and Loan owned by Charles Keating. Fed Chairman Alan Greenspan, as a private consultant back in 1985, had himself been hired by Keating to provide an economic analysis of Lincoln designed to persuade S&L regulators to go easy on him.

Greenspan issued his report on Lincoln, certifying the soundness of the institution and the expertise of its managers. In fact, Greenspan authored similar declarations of soundness for fifteen other S&Ls. Fourteen of them failed. In other words, even the chairman of the supposedly disinterested central bank had a strong personal reason not to make a righteous stink about the impending S&L debacle.[4]

Who will tell the people? No one in authority, if they can see no clear advantage for themselves. No one in the political structure—in either Congress or the Executive Branch—has much incentive to mess with somebody else's problem. Typically, they will stand clear and watch, anxious only that the unfolding disaster does not splash up on them.

A member of the Armed Services Committee or Appropriations or Commerce might well have been aware that something was terribly wrong with the savings and loan industry, but this was the Banking Committee's baby. Responsibility has become so particularized in agencies and congressional committees that, in the larger public sense, there is very little responsibility at all.

In theory, the party leaders are supposed to intervene at this point and impose a broader perspective. But Democratic leaders, led by Speaker of the House Jim Wright of Texas, were themselves a large part of the political problem. They lobbied tenaciously to obscure the crisis and protect their friends and contributors in the industry.

In the Reagan administration, Treasury Secretary Baker did not raise a political alarm either. He was perhaps preoccupied, along with Vice-President Bush, in the troubles engulfing their own political clients in finance—the Republican banks in Texas that were failing as dramatically as the thrifts. While the S&Ls were crashing, the federal government simultaneously bailed out most of Texas's largest bank-holding companies, devoting billions to the rescue of some of Baker's (and Bush's) best friends and major fundraisers.

Ronald Reagan, the president, was as usual out of it; he left office without ever once addressing the subject.

Who will tell the people? The question frames one of the most profound and difficult structural problems embedded in the present system. Politics and government are awash in information—facts and studies, propaganda and rhetoric—yet none of it communicates timely warnings to the citizens. The savings and loan issue never rose to the level of a "public issue" because political leaders in both parties chose not to make it one—that is, not to educate and exhort on a level that would arouse popular reaction.

In the absence of that, no one (save lonely voices like Leach or Gonzalez) is intelligently monitoring the action for the taxpayers and alerting them to trouble. The political parties used to perform this role but have abandoned it. The media do report endlessly on the major events of Washington but the style and focus of their news do not fulfill this function either. Neither, for that matter, do the ranks of reformers and civic organizations, which are mostly devoted to their own specific issues.

Without meaningful communication of this kind, democracy is bound to fail. With no one watching, those in power are left free to serve their narrow interests—protecting themselves and their friends.

The ugly political question that explains the politicians' stalling and obfuscation was always this: Would the taxpayers be compelled to put up the money to resolve this financial breakdown? Naturally enough, politicians were reluctant to face that outcome. But, if the taxpayers weren't going to pay for it, then the industry itself would have to. The modest $10 billion bailout enacted in 1987 employed federally guaranteed borrowing to raise the money but the funds were in theory going to be repaid by the S&L associations themselves through the annual premiums they pay to the insurance fund.

Thus, if Congress had provided prompt, adequate financing to solve the crisis, that would have meant raising the industry's premiums sharply or committing public money from the Treasury. Not a pleasant choice, but either approach would have been a great bargain compared to the eventual cost to the taxpayers, approximating $200 billion, not counting the decades of interest that will be paid on the federal borrowing.

The savings and loan industry proposed a political alternative: Paper over the problem for now and let the next president deal with it. M. Danny Wall, who was the Republican staff director of the Senate Banking Committee and became chairman of the Home Loan Bank Board in the final year of the Reagan administration, described the lobbying in 1987:

"The industry was saying very uniformly but quietly that we want to wait for the next president. You won't find that on the record. The hired lobbyists weren't saying it. It was the guys who come to town who were saying it. Every member has got someone in the industry they pay attention to and it's usually the big ones and not necessarily from their own states. Members of Congress are responsive to banks and thrifts because they're the financial system in their districts. Because the financial institutions are regulated, they come to Washington a lot and a lot of members get to know them. Those guys were saying: Let's just have enough money to get through next year.''

The "good ol' boys" from Texas and California and Florida, where the S&L lending has been most reckless and the impending doom was most tangible, had a particular incentive for postponing a reckoning—the more money that was provided to the federal insurance fund, the sooner their institutions would be closed down. Jim Wright and Representative Beryl Anthony of Arkansas, chairman of the Democratic Congressional Campaign Committee, hectored Banking Committee Democrats not to let these Republican regulators close down "our Democratic S&Ls.''

But even executives of the sound and solid S&Ls far distant from Texas had an interest in deferring the problem to the next president: If the mess got big enough, the main burden of paying for it would be shifted from them to the taxpayers. Kenneth McLean, staff director of the Senate Banking Committee when Proxmire was chairman, explained the subtext driving the congressional decision:

"You were talking about taking away industry money and they said, look, we're paying for this mess. We don't think the Bank Board has the capacity to handle any more money than $10 billion. Now, there were others—the good ol' boy crowd—that deliberately wanted to keep the money low so they wouldn't be shut down. So the message was: Let's let the problem build up and dump it on the taxpayers.''

Congress, in effect, acquiesced to that logic and so did the Reagan administration. Sure enough, it was dumped on the taxpayers.

A delicate political problem remained for both Democrats and Republicans. Having temporarily papered over the crisis, now they would have to get through the 1988 presidential election season without the people finding out. This proved to be relatively easy since the only remaining power center that might have turned this into an embarrassing campaign issue was the news media. Politicians in both parties counted on political reporters not to catch on and they were not disappointed.

Yet every financial lobbyist in Washington knew, without being told, that a major taxpayer bailout of the savings and loan industry was in the works for 1989. They began to lay the groundwork for it early by drafting their own self-interested blueprints for how the next president should solve the problem. Distant from the empty politics of presidential campaigns, these bailout proposals were circulated freely among key political players.

The main trade group for commercial banks, the American Bankers Association, started work on its bailout plan in the spring of 1988, while voters were being entertained with news stories about Mayor Koch attacking Jesse Jackson in the New York primary or news-magazine essays on whether George Bush was a "wimp." Executives from the major Wall Street brokerages were busy on Capitol Hill too, helping congressional staffs design the new government debt issues that would be needed to finance the project. So many different financial trade groups produced versions of the coming bailout that the House Banking Committee staff created a huge spreadsheet listing all of the lobbyists' competing proposals side by side.

The financial industry naturally shared the politicians' interest in discretion, but the bailout plans were not closely guarded secrets. An inquiring reporter could obtain copies without any special effort at digging. Robert Dugger, lobbyist and chief economist of the ABA, explained the politics:

"Everyone knew the game was: Democrats don't bring this up, Republicans don't bring this up. Because a firefight on this issue will have more bodies on both sides than anyone wants to lose. The financial community knew that and we knew where the play was: Wage the presidential campaign on all issues, but don't use the thrift crisis. We all know it has to be dealt with. We'll do it right after the election."[5]

The chief S&L regulator, Danny Wall, understood the same terms of play. When Wall appeared periodically before congressional hearings, he was always asked whether the fund for liquidating failed S&Ls would be adequate. He always said yes. "I was asked in a code that everyone understood," Wall said. "The code was: Will $10.8 billion be enough to get you to 1989? My answer was, yes, this is enough for the near future. I was trying to be more explicit and still answer in code. Everybody knew what we were talking about."

At the White House, the immediate goal was to get Ronald Reagan safely into retirement without having his final year in Washington marred by an embarrassing taxpayer bailout for a deregulated industry. When Dan Brumbaugh was briefly considered as a candidate for the job of chief S&L regulator, the word came back to him through political channels: "If this guy really wants this job, he's going to have to sit down with Howard Baker [Reagan's White House chief of staff] and assure Baker that we can hold things together until this president gets out of town."

By the spring of 1988, Henry Gonzalez was, by his own account, "almost hysterical" on the subject. He called a press conference to describe once again the fantastic unraveling he knew was underway. He proposed an emergency $50 billion line of credit from Treasury so that regulators could immediately stop the hemorrhaging losses. Nobody in the press came to his press conference, aside from the trade papers covering the financial industry and Texas reporters. Gonzalez's dramatic proposal went unreported.

Simultaneously, Gonzalez pleaded for action with Representative Fernand St Germain of Rhode Island, then the Banking Committee chairman. St Germain, who was defeated that fall by his own sleazy S&L connections, brushed him off.

Gonzalez remembers telling him: "Freddie, you may think this is just Texas but sooner or later your constituents in Rhode Island are going to be alarmed too. Why don't you appoint a task force and tell people the truth about the size of the problem? Freddie says, 'Henry, you know all that'll do?' What? 'You'll have the president going to Texas and saying you're advocating a taxpayer bailout and you're a Democratic big spender.' "

Everybody knew except the voters—and the thousands of political reporters who were covering the presidential campaign. They were busy covering the Willie Horton issue, Dan Quayle's college record and other complex matters. The corrective mechanism of the press failed the people too, for its own reasons.

Reporters and editors, save for a few rare mavericks, generally take their cues from people in authority; if the people in high places of government say there is no crisis, the media are inclined to accept that answer, even if contradictory evidence is easily available from less prestigious sources. The cultural boundaries imposed on editors and reporters by their own institutions are embedded in their definitions of what is "news." Cries of alarm from lone congressmen like Leach and Gonzalez, notwithstanding their personal brilliance, do not qualify as "news."

Political reporters would surely have written about the prospect of a taxpayer bailout if regulatory officials had announced it or if either the Republican or Democratic candidates had made an issue of it. But, of course, both parties had tacitly agreed not to bring it up.

One of the reasons elections have lost their meaning is that the content of campaigns is confined by this closed loop between the politicians and the reporters. The media define "politics" as the narrow subject of winning or losing elections—not deciding issues in government. So the campaign coverage generally excludes public questions that people may care about—or ought to care about—unless the subject figures in the electoral strategies of the candidates.

This premise reverses the dynamic of electoral accountability: Public questions get on the agenda for public discussion only if the campaign strategists select them as useful devices for winning votes. Issues that might lose votes are, not surprisingly, selected out. The only serious intrusion on this monopoly is the press's tenacious inquiries about personal character, sex, drugs and other provocative subjects.

The media, furthermore, have developed their own forms of protective specialization—a way of defining their responsibilities in narrow compart-

ments that is not so different from the government's. The political reporters
who cover campaigns, having defined politics as elections, are not inclined to
have much interest in the governing questions, especially complicated matters
like financial regulation or economic policy. Meanwhile, the financial reporters who do cover such matters retreat from the broader political implications
of what they are reporting.

Thus, though they work out of the same newsrooms, they do not intrude
on each other's turf. Political reporters and editors dismiss subjects that are the
core of governing as too dense and boring for campaign coverage, while
financial reporters dismiss politics as a lot of empty hot air. As a result, though
many stories were written in 1988 about the growing troubles of the savings
and loan industry, they mostly appeared on the financial pages and were
constricted by opaque terminology and timidity.

An average reader, following the news conscientiously, was given no way
to divine what was coming right after the election—much less know that the
financial industry lobbyists were already at work designing the taxpayer bailout. Most political reporters, if they had read the same stories, would probably
not have figured it out either.[6]

The S&L crisis did almost become a campaign issue anyway, but it was
quickly snuffed out before the political reporters awoke to its meaning. Late in
the day, the Democratic candidate, Michael Dukakis, issued a stinging attack
on the S&L bailouts already underway in the Southwest and blamed the lax
regulatory atmosphere created by Reagan and Bush for producing a costly
scandal. In late September, the Dukakis campaign was prodded into surfacing
the issue by Representative Charles Schumer of Brooklyn, another Banking
Committee member trying to sound the alarm.

The political apparatus quickly shut the door on further discussion. Senator Garn went to the Senate floor the next day and denounced Senator
Proxmire and other Democrats for playing politics with a bipartisan problem.
Republicans in the House threatened to turn the issue around on Jim Wright
and the other Texans who had lobbied so hard to protect their industry friends.
Senator Lloyd Bentsen, the Texas Democrat who was Dukakis's running
mate, communicated to campaign headquarters that this was not going to be a
winning issue for their ticket. So did House Speaker Jim Wright. Representative St. Germain chewed out Representative Schumer for making mischief.
That was the last word heard on the subject from Michael Dukakis.

After the presidential election, George Bush was widely congratulated for
"facing up" to the problem by proposing a solution—a $50 billion taxpayer
bailout. But the public was once again cut out of the action. Just as Democrats
had taken their cues from their special-interest patron, the S&Ls, now the
Republicans turned to their clients, the commercial banks. George Bush's

bailout legislation, proposed in early 1989, is a remarkably good fit with the blueprint the American Bankers Association drafted the summer before.

This transaction represents another critical juncture in the governing process where democracy breaks down—the moment when the dimensions of the public problem are first defined and before any visible action has begun. As smart politicians understand, defining the terms of a problem will usually determine the scope of the solutions. Certain ideas and alternatives become the accepted political agenda; other possibilities are ruled off the table. Smart lobbyists devote their principal energies to this stage because it is often where the contest is won or lost.

In some ways, this moment is when the public at large has the most to contribute—when the discussion is still generalized instead of technical, when the arguments are about broad political choices and public aspirations. In the routines of modern Washington, this is the point where the public is nearly always excluded.[7]

That is what happened in the autumn of 1988. While citizens remained innocently unaware, the newly elected president's team conducted a series of private meetings to devise a bailout plan that would be announced right after Bush's inauguration. The private consultations actually started a few weeks before the election was decided. Treasury Secretary Nicholas F. Brady deputized two lieutenants, both former finance professors from the Harvard Business School, to begin drafting a bailout plan for the new president.

"Most everybody came through and talked to us," said Undersecretary Robert R. Glauber, "the ABA, the league [of savings and loans], a bunch of lobbyists, the guys from the bank board. It was the usual cast of characters." A public problem that had festered for a decade was now going to be "solved" in two months of backroom meetings at the Treasury Department with lobbyists from the financial industry and a handful of key congressional leaders.

Though they were academics, both Glauber and Assistant Secretary David W. Mullins, Jr., were quite familiar with the viewpoints of the leading commercial banks. In the year before he joined the government, Mullins had earned $262,000—four times his Harvard salary—from Citibank and two other banks for conducting executive seminars. Glauber, in addition to his teaching, was paid $415,000 as a consultant to commercial banks, most of it from Morgan Guaranty of New York. Mullins was subsequently appointed a governor on the Federal Reserve Board, which regulates the banking system, among its other roles.

One politically unsettling idea that Mullins and Glauber came up with—a small tax on all depositors to pay for the bailout—was quickly killed as an alternative when it was leaked to the press. Bank lobbyists made certain the proposal was widely broadcast and the ensuing uproar pushed the Bush administration into disowning the idea. Dugger, the ABA's chief economist, thought the episode reflected a misstep by two professors who did not fully appreciate how Washington works.

"The city works in concentric circles," Dugger explained. "There are a limited number of people—I mean probably fifty people in the financial legislative arena—whom you can absolutely trust to keep a secret. That is the inner circle you talk to first. They were unfamiliar with this network at that time so Treasury didn't know which lawyers and lobbyists you can try out ideas on."

After the president announced his bailout proposal and Congress began hearings, other voices jumped into the debate, speaking for other public concerns. But it was already too late. The broad terms had already been decided and their new ideas were ruled out of order.

The Financial Democracy Campaign was a coalition of community-based organizations representing consumers, labor, low-income people, farmers, housing groups, churches and others. The coalition proposed new taxes on the wealthy and financial institutions to help pay for the bailout, but everyone in authority had already agreed this was not to be a tax measure. The coalition suggested radical remedies for the crisis in housing, the declining home ownership and homelessness that were the social corollary of the S&L crisis, but everyone agreed this was not to be a housing measure.

The Financial Democracy Campaign marshaled support from several hundred diverse citizen groups across the country and some local officials like the mayor of Boston, Raymond L. Flynn. The campaign generated lots of angry mail and even local demonstrations. Press conferences were held featuring the Reverend Jesse Jackson, Ralph Nader and Representative Henry Gonzalez, the new Banking chairman, to promote a citizens' agenda for reform. The press generally ignored these pleas, judging that these uncredentialed intruders in the financial debate would not be considered relevant by Congress. The press was correct.

In the end, the FDC's public-spirited lobbyists settled on a much smaller goal, a minor amendment that at least promised some concrete benefit for some ordinary citizens. They asked that the tens of thousands of empty houses that the government now owned as a result of the massive defaults be made available to low-income families and community housing organizations on a preferential basis.

Congress included their modest proposal in the final legislation, but it was an empty victory. A year later, the frustrated citizen groups were still trying to get the federal bailout agency to comply by selling vacant housing to poor people. In the meantime, under the same provision the citizen groups had lobbied for and won, General Electric qualified to buy twenty-eight apartment complexes with nearly six thousand units at a price that was half their market value.[8]

"Congress prefers to regurgitate people like us," said Tom Schlesinger, an activist from Charlotte, North Carolina, who manages the Financial Democracy Campaign. "When it wants to be Lady Bountiful, it throws us a crumb but it doesn't change the substance. Many of the 'white hat' groups in Washington have gotten used to that game and so they play it too—crumbs for the poor—instead of saying: To hell with that, our members are middle class and they're getting screwed. There is a terrible set of mutually interacting traps and our inside-the-Beltway groups fall for them too."[9]

If taxpayers were the obvious losers, the major winners in this political contest were also obvious. The commercial banks, whose basic design had been followed and whose longtime competitors were now in disgrace. The major Wall Street brokerages too, for they got lots of new business by marketing the government's massive new debt issues that they helped to design. Wealthy investors won too, since the government was compelled to pay them premium interest rates on this new borrowing, even though it was guaranteed by the taxpayers.

In the short run, the politicians of both parties were winners too, for they had gotten the gullible electorate to swallow a huge new liability without much damage to any incumbents. In the long run, however, the victory might well prove to be pyrrhic for all these players—the bankers and the politicians—for the financial unraveling continued to spread into banking and other sectors like insurance. As the crisis in banking gained momentum, the same political dereliction continued. Neither politicians nor the press would tell the people in a straightforward way what they were facing.

Impromptu solutions, arrived at in private and without a wide-ranging public debate, often produce embarrassing results for government. Bush's savings and loan bailout, as subsequently became clear, failed utterly to resolve the crisis and, indeed, the bailout itself became a continuing scandal of sorts. One year later—right after the 1990 elections were completed—the Treasury sent a new request to Congress for another $80 billion.

Thus, a perversely undemocratic pattern was established. In the even-numbered years, the politicians ran for election. In the odd-numbered years—1987, 1989 and 1991—they legislated taxpayer bailouts.

At the White House ceremony when the bailout legislation was signed into law, Henry Gonzalez received one of the president's pens. "When he turned to give me the pen," Gonzalez recalled, "I said, 'Mr. President, you realize, don't you, that this is just the beginning?' He looked at me kind of blank. Maybe he had something else on his mind."

3

BAIT AND SWITCH

The political drama of taxation provides what is probably the best measure of democracy's condition, the clearest evidence of where power truly resides in the society. Aside from sending someone to war or to prison, government's ability to make people involuntarily give over their money is its strongest exercise of authority over private citizens and their institutions.

Indeed, the classical case against democracy has always been a theoretical supposition that, sooner or later, the many would use their democratic control of government to violate the property rights of the few. The mob's insatiable appetites would be fed by unscrupulous politicians, who would use the tax system to confiscate the incomes and wealth of those who have more.

This has not been the case in America, to put it mildly. On the contrary, during the past fifteen years, the monied interests and allied governing elites have used their political power to accomplish the opposite result: Federal tax burdens were steadily shifted from them to everyone else. Clearly, governing power does not reside with the people.

From 1977 to 1990, Congress enacted seven major tax bills and many other minor ones, raising or lowering tax liabilities for individuals and corporations. The results of this legislative torrent are startlingly one-sided. Citizens for Tax Justice, a labor-supported advocacy group, calculated the cumulative effects:

If Congress had done nothing since 1977 to alter the U.S. tax code, passed no new legislation at all, nine out of ten American families would be paying less. That is, a smaller share of their incomes would be devoted to federal taxes.

Yet, paradoxically, the government would be collecting more revenue each year—almost $70 billion more—if none of those tax bills had been enacted.

How to explain this? Where did all that money go? Roughly speaking, it went to corporations and to the one in ten families at the top of the income ladder. Their taxes were cut by spectacular dimensions.[1]

The tax burden on the richest 1 percent of the population fell cumulatively by a staggering 36 percent, compared to what they would have owed under the 1977 tax code. As politicians from both parties congratulated themselves on delivering one tax cut after another, families in the very middle of the income ladder experienced a 7 percent increase in their federal tax burden.

Nothing demonstrates the atrophied condition of modern democracy more starkly than those facts. Behind all of the confusion and complexity of the tax debate, democracy's natural inclinations were literally thrown into reverse—rewarding the few at the expense of the many.

For those who blame Republicans for what has happened and believe that equitable taxation will be restored if only the Democrats can win back the White House, there is this disquieting fact: The turning point on tax politics, when the monied elites first began to win big, occurred in 1978 with the Democratic party fully in power and well before Ronald Reagan came to Washington. Democratic majorities have supported this great shift in tax burden every step of the way.[2]

The politics of taxes pulls together everything that has been described thus far about the deformed power relationships in government. While the preceding chapters focused mainly on the losers—the ranks of citizens displaced from politics—this chapter concentrates on the winners, the people and institutions that hold the high ground of power. Though a small minority of the population, they accomplished hegemony on taxation by exploiting all of the systemic weaknesses described in earlier chapters—from the warped social sensibilities in affluent Washington to the special-interest clientism to the vast resources that monied interests deploy for scholarly expertise and manufactured "opinions."

Those are the common ingredients of the power relationships, but the issue of taxes involves more sophisticated elements as well. After all, this is not an obscure issue like savings and loan regulation or junk bonds that affects people in unseen ways. Everyone cares about taxes and most everyone has strong opinions on the subject.

Therefore, in order to accomplish such distorted outcomes, the governing elites and monied interests are required to create a series of elaborate screens around the subject of taxes—a moving tableau of convincing illusions that distracts the public from the real content and gives politicians a place to hide. Meanwhile, behind the screens, the action proceeds toward the results they seek. In public, the two major parties struggle contentiously over tax issues. Yet the reality is the collaboration between them. Expert opinion is marshaled in behalf of broad economic goals that seem desirable to everyone—economic growth and jobs. Meanwhile, elites work out among themselves how these broad goals can be translated into reducing their own tax burdens.

Given the fundamental nature of tax politics, the powerful economic interests have a large and continuing advantage over unorganized citizens at large. The tax contest plays out in the news as dramatic climax—a tax bill is passed, the president signs it. The real drama, however, continues, year after year, and no outcome is ever permanently decided. Thus, the monied interests are always mobilized and working toward better results, knowing that the continuum of legislative action does not stop with one victory or one setback. Citizens may grow weary and move on to something else, but for obvious reasons, the wealthy are always on the case.

Over a period of some years, the politics of taxation degenerated into what looks like a running game of bait and switch—a hustle in which the governing system plays the clever salesman while the taxpayers are the mark. The bait is the continuing political rhetoric that seems to promise tax cuts. The sleight-of-hand involves switching this promise for something else.

During the 1988 presidential campaign, George Bush comforted voters with a manly promise to enact "no new taxes," and his pledge resonated profitably with popular opinion. If voters had wished to know what George Bush would actually do as president, they should have been listening to other voices.

An elite consensus of opinion leaders from both political parties—economic policy gurus, financial and business leaders, strategic lobbyists and, more discreetly, some prominent politicians—had already developed an agenda for what the next president should do to correct the economic imbalances created by the Reagan era. The next president, they declared more or less openly, should reduce both the federal budget deficit and the trade deficit by first slowing the economy and suppressing personal consumption, perhaps even accepting a recession, and then raising taxes on consumers. Americans, it was said, had been on an irresponsible binge of buying and borrowing during the 1980s and now it was time to sober up.

This could be accomplished, these thinkers explained, by raising taxes on consumption—on gasoline and other staples—as well as by cutting back on government benefits such as Social Security, Medicare and Medicaid, assistance to veterans, and civil-service and military retirement. Their logic, roughly speaking, was that if families had less to spend on things, they would buy fewer foreign goods and thus shrink the trade deficit. To encourage savings, they added, the investor classes should be given additional tax relief—a reduction in the taxes on their capital.

The most influential (and most radical) articulation of this case was made by a prestigious Republican investment banker, Peter G. Peterson, in a magazine article, "The Morning After," published in *The Atlantic* in October 1987. Peterson, who served as secretary of commerce in the Nixon administration, delivered a scary sermon on what would unfold if Americans did not swiftly rediscover self-discipline. His painful remedies, however, were entirely directed at the population at large, while shielding his own class, the wealth holders, from sacrifice. Peterson suggested, for instance, repealing the tax deduction for interest on home mortgages that is so important to the middle class and imposing a national sales tax of 5 percent on all goods.

Savings, he declared, could be encouraged "by trading off increases in consumption-based taxes for reductions in investment-based taxes." All Americans consume, of course, but only a relative few have the surplus income and wealth to be investors. Eighty-six percent of the individual net financial wealth in America is owned by 10 percent of the people.[3]

In less extreme form, the same general argument was voiced so frequently by other influential voices that it became something of a cliché among the well-informed minority who listen to elite channels of discourse. The shorthand label given this strategy was "austerity" and its appeal seemed bipartisan. Peterson's partner in investment banking, Roger Altman, a Democrat, served as policy advisor and Wall Street fundraiser for Bush's opponent, Michael Dukakis, and echoed the same ideas. Lawrence H. Summers, a Harvard economist who was the principal economics advisor to Dukakis, coauthored a study making similar recommendations.

C. Fred Bergsten, a former Carter advisor who heads the Institute for International Economics, a Washington think tank funded by major foreign and U.S. financial institutions, prescribed a "consumption recession" for the next three or four years. The Cuomo Commission, a committee of notables assembled by the New York governor to study the nation's economic condition, recommended a more moderate version of the same approach—a gasoline tax, a national sales tax or perhaps higher income taxes on the Social Security benefits of the elderly.

Some analysts at Wall Street brokerages were more blunt: What the country needed was a government-induced recession to clear away the excesses of the eighties and shrink the trade deficit.[4]

Though little noted at the time, the most influential endorsement of this economic strategy came from the chairman of the Federal Reserve Board, Alan Greenspan. Greenspan did not, of course, call openly for an "austerity" regime but he agreed with the others that domestic consumption must be suppressed by government policy, both budget cuts and higher interest rates. "Domestic absorption has to be restrained by macroeconomic policy," he told the Senate Banking Committee in early 1988.[5]

Unlike the other voices, Greenspan had the independent power to carry forward this strategy, regardless of the promises of "prosperity" that both presidential candidates were simultaneously making to the voters. In the summer of 1988, while the two major parties were in noisy convention nominating their candidates for president, the Federal Reserve initiated its own campaign to discourage consumption—by raising interest rates and retarding the pace of economic growth.

The government's campaign to suppress consumption was conducted by the Federal Reserve with the president's acquiescence and occasional kibitzing for two years. By 1990, it was obvious that the Fed had done its job too well: The nation was in recession. Bankruptcies were multiplying and, as many important borrowers failed, major financial institutions fell into trouble themselves.

"Elite debate" is one of the screens that conceals decision making on the largest economic questions—taxes and recession—from the clear view of the general public. The elite discourse goes on more or less in public (though much more explicitly in private), but the talk is disconnected from the formal politics of parties and candidates covered by the press. Ordinary voters are not tuned in (nor are political reporters), since the opinions of various notables have no explicit connection to the candidates.

Neither presidential nominee would address these economic prospects candidly during their campaigns in 1988. Nor were they pressed to do so by the press. The candidates are free to offer woolly platitudes about economic growth and brisk slogans—"read my lips: no new taxes"—while serious men in other places are left to discuss the real terms of governing among themselves.

In early 1988 only sophisticated observers could discern that the two major parties were maneuvering toward another compact on taxes of the sort they had entered into many times before. For obvious reasons, they did not wish to share this postelection surprise with the voters.

Democrats in Congress created a bipartisan blue-ribbon commission— grandly titled the National Economic Commission and composed of "party elders" like corporate lawyer-lobbyist Robert S. Strauss—which was designed to provide political cover for the next president when he had to undertake such unpopular measures as raising taxes and cutting government benefits. The NEC intended to announce its bipartisan recommendations right after the 1988 election. In the meantime, it kept its mouth shut.

"The White House is putting horrendous pressure on the commission to make no public statements on anything substantive before the election,'' a staff aide to one commission member told me during the campaign summer. ''Their logic is that if the commission positions are aired now, the candidates will have to lock themselves into positions of denial—no tax increases, no gas tax, no entitlement cuts. It could be counterproductive.''

George Bush seized that ground anyway. As a candidate, he accused the Democrats, accurately enough, of plotting to raise taxes if they won back the White House. What Bush did not say was that many influential Republicans were in on the plot too. While the Republican candidate exploited the antitax posture, Richard G. Darman was privately advising key players in both parties not to worry. Darman was then a partner in a major Wall Street brokerage, Shearson Lehman Brothers, but insiders assumed he would become budget director if George Bush became president.

Never mind the campaign rhetoric, they were told. At the appropriate political moment, a grand bipartisan deal would still be doable. If the Democrats were there on spending cuts, Darman confided, George Bush would be there on raising taxes. This scenario, widely heralded among Washington insiders, became known as the ''Big Bang'' strategy.

There was only one problem: This elite bipartisan consensus was promoting a policy agenda directly counter to what voters at large wanted. Raising taxes and cutting benefits would be poison for any presidential candidate who touched the subject, which is why such conversations are necessarily private.

''The elite view of what should be done is completely different from everybody else's,'' said Stephen E. Bell of Salomon Brothers, who had formerly served as Republican staff director of the Senate Budget Committee. ''Opinion leaders strongly support a big increase in the gasoline tax. They want big cuts in Social Security and Medicare or higher taxes on the elderly. The public is against all those.''

Bell's analysis was confirmed in a Gallup Poll survey, conducted for the Times Mirror Company, which found opinion leaders from finance, business and government aligned against public opinion on these tax questions and many others. Only 10 percent of the people favored higher taxes on Social Security benefits; 66 percent opposed higher gasoline taxes; 69 percent opposed a national sales tax. If there must be a tax increase, the citizens said, tax the upper-income brackets. Raising income taxes on those earning more than $80,000 a year was favored by 82 percent of the public. Neither Dukakis nor Bush seemed interested in that solution. Business and financial leaders were, not surprisingly, overwhelmingly opposed, for it meant taxing them.[6]

Thus, the only suspenseful political question, as George Bush took office in 1989, was how the elite consensus might work its will in the face of the stubborn resistance of the citizenry. This is usually the core of the action on taxes: how to distract public anger while things get done. The feat had been accomplished many times during the previous decade, but Steve Bell was dubious that it would succeed again.

"Why can't elites do this deal? Because they won't have the votes," Bell predicted. "The elites understand the precariousness of their situation, not just the financial elites, but the governing elites in this town. The alienation between the governed and the governors is starting to have palpable consequences. The politicians no longer have the ability to go home and persuade their folks to follow when they lead. They know the response will be: Fuck you."

The distorted federal tax code is, as Bell suggested, a central element feeding the popular disenchantment with government and politics. For well over a decade, ordinary voters had heard the perennial chatter from Washington about tax cuts. While they might not know any of the statistics, they knew at least that their own taxes had not been cut. The public's fierce resistance to new taxes, derided by elites as selfish and short-sighted, is firmly grounded in the facts of their own experience.

Popular anger toward the federal tax system was not always the case, as some assume. In the early postwar years, when income-tax rates were steeply progressive, the public overwhelmingly described the federal tax code as "fair"—85 percent, according to the Gallup Poll. By 1984, according to an opinion survey conducted for the Internal Revenue Service, 80 percent believed the contrary: "The present tax system benefits the rich and is unfair to the ordinary working man and woman."[7]

Among the "benefits" reserved for the rich is the fact that even the enforcement of the tax laws was seriously compromised during the Reagan era. The Internal Revenue Service reported that, as of September 1989, the government was owed $87 billion by taxpayers who had underreported or simply not paid their admitted obligations (compared to $5 billion in 1973 and $18 billion in 1981). The chance of getting caught at grand-scale tax evasion was reduced substantially because the sample of income-tax returns that are closely examined by the IRS has been shrunk by 42 percent, thanks to Reagan's severe cuts in the IRS enforcement budget.

The "tax cheats" are not, on the whole, "little guys" who depend on wages and salaries. Most citizens pay their federal income taxes involuntarily through payroll deductions and they file the simplified reporting form that leaves little opportunity for evasive tactics. Only $1.4 billion of the missing $87 billion was attributed to wage earners.

Among the delinquents were 17 taxpayers who owed more than $100 million each and 3,335 taxpayers who each owed more than $1 million. About

$10 billion of the uncollected taxes involved income from invested capital, stocks and bonds and capital gains. About one fourth of the missing revenue, $21 billion, was owed by business—mostly major corporations.[8]

Washington insiders were not unaware of the public anger that had accumulated on these matters. "The American people didn't understand what was happening at first, but now they are beginning to get it," Charls Walker, the premier tax lobbyist for corporate interests, acknowledged in early 1990. "This is an explosive situation we've got here. The political leaders may be able to stanch it this time, but it could blow up if Tom Foley and George Mitchell [the Democratic leaders in Congress] aren't sufficiently responsible."

Something much more complicated than greed is driving the modern tax contest—an economy that no longer produces enough returns to provide ample shares for everyone. In this economic environment, tax politics is a way to protect oneself or to stick someone else with the loss. For nearly thirty years following World War II, the growth and distribution of incomes in American society had been fairly constant (though grossly unequal). Economic expansion was widely shared among citizens of all classes.

Since 1973, however, wages in real terms, discounted for inflation, have been stagnant or declining. Factory workers in Italy now earn more per hour than U.S. workers. The rewards changed most dramatically in the 1980s—at the very time government was cutting tax burdens for the well-to-do. During the last decade, the top 1 percent of American families grossly increased their share of total U.S. income—from 8 percent or 9 percent to more than 14 percent.[9]

"Something's gone wrong with the American dream, at least in material terms," Walker observed. "This is part of the source of the political resentment."

Republicans, historically the party of money, naturally demurred and denied this new reality, at least so long as Republicans were in the White House. But Democrats, supposedly the party of working men and women, turned away from it too. Senator Daniel Patrick Moynihan of New York expressed his own distress:

"The people to whom this is happening know that it's happening to them and they also know that the Democrats don't know it. At least, we don't talk about it. If this were the 1960s, that's all we would be talking about. Good God, what's happening to our country? We're losing touch with that kind of reality. If this is not a crucial proposition for the Democratic party, then our politics have changed."

When the pie is shrinking, someone has to give up his or her slice. Starting in the late 1970s, a fierce political contest ensued on many fronts around this never-acknowledged question: Who will hang on to their share and who must lose theirs? The U.S. tax code, as revised over the last fifteen years, reveals the winner.

This broad economic explanation, however, does not answer the question of politics: How could this betrayal of the many be accomplished in an ostensible framework of democracy? The short, though overly simple answer is: collusion, artful collusion among governing elites and the politicians who claimed to be adversaries. A government that is ostensibly divided between the two parties has learned to work as one.

As Richard Darman once baldly explained, important tax legislation can be achieved by "the political equivalent of an immaculate conception: a compromise that materializes without any politician having to take blame."[10]

The politics of taxation creates its own ideologies and, through most of the twentieth century, the argument has often pitted elite groups against the general population. The graduated income tax, in which the burden rises in relation to one's wealth and income, was the Populists' answer to the gross maldistribution of economic returns generated by modern industrial society. Its justifying principle, stripped of corollary arguments, is that government's core function is to preserve the social order. People of great material wealth inevitably benefit from that service more than other citizens—since social chaos would put their private property at risk.[11]

The monied elites' counterargument was first effectively framed during the 1920s by Andrew Mellon, the wealthy banker who served as Treasury secretary under three Republican presidents. Soaking the rich, Mellon argued, was bad for the economy and, therefore, bad for everyone. His goal was to eliminate the graduated tax system altogether and replace it with flat taxes on consumption, in which rich and poor would pay the same toll. This is not very different from the contemporary tax arguments, except that Mellon enunciated his purpose more candidly than modern conservatives would dare.

"The prosperity of the lower and middle classes depends upon the good fortune and light taxes of the rich," Mellon declared.[12]

The opposing view was expressed by remnant populists like Senator Ralph Yarborough of Texas, who employed this flavorful campaign slogan: "Put the jam on the lower shelf where the little man can reach it."[13]

In most seasons, the politics of taxes plays out between those two poles—an argument for social equity versus the economic hegemony of the investor classes. This might be called the ideology of taxation, and it provides another important screen that the public cannot see through. Once a politician has accepted the ideological assumptions proffered by the monied interests, then he may proceed on a straight path to their conclusions about whose taxes should be reduced. Since the late 1970s, Andrew Mellon's side has won nearly every contest, but with an ingenious twist—tax cuts for the rich are sold as tax cuts for the "little guy."

The Reagan conservatives' celebrated doctrine of "supply-side" economics was, one might say, Andrew Mellon in drag—dressed up in populist denim. The economic logic was Mellon's, but the covering rhetoric justified reducing the tax burdens of the wealthy by promising to spread the jam around a little—to cut everybody's tax rate at once. The regressive effects of the proposal were transparent (and freely acknowledged afterward by the Republican draftsmen), but the basic logic was not challenged by the Democratic opposition. They had already bought into it.

The most dramatic political shift of the 1980s was not in the Republican party, which, after all, had always sided with money. It was among the Democrats who employed facile arguments to abandon the goal of social equity in favor of "trickle-down" economics.

This ideological transformation was accomplished within a political structure very different from what had existed a generation ago. Political parties, whose internal control had been weakened over twenty-five years, were less able to dictate terms to rank-and-file members. In this environment, the political labor necessary to sell a program door-to-door, so to speak, is naturally best suited to the interests with the resources to deploy coordinated networks of lobbyists and churn out the supporting propaganda. In this new environment, business was more creative than organized labor or its other adversaries. It developed new modes of salesmanship—the myriad clusters and temporary coalitions formed among corporations and across trade sectors, always accompanied by systematic money giving.

With no reliable party structure to defend them or poke holes in the deceptive arguments, unorganized voters were hopelessly outgunned. Whatever its other virtues, the new politics of liberated individuals in Congress has not proved to be a reliable defender of the people on the core question of taxation.

The elites also recognized, however, that intensive lobbying is not sufficient by itself. They must also advance a broad public purpose for their objectives—a screen that will distance the specifics from their own obvious self-interest. Yes, the wealthy will get a larger tax cut, but that's not the real purpose. The real purpose is to create jobs. To broadcast this disinterested assurance, they create such mechanisms as bipartisan study groups and so-called "blue-ribbon commissions" composed of public-spirited opinion leaders.

"How do you get around the problem that we don't have a Sam Rayburn or a Lyndon Johnson to ram this thing through?" Charls Walker asked rhetorically. "You go the route of the blue-ribbon commission."

The loss of centralized control has left governing elites in a seemingly permanent state of anxiety. Despite their repeated victories on taxes, opinion leaders, with evident sincerity, regularly lament the government's inability to govern—that is, to implement their far-sighted solutions. Since they never get everything they want, they plead constantly for more courageous "leadership." While citizens generally feel abused and ignored by politics, the political elites describe the opposite condition—a "plebiscite democracy" ruled by the fickle impulses of the voters.

Bush's budget director, Richard Darman, spoke of the public's "self-indulgent" attitudes with droll condescension. "Now-nowism," he called it. "Our current impatience is that of the consumer not the builder, the self-indulgent not the pioneer," he complained. The Reagan tax cutting had begun with the Great Communicator's paeans to the energies of everyday working people. A decade later, with the government mired in debt, Darman likened the American public to a "spoiled child."[14]

Disparaging public opinion is, of course, a necessary prelude to ignoring it. The elites' language of despair over the commonweal is a vital element in their politics, for it creates another screen—a climate that encourages political leaders to be "responsible" by going against the obvious wishes of their constituents. The hesitant are scolded. Gross deceptions are legitimized in pursuit of the greater good. The oblique dialogues that surround the subject of taxation can then be conducted with a broad wink among the players. Over fifteen years, the screen has worked again and again.

The last progressive tax measure proposed by a U.S. president came from Jimmy Carter in fall of 1977. It was decimated—in a Congress controlled by Democrats. Egged on by corporate lobbyists, an uprising in congressional ranks led by right-of-center Democrats turned on their leaders and prevailed. Campaigning for president, Carter had called the tax code a "national disgrace" and promised to eliminate many of the most flagrant loopholes for corporations and the wealthy. He proposed to raise the tax on capital gains and lower rates for individuals. A year later, Congress cut the capital-gains rate in half, lowered the corporate tax rate and made the temporary investment-tax credit for business permanent.

"Carter was screaming that this was a handout for rich people and peanuts for poor people," said Charls Walker, whose Council on Capital Formation helped to inspire the revolt of the haves. "We beat their ass two-to-one on the House floor."

The turning point was the 1978 tax bill, in which governing elites changed the premises of tax policy from achieving equity to augmenting the returns on capital. Amid the aggravations of rising inflation, Walker's corporate clients and like-minded economists persuaded politicians that the problem of lagging productivity in the American economy was caused by the cost of capital. Merrill Lynch, the New York exchange, the Brookings Institution and others all produced expert studies, seconded by influential senators in both parties, that proclaimed the "capital formation problem."

The liberal response to this was quite limp, partly because the Democratic party had been playing its own deceptive game of empty "tax cuts" in prior years. As the persistent inflation of the 1970s swelled government revenues and pushed many wage earners into higher tax-rate brackets, Democrats would magnanimously enact a new "tax cut" every couple of years—in effect, giving back some of the money to the taxpayers while devoting the remaining surpluses to narrow tax loopholes for special interests or for new government spending. Democrats were not in a position to be too self-righteous about either equity or economic growth.

The Democratic party, furthermore, was getting more distant from its traditional working-class constituencies. A swarm of newly elected younger Democrats who came to office after the 1974 Watergate scandal were mostly not from working-class neighborhoods, but from the suburbs and often from Republican districts. They were intellectually inclined to be more sympathetic to the business argument and also anxious to dissociate themselves from their party's fading power centers, organized labor and the big-city machines.

Newer Democrats, as Thomas B. Edsall has pointed out, were also reading the election returns. As voter participation declined year after year, most dramatically among lower-income citizens, the remaining active electorate became increasingly skewed toward the upper brackets—the people who cared most about tax provisions like capital gains. In the process, a large, unorganized bloc of citizens was being left behind.[15]

But the conservatives' attitudes toward tax politics were changing too. Robert S. McIntyre, director of Citizens for Tax Justice, explained the shift:

"Typically, prior to the seventies, Republicans were not big fans of tax breaks for business because it was economic tinkering by government. And Democrats weren't for them because it went against their constituents. In the 1970s, there was a flip-flop. The Republicans started playing constituency politics—appealing to the people who contribute to their campaigns and their core constituency. Democrats, as big-government types, like to tinker around with the economy through the tax code. It feels good and, ideologically, they have no problem with it."

In terms of who benefited, the 1978 tax bill was perhaps the most regressive measure since the 1920s, but it was only the beginning. Its ingredients led directly to the feeding frenzy of 1981 and Ronald Reagan's famous victory—a tax measure that would deprive the government of $750 billion in revenue over the first five years.

The across-the-board reduction of 25 percent in individual tax rates was transparently regressive since, as a matter of simple arithmetic, the larger one's income, the greater would be the reduction in the tax burden. The corporate tax code was so thoroughly gutted in 1981 that hundreds of profitable corporations became free riders in the American political system—paying no taxes whatever or even collecting refunds.

The 1981 tax legislation was so generous in the tax breaks for commercial real estate that it launched the nation's gaudy boom in new office buildings— the boom that collapsed in bankruptcies at the end of the decade. The new tax rules for depreciation were such that developers and investors found they could put up a new building and make money on it, even if it was half empty. They built lots of them. When the real estate–lending regulations were loosened for commercial banks in the 1982 financial legislation, the stage was fully prepared for the great financial collapse that engulfed both builders and their bankers later—and led to another taxpayer bailout.

By focusing on the partisan combat over internal disputes, the media portrayed the 1981 legislative showdown as a test of strength between the two political parties, as it was on the surface. The Republicans won on that level. But the partisan clashes obscured the deeper bipartisan consensus that already existed. Most Democrats in the House and Senate had already endorsed the general concept of a regressive "supply-side" tax cut, many of them before Ronald Reagan was even elected. In the end, only a handful of Democrats voted against the idea.

It was not Reagan, for instance, who opened the floodgate of tax giveaways for business interests but Representative Dan Rostenkowski, Democratic chairman of the House Ways and Means Committee. Prompted by Walker and the corporate lobbyists, Rosty initiated the bidding war over tax favors that Republicans were hoping to avoid. In the end, Democrats lost the contest to the more generous Republican White House.

When neither party attempts to impose restraint, power always flows to the margins—the handful of swing votes that can decide an issue—and opportunistic representatives made deals for scores of clients, trading their votes for tax concessions. "The hogs were really feeding," as budget director David Stockman said. The problem, he added, "is unorganized groups can't play in this game."[16]

Further, it was the Democrats, not the Republicans, who first proposed bringing down the top tax rate on unearned income—eliminating the traditional distinction that passive earnings from dividends or interest should be taxed at a higher rate than wage income derived from human labor. The Reagan White House graciously accepted the Democrats' proposal and the marginal rate of 70 percent on unearned income was abolished.

"The people who are really active politically are the upper-income people," Walker explained, "and a lot of them happen to be Democrats."

The general public, however, opposed this change at the time and, indeed, still favors a tax code that treats income from work more generously than income from capital. A *Wall Street Journal* poll in 1990 found that, by 59 percent to 22 percent, people still think earnings from investments should be taxed at a higher rate than income from wages and salaries. Even two thirds of the upper-income people think so.[17]

These details and ambiguities did not get through to most citizens at the time, especially if they depended on television for their news. The contest was portrayed in simpler terms: President Reagan and the Republicans want to cut your taxes and the Democrats are trying to stop them. Not surprisingly, the public rallied around the president. Beneath that broad umbrella, special interests could accomplish quite a lot for themselves. John D. Raffaelli, a tax lobbyist and former staff counsel on the Senate Finance Committee, once explained the "Dan Rather rule" that governs the politics of complex tax provisions: "You can do taxes as long as Dan Rather can't explain them in 10 seconds."[18]

The orgy of 1981 defined everything that has followed since: The perennial tax debate is still preoccupied with finding ways to correct the embarrassing excesses of Reagan's tax legislation and reduce the huge deficits that "supply-side economics" created. Two major tax bills were passed in 1982 and 1984, taking back some of the most egregious loopholes and benefits provided to business in the original Reagan legislation. The projected losses in federal revenue were thus reduced, but not enough to fill the hole, especially given the soaring defense budgets.

Who will have to give the money back? That question has driven all of the subsequent tax debates.

For ordinary wage earners, the question was answered quickly. They would. Even before the Reagan tax cuts were fully phased in, working people were socked with a tax increase much larger than what they had supposedly just been given. In 1983, with a minimum of controversy, Congress raised their taxes by roughly $200 billion—more than erasing any gain they might have anticipated from the Reagan income-tax cuts. This was among the largest tax increases in history, but it was accomplished without much fuss by increasing the payroll tax collected for Social Security.

This was bait and switch on a grand scale. The payroll tax for Social Security is one of the most regressive levies the government collects from citizens because it has a fixed ceiling that exempts all income above a certain level. A middle-level manager earning $50,000 a year will pay exactly the same amount as his company's CEO, who makes $5 million.

The deal was sold through the mechanism of a "blue-ribbon commission." Right after the 1982 elections, a bipartisan presidential commission, chaired by Republican economist (and future Federal Reserve chairman) Alan

Greenspan, recommended the tax increase and other "reforms" to insure the soundness of the retirement system far into the next century. Social Security would be shifted from its traditional structure of pay-as-you-go financing to one that would accumulate vast surpluses—hundreds of billions collected now from workers and set aside for future beneficiaries.

Three months after the commission reported its ideas, the reforms were law. Ronald Reagan, who had built his career on defending working people against taxes, endorsed the payroll-tax increase after he was told by White House insiders that the rising tax burden on young working people would eventually lead to a taxpayer revolt and the demise of Social Security. "In time, these reforms will sink this thing of its own weight," the president was advised.

Reagan was reportedly cheered by that prospect. Deep in the Republican soul lurks an abiding contempt for the Social Security system, a prejudice lingering from New Deal days when conservatives saw it as the vanguard of socialism. While Democrats used Social Security as an effective scare issue in the 1982 elections, they threw in with the Republicans right afterward and endorsed the tax increase.[19]

The general public, though uneasy, was essentially not represented in the Social Security debate. The two major parties agreed to run this through the system quickly and without alerting working people to the tax implications for them. The media accepted the bipartisan accord as evidence that the issue lacked controversy and treated it routinely.

Even so, there was more public resentment on the issue than the bipartisan harmony indicated. A *Washington Post*/ABC News survey found that 38 percent of the public felt the Democrats, supposedly the defenders of Social Security, had given away too much to the Republicans. Young people, eighteen to thirty years old, were overwhelmingly skeptical that Social Security benefits would still be available when they reached retirement. Given the drift of politics, their suspicion seemed well founded.

Among governing elites, however, the adroit enactment of the 1983 tax increase is remembered as a triumph of political management. At Harvard's Kennedy School of Government, the episode is used as a case study in good government, illustrating how decision makers can make forward-looking policy and work their way around what the professors call "the fickleness of politics."[20]

For most taxpayers, this event was pivotal—as well as costly—to their personal tax equation. The Social Security increases rendered the continuing talk about reducing the income tax largely irrelevant to most working people—since roughly three fourths of wage earners pay more each year through the payroll tax than they will pay through the income tax. Because the payroll tax was now set to increase in regular increments, no amount of tinkering with income-tax rates, deductions or tax credits was likely to offset the rising burden for average Americans.

The terms were now established for the great shift in the way that the government is financed. From 1980 to 1988, revenue from the Social Security payroll tax increased by 23 percent as a portion of total federal revenue, while the personal income tax declined by 6 percent and the corporate income tax by 23 percent. By 1983, the winners and losers were clearly identified.[21]

Yet the contest did not end. Indeed, notwithstanding the facts of what had already occurred, elite commentators like Robert Strauss and Pete Peterson continued to commit gross distortions, as they tried to explain the huge federal deficits that had been created when their own taxes were reduced. The problem, they kept complaining, was the soaring cost of "entitlements," especially Social Security.

Yet that problem had just been "fixed" and workers were now paying for it. In fiscal terms, ordinary wage earners were now covering the hole left by the excesses of business and wealthy individuals. Social Security was not only paying its own way, but would now accumulate growing surplus revenue each year—$74 billion in 1991, $126 billion by 1995 and $225 billion by 2000. This mounting hoard collected from workers helped the government to obscure the continuing deficits in the operating budget and to offset the economic consequences.

Nevertheless, the influential "party elders" persisted in portraying Social Security as a dangerous drain on the society's resources—an example of the self-indulgence that politicians must be brave enough to correct. It was as though the 1983 tax increases hadn't happened.

The next great bait-and-switch transaction—the celebrated "tax reform" legislation of 1986—involved all the same elements, including active collusion between the two political parties. But this contest was not really aimed at the general taxpayers. It was essentially a dispute between the two overlapping power blocs within the monied interests—wealthy individuals versus corporations—over who would get the money. The individuals won, but the corporations did not entirely lose either.

For the general public, the usual screens of large-minded distractions were constructed. The purpose of this legislation, Republicans and Democrats jointly announced, was "tax simplification." That theme became a bad joke as the process unfolded and even the president abandoned it. As income-tax rates were reduced, the tax code became so weird that people who make $80,000 a year were left paying the highest tax rate, 33 percent—higher than all the wealthier people above them, who pay only 28 percent.

The other announced objective was "fairness"—closing loopholes to force all those hundreds of profitable corporations to start paying federal taxes again. Some progress was made toward this goal, but much less than advertised. The proportion of profit-making corporations that legally avoid taxes declined afterward from 36 percent to 23 percent—still roughly one fourth of them. Tax revenue from corporations consistently fell below the government's expectations in subsequent years, as corporate tax lawyers exploited a tax code porous with the exceptions and artful distinctions that the corporate lobbyists had helped craft.

The gravest injury to the general taxpayers, however, was in what the 1986 tax reformers decided not to do—to confront the federal deficits and reduce them significantly. Instead, President Reagan declared up front that the measure must be "revenue neutral"—neither increasing nor reducing overall federal revenue—and the Democratic party swiftly embraced his terms. Walter Mondale, the Democratic candidate for president, had been devastated in the 1984 election by talking about tax increases. This time, as Danny Rosten-kowski told me, "You won't see any profiles in courage."

A vast rewriting of the tax code would be undertaken without addressing the fiscal problems that elites were always lamenting. This central political evasion meant that the huge deficits would continue unabated (and indeed would grow to $360 billion by 1991). But the evasion also meant that ordinary taxpayers remained a vulnerable target for future tax politics, when the day came that the political community decided to get serious about restoring the government's revenue base.

To confront the deficits would have required much tougher politics—closing the major loopholes *and* raising the top-bracket rates, but without giving the monied elites anything in return. No one in power wished to take that on. Instead, enormous political energy was expended on behalf of the competing interests, while the central governing problem was deferred to future years. Where were the elite scolds who complained so regularly about the deficits and American profligacy? They were busy in the tax debate too, defending their own tax benefits.

The general public, having been burned repeatedly by the bait of tax rhetoric, did not buy it this time. Despite the popular president's barnstorming and the political community's enthusiasm for "tax reform," citizens remained skeptical or even hostile. Opinion surveys found only small minorities (as little as 18 percent) supporting the drastic reduction in the top tax rates.

"Tax reform to the American people means fairness, and their perception of fairness is more progressive, not less progressive," said pollster Burns Roper. His firm found that 77 percent of the people thought the upper-income brackets were already paying too little.

The debate proceeded without them to its predetermined conclusion—the drastic reduction of individual tax rates, offset by the restoration of some of the taxation on business. These changes, of course, often affect the same people, so that, while the corporations lost, their highly paid executives and major stockholders won. Indeed, the most spectacular beneficiaries in 1986 were a select group of 390,000 Americans whose incomes were $200,000 or higher but who were not giving up any significant loopholes. On average, the lowered rates gave these citizens a tax windfall of $50,000 each—a total of $20 billion, or roughly ten times what the measure devoted in tax relief for the poor.

One corporate CEO confided to Senator Paul Simon of Illinois that, according to his accountant, he would get a tax cut of $250,000 on his $1.5 million salary. Presumably this softened his objections to the higher taxes being imposed on his company.[22]

Most Democrats sided with the rich people, on the righteous grounds that they were going after the tax giveaways for business. Some liberals argued weakly that, while they were voting for the rich people, they would come back in a year or so and rescind the action by restoring the higher rates. The history of the income tax mocked this wishful thinking. Since 1913, Congress had gotten up the nerve to raise the top income-tax rate substantially on only four occasions—during World War I, the Great Depression, World War II and the Korean War. In other words, it required a seismic event for politicians to go after rich folks.

The new social and political reality was that most Democrats in Congress appeared to be closer to the wealthy (especially the wealthy who were campaign contributors) than to working stiffs. Robert McIntyre observed this phenomenon whenever he proposed various progressive tax measures to Democrats.

"Democrats don't mind talking about the top fifth of the economy, people making over $50,000 a year, but if you talk about the top 1 percent, people earning $200,000 or more, they get nervous," McIntyre said. "They get cold feet partly because that's where their campaign money comes from. Staff people tell me the politicians don't want to take on the very richest people. In many ways, they are the people the congressmen think of as their peers—or whom they'd like to think of as their peers."

The major corporations represented by Charls Walker and other lobbyists lost a lot in 1986 when many of the major tax concessions they had won back in 1981 were scaled down. Still, they were not exactly grieving either. After all, they were still way ahead on taxes for the decade. And Walker found many of his CEOs so enthused about their individual reductions that they were uninterested in mounting an all-out campaign to defeat the bill.

"People asked me, would you vote for this bill if you were a member of Congress?" Walker recalled. "I said I probably would. I didn't like the higher rate for capital gains but I loved the lower personal rates. I never dreamed we could get a top personal rate of 33 percent and a corporate rate of 35 percent. If I thought this was the last chapter in federal tax policy, I would be desperate. But I've seen the pendulum swing before." Business would win back the investment tax credit, Walker predicted confidently, when the economy was in its next recession.

Indeed, a few months after the 1986 legislation became law, Walker and other business lobbyists were back on Capitol Hill, recruiting influential co-sponsors from both parties for a measure that would undo the grand compromise they had just fashioned. Congress had just raised the rate on capital gains, the tax collected on the appreciation of stocks and real estate when these and other assets are sold. Now, Walker proposed, it was time to cut capital gains.

Bait and switch. Once the wealthy achieved a lower tax rate, they started to work on getting back the loopholes and exceptions they had given up. Andrew Mellon's hoary logic was dragged out once again, this time dressed again as the "capital formation problem," and subsequently embraced by George Bush. The American economy suffered from lagging investment, it was said, because the cost of capital was too high. Reducing taxes on capital would encourage the wealthy investors to create more jobs for everyone else. If this argument sounds familiar, it is because it is where the story began back in 1978.

Among all their other disadvantages, citizens are particularly handicapped because the tax debate never ends. It is a continuum of politics that stretches over years. As Walker said, the monied elites understand this and know that they can afford to accept trade-offs in one season because they will be back again next time, with new reasons to plead for tax relief. If political parties were reliable organizations, they would defend the citizenry against these perennial raids on the public treasury. The present reality is that both political parties collaborate with the raiders.

There were at least two obvious things wrong with invoking Mellon's economic logic at this point. First, it had already been applied in the grossest terms during the previous decade—and failed to produce the promised results. New investment during the 1980s was not stimulated by the tax cuts awarded to the wealthy; on the contrary, the pace of investment actually fell below the previous average. A lot of the money flowed, instead, into financial speculation and inflated real-estate values—the excesses that were unwinding in bankruptcy and financial crisis by the end of the decade.

Second, the business advocates were correct about the high cost of raising capital in the United States—it was two or three times higher than in Germany or Japan—but the principal explanation for this was not federal taxes, but the historically high level of interest rates during the decade. Real interest rates in the 1980s—the nominal interest rate discounted for inflation—were the highest of the twentieth century. And what caused interest rates to remain so high? If one asked the Federal Reserve, the Fed blamed it on the federal deficits—the deficits created by the huge tax cuts.

In other words, the facile economic arguments advanced by elites were inducing the political community to chase its own tail. However, from season to season, the chase always ended at the same place—more tax reduction for the wealth holders.

In another era, Senator Pat Moynihan's remarks might have been passed over as the usual rhetoric one expected from liberal Democrats. Yet, in the political context of the late 1980s, his words sounded like populist thunder. All Moynihan said was: "I think it's about time the American workers got a break." With that, the New York senator proposed to give the wage earners back their money—that is, to cut the Social Security payroll tax back to its prior levels and to stop the regressive charade surrounding federal taxation.

The senator himself was a bit taken aback by the storm of reaction. He was swiftly acclaimed by voices from left and right, but also denounced as "irresponsible" by tax authorities in his own party as well as the Republicans in the White House. The people who had shaped federal tax policy for fifteen years—who presided over the betrayal—were preparing to do so again and they recognized the threatening nature of Moynihan's proposal. Though it was not enacted in 1990 and only cursorily debated, Moynihan's idea crystallized what Charls Walker had called "an explosive situation."

What Moynihan did, in effect, was to put the stinking reality on the table where everyone had to look at it. By formulating a dramatic tax reduction that would be genuinely progressive—putting real money in the hands of the broad middle class—Moynihan automatically brought the ranks of the unrepresented into the debate. He may, in fact, have created the political climate that kept the elite consensus from fully accomplishing its agenda in 1990. Some believed—hoped, at least—that his provocation would become a new turning point in the deep politics of taxation.

Moynihan seemed an unlikely tribune for popular revolt against the status quo. For one thing, he himself had served on the bipartisan commission that proposed the Social Security tax increases back in 1983. Now he was belatedly denouncing the arrangement as a hoax perpetrated on working people. While the senator liked to invoke his own working-class origins, he was better understood as a public policy intellectual, fully credentialed and comfortable with the governing elites, a Harvard professor who had dipped in and out of government as a policy thinker for three presidents, before coming to the Senate in 1976.

Moynihan recognized—and had the nerve to declare—that the evasive tax politics of the 1980s was leading toward a future fiscal crisis, in which the public at large would be confronted with monstrous alternatives—either a huge tax increase to fill the hole that was now being masked by the Social Security surpluses or a drastic cutback in the Social Security benefits (thus fulfilling young people's skepticism about the future of the retirement system). Or perhaps both. Moynihan's purpose was to force the crisis now—and make the political system face it honestly.

His initiative did not have that effect, but it at least exposed the feckless-ness of his own party. Ways and Means Chairman Danny Rostenkowski, who presides over tax decisions in the House, belittled Moynihan's proposal as competing for "worst idea of the year." Democratic Senate leaders were struck mute, as though Moynihan had told an obscene joke on the Senate floor. House Democrats appointed a committee chaired by the majority leader to study the idea. The committee never met.

The party's two most powerful constituency groups—organized labor and the elderly—expressed their coolness to the idea of cutting young workers' taxes. The American Association of Retired Persons worried about the actu-arial tables. The AFL-CIO worried about financing big government. As in-dustrial unions have declined in size, public employees have become a larger and larger proportion of the labor federation's membership.[23]

The tax debate, in any case, was proceeding toward a different goal—how to embrace the nettle of additional tax increases and spending cuts, as outlined by the elite consensus, without inciting a damaging backlash from voters who would feel betrayed again. Doing the "right thing" required an extended dance of feint-and-parry between the two political parties—the story that provided the main focus for news coverage—since Republicans and Demo-crats were mutually suspicious of getting trapped in blame by the other side. If the Republican president and the Democratic Congress were going to stick the people once again with unpopular and regressive measures, they must agree to hold hands when the deed was done.

The National Economic Commission, created by the Democrats to provide just such political cover, stalled out in stalemate when the newly elected president declined to cooperate with the "blue-ribbon" approach. On the other hand, Democratic leaders succeeded in blocking Bush's capital-gains tax cut, trying to force him into a public admission that taxes must be raised, notwith-standing his campaign promise.

In early 1990, Danny Rostenkowski started the action by offering an olive branch and a broad wink to his old friend George Bush. Rostenkowski pro-posed what he called a "cold turkey" plan for deficit reduction—a plan that was a reasonable replica of what the elite opinion leaders had recommended. The idea of a national sales tax was left out—still too volatile for politicians to embrace in public (though Charls Walker said Rostenkowski has assured him privately that "it's coming, it's coming").

Otherwise, Rosty's "cold turkey" prescribed a familiar list of sacrifices— $20 billion in new consumption taxes and $22 billion saved by cutting "en-titlements" and other federal programs. While he also proposed to nick the highest income earners with a small rate increase, this was interpreted as a proffered trade-off for George Bush in exchange for granting the president's capital-gains cut.[24]

Rosty's ploy set in motion the high-level action that led to a summer of "budget summit" negotiations between the White House and Democratic congressional leaders. These private parlays were meant to serve as the new equivalent of a blue-ribbon commission. The president, rather clumsily, agreed to withdraw his "no taxes" promise to the American people so the discussions could proceed in mutual trust.

Party leaders closeted themselves at Andrews Air Force Base for the tedious back-and-forth on details. For all the many complications and false starts, these negotiations produced an agreement that should not have surprised any patient observer of tax politics. Just as Darman had suggested two years before, by the grace of "immaculate conception" in which no one could be blamed, Democrats and Republicans produced a "Big Bang" for the voters.

The proposed tax increases and spending cuts of the bipartisan "summit" announced in late September were less extreme, but remarkably consistent with what Rosty had proposed in March. They mirrored in moderate outline what the elite opinion makers had recommended in their "austerity" sermons before the 1988 election. The burden of sacrifice would be distributed regressively, hitting the least among us with the most injury. No increase in the top tax rate. A capital-gains reduction, poorly disguised as investment incentives for small business. Regressive increases in taxes on gasoline, alcohol, tobacco and other items of everyday consumption. A huge reduction in Medicare benefits. The conservative logic of Andrew Mellon had won on nearly every point.[25]

Democratic leaders said it was "the best deal" they could get. *The Wall Street Journal*, which always covers taxation with more precision and depth than other news media, swiftly put the relevant facts on the table for its well-to-do readers. According to the Joint Committee on Taxation, the top of the income ladder—people earning more than $200,000—would escape once again with the least sacrifice, a tax increase of only 1.7 percent, while people making $30,000 to $40,000 would be hit for 2.9 percent. The poorest families, under $10,000, would suffer a 7.6 percent tax increase because of the regressive nature of consumption taxes.

Rank-and-file Democrats choked on those numbers. So did some back-bench Republicans. The next day, the *Journal* published a devastating account of how the new tax incentives for investment would actually work—spawning a new tax-shelter industry and allowing wealthy investors to harvest millions in upfront tax breaks. "Although the text of the bipartisan agreement carefully avoids describing these as a capital-gains tax break, that's what they are," the *Journal* said. In other words, Democratic leaders were giving President Bush what he most wanted and what they had vowed to resist.[26]

The "Big Bang" blew up in their faces. A rump coalition of younger Republicans, angry that Bush had abandoned the GOP's posture of "no new taxes," and liberal Democrats, disgusted by the proposal's gross inequities, united on the House floor to defeat their leaders. This was perhaps the first House roll call of any consequence in fifteen years where the broad interests of the general public defeated the elites, head to head, on a question of taxes. Among other things, it demonstrated the value of democratic process—making decisions in public, with up-or-down votes that are recorded, instead of the "immaculate conception" of backroom deals.

Some thought these events represented a new current in American politics, the beginning of resurgence for popular opinion. Others (including myself) remained skeptical. The collapse of the "Big Bang" package did at least demonstrate anew how alienated the leaders of both parties had become from the lives of ordinary Americans.

Senator Moynihan's jarring candor had perhaps altered the atmosphere of tax politics and made the real trade-offs embarrassingly visible. The senator, having made his point, was less ardent about forcing the question on his colleagues. In order not to inconvenience the Democratic leadership, Moynihan agreed to offer his own tax-cut measure for a Senate vote at a time when it was certain to be ruled out of order. The measure carried the Senate roll call, fifty-four to forty-four, in October 1990, but that was short of the sixty votes needed under the parliamentary rules then in force. The next year, Moynihan brought it up again and it was soundly rejected.

Two weeks after the rank-and-file revolt, the party leaders came back with a new package of tax increases and a better deal for the people. Gasoline and other consumption taxes were still raised, but the sting was reduced and some of the pain was shifted upward to hit the wealthy as well. Tax credits gave the poor modest relief; luxury taxes and a small rate increase were aimed at the top brackets. Medicare and Medicaid were still trimmed, but much less drastically.

Danny Rostenkowski overcame his momentary embarrassment and began styling himself as a righteous convert, ready to go after the millionaires on behalf of the people. But the habit of deception was deeply ingrained in Congress and still at work. As *The Philadelphia Inquirer* revealed, one of the 1990 tax provisions, supposedly aimed at raising $10.8 billion from wealthy people, was actually already in the tax code—enacted during the 1986 "tax reform." All Congress did in 1990 was to change it from permanent to temporary.[27]

The warped social vision of the political community also endured. Some Democrats began preparing tax proposals for 1992 designed to hit the rich and reward middle-class families—a promising issue for their next campaign. But some Democrats' idea of what is middle class seemed to hover around families with incomes of $80,000 a year, not the actual middle of American society down around $35,000.

In any case, the sum total of the final package in 1990 or the new tax proposals hardly made a scratch on the gross maldistribution of tax burdens that had been accomplished in the previous seasons of tax legislation. The elite consensus failed to win the full dimensions of its "austerity" agenda, but it did not lose either. It would require a much larger political struggle—genuine popular revolt and new leaders with a different sense of loyalty—to overcome the full legacy of collusion and betrayal.

Given the darkening economic prospects, the broad public is likely to lose again in the future, so long as the tax debate is framed in conservative terms as an argument of equity versus investment. "Fairness," as Charls Walker said, always loses to "economic growth" in tough times. The hegemony of the investor classes depends upon convincing politicians and citizens generally that this is the only choice. For most of the century, when American economic strength was ascendant in the world, the equity argument could now and then prevail. Now that the U.S. economy is embattled by global competition, "fairness" has become a much harder sell.

The facts of economic history do not support Andrew Mellon's logic, not in the contemporary experience nor during the 1920s. Reducing tax burdens for the wealth holders is a political program that will reward some citizens and penalize others. As an economic program, it does not yield the increased savings and investment and faster economic growth that the conservative logic promises. This is not entirely a secret. Conservative economists have pored over the numbers for years, searching for evidence to confirm their conviction that taxing the wealthy lightly benefits everyone else. In theory, they are sure it is right. Only they can't find much in the way of facts.

For example, two economists, Robert E. Lipsey and Irving B. Kravis, examined the role of savings and capital formation in economic growth in a study jointly sponsored by the American Council on Life Insurance and the Conference Board, an industry-sponsored research group. Lipsey and Kravis reviewed growth rates in the United States and other leading industrial nations, decade by decade through the twentieth century, searching for correlations with taxes on capital, savings rates and capital formation. They reported some awkward conclusions to their business sponsors:

"We suspect that differences in taxation are not likely to explain the differences in saving rates," Lipsey and Kravis concluded. It is difficult, they said, to find any evidence linking tax rates on capital to subsequent rates of savings, investment or economic growth.

On the contrary, a rapid buildup of capital formation typically follows a rapid expansion of incomes and employment rather than the other way around.

The strongest factor predicting increased capital investment is expansion of incomes and employment.

"The relationship was typically stronger between income growth in one period and capital formation in the following period," they wrote. "This finding undermines the idea that a spurt in the capital formation ratio is a necessary prerequisite for growth."[28]

In other words, Mellon had it backward and so do later generations of his apostles. A growing economy with widely distributed incomes and full employment creates the effective demand that leads investors to increase capital investment—new factories and more jobs. Capital will not build new factories to make goods that no one can afford to buy. My intent here is not to settle this central dispute of economics, but to demonstrate that this is the real ground on which tax politics ought to be fought. Is "fairness" in the distribution of tax burdens and incomes an enemy of restoring stable economic prosperity? Or is a progressive tax system a necessary precondition for a healthy economy?

And why is this perspective seldom heard in contemporary politics—especially from the party that ostensibly represents working people? The argument for social equity is, in fact, a much stronger case as an economic argument for balanced growth. This case, of course, would have to be documented anew and marshaled on many political fronts before the deeper tides of tax politics are likely to be reversed.

When untutored public opinion expresses its desire for a progressive tax system, people are articulating commonsense wisdom that elites seem unable to grasp: As ordinary people understand it, the American economy cannot be considered healthy when most of its workers and consumers are not.

A few lonely voices do try to cast the debate in those terms, but they are drowned out by the general chorus of conventional wisdom. Old liberal-labor Democrats of an earlier generation have been replaced by younger Democrats who treat tax concessions to the broad public or the poor as pious gestures of political charity, not as components of good economic policy. In the present context, one side of the debate holds the floor, year after year, and the other is held silent.

That bleak statement, of course, sums up the general condition of politics. It is the conclusion of everything that has been recounted up to this point—the how and why of the deformed power relationships that govern decisions across a wide variety of public issues. In the elaborate machinery of modern government, surrounded by expensive experts and lobbying mechanisms, it is very hard for the people's case to be heard.

If the complicated facts of these relationships can be reduced to a single message, it is this: The present system provides no reliable mechanism to represent the people on the most important governing questions—no institution that is committed to listening to them and to speaking for them, no organization that mobilizes the potential strength of people and uses it to confront the rival power of organized money. The problem of modern democracy is rooted in its neglect of unorganized people.

Unfortunately, even this summation does not describe the full scope of the democratic problem before us—or even its most daunting dimensions. Beyond the visible legislative debate and the familiar arenas of decision making examined thus far, there is another, more complicated realm of government, where the politics and power relationships are much harder for people to see. That realm is the modern labyrinth of decision making within the Executive Branch, where the laws are enforced or not enforced on behalf of the public. It is this complex territory where citizens lose again.

4

THE GRAND BAZAAR

The gleaming temples of democracy that tourists visit in Washington, the marble shrines to great leaders and great ideals, are no longer an appropriate emblem for the nation's capital. Washington now is more aptly visualized as a grand bazaar—a steamy marketplace of tents, stalls and noisy peddlers. The din of buying and selling drowns out patriotic music.

The high art of governing—making laws for the nation and upholding them—has been reduced to a busy commerce in deal making. Thousands and thousands of deals are transacted every day in diffuse corners of the city. The rare skills required for politics at the highest level are trivialized as petty haggling, done with the style and swagger of rug merchants.

The Department of Transportation dickers with Detroit over automobile safety. The Department of Agriculture makes deals with farmers on the price of corn and the permissible poison level in pesticides. The Treasury Department haggles with important taxpayers. The Department of Defense buys rockets and airplanes and sells them too.

In the grand bazaar, the two staples of trade are the myriad claims on the federal treasury and the commercial rights and privileges that only the government can bestow—licenses for television stations or airlines, the use of public assets like land or water or timber. All may produce vast good fortune for the winners and the competition for them naturally draws many eager contestants.

It is bargaining over the law itself, however, that provides the richest commerce and has the greatest consequences for democracy. While the news media focus on the conventional political drama of enacting new laws, another less obvious question preoccupies Washington: Will the government enforce the law? Does the new law enacted by Congress really have to mean what the public thinks it means? Or is there a way to change its terms and dilute its impact on private interests? Lawyers inquire whether exceptions can be arranged for important clients. Major corporations warn enforcement officers of dire economic consequences if the legal deadlines are not postponed for a few more years. Senators badger federal agencies to make sure the law is treating their clients and constituents with due regard.

Washington, in other words, engages in another realm of continuing politics that the public rarely sees—governing contests where it is even more difficult and expensive to participate. This is where the supposedly agreed-upon public objectives are regularly subverted, stalled or ignored, where the law is literally diverted to different purposes, where citizens' victories are regularly rendered moot.

Confusion spreads across almost every function of the government, a continuing uncertainty about whether laws will actually be implemented. Those interests that have the resources and the incentive to stall the law's application do not always succeed, of course, but their persistent efforts keep government authority always in doubt—often long after the public was assured that a problem had been addressed.

The transactions where this occurs are mostly submerged in the Executive Branch, scattered across hundreds of bureaus and agencies and focused mainly on the esoteric language of federal regulations and enforcement. The regulatory government is a many-chambered labyrinth, staggeringly complex and compartmentalized in its thousands of parts. But one does not have to study a dizzying organizational chart of federal agencies to understand how it works. One need only visualize what happens to a law after it is enacted to grasp the antidemocratic dynamic.

The deal making is the principal source of the money scandals that occasionally ensnare senators or representatives. When a politician is caught trying to fix things for a campaign contributor, he usually reacts with injured innocence. He was only doing his job. Besides, everyone does it. As morally unsatisfying as these excuses seem, the crooked politicians are articulating an unpleasant truth about modern government. Everybody does do it, including especially the politicians of the Executive Branch.

For democracy, the result is a kind of random lawlessness. Corrective mechanisms that are supposed to prevent irregular political manipulations have

been purposely weakened. And the public inherits grave injustice: a government that will not faithfully perform its most basic function—enforcing the
laws.

The regulatory government is arguably the largest or second largest component
in the political commerce surrounding the federal government, rivaled only by
the defense sector in terms of the human and financial resources it consumes.
Professor Robert B. Reich of Harvard attempted a precise census in the early
1980s and found that the "regulatory community" in Washington consisted of
92,500 people—lawyers, lobbyists, trade-association and public-relations specialists, consultants and corporate reps. Their primary function is to argue over
the content of federal regulations—the precise meaning that will flow from the
laws that Congress has enacted. A decade later, Reich's head count doubtless
understates reality.[1]

The general-interest press does not try to cover the regulatory government,
except for an occasional controversy, mainly because regulatory politics seldom provides a concise, convenient event. These contests are stretched out
over years—a continuum of tedious actions that confounds the standard definition of "news." The regulatory details, moreover, do not look like "politics," but generally surface as mind-numbing arguments over law, science
and economics.[2]

The explosion of modern regulation, more than anything else, is what
brought the money to Washington and transformed the capital from a sleepy
small town to a glamorous power center. During the 1930s, Roosevelt's New
Deal created 42 major regulatory agencies and programs. Most of these involved economic regulation of specific sectors (airlines, broadcasting, oil and
agricultural production and others), arrangements usually created in cooper-
ation with the affected industries. During the 1960s, 53 regulatory programs
were enacted, as consumer issues and environmental protection gained political momentum. From 1970 to 1980, 130 major regulatory laws were enacted.
That is what brought the Fortune 500 to Washington, along with the tens of
thousands of lawyers.[3]

Unlike most of the earlier regulatory laws, the modern generation of
regulation was primarily aimed at curbing the antisocial behavior of businesses
and was equipped to act in much more intrusive ways. New agencies like EPA
or OSHA were not confined to specific industrial sectors like airlines or broadcasting, but were responsible for policing conduct across the entire spectrum.
In that sense, the purposes were truly national.

This design presumably made it harder for a single industry to capture its
regulator and control the agency's decisions, but it also had a unifying impact
on corporate politics—an incentive for diverse business interests to collaborate
in campaigns to thwart new laws. Coalition building among different compa-

nies and industrial sectors became the preferred mode of corporate pressure, and these alliances now deploy battalions of lawyers and lobbyists armed with their expert testimony.[4]

While regulatory laws have accomplished many things, the cumulative result is a civic culture that is quite different from the classical version of government described in civic textbooks. The arrangements of regulatory laws invite—and often require—that all things be negotiable later in the fine print. In time, once that assumption permeated government, the interested parties established that no principle was exempt from tampering. Theodore J. Lowi, the Cornell political scientist, captured the spirit of modern Washington when he described it as governing by "universalized ticket fixing."

The bargaining mode of governance, as Lowi explained, originated in the pluralist logic that fostered many of the New Deal's innovations—reforms and economic interventions intended originally to share governing power with the weak and unrepresented. The goal was to create new forums and agencies for decision making in particular fields of interest, which would provide a place at the governing table for groups of citizens that could not hope to win in the larger political contests over general law. Struggling labor unions were given the National Labor Relations Board. Farmers were given an elaborate committee system with which to influence agricultural policy. The fledgling airline industry was regulated but also protected from competition by the Civil Aeronautics Board.

The idea, roughly speaking, was to encourage people to organize themselves into identifiable interest groups whose claims and aspirations the government could address, one by one. Out of the many voices, it was supposed, an equilibrium of just results would emerge from the competition among different groups. Lowi called it "interest-group liberalism." This civic philosophy is now fully internalized by both political parties and, indeed, by most citizens too. However, as Lowi said, it "corrupts democratic government because it deranges and confuses expectations about democratic institutions."[5]

This approach, multiplied and elaborated over time, produced a rudderless vessel—a government designed to fix things at many different tables in the grand bazaar. At the dawn of the New Deal, principled conservatives (as distinct from those conservatives merely fronting for monied interests) had warned that a government that dabbled in every corner of the society would be unable to sustain a classical sense of general law. Political decisions would resemble, instead, particular deals, made piecemeal across every front. In those terms, the old conservative nightmare has come true.

But so has the liberal nightmare. Instead of containing the political influence of concentrated economic power and liberating government from its clutches, the steady diffusion of authority has simply multiplied the opportunities for power to work its will. The original progressive purpose of the New

Deal has been stood on its head and now the weak and unorganized segments of society are the principal victims. In the liberal nightmare, pluralist deal making continues in the guise of governing—but now the entrenched monied interests are back in charge of the marketplace, running the tables in the grand bazaar.

The practical result is a lawless government—a reality no one in power wishes to face squarely since all are implicated, one way or another. The clear standards that citizens expect from law—firm definitions of right and wrong, commandments of thou shalt or thou shalt not—are corrupted by a fog of tentative declarations of intent. The classical sense of law is lost in sliding scales of targets and goals, acceptable tolerances and negotiated exceptions, discretionary enforcement and discretionary compliance.

To say that government is lawless does not mean that the laws are never enforced or never obeyed. Of course they are. It means that law is applied with such randomness that its reliability is betrayed. It means that the certitude citizens expect in law is now routinely subverted by the application of political influence. The political interventions are generally not themselves illegal, however. Indeed the processes of law often invite them.

This reality betrays the principle that is most necessary to democracy—equal protection of law—and, for that reason, it is perhaps the gravest disorder in the governing system. A shared confidence in just laws is the prerequisite social faith supporting every other function in democracy. Citizens are entitled to the presumption, regardless of their own economic and social status, regardless of whether they personally participate in the processes of elections and public debate or decline to do so.

As people everywhere now sense, this presumption has been grossly compromised. Though the problem is seldom addressed in public-opinion studies, I suspect that the general awareness of corrupted law is an important factor feeding the popular alienation from government and politics. This may be part of what people mean when they tell the polls that the government is devoted to serving a "few big interests."

"There is one set of laws we are all supposed to follow and then there's another set of laws determined by calling your buddy and asking him what he thinks," said David Vladeck, a lawyer with Ralph Nader's Public Citizen. Vladeck, like scores of other public-interest lawyers in Washington, devotes most of his energy to suing the government—trying to get various federal agencies to enforce their own laws. The same agencies are sued endlessly by the other side as well, the corporate lawyers trying to block and dilute the force of those laws. Whether in courtrooms or in bureaucratic forums, this contest over law enforcement, more than anything else, is what consumes the persuasive energies of the capital's many lawyers.

William D. Ruckelshaus, the first administrator of the Environmental

Protection Agency in 1971, described the continuing uncertainty of law he found when he returned to the job in 1983:

"When I came back into EPA, I hadn't been in office twenty-four hours when I was sued three times. I asked the general counsel to study it and he found that 85 percent of the decisions made by the EPA administrator that are appealable were appealed. Each case takes three to five years to work out in court and the way it's worked out is a settlement negotiated between the industry and the environmentalists with the government sitting on the sidelines as an arbitrator."

What Ruckelshaus did not mention is that, according to another study, 68 percent of the challenges against EPA decided by judges were ultimately won by the environmentalists. Ruckelshaus himself was once held in contempt of court by a federal judge who called the EPA administrator a scofflaw and threatened to jail him because Ruckelshaus was deliberately ignoring a court order to quit stalling on enforcement. "The judge was right," Ruckelshaus acknowledged cheerfully, though he defended his rank evasion.[6]

The lawless bazaar existed long before Ronald Reagan came to Washington and so did its permissiveness. But the political favoritism and insider fixes of the Reagan-Bush years were so flagrant—and crude—that they encouraged the impression that lawless behavior was a partisan problem, peculiar to a Republican regime indebted to big business. The Reagan appointees, it is true, did bend laws and ignore them with more zeal and thoroughness than any of their predecessors, but the roots of this governing disorder are much too deep and bipartisan to be explained away so easily.[7]

In the simplest terms, the lawlessness is another expression of concentrated political power, in most instances the power of corporations to resist the law. Stated another way, corporate interests, on the whole, still do not accept that they must comply with the new regulatory controls enacted during the last twenty-five years. Corporations do comply with laws, of course, and have spent billions to do so (and also paid many millions in fines for their violations). But major business interests have a choice that is not available to most citizens. If they regard the law as unworthy, irrational or too demanding, they have the ability to fight on.

That's real political power—choosing whether to honor a law or resist it. Since the cost of resistance is often quite modest compared to the cost of compliance, companies benefit in real dollars from any success at political stalling, even if they know that they may eventually lose the fight. Thus, what often looks like a legal contest on the surface is really a political struggle in its deeper dimensions.

Curtis Moore, a lawyer who served fifteen years as Republican counsel on the Senate Environment and Public Works Committee, described the tortuous struggle to make the laws meaningful in the face of corporate tenacity:

"Twenty years ago, we set out to eliminate sulfur dioxide from the air. Here we are twenty years later and more than 100 million Americans are still breathing air with unhealthful levels of sulfur dioxide. Why? Because the companies fight you when you try to pass a law. They fight you when you try to pass a second law. They fight you when you try to write the regulations. They fight you when you try to enforce the regulations. Nowhere do they ever stop and say: 'Let's obey the law.' "

The very first secretary of transportation to order airbags installed as life-saving devices in automobiles was John Volpe in 1970 during Richard Nixon's first term. Henry Ford and Lee Iacocca, then Ford's top executive, called on Nixon at the White House the following April and delivered a blustery attack on airbags and other federal safety and environmental laws.

Their visit marked the beginning of a successful twenty-year stalling campaign by the auto industry—political pleas followed by postponed regulations, more studies, court challenges and watered-down proposals and more litigation. The industry's evasive tactics blocked airbags through four presidencies. The episode is revealing because the Nixon-Ford-Iacocca dialogue was recorded for history in the Watergate tapes. Yet it is also a commonplace story in modern government—a law in name only, a law deferred to please a political friend.

"We're not only frustrated," Iacocca exclaimed to Nixon, "but we've reached the despair point. We don't know what to do any more."[8]

Airbags, he told the president, were another untested "gadget" that Ralph Nader and other safety zealots wanted, but they would merely increase auto prices and feed inflation. "We are in a downhill slide, the likes of which we have never seen in our business," Iacocca warned. "And the Japs are in the wings ready to eat us up alive.

"So I'm in a position to be saying to Toms [the highway safety administrator] and Volpe, 'Would you guys cool it a little bit? You're going to break us.' And they say, 'Hold it. People want safety.' I say, 'Well, what do you mean they want safety? We get letters. We get thousands on customer service. You can't get your car fixed. We don't get anything on safety!' "

Richard Nixon responded sympathetically with his own diatribe against Nader and the reformers. They are hostile to industrial progress, per se, Nixon complained, and would like to go back and live like the Indians. "You know how the Indians lived?" the president said. "Dirty, filthy, horrible."

The Nixon-Ford-Iacocca dialogue is instructive for its rambling, semicoherent quality—a series of unfocused grumblings. Neither Nixon nor Henry Ford seemed to know much about how the regulatory process works. Iacocca tried to instruct them, but his task was confused by his own scattershot invective and rambling asides. Reading the transcript of their conversation will be disturbing to anyone who thinks of the Oval Office as a place where the best minds come together to address the most serious matters.

At the conclusion, Nixon instructed his aide, John Ehrlichman, to take care of "this airbag thing." It was taken care of, and for a long, long time. Through Nixon, Ford, Carter and Reagan, the auto industry successfully kept airbags out of automobiles, making the same arguments at every step to administrators, courts and presidents. Airbags didn't work. They would increase prices. Consumers didn't really want them.

Finally, by 1990, the legal and bureaucratic evasions were exhausted and airbags were at last made available for American consumers. Their effectiveness was demonstrated immediately in dramatic incidents in which motorists survived terrible head-on collisions because their cars were equipped with airbags.

And Lee Iacocca, now CEO of Chrysler, appeared in Chrysler's TV commercials, boasting that his auto company was the leader in making airbags available to American car buyers.

Aside from Iacocca's rank hypocrisy, the story of airbags is unexceptional. It is possible to collect dozens, even scores of similar examples of laws that were bent or stalled in regulatory limbo or simply never enforced at the behest of selected clients.

At the Food and Drug Administration, it took more than twenty-five years—and twenty-eight postponements encouraged by industry pressure—before the agency decided to restrict the use of cancer-causing red dyes in food products, a danger the FDA scientists first identified in the early 1960s.[9]

At the Nuclear Regulatory Commission, the regulators issued only 350 fines during the 1980s, though public utilities had reported approximately thirty-four thousand mechanical malfunctions, worker errors and security infractions at nuclear-power plants.[10]

At the Department of Labor, the Occupational Safety and Health Administration referred only forty-two cases of industrial negligence for criminal prosecution over nearly twenty years. Only fourteen of those were actually prosecuted, with ten convictions. No one was ever sent to jail, even for a day, for violating this federal law.

At the Pentagon, exceptions to law were granted routinely to the major defense contractors—General Electric, Boeing, General Motors, Rockwell, Northrop and others—who committed criminal fraud against the government itself. *The New York Times* reported that twenty-five of the one hundred largest contractors have been found guilty of procurement fraud in recent years— some of them several times. The criminal behavior persists because, other than brief embarrassment, there is no significant penalty, at least for the largest companies. Typically, they plead guilty and pay a fine. To appease the public, the Pentagon sometimes "suspends" contractors, but the suspensions are always lifted in time for the company to participate in the next bidding for contracts.[11]

At Transportation, the law enacted in 1975 to require greater fuel efficiency in automobiles was deferred repeatedly by both the Carter and the Reagan administrations at the behest of industry lobbyists. Whenever it appeared that companies might not meet the legal standard, they appealed to the White House for another postponement: Reagan granted three of them.

At the Environmental Protection Agency, the inspector general found that 80 percent of the case files on hazardous-waste violations showed no evidence that the violators had ever complied with the enforcement order. Instead, typically, EPA "enforces" its rules on land, air and water pollution by negotiating with the offenders—bargaining with company lawyers over how much or how little they will do to correct their abuses and how soon.

A senator asked the EPA inspector general: "Is it your testimony that EPA's enforcement policies are so weak that it frequently pays polluters to keep polluting and pay EPA's small fines rather than clean up their act?" "Absolutely," the inspector general responded. ". . . We have found that over and over again."[12]

When federal laws are so malleable and subject to political intervention, they cannot truly be called laws at all.

It is not quite fair or accurate to blame random lawlessness on faceless bureaucrats—the professional cadres who operate the government agencies. In fact, to subvert the authority of law, powerful interests have had to eviscerate the authority of the permanent civil service—those officers and professionals of government who are obliged to provide a fair, impartial rendering of laws. Two decades of propaganda from conservative think tanks assailed bureaucracies as the source of waste and irrational decisions. Republican political candidates promised to dismantle the machinery of big government and, once in office, they tried to keep the promise.

Among other things, democracy requires a strong civil service—government employees who are sufficiently protected from random political influences to carry out the law in a disinterested fashion. This paradox is not exactly new; reformers discovered the same insight in the late nineteenth century when concentrated powers were manipulating government decisions in a similarly shameless manner. In modern political usage, the principle was stood on its head—the permanent bureaucrats were portrayed as the enemy of the public interest and politicians set out to "get control" over them in the name of responsive democracy. They have largely succeeded.

The consequences first became clear in the realm of foreign policy. During the communist-scare campaigns launched in the late 1940s and 1950s, the Foreign Service was accused of disloyalty and individual diplomatic officers were pilloried for expressing inconvenient opinions on the true nature of international conflicts. The diplomatic corps has never recovered.

Over time, as the intellectual independence of the Foreign Service was debased, the quality of its expert judgments became less and less relevant to the political appointees who made foreign policy decisions. Recurring episodes of failure—Vietnam, the debacle in Iran, the war against Nicaragua in the 1980s—all confirmed the problem of high officials who ignored or actively suppressed informed dissent from the Foreign Service. Instead of nurturing honest voices in foreign policy, presidents regularly appoint political hacks who are routinely dispatched to U.S. embassies as a reward for their campaign contributions.

The Nixon administration, as in so many aspects, was more brutally systematic than others in its efforts to defenestrate the domestic civil service. Frederick Malek, a businessman who served as the White House personnel director in 1969, issued an exhaustive manual for political appointees on how to evade the civil-service laws and intimidate or dislodge uncooperative federal employees who did not accept Nixon's political agenda and his idea of what the law required. "There is no substitute in the beginning of any administration for a very active political personnel operation," Malek wrote. He cited Democratic predecessors, Kennedy and Johnson, as his model.

Among other tactics, Malek recommended personal threats to any civil servant who seemed politically disloyal—a transfer to distant parts of the country or damaging reports placed in the employee's personnel file. "There should be no witnesses in the room at the time," Malek warned. "Caution: this technique should only be used for the timid at heart with a giant ego. This is an extremely dangerous technique and the very fact of your conversation can be used against the department."

As a grander strategy, Malek proposed: "Another organizational technique for the wholesale isolation and disposition of undesirable employee-victims is the creation of an apparently meaningful, but essentially meaningless, new activity to which they are all transferred. This technique . . . is designed to provide a single barrel into which you can dump a large number of widely located bad apples."[13]

Civil servants are not oblivious to this sort of purposeful manipulation. Some react with extraordinary courage, carefully protecting their legal prerogatives and making sure that their decisions are technically correct and invulnerable to political assault. Others, more commonly, learn to keep their heads down. John Moran, who served a dozen years as an occupational health expert at EPA and the Labor Department, described the bureaucratic reality that has evolved:

"I was really trying at Labor. I got out safety alerts largely in spite of the system. They kept tightening the screws until they shut me down. My view is that, in the government, the fundamental rule is: Just play the game. Go with the flow. But don't take initiatives or try to go out and solve problems.

"It makes too many headaches for too many people. You get political flak, you get press. A lot of people in the federal bureaucracy are quite happy with that system. They are the ones, by and large, who survive and get promoted. The higher they get, the more cautious they become."

Another technique for subversion, used most dramatically by the Reagan administration, is to starve an agency for funds so that its civil servants cannot conceivably carry out their functions, no matter how conscientious they might be. Overall, regulatory personnel in the federal government peaked at 131,000 in 1980 and fell to 112,000 by 1986, despite the greatly enlarged regulatory obligations that new legislation continued to produce.

In Reagan's first term, EPA's budget was cut by 10 percent and its staff shrank by more than 20 percent (at one point, EPA's office of enforcement was abolished in one of those "reorganization" ploys recommended in the Malek manual). The Interior Department reduced strip-mine enforcement by nearly 60 percent. OSHA cut four hundred inspectors and its citations declined by half. The National Highway Traffic Safety Administration's budget was cut by 22 percent and its formal investigations into potential car defects shrank from eleven a year to four. At the Food and Drug Administration, the number of "emergency exemptions" granted to new pesticides was tripled.[14]

More insidious is the way in which government has put some functions in the hands of private parties—"privatized" them, as the conservative scholars would say—by contracting out the work to companies and consulting firms. This trend was promoted in the name of efficiency and reduced costs, but it has inevitably deepened the irresponsibility of government—private contractors are often asked to recommend the rules and standards that will govern their own behavior.

The Department of Energy's flagrant abuse of environmental laws stemmed largely from private companies like Du Pont that were hired to do the government's work for it. "Some of the severity of DOE's predicament stems from the fact that structurally it is a supervisory agency," Gregg Easterbrook wrote in *The Washington Post*. "Its budget puts bread on the table for about 165,000 people but only 16,000 of them are government employees; the majority work for contractors and consultants."[15]

Despite occasional scandals, government contracting has become a popular remedy for governmental breakdown and tight budgets. If money is saved in the process, this is usually achieved by avoidance of the wage-and-benefit requirements of federal employment. Privatizing governmental functions provides rich contracts for private enterprise, but evades the more difficult questions of authority. It plays to the inherent popular distrust of government bureaucracy, but it also further confuses the public accountability.

Senator David Pryor of Arkansas, a persistent critic of the practice, noted that congressional testimony given before the House Armed Services Committee by the secretary of energy was actually prepared in part by a private defense contractor, unbeknownst to the secretary of energy himself. "Who is running our government?" Senator Pryor asked. "My no. 1 concern is totally unaccountable decision-makers. We don't know who they are, how they got there or why they got there."[16]

Farming out the government's responsibilities to private contractors—while simultaneously holding federal pay for senior executives and technical professionals below that of the private marketplace—naturally encourages a "revolving door" in personnel. Young bank examiners typically put in a few years as government regulators, then join regulated banks at much more substantial incomes. Justice Department attorneys take their expertise to private law firms where they represent the violators.

The federal government, as a whole, has been reduced to a training camp for private enterprise—a school in which the students learn the skills and inside knowledge that will be most valuable to outside employers. Under those circumstances, only the most dedicated civil servants—or the most incompetent—are willing to remain in the public's hire.[17]

In a world of unreliable laws, the news media have become a principal agent of law enforcement. Wherever the press turns its beacon, embarrassed officers of government are compelled to follow. The routine of law enforcement has become a hit-or-miss system dependent upon exposure and scandal.

During the last three months of 1988, *The New York Times* published 108 stories, thirty-seven of them on its front page, devoted to a single scandal. A young reporter named Keith Schneider had discovered the gross and dangerous radioactive pollution emanating from the federal government's own nuclear-weapons production plants. At his urging, the *Times* made a major project of exposing the full dimensions of neglect and deceit. The cost of cleaning up radioactive contamination from forty years of reckless mismanagement at the seventeen federal plants was subsequently estimated to be as much as $155 billion.[18]

The story itself was not entirely new or even secret, despite the rigid national-security classifications that surround the nuclear weapons plants. Congressional committees had investigated the subject for years and voiced their alarm. Freelance documentary filmmakers had produced devastating films exposing the radioactive contamination at Savannah River, South Carolina; Rocky Flats, Colorado; and other installations. Still, it was *The New York Times* that single-handedly made the nation sit up and take notice.

"Congress doesn't have the ability to get an agency to respond," said Representative Mike Synar of Oklahoma, a member of the House Commerce

Committee who has led many of its aggressive oversight investigations. "There's only one way to make them respond and that's to get them on the front page or on the evening news. I was pounding hard on the Department of Defense and Department of Energy installations for six or seven years and nothing happened.

"Then Keith Schneider picked it up and wrote stories for thirteen days in a row on the front page of *The New York Times* and that changed everything. He has more power than any congressman over regulatory agencies."

Congressman Synar may not be exaggerating. Press exposure is a powerful therapeutic agent against the lawless behavior in government, but it is also quite random. Citizens' groups, large and small, work hard to alert news organizations to their complaints, while government regulators and the regulated industries live in perpetual dread that the roving eye of the media will, for some reason, stop on them. When it does, they are required at a minimum to prepare rituals of responsiveness that will appease the public outrage.

But, as every reporter and editor appreciates, the media's glare is essentially a transient, accidental force. It picks and chooses among many possibilities and usually settles on the most visibly alarming ones. Certain kinds of stories—dead fish floating in the river or workers who lost their hands in unsafe machines—are visual and accessible to press exposure. The more complicated, systemic scandals usually are not.

Depending on the media to make government agencies enforce the law is another aspect of randomness. People are often disappointed by the media's fickle attention span, their devotion to certain issues and indifference to others. But frustration with the press is directed at the wrong target. The government is supposed to enforce the law, not the newspapers.

The government, however, is a principal violator itself. As the *Times*'s exposure of the nuclear weapons scandal suggested, major scandals of lawlessness often involve not just private companies, but installations of the federal government itself. During a generation of enacting ambitious environmental protection legislation, the government has been, without doubt, the single worst polluter in the nation. Private corporations can always plead that they were merely following the example set in Washington. The attorney general of Maine, James A. Tierney, compared the two major boatyards in his state— Bath Iron Works, a private corporation that builds destroyers, frigates and cruisers for the Navy, and the Navy's own Portsmouth yard that overhauls and maintains nuclear submarines—both of which generate dangerous hazardous wastes.

"One of these yards obeys the law," Tierney said. "One pays penalties when they do not. One pays fees. One has taken a responsible attitude toward the handling of hazardous waste. And that, sad to say, is the private yard. With our public yard, the Portsmouth Naval Shipyard, we have had an exact opposite situation.'' Shellfish in the Piscataqua River estuary, he said, have been contaminated with PCBs, lead and other heavy metals from the U.S. Navy.

In Minnesota, the Twin Cities Army Ammunition Plant was responsible for contaminating more than twenty square miles of the principal aquifer underlying the northern suburbs of Minneapolis. In the state of Washington, authorities estimate that as many as thirteen hundred hazardous-waste sites mixing radioactive materials with other industrial wastes qualify for Superfund cleanup on the Hanford nuclear weapons reservation; numerous ''contaminant plumes'' have been observed in the ground water, carrying such deadly chemicals as cyanide and carbon tetrachloride. In Arizona, pollution of an underground area four and a half miles long, contaminated with toxic chemicals that threatened Tucson's sole source of drinking water, was traced to an Air Force plant operated by Hughes Aircraft.[19]

These were not exceptional instances. A survey by EPA in 1988 found that half of all federal facilities caused environmental damage. The General Accounting Office estimated that federal departments violated the clean-water law at twice the rate of private industry.

Many of these federal facilities are in practice operated by private industry—companies like Du Pont or General Electric that managed the nuclear weapons plants—but the companies, until recently, were indemnified in their government contracts against any liability for the pollution damage they caused. DOE would pay the fines levied against its contractors—which put the taxpayers in the role of underwriting violations of law.

The federal government, of course, enjoys a crucial advantage in its ability to evade laws. It owns the prosecutor. Every regulatory case that reaches the stage of formal charges or lawsuits must first pass through a narrow funnel at the Justice Department where the constraint of limited resources encourages negotiation and settlement instead of litigation.

Agencies are told to negotiate a compliance agreement with violators because there simply aren't enough lawyers to go around. During the Reagan years, the Justice Department went much further. Aligning itself with the Pentagon and the Energy Department, Justice argued that their violations were not subject to EPA enforcement action at all. How then would these federal departments be required to comply with the laws? The Justice Department suggested that EPA bargain with them.[20]

The cruel legacy of compromised law is that the task of making laws a reality frequently falls to the weakest parties involved—the ordinary citizens who are the victims. The law enacted in 1970 to protect workers from occupational health and safety hazards has, for instance, been a well-documented scandal from the beginning. When OSHA is enforced, it is often because injured industrial workers, the unorganized rank and file, have decided to mobilize themselves in protest.

A group of such workers from Ohio's Mahoning Valley gathered one Saturday morning in 1990 in the vestry hall of the First Presbyterian Church of Warren to stage their own "public hearing" on the subject of occupational health and safety. A stenographer recorded their testimony for several hours— bitter recitals about disease and death in the Youngstown area's major factories, involving such well-known corporate names as General Motors.

Dave Webb, lean and gray-haired at sixty-one, described the plating department at Thomas Steel and the long exposed tanks of acid where he worked many years amid deadly fumes. "I just went through the seniority list since 1966," Webb explained. "Out of twenty-four people who died out of the plating department, fourteen died from cancer. Three are still living with cancer. January, two other people died of cancer. So you're getting up around nineteen people."

After his closest friend died, Webb filed a complaint with OSHA, the federal agency created to protect the health and safety of workers, and Webb said OSHA fined the company $11,000, later reduced by $5,000. His arms flailed angrily in every direction as he recounted his complaints:

"We want a yearly physical, they haven't done anything about that. We want warnings put up all over that you are entering a toxic area, they haven't done that. And we asked them to replace the hoods over the plating tanks, they haven't done that. But they always say it's the cost. What's the cost of one person's life? I can't see where you put a monetary value on a man's life if you are not doing safety-wise what you're supposed to be doing."

Alberta Faber, a frail woman in sunglasses and a white painter's hat, kept a diary of her experiences with blackouts, dizzy spells, bleeding at the mouth and other symptoms when she worked in the paint shop at General Motors's huge assembly plant in nearby Lordstown, Ohio.

"I worked right by the oven," she testified, "so of course at night when the fumes came back, they watched to see when my eyes rolled back and I painted the wrong colors. Then we were relieved . . . I felt like a canary in a coal mine, really."

Leonard Grbinick, a millwright for twenty-six years at a mill that was first Republic Steel, then LTV, then Warren Consolidated Industries, complained about the "red dirt" that settled on workers' hair and skin. For people with sensitive skin, it caused "sores all over their skin about the size of quarters," he said. Injured workers were reluctant to complain or file for workmen's compensation for fear they might lose their positions. "Like in Tom's case, he couldn't afford to take off," Grbinick said. "He had five children at home to feed. And I felt bad for him." As the union rep in the department, Grbinick took the complaints to OSHA.

"We complained and bitched and moaned about it," he testified, "and OSHA just says, 'This is a nuisance dust.' Well, yes, it is a nuisance. When you get it on your skin, if you're sweating or if you get wet, it will burn you just like somebody put a match to you. . . . I would like to take some of that nuisance dust and spread it on some of those OSHA officials' desks and let them breathe it for a while."

The most grisly testimony came from John Wilson, who at thirty-three is incapacitated after working several years as a lacquer sprayer at GM Lordstown. "Basically, forty hours a week, I worked in a cloud of lacquer," he related. "At one point, I found a respirator and put it on and was told I wasn't allowed to wear it because there wasn't good air in the booth and I would probably pass out and be hurt . . . I started getting bloody noses . . . so I complained to my fellow workers and they said, no problem, some of them had had bloody noses for fifteen years. So, unfortunately, this sounds stupid, but I went along with that program."

Wilson displayed a darkly hallucinatory oil painting he had done to depict the symptoms that have incapacitated him—recurring painful headaches, constant listlessness and disorientation. He receives disability benefits of $500 a month. "I have a tendency to want to smash everything in sight now," he said. "I am fatigued all the time. I wash the dishes and, when I'm done, I have to sit down and take a nap or rest. I am really pissed off, this really makes me mad, I'm sorry."

These witnesses and others were drawn together by anger and also by their personal courage. The sharing of testimonials buoyed their spirits, but the hearing demonstrated just how isolated they were. Among auto and steel workers in the Mahoning Valley, raising complaints about unsafe working conditions is considered a threatening act. Thousands of local industrial jobs have been eliminated by plant closings during the last fifteen years; survivors who still have jobs fear that complaints from workers will simply target their plant for the next closing. The United Auto Workers, once one of the most aggressive unions, now treats the subject gingerly too, fearing the same consequences.

When the federal government created OSHA, one of its purposes was to eliminate this grim trade-off between jobs and health that often faced individual workers and their unions. Federal standards and nationwide enforcement would supposedly make it impossible for companies to squeeze economic advantage out of dangerous working conditions.

For most companies, however, the odds of even getting caught are quite remote since OSHA has only eight hundred inspectors nationwide—one for every forty-five hundred employers. When violators are cited, the fines are usually inconsequential—averaging $239 per violation in 1987. OSHA's huge corporate fines that are sometimes well publicized will normally be reduced drastically in subsequent negotiations with company lawyers. The agency won big headlines when it fined Union Carbide $1.3 million for the catastrophic release of toxic chemicals at Institute, West Virginia, when 141 people were injured in August 1985. The bargaining later reduced the fine to $400,000.[21]

"It's a goddamn joke," said John Moran, a safety authority who worked nearly a decade at the National Institute of Occupational Safety and Health, OSHA's research arm, and who now heads an industry-labor safety committee in the construction industry. "In construction, nobody worries about OSHA anymore. They don't take it seriously. The average construction worker has a life expectancy ten to twelve years less than the average. In Indiana, the average construction worker dies at sixty—before he even collects Social Security.

"The bottom line is the working man and woman in this country come in last. The regulators at EPA and OSHA never talk to the working man or the small businessman. They're dealing with big corporations and trade associations and labor unions."

In construction, for instance, the serious injury rate was actually higher in 1988 than in 1970 when OSHA was created. But, as Moran points out, this outcome is not dictated by market economics but by company decisions. Bechtel, one of the world's largest and most successful construction companies, has a health and safety record "ten times better than other companies," Moran said, because Bechtel executives committed their company to high standards in the workplace.[22]

In the case of the Mahoning Valley, the "public hearing" was organized by a handful of auto workers from GM's Lordstown plant who pulled together a little group they called WATCH (Workers Against Toxic Chemical Hazards) and set out to make the authorities pay attention—their union, their company and their government. Charles Reighard, one of the workers, described how WATCH got started. "We were startled at how many names we saw in the paper were people from the auto plant who had died and at their ages," he said. They asked Staughton Lynd, a local labor lawyer and former historian at Yale, how to proceed and Lynd advised them to dig out their own facts.

So Reighard and three companions went down to the local library and pored over eighteen months of the obituaries printed in local newspapers. Even they were stunned by what they found. Between January 1987 and July 1988, they counted seventy-five of their coworkers from Lordstown GM who had died of cancer, leukemia, kidney and heart diseases. The average age was fifty-six years; the youngest was a twenty-nine-year-old woman who worked at Lordstown for ten years before she died of cancer.

"We made copies of every one of those obituaries and we have them to prove that the person did die," Reighard testified. "He wasn't killed. He wasn't shot. He wasn't killed in a car accident. He didn't die ten years ago like the union first said. And every one of them is documented that they died of cancer, leukemia or heart disease, kidney failure, and we feel that it's directly responsible from the chemicals they work in.''

Their unscientific research did not prove, of course, that toxic chemicals killed these people, but the workers held a press conference to reveal their dramatic findings. The local news coverage produced official embarrassment. The United Auto Workers and General Motors, both originally hostile toward WATCH's agitation, agreed to cosponsor an expert study on mortality rates among Lordstown workers.

''We are confident the study will reveal that there are no problems out there,'' a GM Lordstown spokesman declared. A month before the study was made public, the plant manager announced that, in any case, the company's continuing efforts had already achieved ''zero hazardous materials'' in Lordstown's fabrication plant.

When the official joint study of ''proportional mortality rates'' was completed, it confirmed what the four auto workers had documented for themselves at the local library. The death rate from cancer among the auto workers at Lordstown's two assembly plants was nearly 40 percent higher than normal. At the fabrication plant, it was 50 percent higher. GM and the UAW agreed jointly to dig deeper into the causes.

Three months later, OSHA belatedly swooped down on Lordstown and did a ''wall-to-wall'' inspection, found 750 violations and announced fines totaling $211,000 (subject to negotiations). The company and the union have since reported progress on dealing with the health problems, though workers inside the plant said they could not see that much had changed.[23]

The only certain political consequence of WATCH's agitation was its effect on workers at other factories in the Mahoning Valley. They were encouraged to come forward to tell their own stories of dangerous working conditions and recount how the government had ignored them too.

5

HOLLOW LAWS

For democracy, the enduring consequence of random law is the culture of permissiveness and deception that permeates the highest levels of government. The general political climate is now infected with a cynical understanding that things need not be real in order to satisfy the public's desires and demands. Instead, both political parties and the webs of client-representative relationships surrounding them have perfected the practice of concocting hollow laws—promises the government makes to the people which it does not necessarily intend to keep.

The political community as a whole, including the media and even many reformers, has come to accept the legitimacy of this and even celebrates new laws that are really no more than gestures of good intent—grand declarations of what would be nice to accomplish someday. The reality, as every insider knows, is that the laws lack the precision and capacity to deliver on the intentions.

The legislative arena, including the presidency, has become addicted to these artful charades, which are now commonplace, both for regulatory issues and for general subjects like education or social welfare. Every few years, for example, usually just before presidential elections, a new "crime bill" is enacted with bristling resolve in response to public fears. Over two decades, these measures have had no measurable effect on crime or its causes, but they are popular in Washington as election-year gestures to the anxious voters.

Likewise, various social programs are enacted in response to obvious areas of concern—hunger or homelessness or disadvantaged children—but none of them is equipped with the funds to accomplish what they promise. These too are merely political gestures. Even a supposedly popular program like the Head Start preschool education program for poor children (universally applauded by both parties) is funded at a level that reaches only one in five of the eligible children.

Symbolic legislation is passed with fanfare, self-congratulation and the knowledge that the real political fight has only just begun. The participants will decide later, elsewhere, what will actually happen. Citizens at large cannot usually see the details of these evasions, but they observe, in time, that nothing much seems to have happened.

"One of the best ways to kill a civil rights concept is to pass a law and not enforce it," Mary Johnson, editor of *The Disability Rag,* wrote after the Americans with Disabilities Act was enacted in 1990 with huge bipartisan majorities and George Bush's blessing. After all, she noted, federal agencies were still not observing the terms of disability laws that Congress had passed in 1986 and 1973.[1]

The standard reasoning behind these grandiloquent laws is that the approach leads to some incremental progress. It establishes broad public goals that may be fulfilled sometime in the future. But the political price for this is enormous. The approach fosters public deception on a grand scale and a legacy of deepening cynicism among citizens who thought something might actually be accomplished by government.

Richard C. Fortuna, a microbiologist who spent six years drafting environmental laws as a staff aide on the House Public Works Committee and now works for private industry, described the legacy of deceitful law:

"The worst situation is not the absence of laws, but the presence of laws in name only. Right now, we have lots of laws in name only."[2]

The shame of modern government was conveyed with appropriately dry authority in a statistical printout EPA provided to inquiring congressmen in early 1990. With some reluctance, EPA identified 149 industrial facilities in thirty-three states where the surrounding air was known to be quite dangerous, even deadly, due to extraordinary emissions of butadiene, carbon tetrachloride, chloroform, ethylene oxide and other toxic chemicals.

The worst facility was in Port Neches, Texas, where Texaco operated a chemical plant that dispensed butadiene so freely that the lifetime risk of cancer for neighboring inhabitants was rated at 1 in 10. Asarco, Mobil, Shell Oil, Goodyear, Uniroyal and American Chrome each operated smelters, refineries or factories that created a cancer risk for their neighbors greater than 1 in 100.

The EPA printout listed another 45 industrial plants where the cancer risk was less than 1 in 100 but greater than 1 in 1,000. The remaining facilities on the list posed a risk greater than 1 in 10,000. As a matter of public policy, Representative Henry Waxman of California noted, an environmental health risk greater than one cancer per million is considered unacceptable.[3]

The repetitious details of the EPA list were enlivened only by the presence of some well-known corporate names, including some companies that appear regularly in television commercials proclaiming their devotion to the environment. Weyerhaeuser, which calls itself the tree-growing company, operated four mills with acutely dangerous emissions. Du Pont and General Electric each had four plants on the list. Dow Chemical depicts itself in TV commercials as an enlightened company that recruits idealistic young people to go forth and save the earth. In real life, Dow operates eleven factories where the risk of cancer is alarmingly high.

For twenty years, this sort of behavior has ostensibly been against the law, under the terms of the Clean Air Act of 1970. Yet the toxic air pollution continued with virtually no interference from government regulators. How could these companies get away with it for two decades? The sorry history of the regulation of toxic air pollution provides a convenient vehicle for understanding the tangled politics of debased laws.

The Clean Air Act of 1970 empowered EPA to curb toxic air pollution from industrial sources in order to guarantee "an ample margin of safety" for the citizens who live nearby. Yet, by 1990, none of the toxic pollutants listed on the EPA printout was being regulated by the agency. Over two decades, EPA had managed to promulgate emissions standards for just seven of the more than 275 dangerous substances emitted by industrial plants. The continuing violations were not a secret to anyone. For instance, both Texaco and EPA had known since at least 1984 that the Port Neches plant was extremely dangerous. Nothing had happened.

The high-risk factories and refineries on EPA's printout were the dramatic edge of a much larger and more generalized form of lawlessness. In a separate accounting from EPA, for instance, the steel industry was found to be operating thirty-six coke ovens that posed a cancer risk greater than 1 in 10,000— and six mills where the risk was greater than 1 in 100.

Nationwide, according to the companies' own filings with EPA, a total of 2.7 billion pounds of poisonous chemicals are launched into the air every year by American industries. EPA has estimated that fifteen hundred to three thousand people contract cancer each year as a result but, in truth, the full consequences of this casual pollution, both for human beings and for the natural environment, are unknown and probably unknowable.

A law enacted in 1970 to protect human life from straightforward industrial hazards yielded virtually nothing over two decades. The principal explanation is neither bureaucratic laxity nor scientific uncertainty, but an esoteric
form of political deadlock. The companies did not have to bribe people, since
they could accomplish the same thing by exploiting the evasive opportunities
embedded in the law itself. The evisceration of law is sometimes a story of
dramatic backroom fixes by politicians, but more routinely, the law is neutered
in the tedious details—a process that resembles water eroding rock and makes
no headlines. Democracy, as political scientist Theodore Lowi once observed,
is undone by "administrative boredom."

Enacted with appropriate celebration in 1970, the regulatory terms for
industrial toxics were immediately swallowed up in an interminable legal
argument over the stringency of enforcement. From 1971 on, lawyers were in
court virtually every year punching and pulling at those ambiguous words,
"ample margin of safety." Without ever saying so, EPA decided on its own
that the terms were unenforceable and went into a deep stall. The agency's
evasion was implicitly accepted by the political leaders of both parties, who,
aside from a few persistent critics in Congress, did nothing to resolve the
impasse.

Stalemate, of course, constitutes victory for opponents of the law—the
oil, chemical, steel, timber and mining industries—which did not wish to alter
their behavior and had the legal and political resources to avoid doing so.

In broad political terms, the government's dereliction could be explained
as a function of class bias and geography. Twenty-nine of the high-risk plants
were located in Texas and fifteen in Louisiana—the Gulf Coast industrial belt
that is now popularly known as "cancer alley." Dozens more were in other
southern states, which, given their history of economic deprivation, were
anxious for industrial development on almost any terms. In the South, the
conservative Democrats who dominate politics are closely aligned with business interests and they generally work to fend off any form of government
interference in the name of defending free enterprise and jobs.

In both North and South, the afflicted neighborhoods that suffer from this
toxic pollution are generally the working-class and poor neighborhoods whose
citizens are most neglected in contemporary politics. Other Americans might
sympathize abstractly, but most would not be directly affected. Several important environmental organizations did mount continuing legal battles in
behalf of enforcement, but the environmental movement's major priorities
were elsewhere—the smog problem, the haze over the Grand Canyon and
other competing goals for clean-air regulation. No one ever disputed the
harmfulness of the chemicals themselves or claimed that toxic emissions control was beyond the capabilities of engineering. It was always fundamentally
an argument about whether the risk to people justified the cost of fixing things.

"We're not talking about rocket science," explained Richard Ayres, the Natural Resources Defense Council lawyer who chaired the Clean Air Coalition formed by major environmental groups. "It's just using your brain. Companies don't like it because they never had to pay attention to it before, but basically we're talking about tightening the plumbing—reducing the leakage."

The regulatory debate focused instead on the vague language of the original law. What exactly was an "ample margin of safety" if even a slight exposure to cancer-causing chemicals was potentially harmful? After listing three substances for regulation, EPA decided, with considerable kibitzing from industry, that the law literally required "zero emissions." Therefore, the standard seemed impossible to achieve, not to mention greatly disruptive to industrial processes.

The EPA's practical decision was to not enforce the law, but this was never disclosed in a forthright manner. Instead, the agency pretended for years to be faithfully pursuing the law's mandate.

"The legislation gives the agency an assignment that the agency's own scientists say you can't accomplish," William Ruckelshaus explained. "It had the effect of freezing the agency. Once you started into the regulatory process, it meant you were going to end up banning the substance, which would not have made any sense. So, instead of starting the regulatory process, the agency studied it and studied it as long as they could."

Banning some substances and compelling industry to use less dangerous substitutes might, in fact, be a plausible solution for some pollution problems, but politicians never considered such questions when they passed the original law. Lawyers for environmental groups conceded that the statute was ambiguous and would have to be resolved politically, but they saw the legal argument being used as a convenient tool for gross evasion.

"Industry argues the zero emissions interpretation so the perfect becomes the enemy of the good," said David D. Doniger, a senior lawyer with the NRDC. "Instead of imperially taking it on themselves to rewrite this law, EPA should have carried out the law and developed the regulations and that would have constructively put the question to Congress for evaluation."

Over more than fifteen years, NRDC, the Environmental Defense Fund and the Sierra Club sponsored a series of lawsuits on various toxic chemicals, designed to force the issue to a resolution. "What we were trying to do was deliberately force the literal interpretation of the law in order to force the matter back into Congress and write a law that would work," Doniger said.

Instead, what resulted was more lawsuits—appeals brought by both industries and environmental groups, more judicial decisions and court-ordered deadlines and more missed deadlines. The environmentalists thought they had achieved their goal in 1977 when an EDF lawsuit on vinyl chloride was settled with a negotiated agreement that provided a quid pro quo to both sides. "Ample margin" would be defined so that the regulatory agency could require the "best available control technology" on toxic emissions while the goal of total protection against cancer risks would be treated as a long-term objective.

"We said, let's put aside the argument over perfect protection and concentrate on getting a whole lot of protection for a whole lot of people," Doniger explained.

Nothing much happened. EPA instead began defining the control standards in terms of how much it might cost each industry to comply. Environmentalists complained that this was a violation of the settlement terms. The Carter administration, having listed only four more toxics, announced a "cancer initiative" in 1979 and published a priority list of dangerous chemicals. Then it left office without having acted on any of them.

The environmentalists were afraid to turn to Congress for help. By the late 1970s, industry's political campaign against federal regulation in all forms was at its peak. In that political climate, the environmentalists feared they might get something worse if the fuzzy legal definition was resubmitted to Congress as an abstract question of legal definitions.

The Reagan administration was even more recalcitrant than its predecessors, of course, and did virtually nothing beyond defending itself against lawsuits. In 1983, Ruckelshaus promised Representative John Dingell of Michigan, the aggressive chairman of the House Commerce Committee, that he would act on some twenty toxic chemicals by 1985. But, instead of actually listing the twenty chemicals for enforcement, Ruckelshaus merely announced an "intent" to put them on the list. He was held in contempt of court for refusing to observe a court-ordered deadline on regulating the emission of radionuclides.

"Instead of a quid pro quo, what we were getting was a snail's pace and standards very heavily watered down by cost considerations," Doniger said, "and so we raised the issue again in court and tried to drive the legislative debate to get a clean standard."

The Reagan administration's lackadaisical attitude changed somewhat after December 1984. That was the month when Union Carbide's chemical plant in Bhopal, India, released toxic fumes that killed two thousand people and blinded thousands more. Eight months later, another Union Carbide plant in Institute, West Virginia, had a toxic release that injured 141 people. EPA promptly announced a "Policy Initiative" on air toxics.

"It was all hype and nonsense," Doniger said. "They were basically asking industry to care more and, sure enough, industry had a program called CARE. Then EPA referred the pollutants to the states. Nothing happened."

The legal battles dragged on through most of the 1980s and finally in 1986 produced a court-ordered definition of "ample margin" that was presumably acceptable to all sides. By 1990, enforcement standards were in place for a handful of chemicals—the ones first listed more than a decade earlier.

In a sense, however, the story of air toxics regulation began all over again in 1990. That year, Congress enacted a new clean-air law that largely rendered the previous legal arguments moot. The new legislation sets out different and less ambitious terms for how the government will regulate toxic air pollution. Thus, government begins anew the laborious process of regulation writing and litigation. The new law puts aside the question of health risks and instead attempts a simpler approach—an engineering standard for tighter plumbing. EPA is ordered to devise technological standards for controlling 189 toxic chemicals, based on the emissions control performance already achieved in the best plants.

A decade hence, in 2001, if the control technology proves inadequate, EPA may then take up again the health question of an "ample margin of safety," now defined by law in much more conservative terms as one cancer case per ten thousand residents.

In effect, the complicated deadlines and exceptions in the new clean-air legislation give industries another twenty years—till 2010—to comply with a public-health objective that was first set in law in 1970. The steel industry is given another thirty years to comply on its coke ovens—law for the year 2020.

"The new law gives us deadlines," said Richard Ayres of the Clean Air Coalition, "but it's a nonlaw—making deadlines long enough so that they don't have meaning."

Some leading environmentalists were more confident that, this time, something might actually happen. For one thing, after two decades of indifference and resistance, the chemical industry claimed to have gotten religion on environmental questions, and it launched an aggressive public-relations campaign to persuade the public of its good intentions. The timing was coincidental with the congressional debate on clean air, but some environmentalists like Doniger perceived a genuine change in attitude, at least among some major chemical companies (though not in the oil and steel industries).

Monsanto announced an ambitious commitment to reduce its own toxic emissions by 90 percent voluntarily, regardless of what the future regulations may require. Texaco, Du Pont and others made similar promises. In full-page newspaper ads published on Earth Day 1990, the Chemical Manufacturers Association unveiled its "Responsible Care Initiative," an environmental manifesto signed by 150 companies. Indeed, a number of the companies taking the pledge—Texaco, Du Pont, Dow, Mobil, Exxon, General Electric, Weyerhaeuser, BF Goodrich, W. R. Grace and others—were the same ones that showed up that year on EPA's list of high-risk cancer factories.

What discomfited the chemical companies was not the prospect of stern federal law enforcement—they had been quite effective at neutralizing that—

but the unwieldy threat of aroused public opinion. The regulatory law had proved impotent but another law enacted by some states and by Congress in 1986 had stimulated widespread public alarm by establishing the people's "right to know" about what poisons were being dumped on them. As the plant-by-plant reports on toxic pollution were collected and made public by EPA, community after community became angered by the frightening data.

"It's no secret that a lot of people are unhappy with chemical companies," the CMA advertisement acknowledged. Corporate executives still belittled the health implications of toxic air pollution but, as some of them confided to Doniger, the 2.7 billion pounds of toxic chemicals they distributed each year through America's air had become a "public-relations problem."

The clean-air law itself, nevertheless, is still a doubtful authority. Aside from the virtuous intentions of some companies, the new law does not close off the avenues for evasion and, in fact, the new complexities multiply the litigious opportunities for those who wish to resist by exploiting the fine print. Companies will be free, as always, to choose for themselves whether to comply or keep stalling. If they do not wish to spend the money, they will restart the lawsuits and agency lobbying and can hang up the newly reformed regulatory standards for many years to come.

William Ruckelshaus extolled the new environmental consciousness of corporate management, but he also acknowledged that there are many "bad actors" for whom voluntary compliance is meaningless. "For most companies," Ruckelshaus conceded, "they're not going to spend the money unless the government tells them to. If the government doesn't say what you're doing meets the standards, they won't do anything."

The lawless quality of modern government originates, naturally enough, with the lawmakers themselves. For most members of Congress, the legislative process represents a chance to please public opinion by voting for high-minded legislation while protecting corporate balance sheets or other interests by acceding to the legislation's deceptive details.

As conservative critics have observed, the legislative atmosphere of inflated promises was doubtless encouraged by the grandiose expectations promoted during the presidencies of John F. Kennedy and Lyndon Johnson in the liberal hubris of the 1960s. Great goals for the nation were announced rather regularly—eliminating poverty, for instance. But the objectives often lay far beyond the government's existing capacities or the sponsor's real political intentions. Indulging in hollow pronouncements has become a commonplace of modern politics. President Bush announced, for instance, that his great goal for education is that by the year 2000 (well after he has left office) American high schools will have a graduation rate of 90 percent. Senator Daniel P.

Moynihan mischievously observed that Ronald Reagan had made the very same announcement back in 1984, only Reagan had set the target date for 1990. Both presidents received abundant congratulations and press attention for facing the problems of education so boldly.[4]

In the media age, however, empty promises make smart politics. Enacting grand measures has the appearance of responsiveness to constituents' desires and creates a sense of forward motion. When the law fails, enact another one. "We don't have just a failure of one law, but a series of laws," said Curtis Moore, former Republican counsel on the Senate Environment and Public Works Committee. "Toxic pollution is such a potent issue, we have been able to enact more than one law. By and large, they've all been failures."

Despite years of industry-government propaganda, the general public does not accept the trade-offs between corporate profit and human life or the environment. But the governing elites do. So dozens of statutes have been designed to paper over this basic conflict. Political action driven by intensified public opinion is artfully derailed in the legislative details.

A public-opinion survey by *The Wall Street Journal* and NBC in the spring of 1990, for instance, put the question this way: "Sometimes the laws that are designed to protect the environment cause industries to spend more money and raise their prices. Which do you think is more important: protecting the environment or keeping prices down?" The public believed overwhelmingly—80 percent to 13 percent—that the environment comes before costs.

A *New York Times* survey conducted in the same month sharpened the point further: The public endorsed the view, 71 percent to 25 percent, that "we must protect the environment, even if it means increased government spending and higher taxes." A majority even agreed, 56 percent to 36 percent, that protecting the environment comes first, "even if it means jobs in the local community are lost."[5]

In a healthy democracy, these popular expressions of value choices would be taken seriously. Public desires would at least be confronted in an open manner by those who think them unrealistic. If the government considered a congressional legislative mandate unachievable, it would explain why. If economic discomfort were the real reason why regulations were not being enforced, political leaders would force a visible debate on the question so that the public could at least understand the terms of the trade-off and respond with its own preferences.

Are Americans serious about their new environmental values and willing to accept the deep changes these values imply for American economic processes? In different ways, the public keeps saying it is serious. But politicians respond as though public opinion is merely a transient romantic sentiment to be indulged. The deeper political question about this clash of values never gets answered because the political community has discovered how to have it both ways—appealing to the public's environmental values but without disturbing corporate power.

The Clean Air Act of 1990, for instance, advanced matters on several fronts but it did not even consider the technological breakthroughs that many believe are possible. The new law, in effect, rolled over the deadlines for compliance that were first set in 1970 and promised once again that, by 2010, people everywhere will be breathing healthy air.

"We could deal with all this much faster if we wanted to get it done," Richard Ayres of the Clean Air Coalition said. "The government could figure out substitutes for toxics that pollute or it could go 'upstream' and make the chemical companies responsible for the pollution that results from their products and processes. None of that has ever been done. That would be attacking the problem like you really wanted to solve it."

Defenders of the status quo argue that, notwithstanding the evasions and delays, substantial improvements were derived from the original clean-air law and, in time, the system will achieve its goals, however imperfectly. The public at large does not share that optimistic view and even some scholars regard the claims as dubious. Robert W. Crandell of the Brookings Institution wrote, for instance, that "because of delays, poor enforcement, and imperfectly understood dispersion and transport characteristics, it is possible that the entire program has generated little reduction in air pollution. . . . The data on air quality are so poor that one cannot confidently assert that air quality has improved because of the 1970 Clean Air amendments."[6]

All of the interested parties, however, have learned to coexist comfortably in a system that relies on public deception—the legislators, the regulators, the regulated industries and even many of the reformers in the environmental movement. Forcing an honest debate would be disruptive and unpopular among political elites, in and out of government.

At their core, the continual evasions are about "the problem of power," as Theodore Lowi put it. What was missing in the modern era of legislation was a straightforward determination to use the government's power to achieve certain results and accept the burdens of doing so. The purpose of representative government, Lowi wrote, was "to bring the democratic spirit into some kind of psychological balance with the harsh reality of government coerciveness."

Does the government really intend to use its power to force these changes or doesn't it? When that hard choice is deflected into murky bargaining arrangements and endlessly negotiable standards, it reflects a breakdown of the representative process itself.

Sophisticated members of Congress know how to evade the hard choices about power. The imperfections and impediments built into the laws are not

accidental or unintended, but usually represent silent concessions to the lobbyists who were ostensibly the losers in the overall battle. From the perspective of legislators, enacting incoherent laws has a rational purpose—it allows
them to have it both ways. Representative Mike Synar of Oklahoma, himself
a vigilant overseer of health and safety laws, explained:

"We're really pretty smart around here and we know pretty well who's
going to get mad, so we know how to avoid getting them mad at us. The
easiest way is to not decide. It's like a golf game—you score well by not
making bad shots. So we defer the tough decisions to the regulatory agencies.
If we're really deadlocked, we say: Let's defer to EPA for a six-month study
and let EPA tell us what to do. A lot of people can hide behind that.

"The bureaucrats look at the legislative record and they can see the issues
where we didn't want to make a decision. So they know they're in no hurry
either. Why make a decision that will make the same people mad at them, if
Congress didn't want to make it? Then the lobbyists move in and overwhelm
the agency. If a lobbyist sees he's going to lose in Congress, he'll say to us:
Let the agency decide. Then the regulatory side of his law firm will get another
shot at it."

For most members of Congress, there is very little political risk in this sort
of permissiveness. Indeed, the larger risk for them is on the other side—that
the final regulations will be too stringent and angry clients will come back to
Congress demanding relief. For the most part, senators and representatives
have learned how to deal with this problem too. Senator Dale Bumpers of
Arkansas explained:

"When the regulation writers run amok and constituents start writing and
saying, 'My God, have you guys lost your minds?' you can write back and
say: 'Why, those guys in the agency have gone crazy and this is not what we
intended and I'm going to demand hearings on the matter.' Which is usually
where it ends."

The dysfunctions of the regulatory system were actually becoming the
focus of serious debate in the late 1970s, but ironically, when the Reagan
administration came to power, the debate was foreclosed. The Reagan regime's political fixes were so flagrant that a complex problem of governing
was swiftly reduced to a simple matter of political hacks doing dirty deals for
their corporate patrons.

Yet, if one asks corporate executives about environmental regulation, they
will describe it as *their* nightmare. After all, plant managers are buried in
complex and overlapping legal strictures that did not exist a generation ago.
Companies have spent billions on compliance and small armies of employees
are devoted to keeping up with exhaustive requirements for testing and handling, monitoring and reporting—not to mention the corporate lawyers and
lobbyists who attend to the legal language in Washington.

Lloyd N. Cutler's law firm at one time or another has represented nearly all the major trade groups, chemical manufacturers, petroleum, textiles, motor vehicle manufacturers, pharmaceutical makers and major banks, plus leaders of the Fortune 500 corporations. The suggestion that industry has captured regulatory agencies like EPA seems ludicrous to him.

"It would be wrong to think that corporations are on top or ahead," Lloyd Cutler protested. "They feel very put upon or even defeated. It's true that they manage to survive and deal and push things off—they feel the added costs of regulation exceed the benefits—but they would say the notion that they now control or dominate the health and safety agencies is just crazy. Because all industries are fighting running battles with these agencies."

The explanation, as Cutler suggests, is more complicated than the simple image of a captive agency, bound and gagged by its regulated constituency. The contemporary governing system would be more accurately described as a disorderly bazaar that is not securely in anyone's control—a maze of diffused power with endless opportunities for reversal. If the power to decide things is located everywhere, then it really exists nowhere.

Modern political reforms, combined with the new generation of regulatory laws, had the overall effect of multiplying the decision points within the government—this was often their stated objective—in order to break up concentrations of power. The decision making was splintered into many discrete steps, and authority was shared among many more agents along the way. While this broke up the easy politics of the back room or at least complicated it, it also created many more doors at which influence might knock and enter.

The diffusion of authority, as Lloyd Cutler himself observed, provides an ideal arena for special-interest lobbyists—the more of them the better. Corporations may be perpetually frustrated by modern government, but, in the end, corporate interests are much better equipped to manipulate it.

"If you're against something, you're much better off in this diffuse world," Cutler explained. "It's harder to pass a law than to stop one. On the whole, I would say the professional lobbyists and lawyers prefer to live in this world where there are so many buttons to push, so many other places to go if you lose your fight. In a cohesive government, once you lose, it's over."

A minority of conscientious lawmakers has struggled for years to overcome the gap between appearance and reality. One by one, as regulatory laws came up for renewal, Congress often tried to tighten the legislative plumbing, so to speak, by drafting the legal commandments with much more precision and less grandiosity. If EPA would not set meaningful standards, then Congress would do it for EPA.

When this approach did not produce much improvement, innovative legislators devised an even tougher form of legislative command—elaborate traps written into the statutes that are designed to force the Executive Branch into actually doing what Congress said it intended. These legislative devices became known as "hammers" because they confronted the regulatory agency and the regulated industries with a harsh either-or choice.

If the agency stalled and failed to produce a new regulation by the legislated deadline, then another set of stringent rules—drafted by Congress—would automatically go into effect on a date prescribed by law. The "hammer" provisions were intended to take the profit out of delay and inaction, to persuade the industrial sectors they would be better off cooperating with the regulatory process than endlessly obstructing it.

The first set of "hammers" was enacted in 1984 when Congress renewed the Resource Conservation and Recovery Act, better known as RCRA, which governs the handling and disposal of billions of gallons of hazardous wastes. The scandal of careless disposal—symbolized by Love Canal and hundreds of other despoiled places—had spawned the Superfund legislation to clean up thousands of old dangerous dumps; RCRA was supposed to prevent the creation of new ones.

The legislators' innovation has proved to be a dubious remedy. By 1990, EPA had complied with all of the "hammer" provisions written into the 1984 RCRA law—yet the practical experience was not much different. Industry was given six years' advance notice on what to expect in requirements for pretreating hazardous wastes before disposal. Yet industry again claimed at the eleventh hour that the law would force the sudden shutdown of dozens of refineries and chemical plants.

Once again, the terms of the law were subverted in the final stages by strenuous industry lobbying. Once again, the law's meaning would have to be settled in protracted litigation. The message of this regulatory episode is that restoring reliable authority to law is not something that even the lawmakers are likely to accomplish on their own. The political system itself is stacked against the law—even laws made with reinforced steel.

From the beginning, RCRA has been another story of pliant law. The first version was passed in 1976 and, like so many other environmental statutes, it set deadlines for action that were not kept. The Carter administration gave RCRA a low priority and the bulk of final regulations was not published until four years later, when Congress was already renewing the statute in 1980.

EPA immediately was inundated with fifty-two notices of intent to file lawsuits on the new regulations from industries and environmental groups as well as thousands of specific complaints and questions. The agency began negotiating "technical amendments" with hundreds of private parties, trying to answer their complaints and avoid an avalanche of litigation.

In 1981, Reagan's new EPA administrator, Anne Gorsuch, began suspending and deferring key sections of RCRA's new hazardous-waste rules.

Even when federal courts ordered EPA to reinstate the regulations, enforcement was so anemic and compliance so spotty that even some businesses complained. *Chemical Week,* a trade publication, warned: "In a highly competitive industry, companies cannot afford to spend their resources on environmental protection, however well conceived the rules, unless they perceive those rules are backed up by credible enforcement policy."

By 1984, after the EPA scandals involving hazardous-waste sites, Congress was sufficiently fed up to enact its "hammers"—a series of five do-or-die regulatory deadlines spaced over six years, requiring industries to treat chemical wastes to reduce toxicity and other characteristics before the materials are dumped in the ground.[7]

The first four "hammers" covered treatment of specific subcategories of industrial wastes such as solvents and organic chemicals and seemed to be effective; that is, the regulators produced meaningful regulations. When the first "hammer" came due in 1986, EPA at first issued a weakened version pleasing to industry, but this set off a firestorm in Congress. EPA had failed to require that the best available treatment methods be applied to solvents before disposal—in other words, that the stuff be made as harmless as possible before it is dumped into the ground.

Eleven members of Congress, who had been the key draftsmen of the law, complained vigorously that their intentions were betrayed. After the uproar, EPA reversed itself and adopted the best-available-treatment standard for solvents and the three other subcategories covered by subsequent "hammer" deadlines. On the final "hammer" that came due in May 1990, the most important one because it covers roughly half of all hazardous wastes, EPA took a dive.

"In some ways, we've won all the battles and lost the war," said Richard C. Fortuna, executive director of the Hazardous Waste Treatment Council, a trade group composed of companies that manufacture incinerators and other waste-treatment equipment. "If we can't win this back in court, this country is back where it started in 1980 in terms of preventing more Superfund sites."

Fortuna's trade group had an obvious profit incentive in promoting hazardous-waste regulation that imposes tougher standards, but its critique was seconded by angry environmentalists and disappointed members of Congress. The industry treatment council and the Natural Resources Defense Council jointly sued EPA in 1990, charging that the mandate of the 1984 "hammer" had been subverted by regulatory fiat. Instead of requiring the best available treatment technology to reduce toxicity, corrosiveness and other harmful characteristics before the chemical wastes are put into the ground, the EPA regulation set a much more permissive standard.

Companies, in many instances, would be able simply to dilute the chemical wastes with water before injecting the chemicals into deep wells. Dilution, of course, doesn't really change the harmful characteristics of the chemicals. Once in the ground, the toxics are beyond anyone's control.

Deep-well injection has become a widespread practice for hazardous-waste disposal but, like earlier landfill methods, its eventual consequences for land and water pollution are not fully understood. Companies claim the chemicals are pumped so deep into the earth, sometimes thousands of feet down, that the wastes cannot possibly affect surface soil or ground water tables, but no one really knows what may occur ten or twenty years from now.

The practical experience so far suggests that deep-well injections may be a kind of geological crapshoot with the environment. If an underground formation has cracks or leaks through which the hazardous chemicals may migrate, that won't be discovered until many years later when the toxic wastes show up someplace else, perhaps in someone's water supply. A legendary failure occurred at Chemical Waste Management's deep wells in Vichery, Ohio, where 60 million gallons of hazardous wastes mysteriously "escaped."

Companies like Shell Oil, Vulcan Chemicals, Du Pont, BP Chemicals and Monsanto are sufficiently nervous about the practice that they announced their intention to shift away from deep-well injection. For instance, the manager of Du Pont's Beaumont, Texas, works told EPA's *Pollution Prevention News* that his company "recognizes the public concern about deep-well injection and, for that reason, has set a goal of eliminating all toxic discharges into the ground or verifying that they have been rendered non-hazardous by the year 2000."[8]

In other words, the oil and chemical companies promise to do the right thing and stop polluting the ground—a decade or so hence. In the meantime, however, these same companies do not want government telling them to stop now.

As the "hammer" deadline approached in the spring of 1990, the oil and chemical industries subjected EPA professionals to an extraordinary full-court press—warning them that dozens of industrial facilities would be imperiled if the agency went forward with its best-treatment standard. The advocates of stronger regulation were caught off guard because EPA had already issued a preliminary version of the rule in December 1989 that enunciated the more stringent level of protection. Six months later, after lots of meetings with industry lobbyists and lawyers, EPA reversed itself.

"Between the proposal and the final rule, there was no significant new information," an EPA staff professional said. "It was basically a case of EPA management becoming more nervous about what they'd done."

Geraldine Cox, a vice-president of the Chemical Manufacturers Association, described the industry as "very upset," and therefore it mobilized. "We agree with the objectives of the law," she said, "but we will fight very hard if we think something doesn't make sense."

Environmental regulation often doesn't make sense to chemical companies. "In these matters," Cox said, "there's an awful lot of chasing angels to see how many can dance on the head of a pin. But, if that's what the public wants us to do, we will do it."

A delegation of six lobbyists and experts from the Chemical Manufacturers Association and the American Petroleum Institute first called EPA in October 1989 to open the argument for abandoning the best-treatment standard, even though CMA had just lost a court suit on the same issue. Then another group from CMA came back two weeks later. "CMA believes that EPA can interpret that dilution is permissible for characteristics," according to an EPA official's notes of the meeting.[9]

In early December, experts from CMA, Monsanto and CYRO Industries came in to plead for speedy action on exemptions for fifty-four deep wells that industry claimed would pose no risk of migrating chemicals. J. T. Smith, senior partner at Covington & Burling, a premier Washington law firm, rang up with his own legal interpretations on behalf of CMA. Dow, DuPont, Monsanto and other CMA representatives met again with EPA in mid-January to suggest rules changes for granting the exemptions.

BP Chemicals arranged a teleconference in which it informed EPA staff professionals that its Lima, Ohio, plant would be closed if it received no exemption by the time the new regulation was made final. Vulcan Materials delivered the same message about its Wichita, Kansas, plant.

Many of the same companies appeared once again in early February, accompanied by CMA lawyers, to warn again about the potential economic consequences of a tough standard. ARCO Chemical wrote that its plant at Channelview, Texas, would curtail production in May if its injection wells were not exempted. The plant, ARCO explained, produced waste volume of 142 million gallons a year from the production of propylene oxide and styrene monomer—various waste streams that were highly corrosive. Celanese, Cyanamid, Du Pont and Monsanto provided similar data and warnings on six other southwestern plants.

Beyond the familiar tactic of economic blackmail, there is a deeper point for democracy: the question of power. Who has the power to decide when industry will make these changes—the companies or the government? The corporations naturally wish to retain that power for themselves and, in this case, they succeeded.

Most of the lobbyists' meetings were held with EPA division chiefs, middle-level staff technicians and agency lawyers, who mostly listened as the industry experts advanced legal interpretations meant to intimidate. "We were attacked on a technical basis—the kind of case they felt they could make in a lawsuit if we didn't yield," the EPA professional said. "Industry argued there would be huge costs if we went forward with the proposed rule. Depending on who you listened to, it was the end of the world.''

By late March, industry had evidently won its point. The dialogue was taken to a higher political plane by E. P. Blanchard, vice-chairman of Du Pont's board of directors, who wrote directly to Henry Habicht, EPA deputy administrator and the official who would ultimately decide the matter.

Blanchard wrote: ''We . . . understand you are contemplating revisions to the agency's so-called Third-Third land disposal proposal to provide relief for underground injection facilities. We applaud and support your efforts to resolve our May 8 difficulties and encourage you to revise the Third-Third final rule.'' Copies were sent to four EPA division chiefs, Habicht's subordinates.

Some of the corporate pleadings invoked a threat of political fallout if EPA did not fold. Dow Chemical representatives told EPA in April that ''they felt compelled to advise Congress that, if finalized, this standard would be very expensive, environmentally counterproductive, and impossible to meet on May 9 or in the foreseeable future.'' CMA's lobbyists informed EPA staff professionals that they were ''likely to raise their concerns to senior Agency management and with Hill staff.''

A few weeks after Earth Day 1990, EPA announced its final regulation, which attempted to straddle the argument with half-pregnant logic. The agency claimed the legal authority to impose a higher standard involving best-available-treatment technology, but said it was choosing not to do so in this instance because it lacked sufficient data to justify the tougher rule. In the abstract legal argument, EPA was siding with the environmentalists. In practical terms, it was giving industry what it wanted. EPA, simultaneously, was issuing lots of exemptions for the companies' deep-well injection sites.

The administrative record, typically, is silent on the question of outside political intervention, though EPA staff professionals felt certain that somewhere along the line the White House had added its voice to the case made by industry advocates.

''My understanding,'' an EPA professional said, ''is that there was a lot of back-channel traffic, calls to the White House and to the agency management at every level. I can't prove that because nothing like that is ever said. But we were getting a barrage of questions from EPA management that was almost identical to the questions industry was asking us. When I pushed the management for rational explanations—why are we changing this?—they said: 'Listen, this is the way we're going to do it. We've changed our minds.' ''

The political overtones seemed ''pretty blatant'' to Richard Fortuna of the Hazardous Waste Treatment Council, though he had no direct proof either. Three different firms that were members of the treatment council, he said, reported that oil companies had planned to buy equipment for pretreatment and

reclamation of their hazardous wastes in anticipation of the new regulation—
then they abruptly canceled the orders before the final rule was announced.

"These guys were on the verge of signing contracts and they were suddenly canceled," Fortuna said. "Our salesmen were being told the same thing
by a variety of clients. The oil guys said, 'Hey, Sununu went in and got us a
break.' "

Whether or not John H. Sununu, the White House chief of staff, or other
presidential aides personally intervened in support of the industry's case could
not be determined, but that is not the larger point, in any case. The RCRA
episode demonstrates, in up-to-date fashion, that the law remains vulnerable to
powerful manipulation—despite the best efforts of congressional reformers to
stymie irregular intervention. The "hammer" provisions, invented as the
remedy to political manipulation, had proved as vulnerable as earlier legislative commandments.

Richard Fortuna despaired over the implications, though he believed a
stronger standard would eventually win in court. As a congressional aide in the
early 1980s, Fortuna had spent years on the RCRA legislation and helped draft
the "hammer" provisions meant to insure the law's faithful execution. Now
it was clear that even this device could be defeated by Executive Branch
politics.

"There are ninety-nine ways to lose and only one way to win—the final
rule on hazardous wastes has every form of capitulation to every political
interest imaginable," Fortuna said. "Basically, what they've done is gut the
whole RCRA program because it's very easy to dilute hazardous wastes or
switch the wastes to another category with easier treatment requirements. I
hate to say that about something I've spent a decade of my life on, but I really
think it's that serious.

"What EPA and industry are counting on is that this issue is a little too
complex and people won't get it, even Congress. They're figuring that the
combination of Earth Day and an 'environmental president' will let them slide
by. But they can't get away with this. Sooner or later, people will figure out
what's been done and fight back. In the meantime, huge quantities of hazardous wastes are going to be dumped under these easier rules."

6

THE FIXERS

In Ronald Reagan's White House, it was the office of vice-president that was designated as the chief fixer for aggrieved business interests. Industries that were unhappy with any federal regulations, existing or prospective, were instructed to alert George Bush and his lieutenants. The power of the White House would be employed to intimidate and squelch any regulatory agencies that seemed upsetting to American business.

The official language was less blunt, of course, but the meaning was made clear to every lobbyist and corporate CEO when Bush was appointed chairman of the President's Task Force on Regulatory Relief in early 1981. In collaboration with the Office of Management and Budget, Bush was empowered by executive order to review and suspend—and effectively throttle—new regulations emerging from every agency and department of the federal government. C. Boyden Gray, the vice-president's counsel, told the U.S. Chamber of Commerce what to expect: "If you go to an agency first, don't be too pessimistic if they can't solve the problem there. If they don't, that's what the task force is for."

Bush's office and OMB became a shadowy court of appeals where Republican business constituencies could win swift redress—without attracting public attention or leaving any record of what had transpired. In most instances, the corporations had already lost the argument somewhere else, in

Congress or during the long public rule-making process or in lawsuits. Vice-President Bush privately turned them into winners.

The auto industry managed to kill a package of thirty-four air-pollution and safety regulations, including the one for air bags. The auto companies fed their ideas to James C. Miller III, executive director of the Bush task force, who had been a regulatory consultant to General Motors just before he entered the White House. The Chemical Manufacturers Association contacted C. Boyden Gray, whose old law firm, Wilmer, Cutler & Pickering, represented CMA. In a "Dear Boyden" letter, a CMA vice-president urged Gray to scotch a new EPA regulation on pretreatment of industrial chemicals that are dumped into public waters. The rule had been nine years in the making, first authorized by the Clean Water Act of 1972. The Bush task force suspended it and told EPA to give the matter further study.

The White House apparatus killed, stalled or watered down hundreds of regulations and boasted of the billions it had saved private industry. Warning labels on children's aspirin were abandoned for the drug companies. Safety rules for underwater divers were weakened for the offshore oil drillers (George Bush's line of business before he entered politics). Cotton-dust controls were blocked for the textile industry. Industrial air pollution standards were set aside for the steel industry. And so on across dozens of fields of federal law enforcement.[1]

The White House interveners, intent on secrecy, usually communicated their demands orally to the regulatory agencies. As one said, the absence of any written memos or letters "leaves no footprints." Nor did they ever explain who exactly was demanding the changes. Bush's aides were not discreet, however, about bullying civil servants. James Miller, the task force director, boasted that prudent regulators would not question OMB's power to recast things, for fear of losing their jobs.

"You know, if you are the toughest kid on the block, most kids will not pick a fight with you," Miller said.

The presidency cannot be counted upon to uphold law because the White House has become the capstone of lawless government—an institution that rewrites law behind closed doors for the benefit of the few who have political access. Irregular as it seems, the White House's centralized control over the law's actual language has been broadly accepted by the political community as a convenient "solution" to the stalemated politics of governance. As a practical matter, this irregular new use of power became institutionalized during the last decade and the White House fixes continued unabated when George Bush became president himself.

These unpleasant facts provide the keystone for our larger examination of the breakdown of democracy. The presidency itself has been transformed into something quite different from the civic expectations. Instead of the bully pulpit where a national leader can speak for the broad public interest, the presidency has become the last step in the charade.

In the age of mass media, the president is shielded from scrutiny by qualities that other politicians cannot claim—the mythic powers of his office and his ability to broadcast the largest and most deceptive messages of all. In modern government, starting in the New Deal, the White House accumulated an imbalance of power over the legislative branch because it was always seen as the great protector of the national interest and of the weak and defenseless. Now, the protection is regularly employed on behalf of the powerful.

In principle, regulatory reform could have been an important function when Ronald Reagan took office in 1981. After years of tortuous hearings and litigation, scores of major new regulatory rules were nearing completion. The Bush task force might have undertaken a serious study of the conflicting goals and unfilled promises that Congress had produced.

But this "reform" initiative was driven, not by principle or disinterested analysis, but by a cocky contempt for whatever the regulatory agencies had decided. Lawmaking, in a real sense, would be done in the privileged setting of the White House, cloaked by the executive privilege that protects the president's advisors from public scrutiny. The laws would be reshaped, quite literally, to satisfy the very parties at whom they were directed.

Environmentalists and other reformers naturally protested, joined by anxious members of Congress who understood the power implications. But they couldn't change much. "OMB operates in secret and it's undemocratic," said David Vladeck, a lawyer with Public Citizen. "You have this very important rule-making process that's open and accessible. Then at the end of the process it's subverted by the fact that most of the important decisions are made in secret and nobody knows who influenced the decision.

"Regulations sometimes go into the black hole of OMB and never emerge again. Rules were completed years ago and haven't been heard from since. Other regulations go into OMB looking like trees and come out looking like rose bushes. It's an anathema to democracy to have all these decisions made on the basis of a record the public never sees."

OMB continued to exercise its irregular powers just as zealously once Bush became president himself. During his first year in office, OMB changed, returned or scuttled 24 percent of all new regulations—a slightly higher rate of tampering than occurred during the early Reagan years, according to OMB Watch, a public-interest monitoring group. The leading targets were Labor, HUD, Education and EPA.

Furthermore, Vice-President Dan Quayle succeeded Bush as personal appeals judge for business friends of the Bush-Quayle administration. Quayle became chairman of a Presidential Council on Competitiveness, which promptly ordered EPA to kill an ambitious new regulation on recycling—a pollution-prevention measure the Bush administration had boasted about a year earlier as proof of its commitment to the environment. What happened? An administration source told Michael Weisskopf of *The Washington Post*: "There was the strong sense that they needed to give business something. Business has a lot of concern that we lost our commitment to deregulation."[2]

Quayle's operation was as secretive as Bush's and has tampered with or killed new provisions in law for preserving wetlands, reducing power-plant pollution, protecting workers from formaldehyde (an OSHA regulation ten years in the making) and reducing toxic emissions. The promises made in the new Clean Air Act were swiftly unraveled by White House deal making. "This is not only horrible policy, it is clearly illegal," Representative Henry Waxman, a chief architect of the clean-air legislation, complained.

How does Dan Quayle pick his regulatory targets? The same way George Bush did—business picks them for him. OMB Watch reported: "While the council seems to involve itself in virtually every controversial health, safety and environmental regulation that makes its way through the federal bureaucracy . . . Quayle himself has said that he consults most often with business leaders who can tell him better than economists, 'how the clock is ticking,' and the council's executive director has said, 'When they [industry groups] feel like they are being treated unfairly, they come to us.' "[3]

Business lobbyists and executives, not surprisingly, defend the White House intervention since OMB has become a useful tool for them in the tangled politics of regulation. Most members of Congress, despite partisan divisions, are quite willing to tolerate this irregular form of lawmaking. In 1990, Congress declined to enact legislation proposed by Senator John Glenn and Representative John Conyers of Michigan that would have modestly circumscribed OMB's freewheeling power to rewrite laws. The White House's private intervention provides another safety valve for clients and Congress will not be held responsible. Senators may occasionally rail at OMB for gutting a law, but they can also send disgruntled constituents to OMB for relief.[4]

"OMB does their dirty work for them," said Gary D. Bass, executive director of OMB Watch. "Then when OMB does something outrageous, like on the asbestos standard, they hold oversight hearings and get a lot of press. It's a charade. That's the way the game is played."

If Democrats in Congress have been passive on the issue, it is partly because the Reagan and Bush administrations were doing aggressively what the Carter administration (and Nixon's and Ford's) had attempted to do more timidly. Aping the antiregulation critique from business academics in the late 1970s, Jimmy Carter's Council on Wage and Price Stability defined federal regulation as a major source of inflation and began reviewing new rules and arguing with agencies over whether they needed to be so stringent. The White

House advisors lost the arguments at least as often as they won, in part because Carter himself was ambivalent.

Carter's aides, like Reagan's, responded mainly to industry complaints, not broad principle, but with somewhat less certitude that business was always right. At one point, policy analysts from Carter's Domestic Policy Council were wearing respiratory masks around the Executive Office Building, trying to demonstrate to OSHA that this was a cheap and easy remedy for the brown-lung disease afflicting textile workers. Their stunt did not succeed.

Douglas Costle, then the EPA administrator, observed that in his arguments with the Carter White House over pollution standards, "I would say that probably three out of every four [White House] comments on our rule-making were cribbed right from industry briefs."[5]

The rationale for White House control is usually stated as a principle of sound management. "My perspective is entirely presidential," said Stuart E. Eizenstat, Carter's domestic-policy advisor and now a lawyer for corporate interests. "I want a president, whether Republican or Democratic, with the ability to control executive agencies. The president, as CEO of a trillion-dollar corporation, ought to have the management tools to control."

The trouble with this metaphor is that government is not a business enterprise. It has powers to coerce or penalize (or reward) that belong to no private institution. It has obligations, as well, that are unique—including the obligation to uphold the law. Managing government to save money for industrial corporations versus enforcing a new environmental law is a political question, not an argument for business economists, and, in a democracy, it is supposed to be settled in the regular order of political decision making.

The centralized control in the White House, with no public access or accountability, conveniently escapes those obligations. It also short-circuits all of the other processes by which the law is supposedly fashioned, both in Congress and in the Executive Branch's laborious rule-making procedures.

Even Eizenstat, an advocate of White House control, concedes the dilemma: "There is this problem, no question about it, of going through a full-blown regulatory process in the agency with a full public record and then having the president come in with a club at the end to decide it. It's not fair to let some unseen hand get into the cookie jar at the last moment."

The notion that the president personally decides these questions is, of course, a fiction. More typically, the regulatory laws are being rewritten by anonymous political advisors and eager junior analysts, who may have strong ideological biases in favor of business but very little experience in the complex fields of government they are now presiding over.

Among the thirty-two desk officers reviewing regulations in Reagan's OMB, a quarter had graduated from college less than five years before, half less than ten years before. Nearly half of the regulatory analysts had no federal agency experience at all; another 31 percent had none in their area of responsibility. Typically, they had studied economics or public administration at an East Coast university. These young people heard regularly from business lobbyists and sometimes sought out business's opinions, but they were not confidants of Ronald Reagan.[6]

A young policy analyst who was making large judgments on environmental law in the Carter White House acknowledged, in so many words, that he was winging it. "Since I never knew what decision the President would make or would have made if an issue ever got to him, I had no choice but to pursue my own vision of what was good," the analyst told an academic interviewer.[7]

The other popular argument for White House control is that only the president or his agents can impose rational priorities on the scattered actions and impulses of the various regulatory agencies, whose bureaucrats have a self-interested incentive to augment their own power. Since the private economy cannot afford the cost of unlimited regulation, it follows that someone should make broad choices about how much is too much.

Out of this logic, the practices of cost-benefit analysis have flourished. The Reagan administration was the first to require all agencies to produce a "Regulatory Impact Analysis" for every new rule they promulgated—presumably to determine what society would gain and what it would lose from each new regulation.

Instead of broad priorities, the system of analysis produces its own bizarre inconsistencies and favoritism. The techniques for making these judgments are so sloppy and so vulnerable to special-interest manipulation that the notion of rational decision making has become a bad joke among government insiders.

A Labor Department "Regulatory Impact Analysis," for instance, calculated the reduced costs for employers and government if affirmative-action enforcement was limited to large firms. But the analysts did not examine the losses for women and minorities that would result from nonenforcement. The Department of the Interior's RIA on leasing Alaskan oil reserves acknowledged that local Eskimos would suffer while the nation's energy consumers benefited, but the analysis did not bother to quantify the Eskimos' loss. A General Accounting Office study of fifty-seven Regulatory Impact Analyses conducted under OMB guidelines found twenty-three RIAs that made no effort whatever to calculate the benefits of the proposed regulations.

In other words, under the guise of disinterested analysis, OMB is employing a heavy tilt toward business interests and against any new regulation that would cost them money. The analytic process, in fact, has created a web of skewed facts that OMB casually accepts or even encourages—twisting the data to fit a desired political conclusion.

The Department of Agriculture, for instance, counted higher wheat prices for farmers as a benefit for the national economy in its justification for federal price-support regulation. But the Department of Labor counted lower wages for construction workers as a national economic benefit too, justifying its effort to weaken wage standards on federal construction projects. They cannot both be right, unless one believes that farm incomes are somehow superior to labor incomes. In terms of political preferences, that is what the Reagan administration did believe.[8]

All of these examples have one consistent threat—ideological bias. OMB's behavior, in case after case, is not only strongly guided by the business lobbyists linked to the president's political debts, it is also driven by an underlying ideological assumption that the laws themselves are wrong-headed and ought to be neutralized as much as possible. This is a respectable position in the legislative debate and regularly articulated by free-market conservatives, but it is also the position that lost when the regulatory laws were enacted. The White House has the power to reverse it.

When the Food and Drug Administration attempted to assert control over new health claims that some food manufacturers were making for their products—a practice regulated since FDA's creation eighty years ago—an OMB desk officer complained that it was "antithetical" to the administration's free-market principles. Rather than regulation by FDA, she proposed, "Let the marketplace, not the government, set the agenda for the types of claims that will be made."

When business interests were ambivalent about a new regulation, the OMB analysts sometimes actively solicited opposition. An executive of Fieldcrest, asked to comment on new mandatory commercial reporting requirements for the 1990 Census, requirements her company supported, complained: "It is my fear, however, that the Office [of Management and Budget] has already made its decision in this matter and has polled members of the industry seeking justification for a negative finding."[9]

The most telling evidence of OMB's political favoritism for political clients is revealed when industry changes its mind about a new regulation. In case after case, the OMB analysts dutifully change their minds too.

The food industry opposed the new FDA regulation on health claims in advertising until it began to fear that an aroused Congress might enact something worse. When the food manufacturers dropped their opposition to the FDA proposal, so did Bush's OMB. The textile industry spent years successfully forestalling cotton-dust regulation through the White House until it decided that federal regulation might be a good idea, after all. When the textile industry accepted cotton-dust controls, so did the Reagan White House. The chemical industry, likewise, flip-flopped on the question of OSHA's "right to know'' regulation for hazardous substances, once it became clear that many states were enacting their own tough measures. The Office of Management and Budget abandoned its objections too.

The law, in other words, has been reduced to a continuing political contest—its meaning always subject to eleventh-hour fixes. Every president naturally responds to his own constituencies and his own ideological preferences; White House fixes did not begin with modern government. But what is different and without precedent now is that the shadowy practices of backroom politics have become institutionalized—and even exalted—under the rubric of rational governance. The scandal of these White House manipulations of law is that they provoked no scandal—no fervent inquiries by the press and no general sense that something deeply abnormal had crept into the American idea of democracy.

Stuart Eizenstat, in defending OMB's new powers, argued that environmentalists and other reformers waste energies attacking the White House oversight machinery. Instead, he suggested, they should concentrate on electing the kind of presidents who will be sensitive to upholding the environmental laws rather than serving corporate interests. But, I asked, doesn't that sound as if the law is up for grabs? Eizenstat erupted in exasperation at the naivete of my question.

"Of course the law's up for grabs!" he responded. "The law's always up for grabs. That's why you win elections and appoint judges. That's why Reagan appointed five hundred federal judges. The law is not an inflexible instrument like a cannon that can be lined up and fired. It's a flexible human instrument that responds to political power.

"That's what having political power is all about, for chrissakes. When you have the power of the presidency, you have the capacity to put people in place who will be sensitive to upholding these laws. When you lose that authority, you're left with futile rear-guard actions."

This is not what Americans expect or deserve from their government— that the laws will change with the election returns. Nevertheless, Eizenstat is correct: The law is up for grabs.

Even the White House does not get the last word, since, as many of the cases have illustrated, any aggrieved party can still sue. OMB's supposed ability to settle regulatory disputes in a rational manner has been tested again and again in federal courts during the last decade. More often than not, the White House judgment was found to be in error—that is, inconsistent with the original laws. "We never want to go to the courts," said David Vladeck, the litigator for Public Citizen. "This is our last choice. But the courts are our Maginot Line against industry."

"Many of the cases we win today we win before very conservative judges who are very attuned to the concern about courts overstepping the line between law and policy," Vladeck said. "But they just overturned an OSHA regulation of formaldehyde on the grounds that it had no scientific justification—it was the regulation OMB told OSHA to issue. These judges are very conservative but they're also honest and they too object to that kind of lawlessness."

For the last twenty-five years, it is true, the federal courts have served as the powerful arbiter that enforced legal deadlines on reluctant regulators or brushed aside specious protests from the regulated industries. Scores of court orders and decisions have been issued to uphold the terms of modern regulatory laws, most often in response to citizens who sought strong enforcement.

But pushing political questions off onto the courts is not a democratic solution. It may work well enough for citizens who are lawyers or who can afford to hire them, but it inevitably denies representation to most citizens. Judicial lawmaking encourages brokered decisions, negotiated deals done at tables where only the litigants are represented. Federal judges themselves are not answerable to the voters.

Besides, as the history of regulatory law enforcement demonstrates, fashioning law by litigation doesn't seem to work very well. It produces years, even decades of delay and uncertainty but often ends in laws as muddled as the originals passed by Congress.

Liberal reformers, who are effective litigators themselves, mostly ignored the democratic contradiction when the judicial remedy was working for their causes. Environmentalists and consumer advocates found an open door and sympathetic hearing before a federal judiciary that was mostly appointed by John F. Kennedy and Lyndon Johnson. Now the majority of federal judges are conservatives, appointed by Reagan and Bush, and they are gradually closing the door.

"In the early eighties, we were finding the courts to be very receptive," said David Doniger, lawyer for the Natural Resources Defense Council. "You'd almost go in with a calendar rather than a brief and say, 'The law says this is supposed to happen in six months or a year,' and you'd get a court order. More recently, we've had more trouble. The appeals court in the District of Columbia is being more aggressive in saying, if there is no explicit deadline, we're going to assume Congress did not intend one and we'll give the agency as much time as it damn well pleases."

The D.C. Circuit Court of Appeals, the natural venue for legal challenges against federal agencies, has itself become something of a political battleground, where the ascendant conservative majority argues with the receding liberals over the court's role in enforcing regulatory laws. Chief Judge Patricia M. Wald, one of the liberals, used the same metaphor as David Vladeck but with a different twist: "The [liberal] traditionalists still hold, but like the Maginot Line, the strength of their dedication and the limits of their endurance is in some doubt."[10]

The Supreme Court, now dominated by a majority of Reagan conservatives, is, likewise, changing the ground rules—bluntly warning active litigators like the NRDC that they will be less welcome in the future if they challenge Executive Branch interpretations of the law. The Reagan conservatives are advancing behind the general principle that political decisions should be made by accountable political officers of government, not by unelected judges. It also happens, however, that this principle is compatible with the judges' own ideological biases. The conservative justices are generally hostile to federal regulation, especially if it offends business interests. If the federal judiciary was once dominated by liberal biases dressed up as legal doctrine, it is now captured by conservative biases in the same clothing.

The conservative critics are offended, down deep, by the modern legal doctrine, both judicial precedents and often the regulatory laws themselves, that has given legal standing for citizens at large to intervene, including advocates from generalized "public-interest" groups. The conservative legal strategy reveals which side of the struggle the judges are on. They would like to push the citizens and their public-interest advocates out of court and severely limit or even abolish their right to sue (unless citizens can demonstrate that their own personal injury is at stake in the regulatory issue). The regulated companies would naturally retain their standing to sue since they are directly affected. Former D.C. Appeals Judge (and rejected Supreme Court nominee) Robert H. Bork put their argument plainly:

"These last two decades, it has come to be thought that individuals can go to court to assert their own parochial views of the public's legal rights. This is contrary to the traditional rule that a citizen cannot sue a prosecutor to require him to enforce law in a particular way or even to enforce the law at all. Courts recognize 'prosecutorial discretion,' which means that important aspects of policy are left in the hands of Executive Branch officials who are accountable only to their superiors and to legislative oversight."[11]

A less attractive way of stating Bork's point on "prosecutorial discretion" would be to say: If the president decides to not enforce a law in order to please an industrial client, that's his business. Citizens have nothing to say in the matter unless they can prove they are going to be personally poisoned as a result. If they don't like it, they can write their congressman or try to elect a new president. Bork's doctrine sounds like a jurist's version of "the law is up for grabs."

The federal courts, nonetheless, are gradually moving toward the Bork view of things. In an important 1984 decision, *Chevron U.S.A. v. NRDC*, the

Supreme Court held that an agency's definition of a regulatory law should be accepted as a "permissible construction" that will not be second-guessed by federal courts so long as it does not clearly violate an explicit statement of intent from Congress. Thus, the Executive Branch—led by OMB—will be given far more latitude to decide for itself what the law really means.

As one of the losing lawyers in *Chevron,* David Doniger, not surprisingly, thinks the decision was a damaging precedent. "EPA defined the sources of air pollution, as the law required," Doniger explained, "then, by changing the definition in 1981, it excepted 90 percent of the sources—boilers, blast furnaces and so forth. We brought that up to the Supreme Court and said this is crazy. They did define the sources but nobody would accept that as a reasonable definition. The Supreme Court was almost petulant. They said that, since the term was never defined in the original law, they could not decide what Congress meant and they accepted EPA's definition as a reasonable construction. Reasonable meant: not off the wall. There wasn't anybody in government who expected to win that case and we had no idea we would lose."

An aggressive minority on the Supreme Court, led by Justice Antonin Scalia, is trying to shrink the ground for private citizens even further. Justice Scalia argues that when courts examine congressional intent, they cannot look beyond the language of the statute itself. Thus, the frequent practice of consulting committee reports or reading the floor debate on congressional amendments would be abandoned.

Judge Wald warned that this is really a way to ignore the context in which Congress acted and to let judges tease their own meanings out of the words in a statute. "Several [Supreme Court] opinions this past term that eschewed legislative history replaced it with what sometimes looked like a free-form romp through the 'structure' of a statute or its 'evident design and purpose,' " Wald wrote in 1990. "The phrases 'Congress must have meant this or that' or 'Congress probably did this for that reason' appear often in such opinions without apparent source other than the writing judge's mindset."

Her conservative colleague on the D.C. appeals court, Judge Laurence H. Silberman, embraced the new standard enunciated in the *Chevron* decision but conceded that it implies a "notion of statutory plasticity"—law whose meaning is flexible, from one administration to the next. This permissive doctrine is being promoted by the same conservatives who espouse a strict-constructionist interpretation of the Constitution, based on the original intent of the Founding Fathers.[12]

The real power shift, however, is not to the courts but to the president. The largest losers will be not only citizens but also their elected representatives in Congress. In practical effect, the so-called conservatives are tampering with the fundamental balance of power set forth in the Constitution—shifting the ability to write law from the Congress to the Executive Branch or, more accurately, to anonymous Executive Branch political advisors and policy analysts.

In an era when Congress seems permanently controlled by Democrats, conservative thinkers have decided that the presidency, since it is usually held by Republicans, is the nobler branch of government (a generation ago, when the presidents were liberal, conservative thinkers espoused the opposite view). Modern conservatism, while preaching platitudes about local control, has become a force for centralizing the power of government still further—the same ideological reflex that conservatives once denounced in liberalism.

"There's no limit to the courts removing themselves from issues," Doniger warned, "and at some point our system breaks down. You could have executive decision making with no judicial review. The consequence is a shift of power. Not only are the courts giving up power but they're empowering the Executive Branch at the expense of Congress."

In the extreme case, if this doctrine prevails, the elected representatives could be reduced to a hortatory assembly—passing laws that are no more than righteous pleas to the president, asking him to do the right thing. The chief executive would effectively retain the power to respond or ignore the legislative expressions, as he wishes. This imbalance of political power would resemble the arrangement in underdeveloped nations with authoritarian regimes, but no one mistakes those governments for democracy.

The deeper governing maladies that undermine democracy cannot be resolved by judicial fiat or administrative tinkering. The habits of hollow laws and random nonenforcement are deeply embedded in the political culture and are fundamentally political problems. If these can be solved at all, the solutions will likely be found only in politics.

The ambivalence of modern politics involves a deep ideological confusion about the nature of government and, as Lowi said, "the problem of power." In one dimension, the old conservative nightmare of big government came true and now sprawls in tangled reality before a disenchanted public—a government without limits or priorities or the standards for establishing either.[13]

This proliferation of government activity in the private sphere did not lead to the pluralist sense of justice that liberal reformers sought when they set out to address the claims and grievances of myriad groups and interests. On the contrary, the government's decision making now crudely replicates the same injustices of status and wealth and power found among private citizens and institutions in the society at large. That is the nightmare facing liberals—old liberal reforms that now work to defeat liberal values.

Conservatives, however, were corrupted in the process too. Despite their nostalgic rhetoric about small government, the conservatives' principles are now largely defined by their clients. Over time and with superior resources, conservatives have learned to manipulate the system in behalf of monied interests more efficiently—and brazenly—than the liberals who preceded them in power. Conservatives have perfected the politics of symbolic action first popularized by liberal presidents and taken it to audacious levels, employing deft public relations to mask the compromised laws and special-interest fixes.

Though I have focused mainly on regulatory laws and the power of corporate interests to neutralize them, the debasement of law and governing principles is a much larger problem that, indeed, spreads across the governing landscape. The same compromised standards are displayed, less distinctly, on the spending side of the federal government. A generation of politicians in both parties has learned the art of broad symbolic gestures—enacting programs that do not and usually cannot fulfill their stated purposes. Loose-jointed discretion and interest-group favoritism permeate the federal budget and the tax code as well.

This casual use of governing power sows its own public resentments that eventually come back to haunt the politicians. In every important instance, the government is not spending enough to fill the needs it claims to address, but the general public imagines that these domestic programs are a wildly generous giveaway of tax dollars. The poor, for instance, especially the black poor, are thought to be blanketed in federal handouts. Yet even the best-known federal programs—food stamps or welfare—fall far short of serving the universe of citizens who are in need of help.

To take the starkest example of this public confusion, the majority of the people who are officially poor—more than 60 percent of them—receive no cash assistance from the government whatever. Yet popular resentment assumes the opposite. Nearly 40 percent of the poor receive nothing at all from the government, neither cash nor other kinds of aid. It is difficult to understand how welfare checks have undermined the work ethic among the poor, as conservative scholars claim, when most poor people receive none.[14]

The federal budget is littered with such unfulfilled commitments to different groups of almost every kind, not just those in poverty, and new ones are added annually. The impulse to legislate in this manner is by now bipartisan, and every year Congress and the president agree to extend the charade in some new direction or another. People clamor for it. Politicians wish to respond. Very few public officials have the nerve to insist that, if the government is not serious about addressing the problem, it ought not to legislate at all.

Just as the New Deal era fostered the exceptionalism and special-interest deal making that now permeate government, the New Deal also produced an opposite model of how government should use its power—Social Security. The Social Security system succeeded and endures, both politically and fiscally, because it was created as a universal program, not an interest-group deal. Despite minor internal contradictions, Social Security makes a promise that it has kept for more than fifty years—everyone pays in and everyone is entitled to receive benefits.

Applying the same standard elsewhere—designing universal programs with a conception of social purpose broader than targeting a single afflicted group—is much more difficult, of course, and would no doubt eliminate many marginal programs. But it is the only road that leads to a sense of equity as well as an effective government.

Most industrial nations of western Europe, after all, have largely succeeded in following that principle, whether for health care or family-allowance payments or social protections. The well-developed "safety net" systems in Germany and France, for instance, are not only far more generous than America's and more equitably administered, but they also enjoy nearly unanimous political support, from the left to the right.

To confront the random lawlessness in the regulatory government, some obvious remedies are suggested in the misshapen institutional arrangements. The idea of a centralized regulatory review by the Executive Branch is defensible, for instance, only if it is brought out in the daylight and formalized so that everyone can participate. Since no chief executive will ever surrender the confidentiality of executive privilege, this necessarily means removing the OMB review mechanism from the secrecy of the White House itself. A regulatory oversight agency might still be answerable to the president, but not as a place for private fixes.

Congress, likewise, needs a mechanism, however crude at the outset, for facing squarely the conflicting trade-offs and ambiguities it has written into law. No single legislative committee can digest these questions objectively, since it might be asked to throttle its own baby. A joint congressional committee for regulatory review, as Robert Litan of the Brookings Institution has proposed, could ask broad questions and force the conflicts and fuzzy mandates back into the arena where they belong—the lawmaking body of government. If government is going to make trade-offs between business profit and human life, it at least ought to make them in a public debate.

The federal courts could become a radical and positive influence in forcing this sort of reform—by refusing to enforce laws that are designed to be unenforceable. The conservative judges, instead of protecting business or centralizing power in the executive, ought to develop legal doctrine that confronts the problem of lawlessness directly. If a law is so vague and meaningless that regulations cannot be rationally drafted for it, then courts could throw the law back to the people who wrote it—the Congress. This would produce political embarrassment and eventually greater self-discipline among the lawmakers. It would also short-circuit the long-running sagas of litigation and nonenforcement that are now so commonplace.

The regulatory agencies themselves might be given similar leverage, an ability to declare honestly in some public forum that Congress has given them a legal obligation they find impossible to fulfill. A necessary corollary to that innovation would be a stronger protective mechanism for civil servants so that agency professionals could disclose, without fear of political reprisal, that the law's original meaning was being subverted by political insiders on behalf of their clients. In everyday reality, these new powers would probably be seldom invoked—by either the courts or agency administrators or civil-service professionals—but their mere existence would be therapeutic.

Administrative reforms such as these, however, cannot by themselves erase the permissive culture that fosters the deception and deal making in the first place. These attitudes and reflexes have been formed over two generations of American politics; escaping from them will not be accomplished easily or any time soon. Neither political party has the institutional capacity, much less the ideological inclination, to confront the permissive culture in a seriously critical manner. A modest beginning would be for them to acknowledge what the public already grasps—the status quo is a lawless swamp.

The fundamental solution must originate with citizens outside Washington, for it requires nothing less than to change the political culture itself. Politics has to develop a fierce, new governing impulse to displace the old one—a skeptical perspective toward the reigning assumptions about how government is supposed to govern. Only the people can bring this into the arena and impose it on the governors.

I would describe this impulse as a kind of functional conservatism—as distinct from the corporate interest-group conservatism practiced by contemporary Republicans and most southern Democrats. This temperament would have to dig through the tangle of empty laws in search of the deeper principles that most Americans will endorse. It would have to ask, case by case, if the government really intends to use its legal authority to change things or merely wishes to make pleasing gestures.

Politicians following this new perspective would need the stamina to resist dubious banners and the self-discipline to reject inflated claims that do not correlate with broad purposes or have any plausible chance of actually being achieved. This would be nasty work for a political community used to making indulgent gestures and, against the facts of present behavior, it is very difficult to visualize. Still, the old order is failing and people everywhere recognize it. The next step must be to mobilize the political imagination—and courage—to construct a new order in its place.

If government were serious about environmental protection, for example, it would direct its authority at the sources of pollution, not the symptoms—the production processes and products that throw off the billions of pounds of harmful substances every year. It would ban outright the use of some chemicals or force a radical reduction in other pollution emissions by mandating new technological processes for industry, agriculture, transportation and other sectors. If companies refused to change their own processes, the government might underwrite the creation of high-tech waste-treatment centers and compel industries to use them for a fee.

The principle behind this example is that government ought to use its coercive powers only if it is serious about achieving results. Once the chemical and oil industries began paying the real price for producing their hazardous wastes, they would have a strong incentive to reduce their pollution, an incentive more reliable than public relations. The federal tax code, to cite another example, now subsidizes the exploitation of virgin materials, trees, minerals, raw land, with generous tax preferences while government at the same time is supposedly promoting recycling. If government were serious, the tax incentives would be reversed—to penalize the exploitation and reward the frugal use of resources.[15]

Is the government serious about compliance with the law? Corporations are not the only flagrant abusers of the permissive law but they are the most important ones. If the government were serious, it would create a standardized system for penalizing corporate offenders at the place where they feel real pain—the bottom line. Ralph Nader has proposed a set of reforms for government procurement that would effectively close the window to companies that repeatedly violate laws or defraud the government on contracts.

A broader discipline could be applied to virtually all business enterprises through the U.S. tax code. A corporation that accumulates a record of anti-social behavior, including criminal violations, would be forbidden to cash in on the lucrative tax exceptions that are enacted to subsidize various business sectors. Why should other taxpayers augment the profitability of a company that, year after year, chooses to violate or evade the law?

Withdrawing tax privileges in a systematic way is another example of political remedies that speak directly to power—applying the government's public authority to private behavior in a way that will produce real results. Such a negative tax incentive would swiftly alter the cost-benefit calculations that corporations make on whether to comply with new environmental or health and safety laws. Once the practice of abusing the law carries real costs—with real dollar signs—compliance may seem like a more logical choice.

These and similar ideas, of course, are exceedingly difficult—perhaps impossible—to envision in the present politics of the nation. That is because these ideas speak directly to the power relationships that envelop government and have deformed democracy. Anyone who operates successfully within the status quo will have little incentive, it is true, to disturb the present realities. That incentive has to come from the people.

*   *   *

Asking politicians to be more honest or courageous is an empty proposition by itself. The political system will not suddenly become self-disciplined or righteously skeptical of its own well-worn habits. None of the above ideas will be remotely possible unless the governing elites at the national level, including both political parties, feel threatened by some larger political force or the federal government in all its branches perceives a larger challenge to its dominance.

As it happens, the random stirrings of such a crisis are already visible in the vast deterioration in respect for federal authority. Federal law is now widely dismissed, both by aroused citizens and by local and state governments, as incoherent or unwilling to act meaningfully on public problems.

In some areas, citizens are using state legislatures as a bulwark against Washington, trying to prevent the worst outcomes that flow from the hollow laws enacted at the national level. In other instances, citizens skip over government altogether to confront powerful interests bluntly on their own turf. These shifting lines of struggle are still indistinct but perhaps foretell a historic reversal in popular political attitudes.

For two generations in American politics, Washington was the place where progressive reformers came in search of justice, whether it was civil rights or economic reforms, educational aid or environmental protection. The federal government's reputation as the most reliable source of social and economic justice has been destroyed, particularly during the last decade of Republican presidents but more profoundly over the last twenty-five years. As Professor Lowi predicted, interest-group liberalism "was almost inevitably going to produce a crisis of public authority." The crisis appears to have arrived, expressed by the mutual contempt between the people and those who govern the nation.

Engaged citizens of many different persuasions have concluded that, given the power realities that grip the national government, they must seek redress elsewhere, however limited or inadequate it might prove to be. On the whole, these are not the small-government conservatives following the anti-Washington rhetoric of Ronald Reagan, but people who call themselves liberal or progressive. They include as well countless citizens who wear no particular ideological stripe, but are simply seeking government action on the public problems they care about.

The power to govern still largely resides in Washington, but its centralized authority to decide things unilaterally for the nation is under challenge on many fronts. No one understands this better than corporations, which recognize the threat to their own political power and have largely reversed their own historical hostility to federal power. Conservative pundits still prattle on about the "new federalism," but conservative business interests now regularly lobby to defend Washington against rival centers that are trying to decide things for themselves.

Business sectors, it turns out, want to keep decision making consolidated at the federal level, where they have a better opportunity to manage the outcomes, whether the issue is product-liability lawsuits or pollution standards. Having gained substantial control over their old nemesis—the big government built by liberalism—industry now regularly defends big government against its smaller competitors.

This new struggle is found everywhere and on many different fronts. The state of Maine enacted a statute banning low-level radioactive wastes from landfills in the state—trying to counter the federal government's decision to deregulate these substances as harmless. As Washington stalled, Hawaii and Vermont passed the first laws in the nation to control chlorofluorocarbons (CFCs) that threaten the atmospheric ozone. Portland, Oregon, banned plastic cups. Alabama prohibited out-of-state hazardous wastes from being trucked to a huge chemical dump in the state; industry sued, backed up by the federal government. When Iowa enacted a landmark ground-water-protection law, followed by Arizona and Wisconsin, the food industry lobbied Washington to preempt the states' efforts to regulate agricultural chemicals (the Bush administration endorsed the industry's demand). While Congress dallied for a decade over new clean-air legislation, eight New England states had already adopted California's tougher air pollution standards.[16]

These challenges to federal domination and many others like them have the potential to scramble the old lines of political conflict that for two generations delineated the standard liberal-conservative assumptions about politics. The battlegrounds are at least shifting in provocative new directions. The new battle lines, in effect, reflect people fighting back—trying to accomplish something real in public affairs, despite the deformed power relationships and other obstacles.

The story of the democratic condition is not told by government alone, because there is always the other side of the two-way mirror—the people. The next section of this inquiry turns in that direction—citizens at large who are engaged in their own irregular politics, struggling to be heard and to force power to listen. Many Americans have given up on democracy in Washington, but they are still looking for it elsewhere.

PART TWO

HOW MAY THE PEOPLE SPEAK TO POWER?

7

THE POLITICS OF "RUDE AND CRUDE"

The nature of democracy's breakdown is visible not only in the corridors of Washington, but among the people too. Citizens have been distanced from the formal structure of governing power and they know it. Many are demoralized and resigned to their inferior status. Powerlessness also corrupts.

Others who still care about public questions have invented their own irregular methods for speaking to power. People will play the hand they are dealt and do the best they can with it. But, in the modern scheme of American politics, even active citizens are holding a very weak hand. Many have decided that if anything is going to be accomplished, it has to be done outside regular politics and in spite of government. Some assume the role of perennial guerrillas, staging daring raids on the established political order. The assaults occasionally rattle the centers of power but never manage to topple the fortress.

These citizens' attitudes and actions powerfully confirm this book's argument that the political system we call democracy has lost substantive meaning. They can testify from experience to all the many elements of decay that have been identified as the "realities of power."

They see the major political parties in comfortable alliance with one another, not in principled competition. They know, from tangible experience, how the mystique of information-driven politics is used against them, disparaging their claims and pricing them out of the debate. They perceive the client-representative relationships of Washington as partnerships between government and the powerful economic interests that are arrayed against them. These citizens do not perhaps know the precise ways laws are manipulated, but they certainly perceive the murky barrier of symbolic law and false promises that makes it so difficult for ordinary people to penetrate the reality of governance.

All these factors and some others have incapacitated the citizens of this democracy, rendered them ineffectual as citizens. They are cut off from the real decision making in government and unable to speak to it coherently or find reliable representatives who will speak for them. People do the best they can in these debilitating circumstances, but inevitably many have absorbed their own distorted assumptions about what it means to be a citizen in a working democracy.

A generation of frustrated aspirations has led many citizens to separate themselves from the formal system of power and dwell in righteous isolation, contemptuous of all traditional ways of connecting with government. They no longer believe in elections as an effective lever of power for citizens. They distrust the elaborate machinery of governing. Many no longer believe that federal legislation itself makes much difference; they have seen too many reform laws eviscerated by the powerful economic interests.

Indeed, in many realms, the authority of federal law has become the enemy of active citizens—taking issues away from them and concealing the action deep inside the Washington labyrinth. Cut off from the real decisions, lacking the resources to compete with the insiders, citizens at the community level lose contact with the content of public issues they care about and, as a consequence, their political activism sometimes loses coherence and energy. To overcome this, many have developed their own bluntly practical strategies for how to do politics—rough and direct confrontations with power.

Rehabilitating American democracy thus requires much more than reforming the government. It means that citizens at large must also reinvent themselves. The political culture that fractured governing authority and allowed political institutions to become irresponsible has done the same to the citizenry. The modern methodologies of government have taught people to think of themselves as one more "interest group"—focused narrowly on this or that particular concern, but unable to imagine a larger role for themselves in the power relationships. These deformities, like the government's, are deeply embedded in the society and will also not be susceptible to quick, easy remedies. Some Americans are already working on it, however, trying to restore themselves as citizens in order to repair the democracy.

It is this lively but neglected territory of politics, the weaknesses and strengths of active citizens struggling for democratic meaning, that is explored in this next section. Their stories reveal, above all, the disconnectedness that prevents them from entering into any kind of enduring, responsible relationship with those in power.

This chapter concentrates on their strengths—the varied ways in which citizens do sometimes manage to acquire a limited measure of power, despite the barriers thrown up in their path. Their victories are real, but often amount to a negative form of power—popular vetoes over what the governing elites have decided in their behalf.

Not all Americans suffer equally from the deterioration of politics, and Chapter Eight, ''Political Orphans,'' explains how the imbalances of power penalize one sector of citizens more harshly than all others. They are the working-class people who used to be protected and represented by powerful secondary mediating institutions—organized labor and big-city political organizations. The story of how labor unions were stripped of their representative powers is an essential strand in the story of how citizens were incapacitated in politics.

Chapter Nine, ''Class Conflict,'' turns directly to the citizens' own debilities—the attitudes and approaches that condemn them to a weak position in politics. Just as governing circles are ruled by outmoded and self-defeating mythologies, so are many of the citizens who engage in irregular politics.

The final chapter of this section, Chapter Ten, ''Democratic Promise,'' reveals a hopeful alternative vision—a portrait of citizens who are trying to reinvent democracy from the ground up. In a number of unexpected places, citizens are acquiring real power by coming together and patiently developing their collective political voice. These citizens are a living model of democratic meaning—people speaking to power in a coherent manner. They provide an optimistic example for others, but also a rebuke to the atrophied political institutions that have failed.

Above all, these stories of politics have a redeeming message that is more important than all the subsidiary complications: Behind the empty shell of formal politics, the nation is alive with democratic energies. People are still pursuing the universal impulse for political self-expression. Disconnected from power, they are still searching to find it.

At the Highlander school in the mountains of eastern Tennessee, where black citizens trained for the civil rights movement a generation ago, students of a different sort assemble each month for instruction in political organizing and agitating. Most are white and not poor, though they generally come from the less prosperous corners of America, rural counties and urban working-class neighborhoods. Most are already engaged in the irregular politics of their communities and anxious to learn more about how it's done. The weekend training sessions are called STP, a title that is left open to playful interpretations. Save the Planet. Stop the Poisoners. Shoot the Politicians.

At dusk on a Friday evening in late August 1990, a group of nineteen citizens gathered in a wide circle of rocking chairs in Highlander's rustic conference room and began to educate one another with personal stories of victory and frustration. They had traveled from nine states, points as distant as Brooklyn, New York, and Jonesboro, Arkansas. A young folk singer from Pineville, Kentucky, provided a mournful version of "I am just a weary pilgrim going through this world of sin."

Highlander was founded in the 1930s by radical Christian social activists whose training workshops for labor and black organizers were frequently denounced (and persecuted) as "Communist-inspired" by southern segregationists. The mountain training center endures, a staff member explained to the circle, as "a school for people to learn how to act to exercise their rights, which is what we think democracy is all about." The civic battleground is no longer racial equality, but the injustices of life-threatening pollution.

Larry Wilson, a community leader from Yellow Creek, Kentucky, opened one discussion by reporting some of the insights gleaned from previous STP sessions. "Last group decided, since we're doing what EPA should be doing, we ought to bill the government for our work," Wilson said. "So we all sent EPA a bill. As screwed up as EPA is, they may pay us."

From Greenup County, Kentucky, an elderly war veteran named Daniel Thompson reported on GROWL, a citizens group trying to block a huge nine-hundred-acre landfill believed to be designed for the garbage of New York and New Jersey. "Those hearings they have are just a laugh," Thompson said. "The one we had, people said the hearing officer fell asleep two or three times. . . .

"I think the people in New York's got in mind to make eastern Kentucky and the southern states their dumping ground. If they win, we ain't going to have no water fit to drink because even EPA says there's no landfill that doesn't leak. They may get it—I don't know—but they'll surely know they've been in a fight."

Deborah Bouton, from Murphysboro, Illinois, reported gloomily on the hazards of a local Superfund site created by a military installation and EPA's plan to install a mobile incinerator for the cleanup. "I'm here because I desperately need some encouragement," she said. "I need to hear some success stories. I approach friends and try to get them to come to meetings, but their apathy is so profound. It's like there's nobody home."

Bob Greenbaum, a home-repair contractor from Cleveland, Ohio, described a fight against a new incinerator planned for a poor neighborhood "where the people have about as much political influence as my dog." A wealthy suburb, he said, was persuaded to join the fight because its citizens might be at risk too if the wind is blowing the wrong way. ''I'm for environmental fundamentalism,'' Greenbaum declared. ''Start a lot of big brushfires everywhere you can and let the regulators try to put them out.''

James Ramer, a hospital administrator from Jonesboro, Arkansas, recounted how he became politically activated. ''We had one landfill that hit us before we knew how things worked,'' Ramer said. ''We thought EPA was supposed to protect people.'' The others interrupted with cynical laughter. ''Seriously, we did,'' he said. ''So we lost that one. Then they came in with the second landfill and we nailed that one. . . .

''The governor brushed us off so we got mad and we organized an environmental task force statewide with twenty-one hundred members. We're becoming a political force. The governor can't wall us off in one corner of the state. We're popping up all over the place.''

The lengthy discussions at the STP school are about politics, but not in the esoteric euphemisms that cloud Washington debates. These people do not say ''pollutants.'' They talk about the ''poisons'' in their communities. They do not analyze the statistics of risk assessment. They talk about people they know who died or children afflicted with cancer in their hometowns. The official language of environmental regulation—terms like ''interim permits'' or ''sanitary landfill'' or ''state-of-the-art technology''—sounds to them like purposeful double-talk.

''These people are already radical,'' Larry Wilson said, ''but they're saying things here for the first time to real folks like themselves—things they've never had the nerve to say to their conservative folks back home. It's kind of like Alcoholics Anonymous. Saying something out loud that you've been thinking has a cleansing effect and hearing someone else say it has a strengthening effect. It makes it easier to say it over and over again when you get back home.''

The rough-hewn political sophistication of these ''witnesses'' is obvious. Collectively, these people already know quite a lot about how government really works and, if policymakers ever listened to them in earnest, they would hear a brutally explicit diagnosis of why politics and government have failed. From practical experience, these citizens have mastered many of the procedural formalities and dense technical details, but they have also glimpsed the real power relationships underneath. That is why they are so alienated.

Public-spirited reforms enacted in the last generation (including public hearings and formal access to decision making for ordinary people) have only deepened their skepticism. They can see for themselves that the democratic form is not the reality. ''At public hearings,'' one of them observed, ''most public officials act like they're protecting hidden interests, like the decisions have already been made somewhere else.''

James Ramer went further. "The politicians have pretty well quietly insulated themselves from all the critical issues," he explained. "By turning the decisions over to boards and commissions who are beholden to the industrial interests, the politicians protect themselves from the blame."

"We're playing by their rules," Wilson said. "The system was invented by the people who are poisoning us. The rules say they get to argue over how much cyanide they can put in our coffee, how much poison they can put out before they have to take responsibility for it. That's not a system we can ever win in."

The STP schools, perhaps by design, produce predictable tides of conflicting emotions among the students, some of whom are meeting other community activists for the first time. First, there is elation, listening to the others tell stories of their inventive tactics and occasional victories. This is displaced by despondency as they turn to analyzing the political forces arrayed against them: the federal government, local politicians, the corporations and their hired cadres, the scientific community, sometimes the media, sometimes even their own communities.

In a role-playing exercise, the STP students assumed the parts of the industry spokesmen and government officials attempting to convince a community that the new landfill or incinerator poses no health hazards and promises lots of new jobs. With disturbing ease, the activists found they could expertly mimic the condescending language and scientific bromides that have been used against them. The exercise provoked nervous laughter, then subdued reflections on their own weakness.

After many hours of talk, a renewed sense of anger surfaced—anger that swiftly hardened into audacious political statements. "The law is not on our side, it just isn't," Bob Greenbaum said. "It's our government even though it isn't serving us. We need to seize the moral high ground and ask moral questions. Who made this choice that put us at risk?"

"There are already enough laws on the books right now, if they were enforced," James Ramer said. "I think the only way we're going to do it is to get hold of the power, which is the political power. Even though rich people have the most power, if we seize the political system out from under them, that's when it's going to happen. We have to develop enough clout so the governmental machinery can't be bought off."

In that sense at least, their self-conscious identification with the civil rights movement is accurate enough: These citizens are also utterly distant from power. They are scattered voices expressing hopes and fears for their families and communities, but utterly beneath the notice of the larger structure of formal politics. In their hopeful moments, these citizens also imagine that they are quietly building a political movement—a movement for environmental justice—while political elites dismiss their fears as irrational and disparage their demands as ''misplaced priorities.''

Firsthand experience with how government responds to ordinary citizens can serve as a powerful organizing tool. A vast network of indigenous environmental organizations has ''popped up'' from the grassroots during the last decade—as many as seven thousand, some estimate—fighting everything from industrial smokestacks to ground-water pollution. These citizens were not drawn to environmental activism by abstract ideology or aesthetics, but by their own experiences. They did not come from the well-educated managerial classes that produce so many members for the larger environmental organizations. On the whole, these citizens come from the most alienated and passive ranks of society, middle America, where politics seems remote and pointless.[1]

Typically, these people saw their homes or communities threatened in tangible ways. They turned to the government for help and were confronted by bureaucratic indifference or political sleight-of-hand. The disillusionment eventually led them to ask larger questions about power and the nature of democracy, but also to entertain more ambitious conceptions of their own citizenship.

Lois Marie Gibbs, executive director of the Citizen's Clearinghouse for Hazardous Wastes, a national organization that supports and advises thousands of grassroots groups, explains:

''Generally, people at first have a blind faith in government. So when they go to EPA or the state agency and show them that there is a problem, they think the government will side with them. It takes them about a year before they realize the government is not going to help them. They see the agencies studying them to death. That's when they become really angry—radicalized.''

Gibbs went through the same learning process herself back in 1978 when, as a young housewife and mother, she organized the neighborhood families who were living on top of a chemical swamp known as Love Canal in the suburbs of Buffalo, New York. ''When I started, I believed democracy worked,'' she said. ''I believed everything I had learned in civics class. What I saw is that decisions are made on the basis of politics and costs. Money.''

Lois Gibbs and the Love Canal activists became the model for thousands of other communities because they figured out how to play politics ''very rude and very crude,'' as she put it. The governor of New York came to address their complaints and delivered what Gibbs described as a ''kiss-the-baby'' speech. When it was their turn to ask questions, the mothers flooded the stage with their three-year-olds and four-year-olds. Then they turned to the governor and asked if he intended to protect these children from the deadly chemicals. Surrounded by toddlers, the governor capitulated on the spot.

"Although we won, that was really scary to me," Gibbs said. "My God, do they make all their decisions this way? All you need to do is make it politically advantageous for these guys to do what you want, regardless of whether it's right or moral? So much for civics class."

As thousands of other citizen activists have discovered, rude and crude politics works more reliably than the system's formal processes. Instead of obeying the rules, they stage dramatic confrontations with the people who have power. Citizens chain themselves to the gates of landfills. Or they block incoming dump trucks with caravans of their own cars and pickup trucks. They "blow up" public hearings with noisy disruptions and walkouts. In Braintree, Massachusetts, fifteen hundred people formed a hand-to-hand protest across a river bridge to protest a hazardous-waste incinerator. In Eden Prairie, Minnesota, a school bus filled with women and children blocked a Browning-Ferris landfill entrance for three hours. In Sumter, South Carolina, the local American Legion commander was arrested in community civil disobedience. These flamboyant tactics all won their objectives—after reason and politeness had failed.[2]

"The movement is outside the system," Gibbs explained, "because that's the way to win. If you work within the established system, doing the right thing, more often than not you will lose. The system is put together by the powers that be so they will win. To be outside means not to accept that we will lose."

Many of these activists are convinced they are risking personal retaliation by challenging powerful corporate interests, a fear that is not entirely groundless. Some of them have been hit with multi-million-dollar defamation lawsuits filed by waste-disposal companies, a counterattack designed to silence them with huge legal bills (the activists call them SLAPPs—"strategic lawsuits against public participation"). In an internal memo, a Union Carbide executive invoked the Red scare by warning his fellow managers that Lois Gibbs's organization has "ties into labor, the communist party and all manner of folk with private/single agenda."[3]

Nevertheless, William Ruckelshaus, the CEO of Browning-Ferris Industries and former EPA administrator, has a politician's grudging respect for the grassroots activists—perhaps because his own company, second largest in the waste-disposal industry, has gone up against them on many local fronts and often lost.

"They are the most radicalized group I've seen since Vietnam," Ruckelshaus said. "They've been empowered by their own demands. They can block things. That's a negative power. But it's real power. Right or wrong, you can't bull your way through that kind of opposition."

Across many issues beyond environmental protection, Ruckelshaus observed, the dissolution of governing authority is underway—driven mainly by public distrust. "I think what's happening," he said, "is that people are taking back the power to govern. It's not just symbolic power, it's real power."

Among political elites, including some of the respectable environmental organizations, the community environmentalists are regarded as irresponsible and dismissed with the tired cliché "not in my backyard." In fact, the movement for environmental justice has embraced a public-spirited goal that is more positive and ambitious than the government's—to stop the corporations from dumping their stuff in anyone's backyard.[4]

Gibbs describes a plausible strategy for accomplishing this—"plugging the toilet" of the industrial system—a strategy that is based on an analysis of corporate economics, not good intentions. What policy elites mistake for random irrationality in the grassroots agitators is actually their different way of understanding the power relationships. The activists recognize that political outcomes are not determined by the rationalistic policy processes that elites promote. Do federal regulatory laws have the promise of solving the environmental problem, given their compromised condition in the web of corporate political influence? At the grassroots level, based on their own observations of how the system works, the answer many citizens give is no.

The relevant power, the citizens would say, does not reside in the political system, but in the private corporations that finance and manipulate the politicians. So these citizens have worked out their own strategy for achieving environmental progress—a strategy that, realistically enough, targets corporate power. Given all that has occurred, their approach seems at least as "rational" as trying to enact new regulatory laws. Lois Gibbs explained:

"When companies have proposed new hazardous-waste landfills, our folks have come out and said, no, you can't put it there. As a result, there has not been a single new hazardous-waste site opened in the last ten years. Without passing any new laws or regulations, without getting into the debate, we have stopped the expansion of hazardous-waste sites in this country. In Colorado, BFI has the last landfill that's been approved, but the reason people lost in Colorado is because they turned to the scientists and did their objections within the system. You can't win within the system.

"Our aim is to change the discussion within the boardrooms of major corporations. That's where we will win ultimately, not in the government agencies or Congress. Our strategy is basically like plugging up the toilet—by stopping them from opening new landfills, incinerators, deep-well injection systems and hazardous-waste sites. What happens? Industry is still generating the same amount of chemical waste and, because disposal facilities are limited, the cost of storage and disposal climbs many, many times. That's the American way—scarcity raises the price.

"In the boardrooms at some point, there's going to be this discussion: 'Hey, ten years ago, our disposal costs were X and now they are multiplying and so is our liability and so is the public-relations damage.' That's when real change will come. All they understand is profit and loss. When the cost is high enough, corporations will decide to recycle wastes and reclaim materials, to substitute nontoxics in their products, to change their processes of production.''

It is entirely plausible that these scattered groups of citizens, employing their practical strategy of cost pressures, may succeed where government has failed. As if to substantiate Gibbs's power analysis, William Ruckelshaus announced in the spring of 1990 that Browning-Ferris was going to get out of the hazardous-waste business. BFI would concentrate on the other, less dangerous forms of waste disposal and try to sell its new site in Colorado to some other operator. Hazardous waste, Ruckelshaus explained, was losing money.[5]

Active citizens of any sort are always, of course, a small minority of the population, since they are committed to public affairs at a level of intensity most Americans would probably never reach, even if democracy were functioning. A 1986 study measured the political sophistication of American adults and found an activist core of 5 percent, including the regular cadres within political parties. A fifth of the citizenry, 20 percent, was described as "totally apolitical." The rest were said to be "marginally attentive to politics."

Karen Paget, a political scientist at the University of California, estimated that fifteen million people are engaged in as many as two million citizen organizations, ranging from neighborhood drug patrols to national groups like ACORN, which has seventy thousand members organized in poor and low-income communities in twenty-six states. "Though there is no precise definition of a citizen organization," Paget wrote, "even a narrow conception would disclose phenomenal growth in the last two decades."[6]

In some crude fashion, however, these activists speak for a broader public too, serving as self-selected representatives without the benefit of elections. For them, developing political influence depends crucially on sustaining credibility among the passive citizens who merely sit and listen. Ralph Nader is disparaged by the elected apparatus of politics, but he has continuing influence because he accurately voices the complaints of a much broader audience.

On some matters, the unelected representatives are more trusted than the elected ones. A *Washington Post* poll, for instance, asked citizens to rate the different political voices they hear on environmental issues. The environmental groups came in first: 63 percent favorable; 20 percent unfavorable. Local governments finished second, EPA was third. Business leaders finished last: 33 percent favorable; 45 percent unfavorable.[7]

Ronald Reagan made an ironic contribution to the dramatic growth of irregular politics, not because he preached antigovernment volunteerism, but because his administration's hard-headed assault on federal programs and laws clarified the power relations for people. The fix is in in Washington, they concluded. Nothing will be done there. Why pass laws when the other side has no intention of observing them? Let's try something else. So people turned in other directions, lobbying state and local governments for reform or inventing disruptive new ways to apply ''rude and crude'' politics to a wide variety of issues, from housing to taxation.

The very structure of federal laws, however, including environmental laws, has had the long-term effect of weakening citizen politics by making issues more remote. Leon Billings, an environmental consultant, served as staff director of the Senate Public Works Committee during the reform years of the 1970s when all the landmark environmental laws were enacted. He has regretfully concluded that federal legislation like the Clean Air Act of 1970 had the unintended consequence of smothering political energies at the grass-roots level. Might the nation have made more actual progress on clean air, Billings wonders, if the federal law had not intervened?

''Adopting national air ambience standards in the Clean Air Act was the biggest mistake we ever made,'' he confessed. ''Citizens-for-clean-air groups were beginning to get local governments to adopt tougher standards around the country, much tougher than anticipated, and industry wanted to get out from under these local and regional activists who were coming after them everywhere. The Clean Air Act brought the fight to Washington where industry could manipulate thing much more cleverly.

''The federal law short-circuited the activism. It took away the forum for local activists and they had to become involved in much more technical arguments, an arena where industry is strong and citizens are weak. Once policy issues become engulfed in the federal bureaucracy, the public loses the ability to influence these decisions because local electronic and print media simply lose interest in the issues. The story is suddenly distant and difficult to cover in a local newspaper. There's no local agitation because it's now a 'national issue.' ''

If citizens at large seem ''dumb'' to political elites, including their own elected representatives, it is partly because they have been cut off from knowing and understanding the real arguments. But the citizens' new tactics also condemn them to a more or less permanent state of isolation. They may succeed at delivering potent messages to those in power, but this does not get them any closer to developing a relationship with the formal structure that decides things.

Karen Paget, formerly an official for federal domestic-social programs in the Carter administration, offered this sympathetic critique of nonelectoral citizen politics: ''To be sure, community organizations can play a crucial role in fostering participation, strengthening a democratic ethos, and in making government work. But claims that suggest such organizations can replace the state or the polity are as misleading as the notion that they could eradicate poverty.''

The isolation from power leads to strategies that are oppositional and often narrow or essentially negative. Community organizations can target an offending corporation or veto a government project. But they cannot enter into the ongoing political debate on larger matters like the federal tax code or the national economic policies that fundamentally influence the future of their communities. They can stop a chemical waste dump or postpone the closing of a local plant or perhaps even ban a harmful product from the marketplace. But they cannot reach the government decisions that allow these things to happen in the first place. Citizens may block things, but it is much harder for them to build anything.

In recent years, the two ''hottest'' citizen organizations in America have been Amnesty International and Greenpeace. Both have grown almost frantically, especially among younger people. Both have a brash, direct style that cuts through all the political fog with action that is clear and accessible to individuals. ''An organization like Greenpeace was considered a terrorist organization ten years ago because of its tactics,'' Leon Billings remarked, ''and now it's becoming the mainstream.'' When Amnesty or Greenpeace scores a hit, people can see concrete results from their political engagement. Something actually happens—which is more than one can count on from the normal channels of politics.

Both Greenpeace and Amnesty also do what political parties used to do—educate citizens for politics. Amnesty staged a worldwide campaign to connect young people with human-rights politics by sending Sting, Bruce Springsteen and other rock stars on a global concert tour. Music was the draw but the concerts also delivered a mild education on the issues.

High school kids wrote personal letters to political prisoners and to foreign dictators, asking them to stop torturing people. The political prisoners wrote back. Sometimes so did the dictators, evidently unaware that these politically astute Americans were children.

''When we get someone into our organization,'' John G. Healy, Amnesty's executive director, explained, ''we try to turn them into a human-rights activist. We teach them policy and the hardline issues. We're a democracy ourselves, an organization of people who actually write their own policy. It's very direct: You're a political prisoner, we work for you.

''We work just as Greenpeace does. They see a toxic problem, they put a flag down. When we see a political prisoner we put a flag down. We're both dangerous to the U.S. government because we eliminate the government's ally and friend—business—from the argument. We say the same things to the government's closest allies as we say to its enemies. In Amnesty, we say there should be a single standard in the world for human rights. That's a dangerous idea for a superpower.''

Yet where does all the youthful energy turn, once it has freed a political prisoner? Despite Amnesty's many successes, Healy is gloomy about the prospects for political development. He sees idealistic citizens, young and old, confined to ''direct-action'' hits on narrow objectives.

''I'm so despondent about American politics,'' he said. ''Everyone's lost their curiosity and imagination. In Germany, the Greens came out of Amnesty International—all the Green party leadership was trained in Amnesty—but in America there's no way to feed into politics. There's no place to attach. What would they attach to? I don't know.

''We're almost teaching people antipolitics. If you're a people's movement, you don't bullshit. You don't hype. You don't make glib and easy comparisons. So, if you become one of our leaders, you'll never get anywhere in American politics. Because you'll talk substance, you'll tell the truth. That's the last thing you need to succeed in American politics.''

Many citizens in search of political leverage have decided to skip government altogether and confront corporations on their home turf—in the marketplace. Consumer boycotts are not a new pressure tactic, of course, but the form has been elaborated and multiplied many times in recent years.

McDonald's was vulnerable for its ''clamshell'' packaging, Burger King for buying cattle from ranches created by destroying rain forests, and StarKist tuna for killing dolphins. Each of them folded without much of a fight. As a spokesman for H. J. Heinz, owner of Starkist, explained to *The Wall Street Journal*: ''The idea that the company could be branded as the largest slaughterers of dolphins in the world seemed to us to be dramatically opposed to where the company wanted to position itself as health-conscious and caring.''[8]

Because these companies all live or perish by their brand names and the wholesome images their TV advertising has created in the public mind, they are most vulnerable to accusations of antisocial behavior. The smart corporate response, in many cases, is to surrender cheerfully.

According to *Boycott News*, an irregular newsletter, there are now as many as three hundred boycotts a year. Demonstrators dumped Miller beer on the street to protest Philip Morris's campaign support for right-wing Senator Jesse Helms of North Carolina. Black demonstrators targeted Nike shoes, demanding more employment for black executives. Led by conservative preachers, grassroots boycotts aimed at TV sponsors or convenience stores selling *Playboy* have had some success at removing ''blasphemous'' materials from public view. Boycotts are spreading because they sometimes work.

''Most people don't have faith in government's ability to do these things,'' said Steve Beers, an Austin, Texas, activist. ''They're not going to go through the process of petitioning the government and working in elections in order to get the government to do something. Frankly, the dollar bill is a lot more effective franchise. It gives people something powerful but very easy to do. If you go to the grocery store, you can choose.''

Corporations are not exactly helpless giants, however. When a campaign targeted Folgers coffee for its economic connections to the war in El Salvador, Procter & Gamble struck back on the bottom line. The boycotters bought TV time on a Boston station for a commercial attacking Folgers. Procter & Gamble responded by canceling all of its advertising on the station—sending a chilling message to every other broadcaster in America. None has since been willing to run the anti-Folgers spot and risk the same result.

A more fundamental weakness of boycotts is that consumer pressure can't easily reach beyond the shelf of brand-name goods. One of the most ambitious boycotts targets General Electric for its manufacture of nuclear weapons, but the only consumer in the bomb business is the U.S. government. The campaign attempts to get around this barrier by promoting a boycott of everything GE makes and sells, from light bulbs to high-tech hospital equipment. IN-FACT, the Boston group that launched the effort, claims to have deprived GE of $50 million in sales, partly by persuading church-related hospitals to stop buying GE medical technology. For a company with annual revenues of $55 billion, even this loss would not constitute grave injury.

The other weakness is the randomness of the boycott campaigns, which hit here and there in narrow and sporadic fashion. The overall effect of these campaigns is broadly educational and raises the awareness of ordinary consumers, especially about their own contribution to environmental problems. But it also requires the politically conscious to take a lengthy list of forbidden products with them when they go to the supermarket. Indeed, a little guidebook called *Shopping for a Better World* is available for those who wish to express their political convictions at the checkout counter.

Denis Hayes, organizer of the original Earth Day in 1970, has launched Green Seal as an attempt to institutionalize the political power of consumers by creating a standard label for environmental concerns, covering everything from egg cartons to autos. "What we find over time is that, no matter what the laws said, they were just compromised beyond belief, and even the compromises were then delayed and weakened with exceptions and exemptions," Hayes said. "In recent days, we have found we can't even get the good laws passed.

"At which point, people start saying, okay, it would be a whole lot easier to do this with federal laws, but at least they can't stop us from doing it ourselves. Consumers can make a real difference. More importantly, Green Seal gives people more involvement than simply sending a check to the Sierra Club. Out of that, maybe we can begin once again to build a movement from the ground up and begin to assert ourselves in the political process in a way that isn't just Tweedledum and Tweedledee.''

In the meantime, consumer boycotts like Green Seal confirm the general distrust of government and business to do the right thing. The Gallup Poll, in a survey commissioned by *Advertising Age*, asked consumers whom they would most trust to design environmental labeling for products—a government agency or corporations or private environmentalists.

"We won," Hayes said.

In 1988, while conventional politics concentrated on electing a new president, an organization called Voter Revolt pulled off an epic David-and-Goliath victory in California. Supported by contributions from two hundred thousand Californians, the group sent college students out to knock on 1.1 million doors. The result was enough signatures to put a radical proposition on the ballot that fall—a mandatory 20 percent rollback in California's sky-high auto insurance rates.

The insurance industry responded by spending more than $60 million to defeat Proposition 103—millions more than George Bush spent in his entire nationwide campaign to become president. Voter Revolt, unable to afford a single TV spot, won.

On election eve, volunteers stood by freeway entrances and held up cardboard signs: "Nader: Yes on 103." Ralph Nader's endorsement of the initiative helped voters cut through the confusion of scare tactics and counterproposals thrown up by the insurance industry's campaign. But Nader's credibility also connected with a general anger that the political system had declined to address: Californians were paying as much as $6,000 a year for car insurance. People did not need Ralph Nader or Voter Revolt to tell them they were being ripped off.

Voter initiatives were invented by Progressive reformers early in the twentieth century for exactly this situation: a way for citizens to free government from the heavy embrace of special interests and to write laws themselves, enacted by a direct vote of the people. Initiative campaigns have always been a staple of California politics, but in the last fifteen years the device has become the most active (and most expensive) arena for the state's political action. The approach now flourishes in dozens of other states and cities nationwide, on every issue from taxes to helping the homeless.

California voters, for instance, have applied real political leverage on the federal government through their state's initiative process. Proposition 65, an environmental measure approved in 1986, requires safety labeling on products—warnings of cancer-causing ingredients, for instance—that goes far beyond anything Washington has dared to consider. Since California is the largest marketplace in the country, companies will have to comply with the state law in order to sell in that market. No longer protected by weak federal standards, some companies changed their products—replacing the toxic contents with benign substitutes.[9]

"Congress seems to be atrophied and so are the state legislatures," said Albert H. Meyerhoff, a San Francisco lawyer with the Natural Resources Defense Council. "If we've learned one lesson from the 1980s, we've learned that you can't trust the federal government to protect the food supply. . . . EPA has become the Environmental Placation Agency."

The modern rebellion-by-referendum was launched by fed-up conservatives who in 1978 proposed California's now-famous "Prop 13," an initiative that imposed rigid ceilings on state taxes and government spending. Left-liberal groups next began to harness voter discontent on environmental degradation and a long list of other neglected social concerns.

In dozens of states, both liberal and conservative activists are simultaneously popularizing the technique of direct lawmaking, mutually motivated by a deep distrust of elected legislators and governors. In California and elsewhere, the two ideological camps more or less merged behind the cause of imposing term limitations on state legislators. A *Los Angeles Times* survey found that 53 percent of Californians believe their state legislators routinely take bribes from special interests.[10]

Yet left and right are attempting to reform the public sector in roughly opposite directions: The tax-cutting initiatives sponsored by conservatives aim to shrink government's capacity altogether, while the liberals are trying to make government actually do something. In 1990, both sides mostly lost their issues. Environmental measures like the omnibus "Big Green" proposal in California were rejected by wary voters as overly ambitious, but so were most of the tax-cutting measures that conservatives sponsored in many states.[11]

The basic weakness of voter initiatives (and also their great virtue) is that enacting laws by referendum skips over the hard part of representative democracy. Lawmaking is supposed to be a deliberative process of conflict and resolution—debate, negotiations and compromise—that requires all sides to face the contradictions in their own positions. At least that is the ideal. Packaging laws by popular vote evades this obligation—the accountability embedded in the legislative process itself.

Anyone with enough money to collect the necessary qualifying signatures can get a proposed law on the ballot without ever having to address the arguments against it or the people who might be injured. In California, the business of gathering citizen signatures costs as much as $1 million for a statewide referendum and has spawned its own industry of professionalized consultants. Every year, ballot propositions consume more campaign spending than the contests for California's top elective offices.

Furthermore, as California's eminent pollster Mervin Field has explained, the referendum approach to governing generates its own form of class bias, given the atrophied condition of electoral democracy. The minority who actually turn out to vote are dominated by the well-educated, propertied classes and, because of the low election turnouts, they can impose their values and political objectives on the passive majority. Prop 13, which launched a ''taxpayer revolt'' nationwide, was supported by just 27 percent of the California electorate. A companion proposition, enacted the following year, was supported by only 16 percent of the California electorate.

''Taxpaying voters,'' Field wrote, ''represent a declining proportion of all taxpayers and are, increasingly, a different breed of people. They are older, much more white than the rest of the population, they earn more, they have accumulated more wealth, and have different needs than the large majority of taxpayers who happen not to vote.'' Conservatives might argue that similar class biases are embedded in many of the environmental ballot measures—imposing ''green'' values that appeal to a certain stratum of economically secure citizens.[12]

In the modern political condition, however, many popular ideas must bypass the state legislatures (or the Congress) in order to get on the political agenda. ''The government is deadlocked, the people are not represented,'' Bill Zimmerman, a founding organizer of Voter Revolt, explained. ''If you can threaten the legislature credibly with an initiative, you're much more likely to provoke the legislature to do what you want.

''We're supposed to have a government of checks and balances, but we need a check on government for the people because their original check—elections—has been invalidated by modern campaigning, the high-tech, high-cost campaigns that merely manipulate voters.''

However, Voter Revolt's auto-insurance measure, Prop 103, did not produce a substantive victory for the angry voters who enacted it into law. After the referendum, the insurance industry sued and persuaded a court to invalidate the 20 percent rate rollback. A new insurance commissioner was elected in 1990, as prescribed by Prop 103, but the winner was closer to the insurance industry than the proconsumer candidates who lost. The short-term consequence of these setbacks, Zimmerman conceded, was to deepen public cynicism.

''But the battle isn't over yet,'' Zimmerman said. ''We have another insurance proposition in circulation for June of 1992. It says, if rates aren't reduced, the state will create a nonprofit agency that sells auto insurance at a reasonable price. We've already done our own poll and it's 61 percent approval.''

Initiatives by themselves will not alter the balance of power, Zimmerman agrees, but like consumer boycotts, they might help to foster a political mobilization of citizens.

"It's not that one initiative either works or doesn't work," he said. "It's that one victory launches a political force and then you've got to fight like crazy to keep it alive and try to cross the threshold where the reform becomes real. You start with radical initiatives that people want, that state government will never do itself and that can work. Then you can start to build a political force, not with rhetoric and ideology, which nobody buys anymore, but with results."

In many matters, as these examples suggest, the politics of American governance now resembles the rough comedy of a Punch and Judy show. Without a coherent center for collective decision making and shared principles, political conflict becomes a series of rude and crude ambushes. People stage surprise attacks on public policy, then find themselves hit by body blocks or below-the-belt punches. Everyone feels bruised and disappointed, even the powerful.

Over the last two decades, using their superior resources and political skills, business interests succeeded in neutralizing the force of many federal laws and even capturing the democratic arena where national policy is determined. Now, however, corporate interests appear to be particularly distressed by what they have wrought—a governing system that responds to their desires before the public's, but still cannot quite protect them from the people's hot breath. Corporations frequently find themselves cross-checked by the irregular tactics of the citizen guerrillas.

In many states, governors and legislatures have become more responsive to the home-grown agitation and, even in supposedly conservative states, they sometimes take up the citizens' complaints and build legal barriers against the offensive federal policies. In Alabama, the Republican governor closed the notorious hazardous-waste site at Emelle to out-of-state waste. In Texas, the Democratic governor ordered a temporary ban on opening any new chemical dumps or expanding old ones.

Business interests now turn routinely to the federal government and demand that it protect them from these unruly folks. The distress of corporate interests is quite real, though ironic, considering how they systematically accumulated political power to contain this sort of disruption.

The president of the Society of the Plastics Industry, Larry Thomas, issued a dire political alert in 1990 to the plastics manufacturers: Forty-nine states are considering or have already enacted laws that ban or restrict plastic products. Individual consumers are avoiding plastics out of concern for health and environment. Organizations like the Citizen's Clearinghouse for Hazardous Wastes are attacking the industry's "recycling" standards as fraudulent.

"The image of plastics among consumers is deteriorating at an alarmingly fast pace," Thomas wrote. "Opinion research experts tell us that it has plummeted so far and so fast, in fact, that we are approaching a 'point of no return.' . . . There is a growing consensus among plastics executives that we must immediately undertake a major program of unprecedented proportions to reverse this fast-moving tidal wave of growing negative public perception."[13]

A similar sense of alarm was expressed in the food industry. Despite the official assurances periodically issued by such federal regulators as the EPA, the FDA and the Department of Agriculture, the food industry is also suffering a rapid loss of public confidence. A 1989 survey conducted for the Food Marketing Institute, a trade association for major food retailers, found that nearly four in ten consumers do not think the food sold in their supermarkets is safe to eat.

"Who is setting food policy today?" FMI President Robert O. Aders asked plaintively, in a speech to the Produce Marketing Association's convention. "Are the critical decisions being made in the halls of government or in the aisles of the local Safeway or IGA? Environmentalists would grant that authority to the supermarket. It's a clever strategy and it could succeed without decisive countermeasures."[14]

Private interests, Aders warned, "are assuming the government's role in testing for pesticide residues . . . [and] supermarkets advertise that their produce has no detectable residues and consumers respond. The fact that such an ad message has any clout at all is cause for concern among food regulators. It shows a lack of faith in the government systems to safeguard the food supply."

While Aders blamed the industry's problems partly on inflammatory accusations, he also candidly acknowledged the central cause—the breakdown of government. "Government inaction or slow action or indecision creates the void," he explained. ". . . We need a more coordinated [federal] system where the overriding concern is the safety of the food supply—a system that instills confidence in consumers that the food they eat is safe."

EPA, he noted, declares that a cancer-causing pesticide poses an "unreasonable risk," then allows the chemical to remain in use for another eighteen months. Federal regulators promise to "expedite" the removal of dangerous food contaminants, but "expedite" turns out to mean eight or ten years or longer. "That's a long time," Aders said, "even in the time frame of scientists and bureaucrats. And completely unacceptable to consumers."

Corporate interests are now stuck in the ironic position of trying to prop up the federal government's authority. Yet the underlying source of this problem—government inaction and the loss of public confidence—is business's own political behavior. If people have stopped taking the federal government's word as reliable, that is partly because corporate lobbyists subverted the objectivity and integrity of government agencies. If federal law no longer functions in a convincing manner, that is precisely the result that corporate interests intended.

In short, companies that are now afflicted by chaotic political assaults have only themselves to blame. If corporate interests genuinely wished for citizens to defer once again to the authority of the federal government, they would reform their own way of doing politics. This does not seem a likely prospect, to put it mildly.

Instead, business interests are concentrating their political influence on a different goal—nullifying the citizens' political energies with the force of federal law. On issue after issue, alliances of corporations and business sectors are lobbying to enact preemptive federal laws or regulations that will establish Washington as sole authority to govern in those areas. Conflicting state laws, they claim, are creating a "legal balkanization" that Washington must supersede.

"The reason Lincoln went to war was to keep the Union whole," Geoffrey Hurwitz, government-relations director of Rohm and Hass, the chemical company, told the *National Journal*.

His metaphor does not seem too extreme. In terms of national policy on chemical wastes, for instance, a kind of civil war has broken out—especially in the South, where so much of the dangerous industrial refuse is produced and eventually buried in the ground. State governments, egged on by local activists, are blocking the hazardous-waste developments approved by EPA or superimposing their own more stringent standards on top of federal law.

California's voter initiative on product-warning labels, likewise, would be nullified if business can persuade Congress that Prop 65 is an unnecessary nuisance. Thomas J. Donegan, vice-president of the Cosmetic, Toiletry and Fragrance Association, complained: "In effect, you are letting California call the shots [on product labeling] that ought to be called by the federal government in regard to a consistent policy."[15]

A coalition of eleven trade associations, worried about marketplace intruders like Green Seal as well as state laws, petitioned the Federal Trade Commission to produce official federal guidelines on such marketing terms as "recycled" and "compostable." Lever Brothers, Procter & Gamble and Kraft General Foods were prominent in the business alliance, which ranged from the advertising industry to retail packaging.[16]

Autos, drugs, retailing, chemicals, food, insurance, waste disposal, plastics, general manufacturing, small business—all these sectors and others have lobbied for federal preemption in one form or another, sometimes with success. "The business community has tamed the federal regulatory beasts," explained Bruce Silverglade, of the Center for Science in the Public Interest, ''so now the cry for further deregulation is synonymous with a cry for pre-emption.''

This posture naturally requires the conservative business leaders to abandon their traditional position—the defense of states' rights—and to argue, with flagrant hypocrisy, that only the government in Washington can resolve these difficult social questions.

On the other hand, their adversaries—the environmentalists and other citizen reformers—have also had to reverse their old political logic, now that they see state and local governments as their best hope for real change. The Advocacy Institute and Congress Watch issued their own political alert to the grassroots:

''Citizen advocates are fighting and winning battles at the state and local level—battles for clean indoor air, warnings on hazardous products, the disclosure of toxic hazards. But while they are winning on one front, their gains are too often eroded on another, preempted by laws that do little to accomplish their stated goals, but choke off effective regulation at local levels of government.''[17]

Given their pious sermons about returning power to the states, it requires a wrenching political flip-flop for conservatives to embrace the business position. Many of them, nevertheless, nimbly overcome the awkwardness and vote for federal preemptions. Liberal Democrats are, likewise, caught in the middle: They are ideologically disposed to uphold the supremacy of federal authority, yet many of their most active constituencies are now pulling them in the opposite direction.

This struggle defines a new faultline in American politics. Some sincere conservatives oppose the business campaigns for federal preemptions as a matter of principle and, when conservatives join with liberal votes in Congress, the corporations find it most difficult to prevail. On the other hand, business appears to be winning gradually on scattered fronts, at least more than it is losing.

During the 1980s, the era when Ronald Reagan was supposedly turning over power to state and local governments, the enactment of federal preemptions on business regulation and health and safety laws actually accelerated, according to the Advisory Commission on Intergovernmental Relations. So much for the ''new federalism.''[18]

The dissolution of federal authority—people taking back the power to govern, as William Ruckelshaus put it—is an untidy process and essentially negative in the sense that it will indeed create a crazy-quilt system of conflicting laws, at least in the short term.

Yet this disorder flows inevitably from the existing realities of power. As local activists would say: What else can we do? If Washington will not listen or act, then democratic energies will seek redress wherever they can find it. The national industrial system will have to cope with that chaos, like it or not, so long as it uses its political power to abort effective law at the national level.

Business interests, of course, are not exactly impotent at the state and local levels either, but decentralized politics at least multiplies the points of attack for citizens as guerrillas. When citizen reformers find a sympathetic state legislature or an attorney general ready to pursue strong enforcement, they can at least create new points of leverage—start some "big brushfires," as Bob Greenbaum put it, that will excite public opinion and complicate politics for their more powerful adversaries.

In this struggle, as with other political issues, the corporate interests have one big advantage: They will come back, year after year, making the same arguments for federal preemption. They have the resources and patience to stay with it until they get their way. Meanwhile, the citizens who have gravitated to other political arenas in search of victories discover they must still fight a rear-guard battle in Washington—trying to keep the feds from nullifying the victories won by their grassroots politics. The system, as Lois Gibbs observed, is designed for them to lose.

It was not always thus. The American system, as everyone knows, has always fallen short of its democratic ideals in different ways. But, a generation ago, the ordinary people who lack social status or economic advantages did have a much stronger claim on the political system, mainly because they were represented by powerful, permanent voices. The decline of organized labor, as we shall see next, created an entire class of Americans who are effectively orphaned by politics—the working people who are most in need of equitable representation.

8

POLITICAL

ORPHANS

The quality of democracy is not measured in the contentment of the affluent, but in how the political system regards those who lack personal advantages. Such people have never stood in the front ranks of politics, of course, but a generation ago, they had a real presence, at least more than they have now. The challenging conditions they face in their daily lives were once part of the general equation that the political system took into account when it decided the largest economic questions. Now these citizens are absent from politics—both as participants and as the subjects of consideration.

These citizens are not the idle poor, though many hover on the edge of official poverty and virtually all exist in a perpetual condition of economic insecurity. These are working people—the many millions of Americans who fill the society's least glamorous yet essential jobs and rank at the bottom of the ladder in terms of compensation. A large segment of working-class Americans has effectively become invisible to the political debate among governing elites. They are neither seen nor heard nor talked about.

Their absence is a crucial element in the general democratic failure of modern politics. There are different reasons why this has occurred, including all of the deformed power relationships already discussed. But, above all, they are missing because in the past the weak and disorganized segments of society always depended on strong mediating institutions, such as organized labor, to speak for them, to make certain that their particular grievances were included in the whole. When those mediating agents lost power, these people were abandoned too, with consequences more starkly unjust than the injuries done to any other class of citizens.

This loss of power, as the evidence will demonstrate, was not entirely an accident of history or the result of ineluctable social change. The laws that protected the rights of workers to organize and defend themselves in politics have been systematically disfigured by political manipulation, much like what happened to other kinds of law. The governing system, likewise, displays the same cynical penchant for symbolic responses to the plight of working people that it has demonstrated in other areas. And the most difficult irony to grasp is that reforms enacted a generation ago to help the very poor are part of what obscures today's working-class citizens.

Like other citizens who have lost power, the humblest working folk have figured out how politics works in the modern age. They know that their only hope is "rude and crude" confrontation. To illustrate this reality, we turn to a group of citizens in Washington, D.C., who are utterly remote from power—the janitors who clean the handsome office buildings in the nation's capital. In a sense, they clean up each night after the very people and organizations that have displaced people like themselves from the political debate. While they work for wages that keep them on the edge of poverty, their political grievances are not heard through the regular channels of politics.

Like other frustrated citizens, the janitors have taken their politics, quite literally, into the streets of the nation's capital.

In late afternoon on a warm June day, while the people in suits and ties were streaming out of downtown office buildings and heading home, a group of fourteen black and Hispanic citizens gathered on the sidewalk in front of 1150 Seventeenth Street Northwest and formed a loose picket line. They were the janitors who cleaned this building every night and, though hardly anyone noticed or cared, they were declaring themselves "on strike" against poverty wages.

"Fire me? Don't bother me one bit. Can't do worse than this," Lucille Morris, a middle-aged black woman with two daughters, said. She was passing out picket signs to hesitant coworkers, most of them women. "Hold 'em up!" she exhorted the others. "Let 'em know you're tired of this mess."

Others grinned nervously at her bravado. An older Hispanic woman dressed in work clothes started into the building and was intercepted by one of the strikers. "She says she's just going in to use the bathroom," Leila Williams reported, "but she's coming back out." Williams, a sweet-faced grandmother who lives with her sixteen-year-old grandson in one of the poorest wards of southeast Washington, was wearing a bright red union tee-shirt that proclaimed: "Squeeze Me Real Hard—I'm Good Under Pressure."

"No one is working—this building isn't going to get cleaned tonight," the organizer from the Services Employees International Union announced with satisfaction. "And nobody's going to get fired," Jay Hessey reassured. "The company can't find enough people to do these jobs at this pay."

"I've been here eleven years and I still get the same pay the newcomers get—$4.75 an hour," Lucille Morris said. "We be doing like two people's work for four hours a night. We don't get nothing in the way of benefits. You get sick, you sick. You stay out too long, they fire you."

"One lady been here for fourteen years and she still get five dollars an hour for doing the bathrooms," Leila Williams added. "They give you another quarter an hour for doing the toilets. When we pass inspections, you know, they always treat us. They give us pizza or doughnuts, like that. We don't want no treats. We want the money."

The SEIU, a union that mainly represents people who do society's elementary chores, launched its "Justice for Janitors" strategy nationwide in 1987 and has staged scores of similar strikes in downtown Washington as well as other major cities. Because of the way federal government now regulates the workers' right to organize for collective action, regular union-organizing tactics have been rendered impotent. So the workers mostly stage symbolic one-night walkouts to grab attention.

The real organizing tactic is public shame—theatrical confrontations intended to harass and embarrass the owners and tenants of the buildings. The janitors will crash the owner's dinner parties and leaflet his neighborhood with accusatory handbills. They will confront the building's tenants at social events and demand help in pressuring the owners.

They, for instance, targeted Mortimer Zuckerman, the real-estate developer who owns *The Atlantic* magazine and *U.S. News & World Report*, with a nasty flier that declared: "Mort Zuckerman might like to be seen as a public citizen, responsible editor, intellectual and all-around good guy. To the janitors who clean his buildings, he is just another greedy real-estate operator." They hounded Zuckerman at important banquets and even in the Long Island Hamptons at celebrity softball games, in which he is a pitcher.[1]

The owners and managers of some five hundred office buildings in Washington have developed an efficient system that insulates them from both unions and higher wages. Each owner hires an independent contractor to service the building and the competitive bidding for contracts is naturally won by the firm that pays the least to the janitors. About six thousand workers—most of them black or Hispanic—are left without any practical leverage over the arrangement. When the union signs up workers and demands its legal right to bargain for a contract in their behalf, the building owner promptly fires the unionized cleaning contractor and hires a new one who is nonunion. Old janitors are fired, new ones are recruited and the treadmill continues.

This management device keeps janitors like Lucille Morris stuck permanently at the same wage level year after year, hovering just above the legal minimum required by law, a wage level that provides less than $10,000 a year at full-time hours.

But these janitors do not even get full-time work from their employers. By doubling the size of the crews, the contractors can hold the workers to a four-hour shift each night and, thus, legally exclude the janitors from all of the employee benefits the firms provide to full-time employees—health insurance, pensions, paid vacations, paid sick leave. The law protects this practice too.

In order to survive, these women and men typically shuttle each day between two or three similar low-wage jobs, all of which lack basic benefits and other protections. Some of the janitors, those who are supporting families, qualify as officially poor and are eligible for food stamps, public housing or other forms of government aid. In effect, the general taxpayers are subsidizing these low-wage employers—the gleaming office buildings of Washington and their tenants—by providing welfare benefits to people who do work that is necessary to the daily functioning of the capital's commerce.

In another era, this arrangement might have been called by its right name—exploitation of the weak by the strong—but in the contemporary political landscape that sort of language is considered passé. Exploitative labor practices are subsumed under the general principle of economic efficiency and the consequences are never mentioned in the political debates on the great social problems afflicting American cities. The government may authorize welfare for the indigent, but it will not address the wages and working conditions that impoverish these people.

In another time, unions might have been able to achieve a larger political remedy for these conditions—increases in the minimum-wage law or labor laws that truly protect collective bargaining rights and prevent the profitable abuse of part-time workers. In the present political climate, labor is too weak and divided for such a straightforward assault.

The way is now blocked by others, including the array of Washington policy experts who speak on the subject of economics with scholarly authority. They have assured the political community that it would be counterproductive to address this matter concretely as a political issue, that the minimum-wage issue is no longer relevant to the modern economy. It is these voices that dominate the larger political debate, while the janitors cannot make themselves heard.

For the city of Washington, the political neglect constitutes a social irony, for many of these janitors live in the same troubled neighborhoods where the vicious street combat over drugs occurs. The community is naturally horrified by the violence among the young drug merchants and, without much success, has deployed both police and National Guard to suppress it. Yet the city is oblivious to the plight of the janitors—the people who are working for a living, trying to be self-supporting citizens and must live in the midst of the dangerous social deterioration.

Economists might not see any connection between these two social problems, but any teenager who lives in one of the blighted neighborhoods can grasp it. One group of poor people, mostly young and daring, chooses a life of risk and enterprise with the promise of quick and luxurious returns. Another group of poor people, mostly older men and women, patiently rides the bus downtown each night, and in exchange for poverty wages, they clean the handsome office buildings where the lawyers and lobbyists work. When the janitors stage their occasional strikes, they are harassing the very people who have helped block them out of governing issues—the policy thinkers, the lawyers and lobbyists and other high-priced talent who have surrounded the government in order to influence its decisions.

By coincidence, one of the tenants at 1150 Seventeenth Street, where they were picketing, was the American Enterprise Institute, the conservative think tank that produces policy prescriptions for the political debates of Washington. When the service-employees union organizers approached AEI for support, their request was brushed off, but AEI has had quite a lot to say about minimum-wage laws and their supposedly deleterious effects. In recent years, AEI has published at least nine different scholarly reports arguing against the minimum wage. This position faithfully represents the interests of AEI's sponsoring patrons—the largest banks and corporations in America.[2]

But the SEIU organizers insisted they were not trying to make an ideological point by picking on AEI. The real target was the building owner, which operated a dozen downtown buildings in a similar manner. Besides, they explained, most of the ostensibly liberal policy groups in Washington are no different, from the janitors' point of view.

Indeed, the next strike was planned against another building, also owned by the Charles E. Smith Management Company, which served as the home of the Urban Institute, a liberal think tank that specializes in studying the afflictions of the urban poor. The Urban Institute, though presumably more sympathetic to the working poor, has also published scholarly pamphlets questioning the wisdom of laws to improve their wages.

The Urban Institute scholars are regarded as a liberal counterpoise to such conservative institutions as AEI but, in fact, the liberals are financed, albeit less generously, by the same business and financial interests that pay for the conservative thinkers—Aetna Insurance, $75,000; Chase Manhattan Bank, $15,000; Exxon, $75,000; General Electric, $35,000; Southwestern Bell,

$50,000 and so on. The commonly held illusion in Washington politics is that supposedly disinterested experts contend with each other over defining the "public good" from different viewpoints. Yet many of them get their money from the same sources—business and financial interests.

Like other tenants, officials at the Urban Institute insisted the janitors' pay was not their problem. It was a dispute for the cleaning contractor or the building owner to resolve. The SEIU organizers were twice turned down in their efforts to meet with the Urban Institute's officers, so they went out to picket their private homes and tried to crash the institute's banquet for its board of directors.

"Isn't it the same kind of issue any time you pass someone on the street who's homeless?" asked Isabel V. Sawhill, a senior fellow at the institute who is an authority on the "underclass" and related social questions. "It's hard to get involved as an individual in all these microdecisions to change the system. It can't be done at that level. Laws and policies have to be changed."

But these weren't exactly distant strangers one passed on the street. They were the very people who cleaned the office each night, carried out the trash, vacuumed the carpet and scrubbed the sinks and toilets.

"Actually, we never see them," Sawhill allowed. "I do sometimes see them, I admit, because I hang around late, but most people don't."

The janitors, it is true, were mostly invisible. Despite several years of flamboyant efforts, the janitors' campaign had gained very little presence in the civic consciousness of Washington. Public shame is not a terribly reliable lever of political power. For one thing, it only works if widely communicated, and the major media, including *The Washington Post*, had largely ignored the fractious little dramas staged by the janitors.

"People are yawning at them," said Richard Thompson, president of General Maintenance Service, Inc., the largest employer of low-wage janitors. "If there were really a justice question, people in this city would react. There are a lot of government and city government folks who wouldn't stand for it."[3]

The janitors thought they would embarrass both local politicians and congressional Democrats when they targeted a strike at the new shopping complex in Union Station, which is owned by the federal government. Instead, the janitors were fired and commerce continued without interference from the government. Though the Democratic party is ostensibly sympathetic to people like the janitors, Democrats also rely on the real-estate industry as a major source of campaign money.

After an hour or so of picketing on Seventeenth Street, the janitors got into vans and drove over to a museum at New York Avenue and Thirteenth Street where a local charity was holding its annual fund-raising gala. The strikers had no quarrel with the charity, but they did wish to embarrass David Bruce Smith, a young man who is an officer in his grandfather's real-estate company and was serving as chairman of the benefit dinner.

The women in red tee-shirts and the union organizers spread out along the sidewalk and began giving handbills to any who would take them. "Talk with David Bruce Smith," the leaflet asked. "The Janitors Deserve Some Benefits Too!"

The encounter resembled a sidewalk parody of class conflict. As people began arriving for the event, an awkward game of dodging and ducking ensued between the black janitors and the white dinner guests in evening dress. Women from the charity dinner stationed themselves at curbside and, as cars pulled up for the valet parking, they warned the arriving guests about what awaited them. The black women came forward offering their leaflets, but were mostly spurned, as people proceeded swiftly to the door.

"Look, we are a charitable organization and this is political," a man complained bitterly to the union organizers. "People are going to see this and say, what? Are you trying to embarrass me? They're coming here to enjoy themselves."

Jay Hessey reminded him of the constitutional right to petition for redress of grievances. Three D.C. police cars were on hand in the event the janitors violated the law by blocking the doorway or waving placards. It's unfair, the official sputtered, to target an organization that is devoted to charitable activities. It was unfair, the janitors agreed, but then so is life itself. Some people get valet parking. Some people get an extra quarter for cleaning the toilets.

As tempers rose, Hessey stood toe-to-toe with the angry officials and rebuffed them with an expression of utter indifference to their distress. Hessey's colloquial term for the janitors' rude theater—"In your face"—was the essence of their politics. Cut off from the legitimate avenues of political remedy, the janitors had settled on what was left. Like it or not, fair or unfair, people were going to consider, at least for a few uncomfortable moments, the reality known to these janitors.

Most of the guests followed instructions and darted past the demonstrators to the door, but this greatly amused Lucille Morris and Leila Williams and their companions. It had taken considerable courage for these black and Hispanic cleaning women to stand on a sidewalk in downtown Washington and confront well-to-do white people from the other side of town. Once they were there, the women found themselves enjoying the encounter.

It was the white people who turned grim and anxious. Without much success, the black women followed couples to the doorway, urging them to read the handbills. An elegantly dressed woman in silk turned on them and snapped: "You know what? For three hundred dollars, you should be able to enjoy your evening!"

When a mother and daughter streaked past Leila Williams, refusing her handbill, she called after them: "All right, ladies. But you might be standing out here yourself sometime."

"That's right," another janitor exclaimed. "The Lord gave it all, the Lord can take it away."

Their exercise in public shame was perhaps not entirely futile. The elegant woman in silk evidently thought better of her harsh words to the black women because, a few minutes later, she returned outside and discreetly asked them for a copy of their leaflet. She mumbled an expression of sympathy and promised to help, then returned to the banquet.

The janitors may lack formal educations and sophisticated experience with finance but they understand the economic situation well enough.

They know, for instance, that unionized janitors in New York City or Philadelphia will earn two or three times more for doing the very same work. They know that in Washington the federal government and some major private employers, like *The Washington Post* and George Washington University, pay nearly twice as much to janitors and also provide full employee benefits. They know, because the union has explained it for them, that janitorial services represent a very small fraction of a building's overall costs and that even dramatic pay increases would not wreck the balance sheets of either the owners or the tenants.

The problem, as they see it, is not economics. Their problem is power and no one has to tell the janitors that they don't have any. Collective action is the only plausible means by which they can hope to change things. But even the opportunity for collective action has been gravely weakened for people such as these.

The janitors' predicament provides a melodramatic metaphor for a much larger group of Americans—perhaps 20 million or more—who have also lost whatever meager political presence they once had. These are not idlers on welfare or drug addicts, though they often live among them. These are work-ing people, doing necessary jobs and trying to live on inadequate incomes.

These Americans have been orphaned by the political system. They work in the less exalted occupations, especially in the service sector, making more than the minimum wage but less than a comfortable middle-class income. Most have better jobs and higher wages than the Washington janitors—office clerks, hospital attendants, retail salespeople—but are trapped by similar cir-cumstances. Among health-care workers, for instance, one third earn less than $13,000 a year. Some occupations that used to be much higher on the wage scale—airline stewardesses or supermarket clerks—have been pushed closer to the low end by the brutal giveback contracts that labor unions were compelled to accept during the 1980s.

The incomes of the group I'm describing range roughly upward from the poverty line (around $10,000 for a family of three) to somewhere just short of the median household income of around $35,000. "Working poor" does not accurately describe most of them but then neither does "middle class." The poor still suffer more in their daily lives, of course, but even the poor are represented in politics by an elaborate network of civic organizations.

If one asks—Who are the biggest losers in the contemporary alignment of governing power?—it is these people who are economically insecure but not officially poor. During the last generation and especially the last decade, they have been effectively stripped of political protections against exploitation in the workplace. Neither party talks about them or has a serious plan to address their grievances. In the power coordinates that govern large national questions, these people literally do not exist.

The consequences of abandonment are profound and extend to many other conflicts beyond work and wages. On issue after issue from taxation to environmental protection, these are the people who suffer most regularly from political neglect. When EPA did nothing to enforce the law on toxic air pollution, these people absorbed the results—the increased cancer rates in their neighborhoods. When the Labor Department allowed the law on occupational health and safety to become a scandal of nonenforcement, these were the people who suffered the injuries and disease. When Congress and a series of presidents played "bait and switch" with the tax code in order to reward the wealthy, these working people were the taxpayers who were penalized most unjustly.

How might their voices be heard? Only utopians imagine a democracy in which each and every one of these people is someday able to appear in person before the higher forums of government, where the larger questions are debated and decided. Most citizens, regardless of status, have neither the forensic skills nor the time and inclination to participate at that level. That is not what they want or expect from politics.

For most people, democratic expression requires the strength of collective action—a mediating mechanism that will listen to them and speak faithfully on their behalf in the official forums. It is such institutions that accumulate power from their organized numbers, that hold a place for people in the debates and serve as surrogate spokesmen and intelligent monitors of the politicians. This ingredient is the heart of what these people lack and what they have lost.

The voice they lost was the voice of labor. Over the last twenty years, organized labor's political power has declined disastrously—a fact that is central to virtually every economic question fought out in contemporary Washington politics. Labor unions, notwithstanding their rigidities and autocratic crust, were the core liberal force within the old Democratic party and committed their considerable political resources to other progressive causes, including both the civil rights and environmental movements. Their weakness

has weakened many other causes—especially the ranks of unorganized workers.

In another era, the urban political machines also spoke for many of the
citizens who work in unglamorous jobs, but those organizations are now
mostly defunct. People moved to the suburbs. Racial antagonism divided and
weakened their representation. Political structures that effectively served struggling workers when the workers were Irish or Jewish or Italian are now much
less effective when the workers are black or Hispanic or Asian. Labor unions
do still try to organize and represent lower-tier workers but most of these
people are not union members and the labor organizing is frustrated by both
legal and cultural barriers.

A generation ago, leaders of the AFL-CIO could think of themselves, with
only slight exaggeration, as full partners in the power elite that governed
America. Now, they have lost their membership or, rather, they were kicked
out of the club. Unions are mostly reduced to rear-guard battles—fighting
cheap-labor imports or defending the pensions of retired workers or competing
expensively with each other for membership jurisdiction.

Like other mediating institutions that lost authority, organized labor saw
its influence dissipate for many reasons, because of both complex changes in
the society and its own stubborn refusal to adjust to change. More than those
reasons, however, labor unions were decimated by two things: the global shifts
in corporate economic structures and the political confinements imposed on
workers by the law itself.

The ability to move industrial production from high-wage, unionized lo-
cales to cheaper nonunion areas—first to the South and then, more important,
to foreign labor markets—devastated the major industrial unions representing
auto and steel workers, machinists, electrical workers and others. They lost
millions of members and also much of their contract-bargaining power. In real
terms, measured against inflation, the wages of America's premier industrial
workers are declining too.

But the economic forces squeezing labor were complemented by politics
and the force of law itself. The rights that labor's political power first won for
workers in the reform era of the 1930s have been steadily disfigured and
shrunk. The machinery for enforcing labor rights still exists in the federal
government, but functions now as a device for impeding collective action. It
is yet another self-correcting mechanism in politics that has been corrupted to
other purposes.

A union like the SEIU that organizes a majority of workers at a worksite
may or may not ever see a contract with the employer. If the company chooses,
it can undertake years of litigation and, in the meantime, the workers may well
be fired. One in fifteen people who tries to organize a union at a workplace
loses his or her job. The threat alone is enough to impede others from trying.

Over three decades, the AFL-CIO did not shrink in size, but it did not grow with the economy either. The AFL-CIO's 14 million members were roughly one third of the workforce in the 1960s, but only 17 percent by the 1990s. Given the legal risks of union organizing, the growth sector in American labor is now public employees, since, in most instances, they can't be fired for signing a union card.

The National Labor Relations Board has been converted by business appointees into a regulatory agency that adeptly protects management by stalling and suppressing workers' grievances. In the first 150 days of the Reagan administration, the NLRB reversed eight major precedents. Its probusiness decisions in union-representation cases soared to 72 percent, compared to 46 percent in the Carter administration and 35 percent under Gerald Ford. The backlog of undecided cases grew from eight hundred to seventeen hundred— effectively nullifying the workers' complaints by postponing a remedy for years and years.[4]

While unions were crippled, work itself was also reorganized in many fields to undermine the leverage of individual wage earners. "Contracting out" and hiring "part-time" workers who receive no employee benefits have mushroomed as standard labor practices of business, cost-cutting techniques used by even the largest corporations. By 1989, nearly a fifth of the workforce held at least one part-time job. The so-called "temporary" jobs with no employee benefits tripled during the 1980s.

As labor law was compromised, companies figured out, as labor lawyer Thomas Geoghegan wrote, that "they could violate the Wagner Act [enacted in 1935], fire workers at will, fire them deliberately for exercising their legal rights and *nothing would happen. . . .* Maybe, after three years of litigation, the employer might lose, and have to pay a few thousand bucks, if that much: a cheap price, though, for keeping out the union."[5]

By comparison, while U.S. labor was shrinking, Canadian unions grew in the same period from 32 percent of Canada's workforce to nearly 40 percent— mainly because the process for gaining collective recognition is simpler and more direct in Canada. In most western industrial nations, the density of organized labor has increased since the 1960s—a fact that refutes the familiar arguments about labor unions impeding international competitiveness. West Germany, admired for its productive efficiency, has a workforce that is 43 percent unionized.

"European workers enjoy more power, both economically and politically, than their American counterparts," said Michael Merrill, a professor of labor relations at Rutgers University. "They have higher real wages, a stronger and more comprehensive social 'safety net' and a greater degree of political representation than U.S. wage earners do."[6]

Indeed, the astonishing irony of American labor's political condition is that even struggling workers in eastern Europe, bravely led by Solidarity in Poland, have been able to pursue forms of collective action that are not available to workers in the United States. Americans who cheered the triumph of Solidarity perhaps did not realize that the same tactics are illegal in the United States. If an American union adopted Solidarity's methods—seizing the plant with sit-down strikes or forming an interfactory strike committee to coordinate a general strike across different industries—it would be held in contempt and pinned down with injunctions and huge fines. If the tactics persisted, the leaders would doubtless be jailed and perhaps workers too.

These rights were either traded away in exchange for federal labor-law protection or gradually taken away through court decisions and legislation. Labor has tried periodically to win back some of the protection by political action and launched a new effort in 1991 with a measure to prohibit hiring striker replacements in wage strikes.

Its prospects are not good. In 1978, despite the fact that labor provides major funding for Democrats, the Democratic Congress refused to pass labor-law reforms that would have removed some of these barriers. The stereotype of aging white labor bosses still makes it relatively easy for politicians, even Democrats who get so much of labor's money, to scorn them, but the stereotype is no longer accurate. The rank and file of the labor movement is more thoroughly integrated by both race and gender than any other institution in America, except perhaps the armed services or the Catholic church. Furthermore, labor's goals are the very measures that would deliver the most direct relief to the struggling service-sector workers on the bottom rung—workers who are overwhelmingly racial minorities and women.

One crucial fact has been obscured by the long decline of labor as a political force: Millions of American workers want to join a union but, for all these reasons and others, they can't. According to regular surveys conducted by the University of Michigan, 30 percent of the workforce consistently expresses a desire to be represented by a union contract protecting their working conditions and wages. When that number is added to the 17 percent of the workforce who are already union members, it provides a rough measure of how much the power relationships in politics have been distorted. Roughly half of the working population identifies with labor's interests, yet labor is confined by law and politics to a position of weakness.

The statistics also confirm that the yearning for collective expression is alive and widespread, though effectively blocked. Labor is in retreat and unable to defend its own members from further loss, much less the weak and unorganized workers. Yet these two groups represent half of the nation's workforce—the people who are not heard.

*   *   *

In the spring of 1989, various Democratic senators complained privately that Teddy Kennedy was forcing them to cast a ''money vote'' that might hurt them with campaign contributors but wouldn't accomplish anything since President Bush was sure to veto the measure anyway.

The ''money vote'' was Kennedy's proposal to raise the federal minimum-wage floor modestly. Roll calls on such business-labor issues normally follow the obvious party division, but Democrats also feel the underlying tension of voting against business interests that have the power to finance a Republican opponent in their next campaign.

''A senator tells himself: You got an antibusiness reputation and you better work on it,'' Senator Dale Bumpers of Arkansas explained. ''When it's a money vote—minimum wages, mandatory health insurance, the capital-gains tax—and you're perceived as antibusiness, you have to think about it. Even if you know you're not going to get their money, you think about keeping them quiet. You won't get their money but you can at least tranquilize them.''

By 1989, the federal minimum-wage law had not been changed in a decade and, given the yearly erosion from inflation, the real value of $3.35 an hour had fallen by roughly one third during the 1980s—one reason, among others, why the lowest-paid tier of workers was falling behind so drastically. Kennedy proposed only to restore the lost ground—no more than that—by raising the minimum in three stages to $4.55 an hour.

Even that proved to be too ambitious for political consensus. After much back and forth and a presidential veto, Congress settled on $4.25 an hour by 1991. The final deal was brokered between labor leaders and the White House so that no one would be embarrassed when President Bush addressed the AFL-CIO fall meeting. The wage increase, as the reluctant senators had predicted, was not enough to make much difference to anyone.[7]

Despite the elaborate complications piled onto the subject, the arguments about job losses and so forth, the straightforward effect of raising the minimum wage is not disputed among economists. Overall, it produces a net shift in incomes from employers to employees, from companies to workers. The secondary effect, if the wage floor is raised significantly, is to push up wage levels for jobs that are above the minimum but compete for workers in the same labor pools.

Thus, this approach is a very direct way to reorder the imbalance in rewards generated by the private economy and get money to those who need it most, not just poor people but the vast ranks of workers, such as the D.C. janitors. The people who pay for this are not the taxpayers, but the business owners and, to some degree, the consumers who have benefited from the cheap labor. Instead of spending public money to compensate for private injustices, it uses public authority to direct private behavior to just results.

Labor and business both understand these effects well enough and that is why they will always be on opposite sides of the question. For different reasons, neither wishes to speak too clearly in public about the underlying transaction. Instead, the issue was treated by all sides as a familiar anachronism and the congressional debate was spiritless and predictable, smothered in false pieties from both sides. Republicans made speeches that sounded like canned material from the Chamber of Commerce or the National Association of Manufacturers. Democrats gave speeches that sounded like boilerplate from the AFL-CIO. Neither side talked about the millions of workers like the D.C. janitors who were paid somewhat above the federal minimum but would benefit directly if a serious measure were passed.

While organized labor is always the main locomotive driving minimum-wage politics, this time it was following more than leading—repeating slogans that no longer stirred its energies. "Kennedy got it in his head to pass a bill and we went along," Rex Hardesty, chief spokesman for the AFL-CIO, acknowledged.

Throughout the Reagan years, labor had been wary of trying to increase the federal minimum wage for fear the outcome would be the enactment of the so-called "training wage" for youth that Republicans and business always push. Creating a subminimum would permit employers to hire teenagers at cheaper wages for the training period, then fire them and hire new ones, thus displacing older workers whose incomes support families.

For the major industrial unions, the minimum wage had never been a core issue, but in the past they always lent their muscle to their poorer cousins, unions like the SEIU, the garment workers' union, the food and commercial workers' union and others that represent the weakest workers. This time, given the new realities of American incomes and global economics, the heavyweight unions were fighting on other fronts that seemed more crucial to them. The AFL-CIO supported the Kennedy bill, but not with its old vigor.

The transformation of labor wages in the last two decades has opened up a new divide between the economic self-interest of industrial unions and the plight of those unorganized service workers at the bottom of the ladder. Both are losing ground, but the bottom tier is falling faster. This divide provides another explanation for why the political voice for those people has weakened.

"When the minimum wage was 50 percent of the average manufacturing wage, as it used to be, you could really push the wage structure up from the bottom," said David Smith, New York City's business development commissioner and a former aide to Senator Kennedy. "But, when the minimum wage is now only 26 or 27 percent of the manufacturing wage and there are virtually no minimum-wage workers in factories except for the garment industry, the gap between labor unions and the working poor is wider. If we push up the wages of cleaning people and security guards and nursing-home attendants by $1.50 an hour, we're still not bumping up against the bottom of the industrial wage structure.''

If Congress were to raise the federal wage floor substantially, bringing it back to a level around 50 percent of the manufacturing wage level, the 20 million or so workers now dispossessed by politics would benefit enormously. Even though most of them earn more than the minimum, the action would inevitably create upward wage pressure in their labor markets too. Yet such action is highly unlikely so long as organized labor's power is atrophying and its rear-guard battles are concentrated elsewhere. That describes the vicious circle the janitors and others are caught in—their only champion is weak and distracted.

During the Senate debate, Republicans needled Kennedy by asking him why, if he wished to help the downtrodden, he didn't propose a minimum wage of six dollars or seven dollars. Kennedy danced away from the debating trap, but it was actually the right question. A steep increase in the wage floor or a shorter work week for everyone would be most disruptive to existing economic relationships, too controversial for even ardent liberals to endorse, but if the political community were serious about attacking the grosser inequities of American life it would require such disruptive measures.

The minimum-wage law is one of those inherited forms that endures from previous reformers, but only as an empty shell. The original purpose has been lost in politics, but the measure still gets passed with appropriate fanfare—and even the conservative president's signature—because it satisfies old bromides and looks like an enlightened act of social conscience. In the real world, nothing much is changed.

If politics ever approached the subject seriously again, the old form could itself be drastically revised. Labor's original purpose in promoting the federal wage law was, in part, to prop up wages in the impoverished South and thus slow the migration of industrial union jobs to cheaper labor markets. That purpose has been obliterated by the changed economy and global production. Therefore, it is now possible, for instance, to draw up a more sensible and flexible version of a federal wage standard that allows for the disparities in regional or rural labor markets, just as federal pay standards now accept that a federal employee in Washington, D.C., needs more income than one in Mississippi.

A modernized minimum wage, furthermore, could redefine the coverage to distinguish between part-time jobs mostly filled by teenagers and the jobs that are filled by those millions of service workers suffering from inadequate incomes. Middle-class teenagers do often fill the jobs in fast-food restaurants. They do not generally work as nursing-home attendants or security guards or janitors.

Some low-wage jobs, it is true, might be driven overseas in search of cheaper labor if the federal minimum were raised substantially. But the overwhelming preponderance of these jobs, especially in the service sectors, are not portable. Companies cannot hire people in Mexico or Indonesia to clean office buildings in Washington or harvest crops in Florida or answer telephones in New York City. A redefined minimum-wage law could make some distinctions between what work is portable and what is not. It would attack especially the exploitation in jobs that are not going anywhere, but are essential to daily life.

The minimum-wage debate in 1989 did not talk about any of these questions or even hint at any of these possibilities. Instead, the discussion was almost exclusively about the "poor"—as officially defined by the federal government—and whether raising the minimum wage would help them or hurt them.

Republicans spoke for the "poor" by opposing the minimum wage on the grounds that a higher wage floor would eliminate some low-wage jobs, as indeed it would. Democrats argued for the "poor" by pointing out that several million full-time minimum-wage workers are officially poverty-stricken, as in fact they are. Nobody talked about those millions who are a bit higher on the wage ladder who might also benefit from a higher floor.

Like the janitors in downtown Washington, not only have the "nonpoor" been rendered invisible, but their identity has been perversely distorted in the public-policy debate. A critique of the minimum-wage bill published by the Progressive Policy Institute, another Washington think tank, pointed out that 85 percent of the minimum-wage workers are not "poor" and, indeed, many are suburban teenagers working in hamburger joints. With facile arithmetic, the institute's policy thinkers described an economy in which it seemed that most of the crummier jobs are actually filled by middle-class white kids.

The institute's report had a devastating impact in Washington political circles. After all, if "progressives" are against the minimum wage, then who can be for it? In this case, "progressive" was a slight misnomer since the institute is aligned with center-right Democrats trying to move their party rightward and it is financed by wealthy business contributors from Wall Street and elsewhere. Among the institute's "progressive" board members was Robert Kogod, president of the Charles E. Smith Company, the same Washington real-estate company targeted by the striking janitors, the same firm that paid its workers $4.75 an hour, with an extra quarter for cleaning toilets.[8]

The unintended effect of the federal government's so-called "poverty line" is to obscure the existence of the vast pool of struggling families who are above the line—the officially "nonpoor"—and to push them out of the political equation. Just as affluent Washington does not see the black and Hispanic janitors in its midst, the political community as a whole cannot see this class of exploited workers. So long as basic economic issues are defined by the government's narrow and misleading statistics on "poverty," the minimum wage and many other effective reform measures will indeed sound anachronistic.

When liberal economists invented the so-called "poverty line" in the early 1960s, it was a brilliant stroke of political imagination. By devising a quantifiable definition of who was poor, they made the vast deprivation in American society instantly visible to others. The public was shocked by the numbers and politicians could proceed to make decisions about government programs based on crisp estimates of how many millions would be lifted out of "poverty."

Over the years, the poverty statistics steadily became less meaningful. The measure was never realistically adjusted to rising living costs, but it remains the focal point of political debate—the 13 percent or so who are identifiably impoverished in the midst of fabulous wealth. Helping the "poor" is considered virtuous, even among Republican conservatives. Helping the "nonpoor" is thought to be wasteful or even fraudulent. In fact, most of the so-called "welfare cheaters" denounced by politicians and the public are actually low-wage working people who collect food stamps or other federal benefits on the sly, even though they earn a bit too much to qualify as officially "poor."[9]

The official recognition of "poverty" has become an especially cruel instance of old reforms that imprison the politics of the present. The "war on poverty," leaving aside its failures and successes, left behind a deformed perspective in public policy that is oddly disconnected from the present realities. Instead of defending the livelihoods of working people who do not make enough money, politics focuses primarily on the most disabled and disaffected group below them—people who either cannot or will not fill the low-wage jobs their neighbors do every day. A convenient ideological stalemate has developed around this perspective, in which the liberal experiments prove ineffective while conservatives will not discuss any alternative that might disrupt business clients.

The illusion that doomed the "war on poverty" was the assumption that education and training could "solve" the problem of poverty, and this illusion still reigns in the higher realms of politics, shared by liberals and conservatives alike. The problem of poverty is presumed to reside in the poor people themselves, not in the structure of wages available in the private economy. It is assumed that the personal weaknesses of the poor must first be repaired in order to prepare them for better jobs and higher incomes.

This reasoning perversely focuses political attention on the most impaired people—the hardest cases—and skips over those virtuous folk who are already working, doing society's dirty jobs for the rest of us every day. The training-and-education approach is popular, however, and much less controversial because it does not disrupt the private labor markets. The ethic of self-improvement and personal effort is central to the American experience and almost everyone believes in it.

"Fixing up" poor people, however, even when the federal programs succeed, does not alter the structure of the wage ladder in the slightest. Some people may climb up, but someone else must still do the same jobs, the ones that pay too little to support families. The logic of this, though generally evaded, is inescapable. Imagine that education programs were so universally successful that everyone in the society was someday magically brought up to a level of higher education and awarded a college degree, even those cleaning women in D.C. If everyone were transformed into computer technicians or lawyers, then who will sweep the floors and clean the toilets? Someone has to do it.

Since politicians will not confront these wage questions in the private economy, they turn instead to the public treasury for relief. Aid is delivered in various forms to people to make up for the shortcomings in their incomes. Since those programs mostly only reach the officially "poor," political sentiment has turned to another approach that will reach some of the low-wage workers—an earned-income tax credit that gives a cash rebate to those who do not earn enough to support families. Even younger Republican conservatives, anxious to demonstrate their social conscience, have embraced the idea. Among its political virtues, the earned-income tax credit is discreet—a subsidy that other citizens don't see.

But using the tax system has the same effect as the other forms of federal welfare that are provided to workers: The net effect is to subsidize the low-wage employers by relieving them of the responsibility for paying living wages. Instead of the office-building owners and their tenants, the burden of providing for the janitors is shifted to the general taxpayer (and may ignite considerable resentment if people ever figure it out). When the federal tax structure was progressive, placing the heaviest tax burden on those with the most income and wealth, the tax-credit approach had much merit. Now it adds injustice—a discreet transfer of money from one group of struggling wage earners to another group just below them.[10]

Most obviously missing from the political debate are the people who will be most affected by these decisions. Their experience and understanding are not present and they cannot be heard through the layers of expert opinion and old political formulas. If the janitors found a political voice, it might or might not alter the decisions, but it would certainly blow away many of the illusions. If they could be heard, what would the janitors say to the politicians? They might say what Lucille Morris said: We're "tired of this mess." And what Leila Williams said: "We don't want no treats. We want the money."

*   *   *

After many weeks of pressure and rude confrontations, the D.C. janitors found that some people do respond to the tactics of public embarrassment. After twice rebuffing them, officials at the Urban Institute agreed to support the janitors' plea for better wages. Mortimer Zuckerman also evidently had a change of heart, for his real-estate company abruptly agreed to bargain with the union for contracts at three buildings. The Charles E. Smith Company retreated too after the expression's of community concern generated by the janitors' appearance at the charity dinner.[11]

These breakthroughs for "Justice for Janitors" might be taken as heart-warming evidence that "the system works," as Washington political columnists like to say. But the real meaning was the contrary. The janitors' union, like others, has figured out that the way politics gets done nowadays is not by electing people to office or passing bills in Congress. Politics gets done by confronting power directly, as persistently and rudely as seems necessary.

For all its weaknesses, the irregular methodology exemplified by "Justice for Janitors" has become the "new politics" of the democratic breakdown. Other labor unions, large and small, have adopted similar strategies designed to "shame" corporations into accepting decent labor relations. They confront prominent shareholders at public gatherings or testify against the companies at zoning hearings and before government agencies. They assemble critical dossiers on a corporation's environmental record that will shock the public and drive off consumers. These and other corporate-campaign strategies are sometimes effective in forcing a company to respond to its workers. Like the "Justice for Janitors" campaign, however, the tactics are driven by the workers' essential weakness, not the potential power that lies in their collective strength. In the present circumstances, what else works?

9

CLASS
CONFLICT

An unpleasant fact of contemporary politics is that many conscientious citizens have created their own barriers to power. They have become "citizens" of a purified form—free to speak frankly on the public issues they value, but utterly disconnected from the power structure where those issues are decided. Disenchanted with the muck of formal politics, demoralized by the existing alignments of power, people keep their distance on principle. They do this for many good reasons, but the withdrawal itself guarantees their weakness.

In other words, citizens with the best intentions have been so battered by events that their own idea of citizenship becomes miniaturized and confused. They have been taught by the realities of modern government to do politics based on the narrow premises of interest groups, organized around isolated issues. As a result, their own experience is fractured into small pieces, their civic values divided into artificial subcategories. Many have lost the capacity to think more expansively about the possibilities of politics.

On one level, the confusion leads to a random politics of theatrical display or attempts to mimic the mass-marketing prowess of the powerful economic forces in opposition. On another level, it promotes an idealized—an unrealistic—conception of what individual citizens are supposed to do in order to make the system function in a democratic manner. Just as politicians evade hard choices, some engaged citizens manage to avoid their own contradictions. They fasten on moralistic themes and pretend that self-interest is an illegitimate motive for political expression. They presume to speak for everyone, but evade the deeper conflicts of class within their own ranks.

The confusion of contemporary citizens is traceable, in part, to a surprising source—the civil rights movement. The civil rights movement was, after all, the greatest triumph for citizen politics in our time. Yet, as a powerful political experience, it left many citizens with the wrong message.

The memory of Martin Luther King, Jr., still looms over the modern political landscape as the heroic model for how powerless citizens can make themselves heard. King, of course, stands in memory as the icon for a much broader political experience—the civil rights movement and all of its disparate aspects—in which the least-advantaged citizens rose up and changed the nation. The movement's methodologies, the moral tone and tactics were so dramatically triumphant that they are now endlessly copied and elaborated, often unconsciously, by citizens of every class and color.

The essential political fact facing black citizens was that electoral politics was a closed door for them. The civil rights agenda had some northern political support, but it was never going to win an election anywhere in the South. Indeed, both in Congress and across the southern states, the nation's formal structure of electoral democracy was the principal barrier to change—resistance supported by racial prejudice and the indifference of the white majority. The black millions in the South were disenfranchised; the racial caste system was enforced by terror and by law itself.

So black Americans had to invent different ways to move the majority—irregular events outside the system. At Montgomery, Alabama, and Greensboro, North Carolina, and Oxford, Mississippi, and hundreds of other places, vastly different approaches to power were tested by brave individuals and groups. Over many years, the competing approaches were refined and gradually coalesced into a cohesive political movement, strong enough to overcome the status quo. The civil rights movement, it is true, did not entirely achieve racial equality, much less economic justice for the impoverished black people at the bottom. Still, as a profound expression of the democratic promise, it surpassed anything accomplished by electoral politics in modern experience.[1]

At its core, the power of this political upheaval was rooted not in its tactics or even King's great sermons, but in what people believed about themselves. Gradually, one by one and then collectively, black people attained heightened self-awareness, and that new sense of themselves led to courageous political expression. The legislative victories they eventually won confirmed this new self-awareness, rather than the other way around. In other words, this was not

the political system doing something for people. The people did this for
themselves. The distinction is a crucial point to grasp—essential to understanding the full, rich promise of democracy and also its frequent disappointments.[2]

The elusive, redeeming paradox of American democracy is that people are
made powerful, despite all of the political obstacles, when they come together
and decide that they can be powerful. The thought flickers like a small candle
in contemporary politics, held aloft hopefully by countless advocates. Its truth
is regularly confirmed in the experiences of ordinary citizens.

More than two decades after Selma and Birmingham and the other dramatic victories, a black auto worker in northern Ohio grumbled to me about
the fear and passivity among his fellow auto workers.

"People don't understand," Lessly Holmes complained, "the ultimate
power is in their hands."

Holmes was talking specifically about the auto workers who were unwilling to go up against General Motors, but he also spoke to the larger context of
American politics. "The ultimate power is in their hands." His words echoed
Tom Paine's famous declaration: "We have it in our power to begin the world
over again."

Lois Marie Gibbs, a leader of the grassroots environmentalists, expressed
the same conviction: "People have more control than corporations if they
choose to use it. The problem is getting people over that feeling that they can't
change things. More and more, as people win these small fights, they do feel
empowered."

The largest legacy of the civil rights movement is its power as a living
example of what can happen when passive citizens mobilize themselves. It
stands also as a constant rebuke to contemporary Americans: If the oppressed
and isolated black citizens in the South could accomplish this, why are other
Americans so inert and helpless?

Beyond the inspiration, however, the movement has probably taught a
generation of Americans the wrong lessons about how to do politics. In contemporary citizen politics, it sometimes seems that people emulate the civil
rights movement in order to re-create its original handicaps. Black people in
the South, after all, started their struggle with the starkest disadvantages—
utterly isolated from political power, through no choice of their own. They had
to invent ways to overcome those obstacles, but their tactics are now copied
by people who are not so handicapped. Those who attempt to duplicate the
movement's style and method usually discover the results are no longer triumphant.

King's genius, for instance, was moral theater. The civil rights movement
created a drama of conflict, sometimes including civil disobedience, that compelled distant bystanders to take sides (even if only in the privacy of their own

thoughts). Sweet-faced school children marching into a storm of fire hoses and police dogs presented the reality of racial segregation, via television, to even the most indifferent Americans. They could no longer claim innocence.

Once confronted by the harsh moral question, people longed to be relieved of the burden of the discomforting contradictions. The formal political system eventually responded. The civil rights movement did not defeat the local sheriffs and politicians who were enforcing segregation laws; it leveraged the national guilt.

A similar drama of moral guilt underlies much of the irregular politics that has flourished in the decades since the 1960s. From antiwar demonstrators to Christian antiabortion activists, many groups have attempted to create a moral message to incite the larger public. The approach seems especially suited to groups like the gay-rights movement—people who were likewise reviled and isolated—because their cause also poses an elemental demand for justice.

But moral claims become hopelessly splintered and confused when citizen groups try to channel them through the larger complexities of governance. Environmental activists may save dolphins by harassing StarKist—dolphins, after all, are objects of universal human affection—but public outrage is not so easily harnessed to the dense task of rewriting federal regulations or the difficult class issues embedded in government economic policy. Moral outrage simply does not reach the fine print of hollow laws or bureaucratic deal making and can be easily deflected into false victories. Meanwhile, the public audience hears so many competing moral claims, it may instead feel benumbed or skeptical.

The politics of moral drama, furthermore, leads invariably to a preoccupation with the news media—even dependency on them—since the political dramas will have no meaning whatever unless someone transmits them to a larger audience and to embarrassed authorities. To capture the media's wandering eye, frustrated causes find themselves escalating the terms of theatricality to the level of bizarre stunts or ersatz versions of civil disobedience. Police everywhere are now quite familiar with the routine of mass arrests and do not use dogs or fire hoses. What was once a stirring event has been reduced to a paperwork problem.

In the competition for attention, the outlandish and fraudulent drive out what is sober and real. A handful of self-styled eco-freaks, calling themselves Earth First!, gained far more celebrity for their vague threats of environmental sabotage than all of the substantive struggles underway by grassroots environmentalists across the country. Political voices expressing serious ideas are eclipsed by the street action that displays simple rage, since rage is always more videogenic.

Mass-media politics worked powerfully for the civil rights drama, but it is a trap for most citizens' political aspirations because it defers to someone else's judgment—the news media's—to decide what qualifies as authentic political expression. By depending on stunts and celebrity to attract the press and television, people are essentially surrendering to the media—and sometimes making themselves look clownish in the process.

J. Hunter O'Dell, one of King's early lieutenants in the movement, recognized the fixation with media developing among civil rights activists and lamented the consequences.

"We all recognize that technologically this is a media age," O'Dell wrote. "But it was disastrous for us to rely primarily upon these corporate forms of mass communication to get our message and analysis out to the public. . . . In the end, it means a new kind of addiction to media rather than being in charge of our own agenda and relying on mass support as our guarantee that ultimately the news-covering apparatus must give recognition to our authority."

O'Dell's point is that the civil rights movement acquired its "authority" to articulate large political aspirations, not because network television came to Selma or Birmingham, but from the hundreds and even thousands of meetings in black churches, week after week, across the South over many years. The dramatic spectacles that appeared on TV were the product of those mobilizing sermons and dialogues, not the other way around.

The movement's organizing processes, O'Dell noted, contained all of the functional elements of a responsible political organization—mass education and communication as well as continuing accountability between the leaders and the supporting throngs. "The power of any movement for democracy," O'Dell emphasized, "is always dependent on such reciprocal relations between the mass of people and their leadership."

These elements are missing, it seems, from much of the irregular citizens' politics that tries to emulate King's heroic model. Activists hold press conferences or arrange dramatic events to prod the political system. But patiently built reciprocal relationships between leaders and followers, the laborious tasks of education and communication, are often not even attempted. To be blunt, there is a hollowness behind many of the placards and politicians know it.

Succeeding generations of political activists, it often seems, copied the glamorous surfaces of the civil rights legacy—the hot moments of national celebrity that are so well remembered—while skipping over the hard part, the organizational sinew that was underneath. In many organizations, of course, real relationships do form and flourish, especially in the groups that arise indigenously in local communities. The further one gets from the grassroots, however, the more likely it is that national leaders are only distantly connected to their own followers or accountable to them.

Many prominent organizations, from labor unions to national environmental groups, have "memberships" that have never met and never will meet.

People become "members" in many citizen organizations simply because they sent in a check—perhaps as their own weak gesture of connectedness or just to get a young canvasser off their doorstep.

Some citizen organizations pull together impressive coalitions of allied groups that are united behind their agenda, but these coalitions exist only as lengthy letterheads. Some popular causes appear in politics (or disappear) as no more than a packet of press clippings—news stories artfully generated by activists pretending to represent vast throngs.

Elected politicians are generally on to this. They are aware of the shallow connection in much of citizen politics and they resent it: These self-appointed tribunes can arouse public opinion on various issues, but where are their troops? Whom do they really speak for? And whom do they answer to?

The organizational weaknesses are well known to the participants of citizen politics and the subject of continual introspection and exhortation among them. To do more is necessary, they agree, and developing deeper roots consumes considerable effort. Yet the task seems overwhelmingly difficult, given their limited resources and the other obstacles. Instead, they take up one thing at a time—one scandalous situation or another—and dramatize it sufficiently to create at least temporary visibility in politics. Sometimes, it works.

In that regard, citizens behave like creatures of the modern governing system, as much as politicians do. The post–New Deal administrative state defines political opportunity in terms of interest groups, so, in order to proceed, citizens organize themselves in the same manner. They define themselves by the policy language of a particular issue, whether it is arms control or child care or abortion, then stand on that narrow ground. In fact, once they have defined themselves this way, they are stuck on that ground, unable to speak beyond it.

People adapted to the confines of interest-group politics find it hard to think seriously about a more inclusive kind of politics. Instead, they often nurture the frail hope that, somehow, someday, a moment of spontaneous combustion will occur in American society—a flash of public consciousness and anger—that miraculously produces the cohesion to unite people of diverse interests and outlooks in genuine collective action. In the meantime, waiting for the miracle, they concentrate on the small contests that might actually be won.

Spontaneous combustion is an extremely unlikely event and the model of Martin Luther King misleads his many imitators most profoundly in this regard. The purposeful cohesiveness achieved by the civil rights movement cannot be easily duplicated by others, regardless of their issue, because what naturally united people in that movement was a single overarching fact—the fact of race. Black citizens, whether they were schoolteachers or sharecroppers, funeral directors or dishwashers, did not need to be told that they had shared interests. The fact of racial discrimination was the everyday burden in all of their lives.

If that point seems obvious, then and now, what is less obvious are the political benefits that flowed to the civil rights movement because of this unifying fact. First, there was no necessity to parse out difficult political arguments between public morality and personal self-interest: The two were fused perfectly. For black people, self-interest was inseparable from their larger moral claim, the demand for justice. Their political task was to demonstrate to the white majority that this would be true for them as well.

In his lofty manner, King actually preached to both morality and self-interest. The white South, he explained, could cleanse its soul, but it would also be freed for self-development. King was right about that in many dimensions, including the economic development of the impoverished South that, as many white southerners now recognize, was made possible by the civil rights movement. Very few other political causes, however, have the capacity to reconcile the tensions between self-interest and morality so easily or universally.

The unifying fact of race served the civil rights movement in another, even more important way—it was the cloak that covered conflicting class interests within the movement's own ranks. All blacks, regardless of their educational or economic status, would gain something if their political mobilization succeeded. That was enough to smother difficult arguments about goals and priorities that might have divided their own ranks.

In hindsight, it has become obvious that, while all blacks benefited, they did not benefit equally. Legal liberation opened vast opportunities, North and South, for black Americans with middle-class skills and aspirations. It did little to alter the bleak prospects for millions of black citizens at the bottom of the economic ladder. In his last years, after the great legal victories, King himself turned to confront the underlying economic questions, but by then the movement was splintering. Some former allies in the white political structure turned hostile once King's sermons began to address basic questions of wealth and poverty and economic power. From the other side, the "black power" militancy derided him as a middle-class reformer who had done nothing for the truly oppressed.

Other political causes that aspire to mobilize a broad assembly of Americans face the same divisive fundamentals—the conflicts of class, the natural tension between moral claims and self-interest—but without the benefit of a unifying cloak. Both barriers are formidable and help to explain why so many politically alert citizens do not really try to develop a broader political base for their enterprises. To overcome these obstacles, active citizens would first have to talk out quite a lot among themselves, searching for the common perceptions that might dissolve their deep differences.

Instead, they mostly stick to their own narrow issue—a grievance that arouses like-minded citizens—and ride its energy as far as it will take them. In time, if they are successful, they will acquire some real influence in public affairs. But they will still not have many people marching in the ranks, a fact that every observant politician will discern.

Faced with these barriers, other citizens withdraw even further from political engagement into a kind of exclusionary fundamentalism. Enormous energy is devoted to discussing millennial visions of what the society should someday look like, but no effort is made to connect the vision with people or everyday political action.

Scores of organizations, on left and right, devote themselves to this sort of "soft" politics—drawing up plans for the distant future, whether the focus is on moral reform or world peace or designing an economy in harmony with the natural environment. Books and pamphlets filled with their provocative ideas are produced in abundance, but mainly consumed by people who already share the vision.

To create a democratic reality with any substance, active citizens have to engage others across these various boundaries. They have to search for real bridges that connect one class perspective with another in common goals. They have to define goals that fuse the broad moral meaning of their politics with the visible self-interest of everyday citizens. This undertaking would put them at the messy center of a democratic dialogue—the arguments between ideas and values and the real experiences of real people. It would entail taking up the burden of teaching and listening and searching patiently for collective resolutions.

Genuine democracy is very difficult to do, regardless of the issue or context, and citizens understandably shrink from a challenge that is so hard. Because it is so daunting, many retreat instead to a kind of moral high ground, from which they can implore and incite their fellow citizens, while hoping for the miraculous day when collective action might spontaneously arise.

If one single governing issue aroused general public anger and promised to unite people across party or class lines, it was the savings and loan bailout for which taxpayers were providing hundreds of billions of dollars. Yet, the efforts of some alert citizens to mobilize the anger into political action mainly demonstrated the impotence of the classic tactics of moral theater and public outrage. The Financial Democracy Campaign rallied others in coalition, staged dramatic demonstrations in dozens of cities, and testified intelligently before congressional hearings. And on the whole, it was ignored.

On Valentine's Day in 1991, the FDC demonstrators appeared on the sidewalk at chosen locations in twelve cities and began handing out heart-shaped red lollipops stamped with the message: "I'm tired of being played for a sucker.'' In Washington, D.C., their target was the Resolution Trust Corporation, the federal agency presiding over the vast billions of the savings and loan bailout. ''No more sweetheart deals,'' the placards declared.

At several locations, a country singer identified as ''S&Lvis'' entertained reporters and curious onlookers with the lyrics of ''Bailout Rock,'' a song mocking the rescue of banks and S&Ls at the expense of the taxpayers. ''When the party ended and the smoke had cleared/ The biggest banks were bigger, the rest disappeared.''

Bureaucrats at the RTC offices in Washington came out on the sidewalk to listen and were so amused, they asked for extra lollipops to give to their colleagues inside. In Abilene, Texas, small-business owners joined the protest because their bank credit had been cut off. In Baltimore, Maryland, the low-income members of ACORN turned out to picket because of the rotten housing available to inner-city black families. In Los Angeles, hotel and restaurant union workers picketed because high-flying financial deals had destroyed many of their jobs. The financial scandals, in theory at least, represented a rare moment of opportunity for political reformers to unite people with disparate interests around a common cause.

Thanks to the Financial Democracy Campaign, Capitol Hill was flooded with brown paper bags sent in by citizens—''Don't Leave Us Holding the Bag.'' The politicians, in fact, were quite nervous about the public anger—fearful that it would turn up on election day in unexpected forms of retaliation.

None of this, however, did much to divert the political system from its usual behavior. Client-representative relationships held firm in Congress and the Bush administration. The press likewise played its accustomed role—ignoring the citizens who were trying to be heard. The bailout agency continued to award lucrative deals to favored banks.

''The real decision making at the RTC didn't miss a beat,'' Tom Schlesinger, the Financial Democracy Campaign's chief organizer, conceded. At forty-two, Schlesinger had spent fifteen years of his life in the laborious politics of community organizing; he has an idealistic commitment to politics but no fanciful illusions about what lollipops and song might accomplish.

Like the civil rights movement, the Financial Democracy Campaign was attempting to foster moral education on a vast scale—teaching scandalous facts that would mobilize the public anger. But this issue was far too complex to be captured in street theater. It was also not going to wait for Americans to wake up and get smart.

''Our objective,'' Schlesinger said, ''is to take our slingshot and hit Goliath in the ankle or the wrist—and then keep reloading.'' Then what? ''Then we hammer on the people who have power in this country,'' he said. ''As a first step, no more sweetheart deals for bankers. As a second step, reverse the drift of government policy and start making the financial system respond to what the public wants and needs from it.''

Educating people on specific outrages, however, does not necessarily lead them to a larger conception of the problem or their own potential. Their anger may temporarily grow, but will remain incoherent if it finds nothing solid to attach to—no organizational framework to provide a continuing relationship to the realms where issues are decided. Unlike many citizen activists, Tom Schlesinger understood the weakness in what he was doing.

''What we're doing is very, very far away from real power,'' Schlesinger said, ''and is blinkered by all the habits and shortcomings we've brought with us in the last twenty years, trying to do special pleadings in grassroots politics.''

Over time, he suggested, a larger political structure would have to emerge, an organizational framework that could mobilize citizens across a much broader front of issues. But no one imagined this stage of political development was at hand. Even the most engaged citizens, Tom Schlesinger observed, find it hard to think of politics in those larger terms.

''By and large, our folks don't have a sense of the main chance—of seizing the moment and changing the country,'' he explained. ''Obviously, some of us have grandiose thoughts like that. But given our limited tools and resources and personal shortcomings, I'll be as surprised as the next person if we even come close to changing the country.''

Ralph Nader, though obviously less influential than Martin Luther King, has been another important political model for active citizens—the man who singlehandedly inspired a generation of resourceful watchdogs for the public interest. Nader's own story provided an exemplary tale of what one person might achieve—a solitary individual who came to Washington fresh from law school, armed only with his own intelligence and idealism. With this humble start, Nader succeeded in spawning an extraordinary system of active citizens—tens of thousands of people examining and challenging the government on behalf of consumers and the broader public interest.

Nader also relied on the media, but his basic technique was critical analysis—assembling the damning facts about government and industry. Nader's investigations were always guided by values most Americans share—honesty and openness, fair dealing and respect for human life—and the shocking revelations repeatedly shamed the government. His style of dramatic exposure has been mimicked endlessly by others, including the environmental movement, and with great success.

The strength of dedicated individuals, it turns out, is not a substitute for the power of ''organized people.'' Because of him and like-minded critics, the government reluctantly amended its processes, opening decision-making chan-

nels to citizen participation and providing more detailed accountings of its
deliberations. But, as the evidence has demonstrated, the reforms did not
succeed in altering the long-term balance of power. Once monied interests
countered with their own escalation of political resources, citizens were
trapped again in a position of weakness. Nader and other public-interest activists were depicted by business apologists as tiresome scolds.

The core of Ralph Nader's politics was an exalted idea of the individual
and what individual citizens could be expected to achieve. If the government
will not enforce the law, he argued, then citizens must do it themselves and
become prosecutors for the public interest.

The idea is now embedded in many federal statutes. The major environmental laws all include provisions for citizen-initiated enforcement. The tax
code provides bounties for those who turn up large-scale evasions. Rewards
are paid to those who "blow the whistle" on cheating in government procurement. Since 1986, for instance, 274 lawsuits have been initiated by citizens charging government contractors with fraud, mainly in defense, and have
recovered $70 million for the government. When the savings and loan scandals
proliferated, Nader's Public Citizen proposed yet another version of the same
approach—citizens empowered to prosecute financial fraud, consumers organized as the watchdogs of financial institutions. "Citizens should insist,"
Michael Waldman wrote, "that they be given the tools to enforce the law
themselves."[3]

The watchdog approach to politics engages the energies of thousands of
citizens and produces regular victories, some of them quite spectacular. But
this approach is based on an idea of citizenship in which individuals are
supposed to share responsibility for fulfilling the government's duties. The
idea usually defines citizens in the narrow role of aggrieved consumers and
assumes that ordinary people are capable of functioning as the equivalent of
bank examiners.

"It's like serving on a jury," said Joan Claybrook, president of Public
Citizen. "Citizens are responsible for enforcing the law—that's citizenship. . . . The concept of citizen involvement means it has a purity that cannot
be corrupted."

The intent is certainly noble, but the net effect may be further dislocation
in the relationships between government and citizens. Once the responsibility
for enforcement is shifted to private citizens, some agencies are happy to let
them do the hard work of challenging violators. When public-interest lawyers
win a court order for enforcement, the political heat is directed at them, not at
the government officers who failed to do their duty in the first place.

Furthermore, only a relative handful of private citizens are equipped to
carry out this form of citizenship—those with the leisure time and professional

skills. Once again, the less educated and less articulate, the people who must spend their energies supporting their families, are left out.

The notion that citizens will bring "purity" to government is another problem: Some do and some don't. Any mechanism created for citizen participation will also be available for manipulation by any other interest group, whether its motives are self-interested or public-spirited. If everyone has to be a watchdog in order to make government work, then the foxes will also volunteer to serve.

The public-interest movement, in fact, revived the civic values of the Progressive reformers from early in the century (reformers who were themselves well-educated middle-class professionals and managers). They distrusted politics in general, just as Nader does, and wished to keep government insulated from its messy influences. The Progressives tried to create a sanitized democracy that would adhere to principles of good government, but they were disdainful of the party mechanisms that gave ordinary people representation in the debate. Their high-minded brand of individualism became a weak substitute for collective accountability.

In public-interest lawsuits, the inevitable bargaining over final decisions often gets left to the capable few who have the capacity to undertake this work, especially those people with law degrees. Whether virtuous or otherwise, these agents bring their own particular values to the table and their own class biases, which may or may not harmonize with the larger public that cannot be present and has lost reliable representation.

Nor should citizenship require people to do the government's work for it. Government, in theory, is constituted to do the things that citizens individually cannot do for themselves, including making the laws and enforcing them. Assigning that function to individuals is not a solution to the democratic problem, but a subtle form of resignation—another way of accepting that the political system will never perform responsibly and that citizens will never be able to make it do so. If ordinary people are supposed to do the work of government, why, they may ask, are they paying taxes?

Citizens remain weak because their inherited ideas of how to do politics allow them to evade the class conflicts within their own ranks. The environmental movement, though its broad values are almost universally shared by the public, is unable to mobilize its potential impact because it cannot resolve its own differences.

The movement is splintered into many different pieces, including different social classes that do not even talk to one another, much less try to work out a common political agenda. On one end are Ivy League lawyers, urbane and well educated and completely comfortable in the inner circles of government.

On the other end are the thousands of home-grown neighborhood activists, utterly skeptical of government and engaged in "rude and crude" politics at the factory gates.

A few years ago, Lois Marie Gibbs of the Citizen's Clearinghouse for Hazardous Wastes tried to build some bridges across this social chasm. She organized a series of roundtable discussions and invited thirty or so community activists from the grassroots to meet with Washington-based lawyers and lobbyists from the so-called Big Ten, the leading national environmental organizations.

"It was hilarious," Gibbs said. "People from the grassroots were at one end of the room, drinking Budweiser and smoking, while the environmentalists were at the other end of the room eating yogurt. We wanted to talk about victim compensation. They wanted to talk about ten parts per billion benzene and scientific uncertainty. A couple of times, it was almost war.

"We were hoping that, by seeing these local folks, the people from the Big Ten would be more apt to support the grassroots position, but it didn't work that way. They went right on with the status quo position. The Big Ten approach is to ask: What can we support to achieve a legislative victory? Our approach is to ask: What is morally correct? We can't support something in order to win if we think it is morally wrong."

Most of the citizens drawn into grassroots environmental activism are unusual; they come from the social ranks that are least active politically, people who are poor or who are familiarly described as "working class." On the whole, these "middle Americans," as sociologist Herbert J. Gans called them, are the most disaffected and culturally inclined to practice "political avoidance." They are wary of elections and formal politics and even large civic organizations, cynical about government at all levels. Instead of political activism, Gans noted, they normally concentrate their energies on nurturing and defending their own small, private spaces—family or church or immediate neighborhood.[4]

On the other hand, most of the citizens who lead the major environmental organizations are the offspring of the affluent managerial class, people who feel at ease in the higher realms of politics and skilled at the rationalistic policy analysis. Many are idealistic professionals, committed to large intellectual conceptions of the environmental problem but not personally confronted by the risks of poisonous industrial pollution.

These class distinctions were playfully delineated by *Outside* magazine when it published a consumer's guide to the environmental movement. Citizen's Clearinghouse: "Typical member: quit the church choir to organize toxic dump protest." Natural Resources Defense Council: "Typical member: Andover '63, Yale '67, Harvard Law '70, Pentagon anti-war marches '68, '69, '70." Environmental Defense Fund: "Typical member: lawyer with a green conscience and a red Miata." Conservation Foundation: "As connected as they come and is quite friendly with many less-than-pure corporations like Exxon and Chevron."[5]

The environmental movement is a complicated spectrum of tastes and aspirations, ranging from the aesthetics of bird watchers to the radicalized politics of angry mothers. All share a generalized commitment to the environmental ethic, but have very different conceptions of what that means and how to accomplish their goals. These differences are rooted in their economic classes. An environmentalist who graduated from an Ivy League law school is more likely to believe in the gradual perfectability of the legal system, the need to legislate and litigate.

However, if one lives on the "wrong side of the tracks," downwind from toxic industrial fumes, these activities look pointless and even threatening. The idea of passing more laws seems a futile diversion. There are already plenty of laws. The problem is political power. "It's not illegal to build an incinerator and it's not illegal to poison people," Lois Gibbs said. "Poor people know that they need to organize and fight to win."[6]

The corrosive consequence of this underlying conflict is lost political power—a popular cause that is unable to realize its full strength because it cannot reconcile its own internal differences. "It does hurt us," Gibbs agreed, "because we don't have any people lobbying on the Hill, while the Big Ten lobby could turn out the people—if they were connected to the grassroots. But they don't have the constituency we have. They don't want to dirty their hands, dealing with these people from the grassroots."

Some leaders in the major environmental organizations recognize the same dilemma. Richard Ayres, chairman of the Clean Air Coalition formed by the Big Ten groups, sees Washington-based lobbyists like himself trapped between the grassroots demands for fundamental change and a political system that will not even consider them. The Big Ten works for incremental victories and, when even those are watered down by Washington politics, the grassroots activists become even more disenchanted. Young people sign up for Greenpeace, not the Audubon Society.

"If the central government won't respond to a situation, it drives the moderates out," Ayres said. "People far from Washington are saying we ought to be doing recycling and changes in the production processes that will prevent pollution. But we're caught in the middle, having to say: 'We can't do that. Congress won't touch it.' "

Major organizations in Washington cannot easily align with the fervor of the grassroots environmentalists: This would threaten their own standing within the political establishment. When a GE lobbyist wanted to cut a deal on CFCs in the new clean-air legislation, he phoned a lobbyist from the NRDC to see if his organization would go along with the compromise. That's real power—having a putative veto on insider negotiations—but it is usually quite limited. The Big Ten groups have such influence only so long as they adhere to the constricted terms of the Washington regulatory debate.

"If I represent an industry, I can always get into the argument in the Executive Branch or Congress by nature of the fact that I have money," Curtis Moore, former Republican counsel for the Senate environmental affairs committee, explained. "But if you're an environmental group, you can't get into the argument unless they want to let you in. And they're not going to let you in if they think you're crazy, if you don't think in the same terms they do. So you have to sound reasonable or you won't even get in the room. And you don't find many people in the major environmental groups who are willing to be seen as unreasonable."

Moore's point is crucial to understanding the compromised performance of citizen politics. The admission ticket to the debate is: "You have to sound reasonable." The broad ranks of citizens whose own views have become "radicalized" by experience, as Lois Gibbs put it, will always sound "unreasonable" to the governing elites. They not only won't get a seat at the table, but may conclude that the Big Ten environmentalists are in collusion too, bargaining settlements with government and business behind closed doors.

Grassroots leaders, for instance, attacked the League of Women Voters for accepting grants from Dow Chemical and Waste Management to finance educational projects on hazardous wastes. The LWV in New England sponsored a series of conferences at which environmentalists and business representatives discussed their differences on key policy issues, but community-based leaders were not invited. "We were told that grassroots people are too ignorant or too hysterical to be able to participate meaningfully," Lois Gibbs complained.[7]

The grassroots suspicion of collusion between big-name environmentalists and industrial polluters is not entirely imaginary. When the CEO of Waste Management wanted to lobby EPA Administrator Reilly in 1989 to block state-enacted restrictions on hazardous wastes, he arranged a breakfast meeting through a mutual friend—the president of the National Wildlife Federation. The industry lobbyists warned Reilly that a "balkanization" was being fostered in many states by the grassroots agitation for tougher restrictions and the federal agency must "make its presence felt." Reilly, himself the former president of the Conservation Foundation, obliged.[8]

Class conflict is, of course, a persistent theme in popular politics throughout American history. Differences of culture and class have always set citizens against one another, separating the people who, in theory, ought to be allies. Racial antagonism remains the most divisive barrier between people, white and black, who have common interests. Differences of region and religion are now much less influential than in earlier eras, but the differences of income and economic perspective are greater now than they were a generation ago. The inability of people to confront and overcome the class biases that divide them is one of the oldest failures of American democracy.

Eras of popular reform usually fail to produce genuine change, political scientist Samuel P. Huntington has argued, because they nearly always embody unnatural marriages of conflicting class interests. "Middle upper strata [of citizens] may have an ideological commitment to political reform, but they also have an economic interest in not permitting reform to alter significantly the existing distribution of income and wealth," Huntington wrote. "The poorer classes, on the other hand, may have an interest in substantial economic change, but they lack the ideological motivation to make that change a reality and, indeed, they are mobilized for political action by appeals to values which guarantee that major economic change will not become a reality."[9]

Citizens from the lower economic ranks seek to preserve the independence of their own community institutions and are skeptical of grand causes that intrude, especially if these seem to be controlled from above. Middle-class reformers, on the other hand, are willing to use governmental power on behalf of good-government reforms, but not in ways that will change power relationships in the economic order. "Upper-class and upper-middle-class hypocrisy combines with lower-class cynicism to perpetuate the status quo," Huntington concluded.

This bleak view wrongly presumes an endless stalemate for democratic possibilities, but it does accurately describe the present reality, both in the environmental movement and in many other public-spirited reform campaigns. Middle-class reformers, whether they are environmentalists or consumer advocates, tend to focus on perfecting the processes of government, not changing the underlying arrangements of power. Grassroots advocates have the advantage of being able to see the underlying power realities more clearly and are therefore willing to confront power directly. But they are handicapped by their own lack of access to the debate—and their "unreasonable" attitudes.

The other great obstacle within the environmental movement has been the inability to reconcile bedrock tensions between its moral claims and economic self-interest. The civil rights movement could finesse this conflict because of the unifying fact of race. The environmental movement has mostly tried to smother it with righteousness. Everyone wants to advance the environmental ethic, of course, but the underlying conflict is about jobs and profit and economic growth versus environmental protection. This is not a question the mainline organizations have wished to face directly, nor have many of the grassroots advocates.

Penny Newman, a community activist who led the fight against the notorious Stringfellow acid pits in Riverside, California, observed: "Too often the only time community-based environmentalists meet the workers is when we are protesting against corporate practices and the workers are bused into public hearings to advance the company's agenda—so that the company can orchestrate the conflict between workers and the community.''

In the Los Angeles basin, for instance, enforcement of the increasingly stringent air-pollution standards needed to free that city of its terrible smog will directly threaten scores of furniture-making factories that release highly toxic fumes in the air—and also employ seventy thousand workers, most of them Mexican-Americans. The companies, especially smaller firms that cannot afford new emissions-control systems, threaten to close down and move their production to Mexico. Some of the upper-class environmentalists regard this as an acceptable solution since, after all, many of the furniture workers were themselves migrants from Mexico. Send them all back to Mexico—the jobs and the people.

Again, low-wage workers wind up paying the price for everyone else's well-being. Groups like the Labor/Community Strategy Center in Los Angeles are trying to mobilize an alternative approach that speaks for both the low-income communities and their workers—that represents both their environmental complaints and their economic interests.

"Industry begins the battle with a captive army of workers whose livelihoods are in some way dependent upon the production of toxics and who are predisposed to believe company claims that environmentalists are well-to-do, anti-working-class crybabies,'' wrote Eric Mann, director of the Los Angeles Strategy Center. "Workers may argue in turn that if life is reduced to a battle between one self-interested force (the environmentalists) attempting to take their jobs versus another self-interested force (corporate management) attempting to 'save' their jobs, then they have no other self-interested option but to side with corporate power.''[10]

Community organizers in many places are trying to break out of this self-defeating conflict by synthesizing the community's overall concerns—the right to protection from industrial poisons and the requirements for promoting stable economic prosperity. This approach entails a much more complicated politics, of course, but it has the virtue of facing the buried conflicts more honestly.

An environmental politics grounded in the perspectives of communities would undoubtedly lead to different kinds of public policies—transitional assistance to threatened workers or small businesses, for instance, or government-sponsored centers for treating hazardous wastes in a serious manner. It would encourage people to ask the larger strategic questions about the production processes themselves. It would assume from the start, as grassroots activists say, that the poisonous stuff should not be dumped in anybody's backyard.

If any of the major environmental groups were to realign their own politics with these positive energies emanating from the grassroots, they would necessarily have to rethink their own policy priorities and methods—and listen respectfully to what these people from the communities are trying to say. Inevitably, this would put at risk the environmentalists' good standing as "reasonable" participants in Washington politics. But they would also discover a source of new political strength—the power that comes from real people.

There is one other, distasteful explanation for why many citizen organizations, including the major environmental groups, are disconnected from the politics of ordinary people and hesitant to advocate far-reaching solutions. That explanation is money. Many citizen groups depend on tax-exempt contributions from foundations, corporations and wealthy individuals to finance their political efforts. The dependency guarantees that they will never move beyond a purified version of citizenship. In truth, much of what passes for "citizen politics" on both right and left would disappear if the wealthy benefactors withdrew.

Under the federal tax code, tax-exempt grants are fully deductible for the donors only if the recipients stay clear of partisan politics, and many organizations accept these limitations on their politics. They may develop "educational issues" or create "civic projects" for citizens, but they cannot take these concerns into the arena of accountability that matters most to those in power—elections. Thus, the tax code itself fosters a limp kind of interest-group politics for citizens—the same splintering that in government has proved so debilitating to democracy.

The law thus draws an unnatural circle around the political ambitions of citizens at large—especially the citizens who are the weakest and most dependent. Every organization that relies on tax-exempt contributions lives constantly with the complications of what it can or cannot do; many flirt at the edges of what the Internal Revenue Service would allow. "Every local project that I've ever been involved in," community organizer Arnie Graf said, "has had a lawyer who was a friend and was always telling us, 'Oh, my God, you're going to get in trouble. You say you're nonpolitical but look what you're doing.' "

The tax-exempt financing provides still another means by which wealth—including corporate wealth—defines the political agenda for others. In the arena of public affairs, private wealth exerts enormous influence over the scope and direction of what citizens will undertake because the giving is conditioned by the giver's own sense of what is an appropriate political cause. Though a few foundations are famous for launching provocative and even radical causes, the overall effect of political charity, as one might expect, is mostly conservative—guaranteed to preserve the status quo. Charity is another form of political power.

Many citizen organizations expend enormous energy packaging "proposals" that will appeal not necessarily to people at large, but to foundation officers and very wealthy citizens. These projects will be accountable not to rank-and-file members but to the sources of financing.

Corporations, including the major polluters, have discovered, for instance, that they can buy into the environmental movement itself through tax-deductible contributions to the mainline organizations. Waste Management, Inc., the largest waste-disposal company and a company frequently fined for its environmental violations, has donated more than $1 million to various environmental groups in recent years. The company's generosity bought its CEO a seat on the board of the National Wildlife Federation. The National Audubon Society, which got $135,000 from Waste Management, expected its corporate gifts to top $1 million in 1989, up from $150,000 a few years earlier. The Conservation Foundation received money from Chevron, Exxon, General Electric, Union Carbide, Weyerhaeuser, Waste Management and a long list of other corporations during the year before its president, William Reilly, became EPA administrator.[11]

Naturally, the companies depict these gifts as a tangible way to affirm their commitment to the environment, but in the usual manner of Washington connections the money also builds political bridgeheads—access to the opposition camp. Some of the Big Ten groups are leery and keep their distance from certain corporations; others take the money and curry favor with the corporate donors.

"American philanthropy is a system of 'generosity' by which the wealthy exercise social control and help themselves more than they do others," wrote Teresa Odendahl, an anthropologist who examined the lives and attitudes of several hundred wealthy philanthropists. Most major contributors, she found, are guided by a very narrow conception of democracy and "do not believe that the common people constitute the source of political authority."[12]

To escape from dependency, citizens would have to learn to depend on their own financial resources (as some already do) or to take only contributions that impose no limits on their political vision. Ultimately, only a general reform of the fraudulent distinctions in the tax code will remove the special political influence that private wealth derives from its charity.

In any case, money is never going to be a reliable source of political power for unorganized citizens. The other side will always have more of it and politics based on the generosity of others can never attain maturity or independence. The political strength of citizens can only be aggregated by assembling the collective aspirations of the many into a coherent, reliable whole.

This is the daunting challenge of democracy and it is difficult to do in any era. But it is not impossible.

In fact, there are many citizens who are already doing this in different parts of America and with tangible success. They are building their own political organizations and formulating their own political agendas and acting on them. They are accumulating real power because their political aspirations have been authenticated, not by experts or opinion polls, but by the authority of real people.

10
DEMOCRATIC
PROMISE

The maldistribution of power in American politics—embedded in the governing processes, reinforced by inequalities of private wealth, protected by the existing relationships—is not the last word. In scattered places, a vibrant minority still believes in the idea of democracy and acts as though its promise is still possible to fulfill. Where would one find these faithful? In the most unlikely places.

Some are in the drug-ridden neighborhoods of Queens and the South Bronx or the Brownsville section of Brooklyn. Some are in the Mexican-American neighborhoods of East Los Angeles. Others live in the west side wards of San Antonio and the black neighborhoods of Houston and the border towns strung across south Texas. Some are in Jersey City and Baltimore, Memphis and Prince Georges County, Maryland, suburb to the nation's capital.

They are not running anyone for public office or even thinking about doing it. For them, democracy means building their own political organizations, drawing people together in a relationship that leads to real political power. In a sense, they are reinventing democracy from the ground up, starting in their own neighborhoods.

In Brooklyn, people first came together in 1978 as East Brooklyn Congregations, sponsored by Catholic and Protestant churches, a synagogue and two homeowners' associations. After years of patient conversations and thousands of meetings, they were, among other things, building homes for real people. Their Nehemiah project has built two thousand moderately priced houses in Brooklyn. Their accumulated political clout arranged a patchwork of public and private financing that provided low monthly mortgage payments for the buyers.

In Southern California, three allied organizations turned out seven thousand people to lobby Sacramento in a successful campaign to push up the state's minimum wage.

In Texas, a statewide network of ten such organizations has won state legislation for health care for the indigent and $100 million in financing to build sewer and water systems for impoverished migrant-worker settlements in the Rio Grande Valley.

In Baltimore, a citizens' organization called BUILD (Baltimoreans United in Leadership Development) canvassed neighborhoods on their political priorities and drafted its own agenda for the city—education, housing, jobs— then collected endorsements from seventy thousand citizens. One political candidate embraced BUILD's agenda as his own and he became the first black mayor of Baltimore.

These victories and many others, though real and substantial, do not quite capture the essence of what these people are attempting: the reconstruction of democratic values in their own lives. Jan Wilbur, a leader in a multiracial Houston organization known as TMO (The Metropolitan Organization), expressed the idea at a meeting of the ten allied Texas groups:

"While the Founding Fathers spoke those values, they did not live out those values. What we're trying to do has never been done before. We're trying to make those values that we've heard all our lives into something real. That's radical and new."

Father Leo J. Penta, a priest who is active in the East Brooklyn organization, described the organizing process as "weaving a network of new or renewed relationships" among alienated and powerless people. The undertaking begins, he said, with "the wounded and struggling institutions which mediate relationships: families, congregations, churches, workers' organizations, civic and cultural associations." The objective is "to establish islands of political community, spaces of action and freedom in the sea of bureaucrats, political image mongers and atomized consumers."[1]

Skeptics, of course, dismiss this sort of politics as hopelessly old-fashioned and impractical in the age of mass media and high-tech campaigns. But what these people from different parts of America have come to understand is a basic idea nearly lost in American democracy: Politics begins in personal relationships. Indeed, without that foundation, politics usually dissolves into empty manipulation by a remote few. People talking to one another—arguing and agreeing and developing trust among themselves—is what leads most reliably to their own political empowerment.

That is the core of what's missing. In an earlier era, the kind of community organizing these people have undertaken would have aroused immediate suspicion and probably hostility from existing political parties. But that no longer happens. Arnold Graf, an organizer who helped to launch several of these organizations, described the reality:

"When I'm out organizing in a community, I always feel like I'm in a vacuum. There's nothing to hook up to. There's no political party or labor movement. We're trying to imagine what all those organizations would do for people because none of them exist. People are just out there—lost.

"In places like San Antonio or Baltimore, we are as close to being a local political party as anybody is. We go around organizing people, getting them to agree on an agenda, registering them to vote, interviewing candidates on whether they support our agenda. We're not a political party, but that's what political parties used to do."

All of these organizations and a number of others are linked by a national organization and a common heritage—the inspiration of Saul Alinsky and the Industrial Areas Foundation. Alinsky created a national team of organizers in 1940 to help low-income communities discover their own political power. He is another important model for contemporary citizen politics, like King or Nader. The community-organizing approach to politics lost favor after the 1960s, partly because the federal government borrowed loosely from Alinsky's ideas and corrupted them in the "community action" programs of the war on poverty. The notion that the government could sponsor citizen organizations in opposition to itself—or that entrenched power would allow them to succeed—was a doomed concept from the start.

A University of Chicago sociologist, the charismatic Alinsky developed his own version of "rude and crude" politics during the 1930s and, for several decades, showed poor people in Chicago and other industrial cities how to use confrontational strength against City Hall and the political establishment. Alinsky-style organizations multiplied for a time but many did not endure, especially after his death in 1972.

The Industrial Areas Foundation lived on, however, and contrary to popular impressions, it has flourished, though its methods are now quite different. During the two decades when conventional politics was atrophying, the IAF organizations began to grow rapidly as its conception of democracy spread to more and more communities. IAF organizers launched a dozen or so organizations between 1973 and 1985, then doubled that number in the next five years. It now has twenty-four organizations in seven states, encompassing twelve hundred congregations and associations with nearly two million members, plus another five or six communities that are in the formative stages. By 1996, it hopes to be operating in fifteen or sixteen states.[2]

Alinsky's radical conviction is still the core premise. He believed that the ignored and powerless classes of citizens are fully capable of assembling their own power and leading their own politics. But the modern IAF has transformed Alinsky's fractious style into a deeper and more patient understanding of human nature. It does not start out with a "policy issue" or political purpose. It starts with conversations in people's homes. It does not spring itself on a city or town, but begins by establishing relations with the enduring community institutions that people rely on—churches and synagogues and civic associations, from Catholic bishops to black Baptist ministers. The modern IAF, unlike Alinsky, espouses a political doctrine that is rooted in the language of the Gospels.

Edward T. Chambers, an Alinsky protégé who is now IAF executive director, explained the approach to the *Texas Observer:*

"Our culture is very simple. We start with family, a congregation. We start with the teachings of the Bible. We start with basic values that are given us. Then we try to practice a genuine democracy—not the artificial democracy of the sound bite."

What exactly does that mean? "You believe that men and women are the most precious treasure this country has," Chambers said, "and the most important thing we can do is to develop them, let them grow, let them flower, let those talents flourish."[3]

This version of democracy still makes house calls—thousands of "house meetings" held in private homes—where organizers get to know people and their ideas for the community and, in passing, scout for those who will become the community's leaders. The organization, as it develops, gives the people a regular place to meet and discuss their ideas with others—a place that belongs to them, not to someone else. Conventional politics no longer fulfills either of these functions, but then neither do most of the prominent organizations in citizen politics.

In other words, this politics starts with people—not scandalous revelations or legislative crusades, not candidates or government agendas, but ordinary people. The overriding political objective, whatever else happens, is to change the people themselves—to give them a new sense of their own potential.

One Alinsky principle, known to all IAF members as "the Iron Rule," is frequently invoked during their meetings: "Never do anything for someone that they can do for themselves. Never." The organizations, for instance, are launched with financial aid from the sponsoring parishes and churches, but the members must immediately develop their own capacity to be self-sustaining and financially independent.

Their concept of the political arena echoes the theology of Paul Tillich—a realm ruled by both power and love. "The world as it is—that's power," said Ernesto Cortes, Jr., the lead organizer for the IAF Texas network. "The world as it should be—that's love."

A citizen schooled in democracy understands that he or she must live comfortably with both forces. "We learn that power and love go together," Cortes explained, "that they are conjugal, that they both come of the need to form relationships." In a sense, that is a more erudite way of saying that self-interest and competing moral claims must become fused in order to produce effective political action. The definition also provides a way to escape the confinements of "purity" that the modern political culture has taught citizens to accept for themselves.[4]

This language has a resonant quality for contemporary America because, in general, Americans are obsessed with the question of "relationships." The bestseller list is dominated by how-to books on the subject; television talk shows and popular experts endlessly examine the dimensions of personal loneliness, alienation, addiction and the frayed bonds of kinship. The popular obsession with relationships, however, is usually grounded in a narrow and egotistical context—repairing one's relationships with husband or wife or lover, with children or parents, even with one's own true self.

The IAF theology of politics asks people to think of relationships in a context larger than themselves. Politics, after all, was originally understood as a process through which people would work out the terms for living with one another—the shared rules and agreed-upon commitments of the social order. A successful family that is bound together by trust and loyalty and mutual purpose can be thought of as an intense microcosm of a larger society that has developed the same capacities. If families are wounded and struggling in modern America, so too is the political order.

The two realms—the personal and the political—are, in fact, intimately related, since much of what decimates contemporary family life originates in the matters that are decided by the larger political realm. The isolation that haunts Americans in their social lives is not really very different from the alienation that also undermines American politics. It is possible that Americans will be unable to repair their damaged personal relationships without eventually facing their deteriorated political relationships too.

"What we're trying to do," said Ernie Cortes, "is to draw people out of their private pain, out of their cynicism and passivity, and get them connected with other people in collective action."

On a weekend in June 1990, 150 community leaders from across the state of Texas met for a day and a half in a San Antonio hotel to discuss and refine what they called their "vision paper" on public education. The first draft had been written a year earlier, based mainly on experiences in Fort Worth, Houston, Austin and other places where IAF groups were working with school systems and particular schools on various self-improvement projects. The San Antonio meeting was one in a series of continuing deliberations, intended to sharpen the document further.

The meeting had a second purpose, which was to ratify plans for a huge statewide convention in October when the Texas IAF network would turn out ten thousand people and formally declare itself "a new power in Texas public life." It had taken sixteen years to reach this point, starting in 1974 with a feisty San Antonio organization called COPS (Communities Organized for Public Service). COPS endures and is now the largest and most experienced among the Texas network's ten organizations. The rally would also mark the fiftieth anniversary of Saul Alinsky's creation, the Industrial Areas Foundation.

Statewide candidates from both parties would be invited to attend the celebration and experience an "accountability night." This is an IAF ritual in which the politicians are required to sit and listen, while citizens stand at the rostrum and do most of the talking. The network's agenda, including the education "vision paper" and others on jobs and housing, would be made public. Both Republican and Democratic candidates would be asked to endorse it.

"You really feel empowered when you see the politicians come to our accountability night," Marilyn Stavinoha of San Antonio explained to some women from Dallas. "Instead of politicians talking to us, we talk to the politicians."

At the planning meeting at San Antonio, community leaders would talk earnestly about these matters for many hours, but not in a manner likely to excite much outside interest. Democracy at this level is simply not very newsworthy. It lacks the sense of conflict that makes "news" in other political arenas, the stories of winning and losing. No angry voices are ever raised. The people arrive at a consensus on things, yet there are never any votes taken—no climactic moments or soaring orations, no drama whatever. That is not what these people come for nor what they take home.

Before the community leaders convened, Ernie Cortes gathered the seventeen other IAF organizers, who are each responsible to specific communities, for a premeeting meeting to critique the preparations. Afterward, the organizers would meet again to critique the meeting's outcome. In IAF doctrine, the organizers submit to a self-conscious process of arduous accountability. Where are people? Do they understand? Do they really agree?

Are the organizers comfortable, Cortes asked, with the quotas assigned to each organization for getting people to the October rally? As he went down the list, the quotas elicited some groans and sarcastic asides, but no dissent. Transporting thousands of citizens across the vast state of Texas is itself a formidable task, but IAF would have to fill the arena in San Antonio (or make it seem full) for its rally in order to make its point.

"The question is how much do we want to put in this," Cortes said. "It means raising money. It means building momentum. It means this would be our big political event of the year, where we literally use all of our political capital to get the candidates to the meeting." An organization-by-organization tally of what seemed doable produced a total of eighty-eight hundred. "Okay, that's short," he said, "but that will be hard to do."

What do the organizers think of the new draft of the "vision paper" on education? Sister Pearl Caesar, a nun who is an organizer for the Metro Alliance in San Antonio, thought it was very good. "It tells you where we want to go," she said. Others were mildly critical. Too wordy, too repetitious, too specific.

Cortes explained the purpose once again. "The reason we're doing this document is to have a tool to build a constituency at the local level," he said. "The audience is you, the key leaders in the organizations, educators and others around the state, legislators and editorial writers. None of these are original ideas. It's a synthesis, but it's an implicit attack on some things."

Ernie Cortes, one might say, is a mellower, Mexican-American version of Saul Alinsky. He has the same charismatic quality—a mixture of the cerebral and the tough—but Cortes seems less brusque and manipulative than the legendary Alinsky. His manner is more patient with other people and, indeed, more democratic. A few years ago, Cortes was awarded one of the MacArthur Foundation's "genius" fellowships and he has become a minor legend among political activists because of his brilliant organizing work in Texas. Slightly balding and pot-bellied, with stringy gray hair, he often has a scowling expression that can seem, oddly, both menacing and sweet.

Ernie Cortes likes to think of himself as a teacher. He dropped out of graduate school at the University of Texas to become a political organizer among migrant workers in the Rio Grande Valley, but he lives for ideas as well as action—a rare type in politics who devours books on an awesome scale (history, economics, philosophy, politics). Cortes sees the IAF organizations as a university for the people—a school for democracy where they learn how the world around them really works.[5]

Politicians in Texas probably see the organization in a less benign way. The IAF network is a strange new force in their midst—potentially capable of disrupting their own power relationships because it includes so many real people. Something is being built in Texas politics that does not respond to the usual alignments of money and influence. The politicians may not understand the theological talk about "love and power" but, when IAF speaks to power, they listen respectfully. After all, those are live voters going to all those IAF meetings.

When IAF started in San Antonio in 1974, its style was by necessity hard-nosed confrontation. Andres Sarabia, a computer technician at the local Air Force base who became the first president of COPS, described the anger felt by the powerless Mexican-Americans on the west side of town. The city was run by the anglos on the north side and the west side's most modest pleas for public service—street lights or decent drainage—were ignored by City Hall. "I'm not a Republican or a Democrat," Sarabia still likes to say. "I'm Angry with a capital A."[6]

"The issue then was recognition," Sarabia recalled. "We were considered Mexicans. There was a statement made: 'Leave them alone, they're Mexicans. They'll be dead in six months because they'll get drunk and kill each other. They can't organize themselves.' "

To get the establishment's attention, COPS organized "tie-up" actions at banks and department stores—overwhelming clerks and tellers with a flood of Mexican-American customers. "People would try on clothes and fur coats and not buy anything—even the sisters," Sarabia remembered. "They had fun. People used to have fun at these actions. It struck me as tragic—here we are doing this to have fun."

The local business elite eventually got the message and, sure enough, City Hall did too, but only after some brutal conflicts. The people who held power accepted that the Mexican-Americans on the west side would have to be given a share too. Over the years, COPS has won many issues and lost some, but its presence fundamentally redirected the flow of political power in the city.

As the people won tangible victories through their new organizational power, they also recognized the connection with electoral power. The voter turnout among Mexican-Americans in San Antonio has risen steadily ever since—a fact that contrasts with those campaigns of empty exhortation mounted periodically by national foundations to encourage voting.

"You have to teach people at a very local level that voting makes a difference right in their own neighborhoods," Cortes said. "In that sense, we are doing what a political party used to do—giving people a reason to vote." In 1981, for the first time, the inner-city wards of San Antonio outvoted the anglos on the north side.

The other IAF organizations that developed later in Texas were usually less confrontational than COPS because the word spread among Texas politicians that it was easier to talk with these people than ignore them. "When somebody is willing to deal with you, for you to be confrontational, you're being a bully," Cortes explained. "We're trying to teach people politics. Politics means negotiating and being reciprocal and thinking about the other person."[7]

Nevertheless, entrenched political power usually does not yield recognition without a fight, whether in San Antonio or East Brooklyn or El Paso.

When Ernie Cortes was organizing along the border, someone fired a shot into his home one night. Utility companies warned their employees not to mess with these new-fangled political organizations. The *Houston Post* ran a series of stories "exposing" the dangers of these agitators.

"We go right for the center of power—governance—and there's always someone in power who fights you very hard and they get nasty," Arnie Graf explained. "Once you fight for three or four years—and I mean really fight and things get really tense and polarized—then it's easier to get to the table and negotiate things. Once you have that fight, then they look at how to accommodate you."

Of the 150 community leaders who gathered in San Antonio to discuss the "vision paper" on education, many had already been through such "fights" to establish their own presence in local politics. Others were still learning the rudiments of power. The hotel conference room was nearly filled with IAF people who had come from all over Texas. They are known simply as "key leaders" in their community organizations—black, white, Mexican-American, middle class and working class and poor. There appeared to be more women than men, with a few priests and nuns and black ministers scattered among them. After the greetings, Cortes immediately called a fifteen-minute recess so the groups could caucus their own members. When the meeting resumed, a roll call of the organizations followed—a procedure that used up most of the evening.

City by city, town by town, leaders introduced their delegations and designated members delivered progress reports on local projects. Fort Bend Interfaith had persuaded local school superintendents to let them do a school-by-school assessment and so far they had talked with forty principals. El Paso reported good news (a higher number of students who achieved a B average) and bad news (the business community was very slow in raising the money promised for scholarships).

Valley Interfaith, representing border towns such as Brownsville and Harlingen, had raised more than $10,000 from member dues—twelve dollars a family. Dallas Interfaith, still in the formative stages, had signed up fifty-one sponsoring congregations, with financial commitments of more than $100,000. Port Arthur, with seven black delegates present, was just beginning the same arduous groundwork and eager to learn from the others.

Jean Marcus gave a more detailed account of the "parental empowerment" project that ACT (Allied Communities of Tarrant) had pursued in Fort Worth schools for four years. "We've become active on eight campuses," she said. "We have schools with a lot of very low-achieving students and we have schools with high levels of violence. Without parental involvement, we aren't going to be able to turn those schools around."

At the middle school where ACT first concentrated, the children's achieve-

ment scores had already risen from last in the school district to third. "We help
the parents to identify their self-interest," Marcus explained. "They already
know more than they think they know about what's wrong with the schools.
As they become more active in the schools, parents become more active in the
community at large."

The organization is also a university, as Cortes said, and the next day the
150 leaders were taught a succinct history of public education in America,
from Horace Mann's "common school" to the "factory model of schools"
that has prevailed in the twentieth century. Sonia Hernandez, a former leader
of COPS and now a national education consultant, was the teacher, providing
a larger framework for people to think about their own schools and the troubling questions about whether their own children are being prepared for the
work of the future.

Schools are also about political power, Hernandez explained. "If teachers
don't have power," she said, "guess who else doesn't have power—parents.
So we wind up in conflict with each other and neither of us has the power to
change things."

The review of the education document was, above all, orderly and good-
natured. Each delegation was given responsibility for a particular section and
they studied it overnight, then came forward the next day to comment and lead
the discussion. The contents of the "vision paper" were a collection of old and
new ideas about school reform, ranging from school-based management to
greater parental involvement to new methods for accountability.

Some people wanted a stronger "moral statement" in the preamble. Others worried that the emphasis on "competitiveness" sent the wrong message
to kids. A spirited exchange developed on the nature of work in the future and
whether schools were preparing children for the next generation of jobs.

Father Rosendo Urrabazo, a key leader from San Antonio, brought the
discussion back to its central purpose—political action. "We have people
trained now so they feel comfortable going into City Hall and talking to the
officials," he said. "But they don't feel comfortable going into the schools.
What we did in City Hall, we have to do now in the schools."

The only discordant note was quickly smothered by Cortes. A priest rose
to speak in behalf of the "school voucher issue"—a means of providing public
financing for struggling parochial schools—and one mother seconded his plea.
The public schools are hopeless, she said, and parents need help getting their
kids out of them. Cortes responded with a soliloquy on Thomas Jefferson and
the need for a unifying "common culture" in America—a diversion that
seemed to close the subject.

Outside in the lobby later, Cortes bluntly warned the priest to back off, lest
he provoke an argument that might break up the multidenominational coalition. "I told the monsignor it was not in his interest to push the voucher

issue,'' Cortes said, ''because we would have to fight him on it. The first thing we have to do is demonstrate our commitment to the common school, to preserve the common culture, or we're going to wind up with a fractured, two-tiered country and that won't be good for any of us.''

The ''voucher issue'' was not mentioned again. Strange as it might seem to anticlerics, an organization that is greatly dependent on the Catholic church was deliberately deflecting a political issue that is most important to the church—in order to preserve its broader political purposes. Such trade-offs are the natural consequence of collective conversation.

When the education discussion concluded, Cortes reminded the delegates: ''This paper is not finished. Go back to your communities and review it. Form an education committee and critique it and come back to us. Are we on the right track in developing a teaching document for ourselves to use?''

Meetings, then more meetings, hours and hours of talking and listening— the process of building political relationships can be almost as exhausting as tending to personal relationships. But the IAF's procedures for fostering deliberation clearly succeed for these citizens. The San Antonio meetings posed a tantalizing question: Is this what the dialogue of a genuine democracy would sound like?

The discussion certainly did not resemble the fractious debates of a town meeting, where everyone pops off on whatever subject moves them. There was no debate to speak of. The format was highly structured and, ultimately, designed to avoid random digressions and encourage consensus. Ernie Cortes was the principal teacher, but also essentially the leader. One could imagine that an audience of hyperactive citizens, full of strong opinions and personal agendas, might rebel impatiently.

Yet it seemed to work. At least, the process worked for the people who were in the room, who had come great distances to join this discussion and dozens of other meetings like it. What did they get from the exchange? A sense of participation and also a sense of sharing in power.

The format, for one thing, is subtly but rigorously all-inclusive. One way or another, before the discussions were over, literally all the people in the room—even the most awkward and shy—were required to be on their feet, facing the entire assembly to make some small contribution to the dialogue, if only to give their names and express solidarity with what their own community leaders had said. For the inexperienced and least articulate, the meeting itself was the teacher.

Beyond the personal transformations, the dialogues also yielded the feeling that something important had been accomplished. Agreement had been reached on important matters. The participants knew that they had collaborated in developing a consensus with very different people from many different places and that the consensus would be put to political use in the future.

The "relationships" that have formed around a set of political ideas will be more important than the details, for as these people understand, the relationships are the source of their political power. It was the desire for this consensus, not a thirst for conflict, that brought these people to the meeting. Year after year, it is why they keep coming back.

On October 28, the months of meetings and countless hours of talk came together in an impressive demonstration of political purpose. The arena in San Antonio was filled with ten thousand people, the newspapers reported, and respectful politicians attended to hear from the people. "Coalition Jells into New Force," one headline declared. "Meeting Signals New Texas Politics," said another.

Clayton Williams, the Republican candidate for governor, did not show (though he met separately with the network's leaders). Ann Richards, the Democratic candidate and the eventual winner, did appear and enthusiastically endorsed the IAF network's agenda on education, housing and jobs. Richards promised, as governor, to consult them regularly (and, once in office, she has).

Were the headlines right? Was this new political force for real? Ernie Cortes demurred slightly.

"If I believed my press clippings, I'd say we are a major political factor," Cortes said. "Off the record, I'd say we're not quite there yet. But I believe we're on the threshold. It's in the interest of the political establishment to let us look strong, so they don't look too greedy. It's not in their interest to let us be so strong that we can stop them from doing what they want to do. We haven't got that kind of power yet. But I think we can get it."

The resonant language of love and power, the earnestness and dedication of the IAF organizations, tempts some to romanticize these citizens into something more than they are. The IAF organizations, from East Brooklyn to East Los Angeles, are succeeding on their own terms, but they are still a long, long way from the centers of power. Their politics delivers on its promises to people and that is why these organizations survive and flourish. But there are still many, many obstacles before them.

These citizens have not overcome all of the barriers to democracy but, one by one, they are at least trying to confront some of them in a straightforward way. They may reasonably be regarded as a living model for the democratic promise not yet realized in America. It is also not unreasonable to imagine them as the vanguard, perhaps one of many, for the restoration of American democracy.

The skeptical questions about a politics that originates with people are obvious. Door-to-door politics takes time, for instance, years and years of it, but established power does not wait for citizens to get themselves in motion.

This tension is felt by the IAF members themselves: Their organizing processes cannot be rushed without subverting the integrity of the human relationships, yet political events are deciding important questions right now.

In a society conditioned by technology to expect instant responses, the IAF methodology assumes that human development requires patience. Their strategy for gaining political power requires, above all, heroic patience and an abiding optimism about the country—a belief that gradually, community by community, the public's voice can be reconstructed in American politics.

In the media age, that approach is widely regarded as obsolete—even reactionary—since it ignores the reality of mass-communications technology and its supposed blessings. But the IAF groups stubbornly insist that the only way to overcome the alienation fostered by the modern political culture is by doing politics the old way—face to face, precinct by precinct. But can the politics built on personal relationships ever make itself heard in the clamor of mass communications? The IAF has not, as yet, found a way nor has it really tried, since it does not wish to dilute its deeper purposes by getting drawn into "sound bite" politics.

The quality that makes the IAF organizations so distinctive is their relentless attention to the conditions that ordinary people describe in their own lives. Their authority is derived from personal experience, not from the policy experts of formal politics. Most other varieties of citizen politics start at the other end of the landscape—attaching to the transient storms of "public opinion" or "policy debate" that play out abstractly on the grand stage of high-level politics. IAF gives up short-term celebrity on "hot issues" in order to develop the long-term power of a collective action that is real.

In fact, because of its obvious strength, IAF is frequently invited to join the coalitions assembled by other citizen groups for campaigns on major national issues, but it nearly always declines, partly because of what IAF leaders see as hollowness in many of those campaigns: Real people are absent from the ranks. The IAF leaders are also wary of using their people as fodder in someone else's crusade. Other citizen groups typically try to form working alliances with the politicians in power and generally define their own goals in terms of what seems possible within the reality of Washington politics. These practical compromises, IAF leaders believe, effectively cut out the "unreasonable" voices of people at the community level.

"We have to build a strong constituency of people who care about things that are important and who free themselves, both spiritually and practically, from either party so that both parties will want them," Cortes said.

Like all other citizen politics, the IAF organizations face the daunting barriers of class conflict and racial differences, but at least they are confronting those obstacles in different ways. The organizing successes to date confirm Saul Alinsky's original conviction—that the poor and powerless can be drawn out of their passive anger and mobilized into effective political action—but it is not yet clear that the same techniques would succeed with other kinds of communities. The process, after all, mainly teaches racial minorities or low-income neighborhoods the sense of political entitlement that already comes naturally to the white middle class and upper middle class—a belief in one's right to be heard on public issues, the self-confidence to speak for oneself.

By itself, the personal enhancement of the disaffected classes is valuable, but insufficient. Alinsky himself conceded, late in life, that "even if all the low income parts of our population were organized—all the blacks, Mexican Americans, Puerto Ricans, Appalachian poor whites—if through some genius of organization, they were all united in a coalition, it would not be powerful enough to get significant, basic, needed changes."[8]

Unless an organization can learn to build bridges across the class divide, it will never attain the kind of political girth that might threaten the status quo. In various places, IAF organizations are already at work on the bridge building. Some of the Texas organizations, for instance, are truly diverse, with memberships that leap across the usual lines of race and class. Many white middle-class members, drawn by their Christian or Jewish faith and progressive civic values, have a conscience-driven commitment to their communities and a sense that this is the only politics that produces anything meaningful.

Cortes does not think the IAF Texas network will achieve full status as a major power in the state until it succeeds at creating a presence among the white blue-collar workers in East Texas and elsewhere—people who have common economic interests but are in social conflict with blacks and Hispanics. The organizers are looking for such openings.

In Phoenix, Arizona, the IAF organization (Valley Interfaith Project) was deliberately founded across class lines—bridging both sides of town. It encompasses Hispanic neighborhoods on the south side of the city and white working-class and professional neighborhoods on the north side. Many white people are drawn to participate, organizer Peter Fears explained, by a sense of the deteriorating quality in their lives—crime and pollution, overdevelopment, traffic jams and the rest. The good life is crumbling and, unless citizens mobilize themselves, the political order will do nothing to stop it.

Such organizing ventures will seem wildly idealistic to cynics who are familiar with the present context of racial and class antagonism in American politics. Still, American political history suggests that this kind of politics, difficult as it is, is the only kind that leads to genuine change. Eras of great reform usually began with the emergence of new political demographics—either newly arrived immigrants who finally found their voice in American politics or large sectors of citizens who had been held down by the system. Their political strength crystallized when they bonded with others unlike themselves with shared political goals.

In history, it is the least powerful, the outsiders, who have often been the principal agents for democratic growth. Therefore, if democratic regeneration is to occur in the years ahead, it is likely to be led by people such as these—women and men who are now the weakest and most disregarded citizens, the politically orphaned—rather than by middle-class reformers with professional skills. Mexican-Americans or blacks, Asian-Americans or working-class whites—these are the people most injured by the decay of democratic representation and the people who have most to gain by restoring equity to politics. It is perhaps the case that the democratic promise waits for them.

One other crucial barrier stands in the way of groups like the IAF: They cannot at present reach beyond their own boundaries. Vibrant democracy has always been easier to accomplish in localized settings, closest to the people, but that is not sufficient to address the present breakdown. In order to imagine a restored democracy, one has to imagine a politics beyond cities and states that can speak convincingly to the national government in Washington.

In other words, how can people create a political presence that links them to large and complicated issues like taxation or the savings and loan debacle? The IAF organizations, like almost everyone else in America, are a long way from establishing that kind of link to power, though they are taking small, careful steps toward the higher realms of politics.

This is absolutely essential. The harsh fact is that the fundamental well-being of San Antonio or East Brooklyn is not determined at City Hall or even ultimately at the state legislature in Austin or Albany. The fate of these communities, their families and parishes, is embedded in a web of distant governing decisions in Washington where elite influence is concentrated.

In their cautious, deliberate manner, the IAF organizations are trying to develop channels with which to speak in unison on larger national or regional questions. For the last couple of years, Andres Sarabia and key leaders from the other cities have been meeting regularly in Washington with their congressional delegations, exploring the landscape of national legislative politics, trying out modest proposals and establishing relationships with those in power.

These contacts are only a first step and IAF now intends to expand its national base more rapidly. Cities in virtually every region of the nation have urged the organization to come in and help repair local politics: The pace of growth depends partly on recruiting able organizers who truly grasp the human dimensions of this politics. Arnie Graf, who is recruiting for the expansion, explained the strategy:

"Generally, our hope is that by 1996 we would be in twice the strategically located states as we are now and that would give us the capacity to develop either the regional or national base to look at national policies. If we were in the right fifteen or sixteen states, we wouldn't have to be in all fifty states. That would give us enough clout to be able to affect policies, whether it was through political parties or corporations.''

With Texas, Arizona and Southern California already well launched, for instance, when IAF adds a presence in Colorado and New Mexico, it will have the beginnings of a common regional base—one that can talk collectively to the region's congressional delegations and also to economic enterprises based in the Southwest. At the very least, it will have a platform larger than the boundaries of communities or even states. Coherent and authentic citizen politics takes time.

What would the IAF communities talk about if they develop a strong voice in national politics? Organizers already know the answer, because the same concerns arise again and again in community dialogues. These are: the terms of work and wages, the precariousness of family incomes.

''In some areas, where there is no hope, we've brought people a certain measure of hope,'' Arnie Graf reflected. ''However, we're not bringing them better incomes. It's our feeling it's all going to be short-lived if we can't do something about getting people a family wage that's livable. What is the wage that a family needs to survive and live well? We have to aim at the incomes of families. We know this about ourselves: We have to look at the large issues and we can't do that from a seven-state base.''

Ernie Cortes envisions that, as the Texas network develops a stronger presence, it can begin addressing large economic issues from the perspective of workers. Some of the ideas may be small and pedestrian, some may be large and radical.

''We can then raise questions about work, which raises questions about investment patterns,'' Cortes said. ''Can we create some fundamental institutions that allow reinvestment in communities? If we all come to a conclusion that the cost of capital is a serious impediment to economic development, then we're going to have to have a new institution to provide low-cost capital.

''People also ought to have some say-so about the conditions in which they work. One of our ambitions down the road is to create some workers' associations that would deal with issues like job safety and workmen's compensation. We don't want to get under the NLRB, but we think we're in a position to negotiate with corporations about an American *perestroika*. We are talking now to a major company about restructuring work, with schools in the plant. Workers need to be paid in accordance with the things they control. They get demoralized when they have no control and produce lousy products. If you have intelligent management of the economy, these things are possible.''

These political ideas are all cast well into the future, not tomorrow or next month, not even next year. But they exist as possibilities—a political program that goes to what most people would say is the heart of the matter, work and family and incomes. The fact that some citizens are getting a handle on politics in order to force these matters into the political debate is perhaps the most hopeful evidence of all.

If they succeed, they will inevitably confront the underlying power relationships in government and, thus, provoke stern resistance. But what makes these ideas plausible, if they do someday invade the narrow national debate surrounding government, is that they will not enter as abstract policy prescriptions. They will have originated from the experiences of real people and real people will be gathered behind them.

The tragic quality of contemporary democracy is that circumstances have alienated the most conscientious citizens from the principal venue for speaking to power—elections. Even the most active citizens' groups have lost faith in the idea that elections are the best means for making government accountable or advancing the public's aspirations.

American democracy is thus burdened with a heavy irony: The nation is alive with positive, creative political energies, yet the democratic device that grants citizens their sovereignty is moribund. Elections exist like a vacuum jar at the center of the political disorder; the most interesting and important action flows outside and around them.

When citizens set out to influence governing decisions, they usually begin with the assumption that electoral politics is inoperable or a trap. The three popular models for citizen politics—Saul Alinsky, Ralph Nader, Martin Luther King, Jr.—all began by distancing themselves from the most direct and legitimate source of political power. This is a fundamental handicap.

Most of the barriers to electoral politics are well known: the daunting cost of entry, the disconnectedness of mass-media political messages, the manipulative marketing techniques of campaign strategists and, above all, the gargantuan flood of money that pays for all these. Mere citizens—even if they recognize a plausible motive for participating in this contest—will find very little they could afford to contribute. Political power, as Ernie Cortes likes to say, comes from either "organized money" or "organized people." In the electoral arena, the money is organized, the people are not.

The citizens who do exert important influence on elections are usually organized around the most narrow objectives and often then in a defensive crouch. The National Rifle Association is famous for exerting negative influence because the issue of gun control arouses deep emotions and class resentments that mobilize its members. The NRA can frighten incumbent representatives, with both its votes and its money, though it cannot legislate much in a positive manner. The antiabortion forces, likewise, rallied crucial swing votes on the margins of close contests and that was intimidating to many elected representatives, until the tide turned against them. The League of Conservation Voters and other environmental groups exert some electoral influence by targeting their campaign contributions on worthy contestants. The pro-Israel lobby works its will much more powerfully in the same manner.

The entry points for citizens, in other words, are quite narrow: either through money, the more the better in order to compete with other interests, or through an intensely organized focus on a single issue. Elections do not work for those who are unwilling or unable to squeeze through those gates. For those who wish for a broader dialogue between the governed and the governors, the electoral route seems barren.

All the electoral barriers are real and formidable, yet they do not fully explain the vacuum. In many instances, it is not simply that active citizens are shut out, but also that they have deliberately chosen to stand apart. The formal handle exists for citizens who wish to share in the governing power, yet many shrink from using it. Why do they turn their backs on the lever that is available and potentially the most powerful?

The blunt answer in some instances, of course, is that, if they participated in elections, they might lose. For some frail causes, it is wiser to stand aloof, claiming to represent the people's unrealized political aspirations, than to submit those claims to an up-and-down vote by secret ballot. Opinion polls, whose results are easily manipulated, have become the surrogate elections for groups that do not wish their true strength to be tested with the voters.

In other cases, the investment of time and energy in the tedious mechanics of the electoral process itself often seems counterproductive—not the best use of people and limited resources. In San Antonio, for instance, COPS put together the equivalent of a full-scale precinct organization in order to campaign for a citywide referendum on reforming city council districts. It won the referendum, but the organization was exhausted by the effort. "It's very mechanical," said Arnie Graf, "and it doesn't get at what politics is really about. It doesn't allow people to talk about the broader issues."

A less tangible, but possibly more important factor that separates citizens from electoral politics is their own sense of purity—the conviction that elections are corrupting (or at least perceived as corrupt by the general public) and that righteous causes will lose their glow if they become entangled in the fortunes of mere politicians. For years, people have implored Ralph Nader to run for office—if only to provide a substantive alternative to the dross of party candidates—but he never took the suggestion seriously. Joan Claybrook, president of Public Citizen, explained why:

"Ralph's presumption is that, if he runs for office, he would lose power because he would then become dependent on the political processes and so forth. So he's willing to rely on less resources and be called a 'national nanny' and lose some battles in order to remain independent."

Sister Christine Stephens, an IAF national organizer and a leader in the Texas network, expressed a similar reluctance: "We think the work of being a citizen is too important to be corrupted by [electoral] politics. Once the person gets in there, they can be corrupted. Even the best people will lose their soul. The most we can do is keep a countervailing force to keep the balance even."

Nader, nonetheless, took a first, exploratory step into electoral politics in the early presidential primaries of 1992—offering voters in New Hampshire and Massachusetts a chance to protest the regular order by voting for him. "I am campaigning for an agenda, not for elected office," he said. Many more such ventures, led by many different insurgents, would be needed to restore the public's voice in elections.

Electoral politics, in its present format, reduces the role of citizens by attaching them to a single candidate's fortunes, not to a political program they helped develop. "I'm not interested in teaching people how to be appendages in anybody's movement," Ernie Cortes said, "because, in the final analysis, a political campaign is a movement. It's built around a single candidate. It will evaporate when he or she gets elected."

On a local level, the IAF groups move deftly around the edges of elections with their "accountability nights" and politicians usually get the message: These are real voters facing them. IAF does not run candidates or endorse them, but it does register people to vote and those voters do not need a TV commercial to learn that a candidate has ignored the community's agenda. If citizen organizations create a new framework for how people think about politics, Cortes argues, then electoral results will follow, not the other way around.

The objections all have practical validity to those citizens struggling to generate an authentic politics. To working politicians, however, the reluctance of citizens seems overly precious—people who want to have it both ways. They wish to influence government, but not to get soiled by the muck of politics. They want to become powerful in the public arena, but without themselves being responsible for the awesome machinery of government. A purified citizen who is above electoral politics, one might say, is someone who has not yet come to terms with the psychological burdens of accepting responsibility for the government's coercive powers.

The disjunction between voters and elections is itself a central element of the democratic problem—another expression of the damaged relationship between people and authority. Elections are the most visible, most legitimate means of maintaining those relationships and the only sure way to establish accountability to the governed and to develop a general trust in those who are given the power to govern. People who want responsible government are bound to be disappointed so long as they turn away from this central mechanism of power.

A genuine democracy will not likely develop until the two realms are reconciled—the irregular citizens and the formal structure of power. After all, like the two-way mirror, democratic accountability runs both ways—between those in power and those who put them there. This requires a reliable organizational framework that at present does not exist—a viable political party that provides the connective tissue between the people and the government.

Conceivably, the steady development of citizen organizations like IAF may eventually create a workable substitute and heal this breach. It is not far-fetched, for instance, to imagine that a decade hence a broad alliance of citizen-based political organizations may have formed that can effectively exercise the power of "organized people" once again in elections. The vanguard is visible now. In the best circumstances, this enterprise will take time—years of patient rebuilding by people everywhere.

In the meantime, the machinery of power is held comfortably in other hands. The principal political institutions that dominate conventional politics—the two major parties and the media—once provided the connective tissue that linked citizens to government but, in different ways, each has abandoned that responsibility. It is to those familiar structures of politics that we will turn next—the main institutions that surround both the electoral process, where the power to govern is legitimized, and the governing process, where the power is exercised. Each of these, in different ways, has lost its connections to ordinary citizens and each has gravitated toward the powerful elites that dominate the politics of government.

The models of democratic politics that some citizens at large have already created may or may not succeed someday in salvaging democracy. But, in the meantime, they exist as a living rebuke to the important political institutions that have failed.

PART THREE

MEDIATING
VOICES

11

WHO OWNS
THE DEMOCRATS?

The empty space at the center of American democracy is defined ultimately by its failed political institutions. At the highest level of politics, there is no one who now speaks reliably for the people, no one who listens patiently to their concerns or teaches them the hard facts involved in governing decisions. There is no major institution committed to mobilizing the power of citizens around their own interests and aspirations.

The principal mediating institutions of politics do still function in a formal sense, of course, but in different ways each has lost the capacity to serve as authentic connective tissue between government and citizens. In different ways, the major political parties and the news media have instead gravitated toward another source of power—the elite interests that dominate government.

This section directly confronts the failure of those political institutions and explores why each, in its own way, falls short in its responsibility to democracy. The analysis begins with the hollow reality of the Democratic party and how economic interests that are most hostile to the party's main constituencies manage to influence the party's direction from the top down. Chapter Twelve, "Rancid Populism," examines the Republican party and how its mastery of modern communications enables it to hold power with an illusory program based on alienation and resentment.

The press fails its responsibility too and Chapter Thirteen, "Angle of

Vision,'' explains the deep economic and social transformations that led the
"news" away from the people it once spoke for and into alignment with the
governing elites. The political impact of the mass-media culture, explored in
Chapter Fourteen, "The Lost Generation," is more paradoxical and, in some
ways, more hopeful. While television trivializes complex political action, its
imagery is also relentlessly populist in its directness—and brutally accurate in
its own unsettling manner.

The empty space left by the failure of these mediating voices has been
partially filled, however. It is held by the powerful political organizations
called corporations. The final chapter of this section, Chapter Fifteen, "Citizen GE," illustrates the institutional reality of corporate power by examining
the awesome reach and capabilities of one corporate political organization, the
General Electric Company.

The distorted power relationships that dominate government and have cut
out citizens are embedded in all these political institutions. At its core, the
democratic problem is a problem of institutional default on a massive scale.

The Democratic party traces its origin, with excessive precision, to the twenty-
third day of May in 1792 when Thomas Jefferson wrote a letter to George
Washington. His letter described political alignments that were already visible
in the young Republic—the yeomanry versus the Tory financiers. Jefferson
urged President Washington to rally the people in a party that would defend
democracy against the corrupt ambitions of monied interests. His text is un-
cannily appropriate to the politics of the late twentieth century.[1]

While historians recognize the letter as a milestone, it was Andrew Jackson, thirty years later, who mobilized the constituencies of farmers, workers
and merchants into a vigorous, effective political party known forever after as
the Democrats. The dual heritage is observed by party stalwarts every year at
their Jefferson-Jackson Day dinners.

If Jefferson's letter is taken as the true birthday, then the party would
celebrate its bicentennial in the presidential election year of 1992. When this
point belatedly occurred to some staff officials at the Democratic National
Committee, they began to discuss what they might make of the event. The
Democratic party's perennial disorganization has always been part of its
charm. If the Republicans were approaching their bicentennial, they would
have already sold ads to the Fortune 500 for a souvenir program guide.

The discussion at the Democratic National Committee followed these
lines: If the Democrats were to stage a two hundredth birthday spectacular,
whom should they invite? Naturally, staff officials thought first of the direct-
mail lists stored in computers—the people who give money to the party more
or less regularly. Then, of course, they would include all the elected officials,
state, local and national, who call themselves Democrats. Why not, someone

suggested, also invite the many thousands of people who are active in party affairs—the "regulars" who serve on county committees or tend to the mechanics of election precincts or campaign operations, the legions of people who faithfully rally around the ticket?

But, it was asked, who are these people? Where are their names and addresses? The DNC staffers searched the party's files and discovered that such lists no longer exist. The Democratic party headquarters did not know the identity of its own cadres. It no longer kept the names of the people who ostensibly connect it to the millions of other citizens who are only nominally Democrats, by virtue of registration. The DNC could not even say how many Democratic "regulars" there are.

Thirty years ago, lists of names—county by county, ward by ward—were the muscle of party politics and a principal source of power. Many were hacks and ward heelers, hanging on to public jobs by doing political chores, but many were also skillful organizers at the humblest level, adept at pulling people into politics by talking to them, listening to them. Political careers, from the courthouse to the national legislature, even the White House, were built on these cadres.

The old lists presumably still existed, but not at party headquarters. They were believed to be in permanent storage at the National Archives—boxes and boxes of index cards from the 1950s and 1960s with the names and addresses of the people who, in that day, made the party real. In the age of television, big money and high-tech candidacies, the "regulars" of party politics have been rendered irrelevant.

The Democratic party, as a political organization, is no longer quite real itself. The various strands of personal communication and loyalty that once made it representative and responsive to the people are gone. It exists as a historical artifact, an organizational fiction. Its inherited status—"the oldest political party on earth"—is the principal basis for its influence, since any candidate who calls himself a Democrat will automatically enjoy certain legal privileges not available to unaligned opponents.

The party's preferred status in the electoral arena is no longer justified, since the Democratic party no longer performs the basic functions of a political party. It acts neither as a faithful mediator between citizens and the government nor as the forum for policy debate and resolution nor even as a structure around which political power can accumulate. It functions mainly as a mail drop for political money.

"If you go to the voter files and ask people who are registered Democrats if they are party members, they wouldn't know how to respond," Michael McCurry, communications director at the DNC, said. "They don't go to any meetings or participate at all, except maybe—maybe—to vote." While 42 million Americans are registered as Democrats, many of them would vigorously deny that they are "party members." Like candidates who run on the party label for convenience, voters would say their registration is a matter of historical necessity, not conviction. Since the two major parties, given their preferential status, are bound to dominate the outcome of elections, one might as well sign up as a Democrat or a Republican.

If one inquires further about the true membership of the Democratic party, a reasonable surrogate is provided by the people who contribute money regularly, sending in their checks year after year, whether for $25 or $1,000. "If you're willing to part with your hard-earned cash in exchange for a newsletter or whatever, that probably qualifies as party membership," McCurry said. "Of course, the number of people who actually go to meetings and take part in debate is much smaller."

By that yardstick, the national party of Democrats is a very small organization indeed—roughly 100,000 people. The DNC knows the number with some precision because 100,000 is the normal response rate for its direct-mail solicitations. It sends out about 400,000 letters to the names in its computer files and usually gets money back from about one fourth. In presidential election years, the response goes up sharply—350,000 in 1988—but even that group is preciously small for a nation with 180 million adults. Amnesty International, by comparison, has 450,000 dues-paying members in the United States, whom it keeps engaged in tangible political activities such as its letter-writing campaigns.

The Republican National Committee has a much broader popular base—750,000 contributors in 1989, 1.2 million during the '88 election season—but even the GOP numbers are unimpressive for a national political party.

The IAF network of community organizations represents 400,000 families in Texas alone and counts more than 2 million in its nationwide base of organizations. The National Rifle Association, with 2.5 million dues-paying members, is larger than both major political parties combined. The National Committee to Preserve Social Security and Medicare, a lobbying group for the elderly, has 10 million members (who each pay ten dollars in dues). Its larger rival, the American Association of Retired Persons, has 32 million members (who pay five dollars a year). The National Parent-Teacher Association has 6 million members. The AFL-CIO unions have 14 million members. The Roman Catholic church, the largest organization in America, has 55 million members.

America, in other words, is a nation of active joiners and givers, as it always has been, and Americans will part with their dollars rather freely if given a plausible reason to do so. They just don't give their money to political parties.

What is it that makes these other organizations different and more convincing to people? Some of the organizations promise to provide direct political representation, a voice in the larger arena on specific matters. Unlike the Democratic National Committee, most know the names of their own cadres and can turn out their troops, quickly and massively. Some of the organizations provide people with valuable services, from economic protection to spiritual solace, from informative newsletters to insurance coverage. One way or another, all of these other organizations promise to take responsibility for their adherents.

The Democratic party does not really make that promise, aside from the rhetorical flourishes in its direct-mail solicitations. Given its weakened vitality, the party would perhaps not be believed if it did. Instead, the Democratic National Committee promises to pursue a narrower goal—winning elections for Democratic candidates. That objective no longer excites most Americans, not enough to open their checkbooks.

The most revealing fact about the Democrats' "party members" is their age. Among the DNC's 100,000 regular contributors, the average age is seventy years old. On the whole, these elderly loyalists are the remnants of the old "regulars"—people who probably formed their attachments to the Democratic party forty or fifty years ago, when it stood for a clear set of ideas and represented well-defined segments of the American public. "The thing that is frightening," McCurry said, "is that it's old and getting older."

Thomas "Lud" Ashley, a former liberal Democratic congressman from Toledo, Ohio, and now president of a powerful financial lobby, the Association of Bank Holding Companies, reminisced gloomily about what has been lost—the party's mediating capacity with citizens. The American system is no longer a democracy, Ashley attests, because "democracy is based on accountability and it's not there now.

"It may be nostalgia, but, when I was elected [in 1954], we didn't count on television," the former congressman reflected. "We counted on what had existed for one hundred years—a political organization. Toledo wasn't Chicago, but we had precinct captains and twenty-two ward chairmen and there were monthly ward meetings that you went home and talked to. They were robust, well-attended meetings—half business, half social. The business took forty-five minutes or an hour and then it was 'let's get into the beer.'

"What you talked about wasn't how much you'd done about getting somebody's goddamn Social Security check or getting their uncle into the Veterans Hospital. What you talked about was public policy. What people thought about things. What they wanted done. Like, are the blacks going to move into the Polish neighborhood? Or why are some federal funds going to the downtown area when they are needed in the neighborhoods? These were Polish, Hungarian, Czech communities and there was a helluva lot of interest in what was going on in eastern Europe.

"Certainly, Vietnam was a ball-breaker. I was pro-Johnson at the time and, Christ, I had my head handed to me. For the first time in twelve years in Congress, I was booed and hissed and practically driven from the hall. So I just had to look at the war from the standpoint of my constituents. That's real accountability and I responded. I had to—if I was going to run again.

"There's no longer the necessity for that. There's no political infrastructure to go back and report to. Members go back now and report on TV. And the local press doesn't have the slightest idea of what you're doing on public policy unless you get caught in a scandal."

The modern Democratic party does provide modest mediating services to a limited number of citizens, but only in relation to the amount of money contributed. The DNC operates an elaborate hierarchy of "donor councils" for individuals and political interests who wish to buy memberships in the party—$1,000 for young people, who are mostly former congressional aides active as junior lobbyists; $15,000 for corporations that want to belong to the Democratic Business Council; $5,000 or more for the wealthy individuals and lobbyists who wish to serve on the National Finance Council. The Democratic Labor Council is for unions, who are still the party's most important financiers. The most gilt-edged circle is composed of the party's three hundred "trustees"—people who give or raise $100,000 each.

In exchange, these citizens are provided social entrée to the Democratic leaders in Congress, influential committee chairmen and their key staff officials. "We like to think we give very significant benefits," said Melissa Moss, one of the DNC's fund-raising officials. "We have an annual meeting where we cover very substantive issues, roundtable discussions, quarterly meetings in the Capitol with congressional leaders. What we try to do is have a flow of ideas and let them have input into the key players. People are motivated for many reasons. Obviously, there are lobbyists who want to have as much contact as possible with key members. Others are private citizens who just want to be active."

The Democratic National Committee is weak because it performs only one function that matters to other politicians: It holds a national convention every four years to nominate someone for president. Even that event has lost most of its meaning, since nominating conventions are no longer suspenseful dramas. Because of state primaries and the decline of powerful local organizations, the outcome is already decided weeks or months before the delegates arrive to cast their votes.

Still, this is the only moment when the Democratic party exists tangibly as a national organization, and the convention gives the DNC leverage over the independently constituted state parties: If the states want their delegations seated at the national convention, they must pick them according to the national party's rules. The rules are decided, ultimately, by the 404 members of the Democratic National Committee, most of whom are longtime party activists, state chairs or people closely identified with labor, racial minorities and other constituencies that still regard the DNC as an important place from which to influence the party's direction.

Most of the state-party structures, though once important power centers themselves, are now as atrophied as the national organization. "A lot of state parties have devolved into dinner committees or debt-management committees or very small-bore local operations to pick judges and that sort of thing," said Paul Tully, the DNC's director of organization. A few states have stronger organizations—Iowa, Michigan, Ohio, New York—but none is what it used to be.

The power of the state parties was gradually enfeebled by the same forces that weakened the national party—social changes that broke up the old neighborhoods and new electoral techniques that enabled individual candidates to invent their own self-centered political parties. The influence of television, among other agents of social change, obliterated the ability of the party "regulars" to mobilize voters and, in that sense, liberated politics from the control of the old machines.

But, in exchange, television politics requires huge amounts of money. Thus, a candidate who knows how to get his own money is free to design his own political agenda, however vacuous, and sell it to the voters, however deceitfully, and enter public office without any obligations to the permanent political structures—local, state or national parties.

Every state as a result now has "networks" of money and activists assembled around individual politicians—senators or governors who reached public office largely on their own. New Jersey has a Bill Bradley network for the senator. In Texas, there is a Lloyd Bentsen network. In Virginia, there is a Chuck Robb network. These personal affiliations are much more potent than the formal party organizations and cooperate with the party only if it serves their leaders. For the last few years, under DNC Chairman Ronald H. Brown, organizer Paul Tully has been working on fostering a higher level of mutual enterprise—encouraging the states to build cooperative campaign machinery that works for the whole ticket.

"We act as a cajoler, seducer, nudge, donor," Tully said. "The old DNC was tied to an age when the old urban organizations were the center of things, with close ties to the AFL-CIO. The DNC was the traffic cop among the big fiefdoms, rather than an organization that created its own agenda. It did what we call 'glue politics' or somebody else might call 'grease politics.' Even in a much more homogeneous party like the Republican party, there's a constant adjusting process that goes on, among personalities and so forth. But by necessity, that's inward looking. That's not looking at voters and elections and the problems of the country."

If the national committee functioned as an outward-looking agent, trying to connect with voters and their problems, it would probably be more reform-minded (and liberal) than the Democratic party reflected in Congress. Many of the DNC's members came of age in the 1960s and entered political activism through civil rights or the antiwar movement or the presidential campaigns of Robert Kennedy, Eugene McCarthy and George McGovern. They started out, like Tully, as insurgents against the old order. If they had the power to do so, the membership of the Democratic National Committee would likely commit the party to a much more aggressive agenda than the one the public now hears from congressional Democrats.

But they do not have the power. The DNC, because it does not attempt to connect with people in any meaningful way, is utterly dependent on the politics of money. The party headquarters is located on the top floor of the Democratic party's building on Ivy Court, a few blocks from the Capitol, but it is not the most important entity in the building. Downstairs are the congressional campaign committees, one for the Senate and one for the House. Both raise far more money and are directly connected to real power—the incumbent members of Congress. Why should a lobbyist dump a lot of money on the national committee, when he can give it straight-out to the people who will decide his issues?

"The congressional party is the only lifeline we've got to money and legitimacy," Mike McCurry explained. "The DNC—the party as a party—does not have an independent base it can rely on. So whatever we do on substantive issues is done with a very close eye to what the reaction of the congressional leadership will be. Because they can shut us down very quickly."[2]

In fact, when DNC Chairman Ron Brown intruded on some issues in a way that was offensive to the Democratic leaders in Congress, he was told, rather harshly, to back off. Brown declared his strong opposition to the Republican proposal for cutting the capital-gains tax—a perfectly orthodox position for the party of working people—and Representative Daniel Rostenkowski, chairman of the House Ways and Means Committee, reacted angrily. Rosty stayed away from the DNC's fund-raising dinner, a nasty signal that communicated his disapproval to every tax lobbyist in town. Brown was, likewise, rebuked by the party's Senate majority leader, Senator George Mitchell, and Senator Bentsen, chairman of the Finance Committee, when the DNC aggressively embraced another idea that might appeal to average voters—cutting the regressive payroll tax for Social Security.

Everyone understands the power relationships: The congressional leaders control access to the money because of their intimate relationships with lobbyists and interests. If the Democratic party began to act like a real political party, the money would be cut off.

"A DNC chairman who gets a little too far out front," McCurry said, "can get slapped around."

When political polls ask voters to describe the Democratic party, the most frequent answer is "the party of average working people." That used to be the overwhelming response, expressed by 50 percent of the electorate, but according to McCurry, this is now an answer given by only 13 percent. Still, it remains the single strongest element in the party's public identity.

The Democrats might more accurately be described now as "the party of Washington lawyers"—lawyers who serve as the connective tissue within the party's upper reaches. They are the party establishment, to the extent anyone is, that has replaced the old networks of state and local political bosses. But these lawyers have no constituencies of their own and, indeed, must answer to no one, other than their clients.

Democratic lawyers who have reached this plateau are mostly veterans of past administrations or old presidential campaigns, though some served as aides to key congressional leaders. They move easily in and out of the various power centers in the Democratic Congress, dispensing political advice on the direction of the party and specific issues and also distributing that important commodity—campaign money. Many major law firms have formed their own political action committees, so that the various strands—party strategy, issues, money—conveniently come together in one location. These lawyers speak, naturally enough, with a mixture of motives—for the good of the party, presumably, but also for the benefit of the clients who are paying them.

Thomas "Lud" Ashley, the former Ohio congressman, speaks of this realm with some contempt, though he functions comfortably within it himself. Ashley served twenty-five years in the House, in the time when local political organizations still had vitality and elected representatives were compelled to listen to them. That system of accountability, he observed, has disappeared and the well-connected law firms have become an unsatisfying substitute.

"Tommy Boggs practically invents a fundraiser for someone and then he invites the member of Congress to attend," Ashley said. "There are half a dozen law firms in town that do that—raise money and lobby. If you ask who is the Democratic party, it's those law firms. Either they go to the members and offer to raise money or the member goes to them and says, 'I'd appreciate it if you will handle my Washington fund raising,' and the collection is all taken care of for the member.

"You put the money out and you collect at the other end. You have access and more than that. Access is really a cowardly word because the legislation is the bottom line. Believe me, the money is not directed at access. It's directed at the bottom line."

Has the party of Jefferson and Jackson been reduced to the political machinations of six Washington law firms? Not quite, but Ashley's point is only modestly exaggerated. When I asked other old hands in Washington to take a stab at naming "the six law firms" who form the establishment of the Democratic party, none of them hesitated or argued with the premise. They had only marginal disagreements about which firms ought to be included.

The ubiquitous Robert Strauss of Akin, Gump, a Texan who was party chairman in the mid-1970s and U.S. trade representative in the Carter administration, was on everyone's list. The news media dubbed him "Mr. Democrat" and often seek his thoughts on party affairs, though Strauss is closer to the Republicans in the White House and to Republican corporate interests than to any bread-and-butter Democratic constituencies. His firm represents everything from Drexel Burnham Lambert to the Motion Picture Association of America, from McDonnell Douglas to AT&T. When George Bush appointed him ambassador to Moscow in 1991, it was widely understood that Strauss would be busy arranging deals for American business to develop markets and resources inside the newly liberated republics.

Others on the list of Democratic influentials would include Tommy Boggs, son of the late House floor leader, and his firm of Patton, Boggs and Blow (Ron Brown, the party chairman, is a lawyer-lobbyist in Patton, Boggs); Harry C. McPherson, Berl Bernhard and Lloyd C. Hand of Verner, Liipfert, law partners who served in government during the Kennedy-Johnson era; J. D. Williams, former Senate aide from the early 1960s, and his firm of Williams and Jensen; Charles T. Manatt, a Californian appointed national chairman by Jimmy Carter, and the Los Angeles–based firm of Manatt, Phelps; Patrick J. O'Connor, a former party treasurer and "money guy" for Hubert Humphrey, and the Minneapolis-based firm of O'Connor and Hannan.

To be less arbitrary, the list could be expanded to include selected influentials from other law firms—Stuart E. Eizenstat, who was Carter's domestic policy advisor, or Joseph A. Califano, Jr., who was Lyndon Johnson's, or Richard Moe, who was Vice-President Walter Mondale's chief of staff, and some others. Older lawyers like Lloyd N. Cutler or Clark Clifford have been influential insiders for so many years that they have acquired the patina of statesmen, although the elderly Clifford looked more like a statesman-fixer, thanks to the BCCI banking scandal.

"Those guys really are the establishment," Mike McCurry said, "and the establishment argument is: Don't rock the boat, stay in the mainstream where everything flows smoothly."

Their accumulating political influence is largely a matter of default— reflecting the decline of other structures within the Democratic party. Stuart Eizenstat, the former Carter aide, explained:

"If you ask me where the power centers are in the party, my answer is there aren't any. They don't exist. There's an utter vacuum of power. The New Deal coalition no longer exists. All that's left are small pieces—a small Jewish piece, the black piece and small intellectual-labor pieces."

Ambidextrous lawyers try to fill the breach. Eizenstat, for instance, lobbies for clients and also works energetically in the role of party advisor. Among others, his Atlanta-based firm, Powell Goldstein, represents high-tech companies, housing developers and the major banks (including Lud Ashley's trade association). Eizenstat sees the political counseling as his conscientious duty to the party, not as a means of enhancing his influence, but the two roles inevitably enhance each other.

"I've spent the last two days calling as many leadership people as I could, advising them on how to handle the budget summit," Eizenstat said. "I do my piece and others do theirs, but it's extremely diffuse. I'm constantly asked privately to come to the Hill and work on things. I worked on [George] Mitchell's maiden speech as majority leader. I worked on [House Speaker Tom] Foley's state of the union response. Dick Gephardt [House majority leader] sends me drafts of his speeches."

While he is on the phone with the key players, Eizenstat sometimes does bring up other matters—the particular political interests of his clients. "I had to make some calls for high-tech clients and get a sense of what impact the budget process will have on them," he said. "I said, as I always do, that I'm calling on behalf of such-and-such client. Then I say: I want to take my lobbyist hat off and say, 'Here's where we ought to stand as a party on this budget situation.' I don't feel any qualms about doing that."

Eizenstat is perhaps more sensitive than most to the potential for conflict, but he does not regard this as a problem for the Democratic party. "I've felt I could take my client hat off at any time and give my unvarnished views," he said. "You'd be hard-pressed to find a relationship between my advice to the Democratic party and my client list."

Eizenstat's client list, nonetheless, does sometimes put him on the opposite side of issues that matter greatly to important Democratic constituencies. When organized labor was pushing for a workers' right-to-know law on toxic chemicals, Eizenstat lobbied for the National Association of Manufacturers (NAM), trying to weaken the measure. "That did raise some hackles with the AFL-CIO," he conceded. "I didn't oppose the bill, I tried to improve the bill."[3]

When Congress enacted the new clean-air legislation aimed at acid rain, Eizenstat represented an Indiana public-utility company, one of the sources of the pollution. The company, Public Service Indiana, liked his work so much that it made him a corporate director. "Now we've got a good one-two punch on the board of directors," a PSI official said, "good Republican clout and great Democratic clout."[4]

When public-interest reform groups urged Democratic senators to stop the White House's secret manipulations of regulations at OMB, Eizenstat lobbied to kill the measure. He represented a business coalition including aerospace, electronics, construction, computers, the NAM and the U.S. Chamber of Commerce. When the largest commercial banks pushed for further financial deregulation, Eizenstat lobbied on their behalf. His firm's banking clients include Chase Manhattan, Citizens & Southern of Atlanta and the Association of Bank Holding Companies, the trade group for the major multinational banks.

Eizenstat's client list is typical of the influential Democratic lawyers, though he is perhaps more punctilious than some others about avoiding the more flagrant intraparty conflicts. It is quite routine for these important Democratic advisors to represent Republican corporate interests on economic issues in opposition to Democratic constituencies. Except for a few labor-union accounts, these lawyers do not speak for the "average working stiff" because they have been hired by his boss.

Tommy Boggs made his reputation as an effective lobbyist in the late 1970s when he persuaded Congress to provide a loan-guarantee bailout for Chrysler, a cause pushed by the United Auto Workers as well as the company. A decade later, Boggs was on the other side—representing Japanese auto imports. The Automobile Import Dealers Association successfully hammered Chrysler and the UAW on trade issues and its Autopac pumped $2.6 million into 1988 congressional races, money that Boggs helped direct to the right places. "We basically pick our customers," Boggs explained, "by taking the first one who comes in the door."[5]

When the United Mine Workers confronted Pittston Coal in its 1988 showdown strike over health benefits, J. D. Williams of Williams and Jensen championed the company side. The Pittston strike was pivotal in the coal industry because the company had walked away from the industrywide contract obligations with the UMW and, if Pittston won, other companies would likely follow. Williams and Jensen, flanked by influential Republican lobbyists, became a clearinghouse for the coal industry, whose ultimate objective was to strip retired coal miners of guaranteed health benefits. Williams and Jensen financed an ostensibly objective study by an independent research institute to attack the soundness of the mine union's pension fund. As J. D. Williams once joked to an audience of fellow lobbyists: "If I get desperate enough, I can usually argue a case on the merits."[6]

When many active party members at the grassroots were campaigning against human-rights abuses in Central America, the Democratic firm of O'Connor and Hannan was doing political public relations for ARENA, the right-wing party implicated in the "death squads" of El Salvador. The firm's lobbying was designed to keep foreign aid flowing to the right-wing government, and it succeeded, despite the murder of six Jesuit priests by the Salvadoran military. Local Democrats on the Minneapolis City Council were sufficiently offended by the connections to cancel the city's legal contract with O'Connor and Hannan.[7]

Bob Strauss, because his firm is so large and diverse, is often in a position where he seems to be counseling both sides in the political debate. As a high-minded statesman, "Mr. Democrat," Strauss played the advocate's role for raising taxes and cutting federal benefit programs and coaxed the two parties to come together for their grand budget summit. But, while Strauss played statesman, his law firm was busy lobbying specific tax issues on behalf of selected industries, from alcoholic beverages to mutual insurance companies. Indeed, while Strauss served on the National Economic Commission, two of his own clients, AT&T and Pepsico, filed comments with the same blue-ribbon group. The law firm dismissed any possibility of conflicting loyalties. "Strauss is clearly doing this as a public servant," his partner, Joel Jankowsky, explained.[8]

On trade issues, the lines of loyalty become particularly tangled. When the Democratic party geared up to enact tough trade legislation, hoping to defend American jobs, influential lobbyists like Strauss were advising the party's leaders on the broad politics of the issue, while their firms simultaneously represented the Japanese manufacturers who stood to lose if the legislation proved to be too tough. Fujitsu, the computer maker, paid Akin, Gump nearly $2 million over three years to assure that it would not be one of the losers.

For that matter, the party's national chairman, Ron Brown, also lobbied the 1988 trade bill on behalf of twenty-one Japanese electronics companies— Hitachi, Mitsubishi, Toshiba and others. As party chairman, Brown has continued as an active member of Tommy Boggs's firm, while insisting he does not personally lobby the government for the firm's clients.[9]

The most notorious episode in which the party's lawyerly establishment ganged up on one of the party's major constituencies involved Frank Lorenzo's campaign to break the labor unions at Eastern Airlines. With a cynical understanding of how Washington works, Lorenzo deployed a virtual galaxy of Democratic influentials as his lawyers and lobbyists, hired to fend off the political counterattacks from the machinists', pilots' and stewardesses' unions. Lorenzo's team included J. D. Williams, Berl Bernhard, Robert Strauss and Tommy Boggs. David Sawyer, campaign consultant to many Democratic candidates, took care of the advertising campaign against the unions. For good measure, Lorenzo hired three former aides of Senator Teddy Kennedy, hoping to influence an important labor ally.

For all that, the Democratic lobbyists did not prevent Democrats in Congress from enacting labor-backed legislation to force Lorenzo into mediation. But the lobbyists won anyway—by persuading the Republican president,

George Bush, to veto the bill. In the end, after Lorenzo racked up $12.7 million in legal bills, his hardball antiunion tactics failed. Eastern Airlines was destroyed and thousands of jobs along with it. The Democratic lawyers and lobbyists had to go to bankruptcy court to collect their fees.[10]

The political clout of the well-connected lawyers is actually strongest on the many public matters where no such visible conflict develops. As Lorenzo's fight demonstrated, they cannot always prevail if they go head-to-head against a fully mobilized constituency like organized labor. But they act like silent watchdogs for various economic interests on a vast range of public issues where citizens are not aroused—insuring that Democratic lawmakers do not intrude on their clients' turf.

If one asks, for instance, why the Democratic party never did anything during the 1980s to confront the various abuses and instabilities unfolding in the financial system, a power analysis of the party establishment might provide the answer. These Democratic lawyers and lobbyists represent many diverse sectors of the economy, but none more comprehensively than banking and finance. The nation's leading banks and brokerages have assembled a formidable team of Democrats to protect them from hostile legislation:

Bob Strauss (Drexel Burnham, Morgan Stanley, Texas S&Ls), Chuck Manatt (California S&Ls, the California Bankers Association, First Bank System), J. D. Williams (First Boston), Richard Moe (Morgan Guaranty), Berl Bernhard (Investment Company Institute, the trade group for the mutual-fund industry), Joe Califano (Bankers Trust, Fannie Mae), Stuart Eizenstat (Chase Manhattan, Association of Bank Holding Companies), Lloyd Cutler (Citibank, Bank Capital Markets Association), O'Connor and Hannan (Merrill Lynch, Paine Webber, Securities Industry Association), Tommy Boggs (American Express, Bear Stearns, Chicago Board Options Exchange, Paine Webber).

Given their client list, one may assume that these party advisors were not counseling the Democratic party to make a political issue of the reckless behavior that characterized Wall Street in the 1980s. They did not urge Democrats to go after Michael Milken's junk bonds and the leveraged buyouts that cannibalized companies or the gutted financial regulations that produced bank failures and taxpayer bailouts or the high interest rates and debt crises that devastated small business, farmers, labor, housing and manufacturing.

One may reasonably assume that, whenever the subject of these financial disorders came up in private political discussions, the lawyers faithfully defended the behavior of their clients and the status quo that proved so costly to the nation. These party counselors would have no incentive to address the financial disorders or even acknowledge that they existed, since their own clients were profitably engaged in exploiting the disorderly conditions. The power to define the outlines of a public problem, as we have seen in other matters, is usually the power to define its solution. The power to keep an issue off the public agenda is just as valuable.

The financial system was further protected by its money, which many of these same lawyers routinely dispense to Democratic campaigns. Anomalous as it may seem, Wall Street is a major source of financing for the party of working people. "Harry Horowitz was Michael Milken's money guy," a congressional staff aide explained, "and, if you started looking in everyone's Rolodex, you'd find Harry's name in every one of them. Because he was the guy you went to when you wanted Drexel's help raising money. The financial industry has this whole infrastructure of money people—and it's the easiest, quickest way to raise $250,000."

"The dependence on Wall Street money really suppresses argument," Mike McCurry explained. "If you have come back from your fifth fund-raising trip of the year, where you schlepped up and down Wall Street with your tin cup, then you listen to these guys making their arguments about the efficiency of financial deregulation and so forth, you begin to say, yeah, they've got a point."

The influential law firms are only part of the money network, of course, but a growing segment. *Legal Times* found that by 1988, 157 law firms had established their own PACs. Common Cause estimated that the Washington lawyers in both parties have spread around nearly $5 million in recent years. More than 70 percent of each major party's contributions now come from corporations, according to Charles R. Babcock of *The Washington Post*.[11]

The most pernicious effect of campaign money is probably not on the legislative roll calls, but in how money works to keep important new ideas off the table—ideas that might find a popular constituency among citizens, but would offend important contributors. Robert Shrum, a campaign consultant to many Democratic candidates, has witnessed many campaign-strategy sessions where new ideas were discreetly buried.

"It costs so much to get elected and re-elected," Shrum said, "that the system inhibits anyone from taking positions that will be too controversial and will make it more difficult to raise money. Do people in a campaign say that directly? No. What they say is: 'What's the responsible position on this issue?' That's a code word for fund raising. Even when it's not consciously used as a code word, that's the effect."

However, the process of giving and getting the money is more casual than many critics imagine and generally not defined by concrete bargains of quid pro quo. A congressional aide described a typical transaction:

In the morning, one of these Democratic bank lobbyists called on the senator's staff to plead the case for repealing federal regulations on commercial banks. Since the senator is a liberal Democrat and, as the lobbyist knew, almost certain to oppose the banks, the conversation was strictly informational and relaxed. In the afternoon, quite by coincidence, the senator's staff tele-phoned the same lobbyist, in the process of trying to raise campaign money for a struggling congressional candidate, an underfunded challenger who was not likely to win.

Though he had no interest in the race, the lobbyist cheerfully agreed to make a contribution and even volunteered to call some other Democratic lobbyists to raise money. It was no big deal, just a bit of back scratching among people with mutual political attachments. The exchange was done, not in return for particular favors, but "for the good of the party."

The popular image of rank bribery misses the supple essence of how political money works. Though explicit bribery does sometimes occur in these transactions, the exchanges are more routinely among friends—not buyers and sellers, but people with shared interests in the long-run political prospects.

The way to understand political money is to think of it as building "re-lationships." Just as the IAF community organizers try to weave new political relationships through personal contact and meetings, the lawyer-lobbyists use their money to nurture their relationships with politicians and party. Nobody is buying anybody—these are old friends. When money passes among friends, they need not ask what it is for. It is for friendship—the bonds of loyalty and trust.

None of these various political transactions poses any questions of legality or even personal ethics for the Democratic lawyers themselves. This is how they make their living; political influence is what they sell to their clients.

The ethical problem belongs to the Democratic party. Relying so inti-mately on Washington lawyers for the party's sense of direction necessarily obscures the grievances of distant constituencies. It blocks awkward questions about large public problems that involve private clients—who is being served and who is being injured?—and leads the party off toward harmless distrac-tions. For disappointed constituents, who are distant and unorganized and unrepresented, the arrangement understandably smells like betrayal from the top down.

Because it operates without a superstructure based on organized people, the Democratic party has ceded another important function of political parties to organized money—the process of developing the big ideas that will form the party's public-policy agenda and campaign strategy. In theory, the two are the same: A political party is supposed to find out what its adherents want as a program for government, then translate those goals and ideas into slogans that will communicate them to the electorate and persuade a majority of voters.

In Democratic circles, the process mostly works backward. Party leaders talk obsessively about how to package the right slogans—the words and phrases that might have won the last election—but they seem awkwardly shy about developing the content of how they would actually govern. The confusion is natural for any party out of power, denied the centralizing focus of the presidency, but for Democrats it is compounded because they still do hold power in Congress—where every splinter of congressional influence clings to its own narrow governing agenda.

Practically speaking, informal exchanges among the party's congressional leaders are often the only time when the party attempts to devise a "national program" of policies and election themes. Even this process is quite random, driven by the need to prepare important speeches or party responses to the Republican president's initiatives. Many voices will be heard in these discussions, from the AFL-CIO to the Black Caucus, but the inner circle of consultants always includes "party elders" like Robert Strauss or Stuart Eizenstat or Richard Moe.

"A set of players always put themselves in play on the words that are going to come out of Tom Foley's mouth," said one party strategist who participates himself. "Eizenstat and Moe and these other guys will show up and you don't know whether it's their clients talking or their intellectual vanity or their own presidential strategic knowledge. They always give the same advice: 'Don't cut defense because you'll look soft on defense.' 'Don't try to do anything big because you'll look like big spenders.' This reflects the limits of their imagination, not crass motives."

The Democratic establishment is understandably burdened by its own past and tends to dwell on what went wrong in the last presidential election. The Republican party has accumulated a thick stratum of experienced managers from winning campaigns for the White House (the late Lee Atwater, the 1988 campaign manager, counted more than twenty-five people in the Bush campaign who had each worked in at least three presidential contests). The Democratic party leadership, meanwhile, is counseled mainly by people who devised strategy for the losers. They worked in the White House when Lyndon Johnson launched the war in Vietnam. They helped Jimmy Carter design his re-election strategy. They were advisors to the disastrous campaigns of 1984 and 1988.

Preoccupied with their old mistakes, they dwell upon the value-laden issues—race, crime, abortion, national defense—that drew millions of Democrats from the ranks of the white working class to the Republican ticket. What they seldom discuss, however, is a coherent economic program and the issues relevant to work, wages and the precarious living standards of ordinary families. New policies in these areas would give disaffected Democrats a real reason to vote Democratic once again, but would also conflict with the interests of the financially powerful important clients.

Beyond the level of these informal conversations, the larger task of policy formulation for the Democratic party is mostly left to others—the private realm of think tanks and sponsored research. Washington is a perpetual stage for self-important conferences and policy bulletins, announcing "new ideas" or exhuming old ones, debating ideological distinctions or proposing new language that might connect with the public's anxieties.

These materials are rich in intellectual argumentation and statistical proofs, but inclined toward an abstract, rhetorical version of politics. They provide the fodder for an enjoyable kind of parlor politics—a running debate that attracts scholars and journalists and some politicians. But the participants tend to view politics pristinely, as an earnest search for correct ideas, not as the fierce struggle for power.

Everyone might be said to have a voice in this dialogue, given the variety of think tanks and front groups. The Children's Defense Fund mobilizes for children. The Economic Policy Institute articulates economic ideas and arguments on behalf of labor. Inevitably, however, the process of policy formulation is dominated by wealth. It requires lots of money, so monied interests naturally can do more of it.

"I call it America's second party system," said political scientist Thomas Ferguson. "All of the thinking about policy that political parties are supposed to do has been off-loaded onto the foundation world. It's very expensive. You have to have a pile of money, you have to be able to maintain it over time. Left-liberal organizations depend on tax-exempt money too, so there's no longer an independent base in the American public for formulating policy ideas."

In theory, as Ferguson pointed out, a political party is supposed to help ordinary citizens overcome these cost-of-entry barriers. The cost of gathering information and developing policies is prohibitively high for most citizens; when the party assumes the responsibility, it spreads the burden among many and thus reduces entry costs for all. American political parties instead delegate the policy process to others, letting them pay for it and, therefore, shape it.

In addition to the established think tanks, most of the "policy commissions" created in recent years to feed new ideas to the Democratic party were invented and manned by figures from the old establishment. The policy papers they produced were predictably unprovocative, reflecting the conservative reflexes of their patrons. Their bland ideas proved to be highly perishable. One of these groups, the Center for National Policy, was run by Kirk O'Donnell, former aide to House Speaker Tip O'Neill, who after the 1988 election left the center to work as a lobbyist in Bob Strauss's law firm. Working for Akin, Gump would be "most exciting," O'Donnell declared with unintended irony, because the law firm's policy agenda "is as broad as the center's."[12]

The lawyer-lobbyist establishment launched a more ambitious effort to redirect the Democratic party when Robert Strauss and others raised corporate money to finance the Democratic Leadership Council, an organization of elected politicians dedicated to returning the party to the "mainstream." The council promoted southern business conservatives like Senators Sam Nunn of Georgia and Charles S. Robb of Virginia as presidential prospects and issued policy papers on what it deemed to be "mainstream" ideas.

The boundaries of the "mainstream" were defined by the DLC's donors from corporate America—ARCO, the American Petroleum Institute, Dow Chemical, Prudential Bache, Georgia Pacific, Martin Marietta and many others. At its 1990 conference in New Orleans, as Paul Taylor reported in *The Washington Post*, the audience was decidedly not enthusiastic when some speakers called for tax cuts for working people, since the majority of the conference audience was composed of corporate lobbyists, many of whom were not even Democrats.[13]

The DLC's main objective, however, was an attack on the Democratic party's core constituencies—labor, schoolteachers, women's rights groups, peace and disarmament activists, the racial minorities and supporters of affirmative action. Its stated goal was to restore the party's appeal to disaffected white males, especially in the South, but the DLC discussions did not focus on the economic decline afflicting those citizens. Instead, it promoted the notion that Democrats must distance themselves from the demands of women or blacks or other aggrieved groups within the party. The Reverend Jesse Jackson and his provocative economic agenda aimed at workers, white and black, was a favorite target of the Democratic Leadership Council and, on Capitol Hill, the DLC was sometimes waggishly referred to as "the white boys' caucus."

Thus, in addition to all its other organizational weaknesses, the Democratic party is divided by nasty ideological combat between the party's Washington elites and its rank-and-file constituencies—the people at the grassroots who are most active in Democratic politics. The establishment's quarrel was with the party's own voters. The people they belittled as "activists" and "interest groups" were the very people who cared most intensely about public issues and who formed the faithful core of the party's electorate, win or lose.

The Democratic establishment did not wish to initiate a dialogue with these citizens, only to make them go away or at least keep their mouths shut. The party elite had no intention of sharing its own policy deliberations with Democrats at large or trying to re-engage people in governing politics by rebuilding the organizational connections that have been lost. The elites wished only to form a governing consensus around the supposed "mainstream"— their mainstream, the one they have already formulated in Washington.

The stubborn and resourceful citizens at the grassroots remain a nettlesome presence in Democratic politics because they do sometimes succeed in disrupting the high-blown policy consensus formed by the elite circles. Because they are real voters and capable of mobilizing other real voters, they can sometimes compel the politicians to address their cause, especially in party primaries when the voter turnout is so weak.

The despised activists are like the organizing cadres of the old politics, except that these new "regulars" operate freelance across the electorate. They are detached themselves, without any formal party structure for debate and compromise, without any way to form relationships of accountability and shared responsibility with those in power.

Their sort of active engagement was once regarded as an asset, the kind of indigenous energy that a functioning political party sought out and nurtured. In the contemporary Democratic party, the "regulars" at the grassroots are regarded as an impediment to governing.

Nothing is likely to change until people decide to change it. This is a truism of democracy, but it has special application to the deterioration of the Democratic party and, ultimately, to the deeper dimensions of decay in the governing processes. If the public's voice has been lost, it cannot be restored without a political party to speak for it. Citizens cannot hope to rediscover their connection to power without exercising the collective power that is available to them through elections.

None of the deeper problems of government described in this book, whatever plausible solutions may exist, are likely to be addressed until this sort of political development occurs. Someone will have to invent a genuine political party that takes active responsibility for its adherents. This is an awesomely large project, of course, for it literally means trying to construct piece by piece, in the fractured modern society, the personal and institutional relationships that might draw people back into the process of democratic governance.

The Democratic party, given the legacy of Jefferson and Jackson, seems a likelier candidate for this sort of renewal. Its advanced state of deterioration makes it vulnerable to change. The Republican party, on the other hand, contains its own reform energies and also has a better intuitive grasp of modern political circumstances. Neither party, however, is going to undertake this regeneration on its own—since democratic renewal would radically threaten all of the existing power relationships in American politics.

To visualize what is required, contrast the hollow organization called the Democratic party with the vibrant and fast-growing political organizations that the Industrial Areas Foundation has fostered in Texas and Brooklyn and Baltimore and many other places. Imagine, for instance, that the Democratic party decided to do for people what the IAF organizations have already succeeded in doing—that is, talk with people face-to-face and listen seriously to what they say about politics.

The political parties spend hundreds of millions of dollars on the empty politics of TV commercials, but nothing on authentic human conversations. Imagine, for instance, if the Democratic party devoted a few million each year to party building from the ground up—talking and listening to real people in their communities, hiring organizers to draw people out of their isolation and into permanent relationships with organizations that would speak for them, that they themselves could steer. Imagine if some of the patience—and the respect for ordinary people—of the IAF's organizations were borrowed by the Democrats.

If a political party started such a dialogue with people in many places, it would no doubt hear the hot discontent of unfiltered public opinion on virtually every subject (including the complaints recounted in this book). This would not exactly be news to elected politicians, since they already collect that information continuously through polling and focus groups and other techniques. But opinion polls and even focus groups are marketing techniques, not conversations. They are designed, not to produce responsive government, but to manipulate voters and harvest enough votes to win elections.

In order to be genuine, a renewed political party would have to start the dialogue with a radically different purpose—taking responsibility for the party's adherents, rather than simply winning elections for the party's candidates. Winning elections and attaining power is essential, of course, to achieving anything for people, but the integrity of a political organization is determined by which of these goals it puts first. As most people understand, the Democratic party (and the Republican party, as we shall see) is now devoted mainly to using people as a means to its own end—winning the elections. Not surprisingly, once people see through this, they do not stick around to become loyal cadres for the long term.

Aggregating the political power of organized people requires an institutional commitment to remaining loyal to them, a commitment they can believe and trust. That would necessitate building a permanent, enduring presence with intimate ties to citizens and communities, not an organization that comes and goes in election seasons. It would require an organization that delivers something real in return for the people's presence.

What would a real party give people? A forum for democratic conversations, a place to say things about public concerns and a place to teach about them, a structure around which political consensus could develop its power. Ultimately, it would also have to promise something larger—a viable channel by which these voices could be carried upward in the structures of power and taken seriously. A political party with these qualities would not have allowed the savings and loan disaster to be evaded, then dumped on the taxpayers. A political party committed to its own adherents would not have stood by silently while elected politicians jimmied the tax code to benefit the few at the expense of the many.

The old party system, of course, was itself far short of genuine democracy, often corrupt or closed to outsiders. But, before its neighborhood cadres were eclipsed by television and big-money politics, they did provide real connections for many people. The party's organizational strength drew upon the permanence of church and neighborhood and union affiliations and other secondary mediating institutions that are now weakened too. Creating a new place for people in politics, one that is truly open to all, is now much harder to accomplish, given the alienation and social distance that have developed.

But no one really knows what might come forth from citizens if a political party set out to create a serious structure for communication and accountability, since neither major party has ever tried it. Judging from the enormous political energies already randomly at work around the nation, the cynics might be surprised by who turns up at the meetings.

Most people, understandably, will not come just to hear more talk. To be real, the party would also have to begin doing real things for people—even the kind of humble services that ward heelers once provided constituents, though these chores would not necessarily involve the usual patronage and street repair issues.

A local political organization might, for instance, undertake the responsibility of overseeing federal law enforcement in its community—assuming the role of permanent watchdog and thereby spreading the costs among many people. Do the federal agencies actually enforce the labor and environmental laws in the community or don't they? If not, why not? It would be most disruptive for a local political party to start asking such questions or showing up at all those regulatory hearings alongside the citizens who are trying to get the government to listen.

Or a local party might become a willing civic agency that volunteers to assist a community with its tangible problems, large or small. Millions of citizens, for example, lack health-insurance coverage for emergencies; the party might arrange pool coverage for those who need it. Labor unions help their young members find bargain rates for mortgages; a political party could do the same. In recent years, the Industrial Areas Foundation's network of community organizations has built four thousand homes across the nation for people who could not previously afford to own one. If that seems trivial compared to the scale of the nation's housing crisis, it is four thousand more homes than the Democratic party has built.

At the Democratic National Committee, Mike McCurry once urged his colleagues to undertake what he calls the "service approach" to politics. He envisioned a national party that would help state and local organizations engage themselves in the most pedestrian civic enterprises—from helping the PTA with its book sale to cleaning up abandoned buildings to working at a car wash for the church remodeling fund. The idea, he said, would be to foster a permanent pool of volunteers called Democrats "so that when people are trying to accomplish something, they would say: Call the Democrats, they always have people."

McCurry's colleagues didn't get it. "Their reaction," he said, "was, 'What would that have to do with winning a campaign? Why should we go out and do bake sales with the Girl Scouts when our problem is getting votes?' If it's not hard-core politics, they're not interested."

The deeper obstacle to reforming the Democratic party from the ground up is that no one who now shares power in the party structure, however marginally, will be in favor of it—not elected senators and representatives who are secure in their seats, not the lawyer-lobbyist establishment in Washington, not major constituencies like organized labor nor even many of the reform groups that surround the party and interact with it.

All of these players have their own discontents and insecurities with the present arrangement, but none has much incentive to seek radical changes. Expecting them to lead the way to democratic renewal is asking them to put their own power at risk, to make themselves accountable to other citizens in new and potentially threatening ways.

Real change, if it comes at all, would likely have to originate with angry outsiders, the citizens who are willing to attack the status quo on its own ground and create an alternative example of how democratic politics ought to function. This makes the challenge even more daunting, of course, because all the usual barriers argue the impossibility of such an undertaking. The history of third parties in American politics, for instance, is that they do not gain power, though they do sometimes create important momentum for new ideas and aspirations. The accumulated protections of incumbent Democrats, from the special-interest money to the campaign laws that favor them, are all formidable barriers to insurgents, whether they attack from inside or outside the party.

The vulnerability of the Democratic party is obvious, however, in terms of the party's own atrophied organizational structure. There are no people left. In many locations, the party organization is tended by a graying cadre of aging loyalists who perform the mechanics and not much else.

The seeds of insurgency are also visible and scattered throughout the party in many places. They are the people who have come into party politics as outsiders—especially women, blacks and Hispanics—and who want the Democratic party to become something more than a mail drop for corporate donations. They are the restless dissidents in organized labor who are fed up with feckless Democrats who take labor's money, then abandon workers on the key economic issues. If the Democratic party regenerates as an organization, it will likely occur because those people have decided to seize control and raise their own concerns to higher visibility.

"In most parts of this country," McCurry said, "anyone who walked in the door with enough people could take it over and do what they wanted. The oldtimers would probably welcome the new blood because they're dying off themselves."

If people undertook such challenges and won control of the county committee, what would they win? Not much of anything, in present terms, since the local and state party organizations have no power either. The only purpose would be to make those organizations into something different—real assemblies of people. Elected Democrats, kept in power by their own political networks, might well react indifferently or hostilely at first. But they would be compelled in time to listen respectfully to a party organization that begins to speak authentically for their own constituents.

Despite the conventional wisdom, my own analysis is that the political status quo is also highly vulnerable to a concerted electoral assault from citizens. The rising popular resentment aimed at all elected incumbents demonstrates the potential for such an effort.

Certainly, many incumbents do feel insecure, despite their comfortable victories in the past. In the 1990 elections, for instance, some senators and representatives who had grossly outspent their opponents by margins as large as eight to one or ten to one found themselves in dangerously close contests, winning by a few thousand votes over unknown opponents.

All politicians, regardless of their ideology or personal competence, understand the same basic thing about power: Losing the election is what matters in politics. Everything else is mood and methodology and fine talk. Any force that threatens politicians with defeat or even raises the percentage of risk can accumulate power.

If not losing the election means raising lots of money in advance, then power flows to the sources of money. If not losing means yielding to the specific demands of a single-issue organization, the gun owners or retirees or antiabortion forces, then those groups will gain some power. If not losing means responding to the agenda proposed by a democratic organization of voting constituents, then most incumbents will try to respond to that too—if not for lofty democratic reasons, then because they do not wish to become former incumbents.

Political power, in other words, flows to the new margins—to the new voters or interests that intrude on the status quo. They may not yet represent a majority but their assembled numbers can force a decisive shift in political behavior if they threaten to disrupt the settled assumptions about what wins or loses an election. This effect is especially true for elections in a representative assembly like Congress, though obviously less so in the broader national contests for the presidency.

In Congress, the power exerted by a relative handful of intruders radiates rather quickly through the entire membership as other politicians calculate the implications for themselves. In my observation, nothing captures the attention of senators and representatives more firmly than the shock of seeing four or five of their colleagues blindsided in an election—defeated by a popular issue no one had anticipated or by an assembly of citizens no one had taken seriously. Typically, regardless of party or political persuasion, the members try to adjust quickly to this new threat, if they can, so that they will not be the next target.

In other words, politicians do respond to the danger posed by newly engaged voters, if only to protect themselves. Conscientious citizens, entering the electoral arena in a purposeful way, would have to pick their shots carefully, but they would not have to organize the entire Republic in order to begin leveraging change in the political system.

The truly difficult part would be to develop focused political objectives that resonate authentically with the army of fed-up citizens—the political ideas that people could call their own and would march behind confidently. In order to accomplish that, citizens would have to get serious about power themselves. Do they really want to be engaged with governing power and take some responsibility for it or don't they?

12

RANCID

POPULISM

The contemporary Republican party seems brilliantly suited to the modern age, for it has perfected the art of maintaining political power in the midst of democratic decay. The party of Lincoln has become the party of mass marketing, applying marketing's elaborate technologies to the task of winning elections. From this, it has fashioned a most improbable marriage of power—a hegemony of monied interests based on the alienation of powerless citizens.

As men of commerce, Republicans naturally understood marketing better than Democrats, and they applied what they knew about selling products to politics with none of the awkward hesitation that inhibited old-style politicians. As a result, voters are now viewed as a passive assembly of "consumers," a mass audience of potential buyers. Research discovers through scientific sampling what it is these consumers know or think and, more important, what they feel, even when they do not know their own "feelings." A campaign strategy is then designed to connect the candidate with these consumer attitudes. Advertising images are created that will elicit positive responses and make the sale.

To understand the basic approach, one has only to watch an evening of television, not the programs but the commercials. There are wondrous things to behold on TV—cars that turn into sleek panthers and stallions, or that take off and fly like jet airplanes. Beers that magically produce jiggling young women in bikinis. Basketball shoes that allow small boys to soar like gazelles. There are patriotic soaps and talking toilets and phallic deodorants. In this dimension of reality, a presidential candidate who is actually a cowboy on horseback seems quite plausible.

The essential transaction in modern marketing is that most products are separated from their intrinsic qualities—since most brands are basically not that different—and imbued with fabulous mythical attributes that attract buyers. Consumers understand (at least most do) that cars will not fly and that underarm deodorants do not increase sexual potency. Still, the advertising's fantasies provide as good a reason as any to choose one brand over another that is just the same.

"Increasingly people buy a product not because of its benefits but because they identify, or strive to identify, with the kind of people they think use it," Karen Olshan, a senior vice-president of BBDO, explained to a business-magazine writer. Paula Drillman, executive director of strategic research at McCann Erickson, emphasized that consumer emotions are a more reliable basis for selling than the "rational benefits" of the product itself.

"Rational benefits are vulnerable," she explained, "because with today's technology it's easy to knock off a competitor's innovation quickly or play on his marketing turf. Emotional bonds, on the other hand, are hard to break."[1]

The same logic has now become the prevailing rule for political competition in the media age. Campaign consultants and managers describe the electoral process in the same dispassionate—and amoral—terms. Elections are for selling, not for governing and certainly not for accountability. The selling depends, not on rational debate or real differences, but on concocting emotional bonds between the candidate and the audience.

"We had only one goal in the campaign and that was to elect George Bush," Lee Atwater, Bush's 1988 campaign manager, told *The New York Times*. "Our campaign was not trying to govern the country."

"Campaigns are not for educating," GOP consultant Douglas Bailey told *The Washington Post*. "They're for linking up with the public mood."[2]

No one gets educated in election seasons—neither voters nor candidates—because provocative new ideas may disrupt the formation of emotional ties. Discussing the actual content of governing issues simply complicates the message. "Pollsters are so good that it is possible to know at every minute what people think," Doug Bailey told a Washington seminar. "No political leader needs to guess at what the people think about any issue and, therefore, there is no need ever to go out and lead."[3]

In this realm, Democrats have had to overcome certain cultural disadvantages. Their political experience originates, for the most part, in old-fashioned organizational settings, labor unions or protest movements or good-government causes. Republican managers came from backgrounds in public relations, advertising and corporate management, all of which are familiar with the contours of advertising messages. Democrat Mike McCurry described his party's handicap: "Our idea of politics is to go out and build coalitions among different groups and so you don't get 'Big Think.' You get 'Big Think' from the corporate culture of mass communications."

Much of what currently passes for strategic planning within the Democratic party is actually a forlorn discussion about how to emulate the Republican party's mass-marketing skills. As Democrats learn to catch up, the content and relevance of election campaigns naturally becomes even less satisfying to those expecting a serious debate about governing agendas. The conduct of contemporary electoral politics is like what would happen if an automobile company decided to fire its engineers and let the advertising guys design the new model. The car they package might sell. It just wouldn't run very well.

The familiar problems that afflict political campaigns and elicit much earnest commentary in the news media—the mushrooming costs and the rise of negative "attack" ads—are actually mass-marketing problems that originate in the domain of commercial advertising. In the last decade, according to *The Wall Street Journal*, the average cost of a thirty-second spot on prime-time television went from $57,900 to $122,000—even though the networks' prime-time audience was shrinking. A major advertiser like Budweiser beer spent three dollars a barrel on its marketing in 1980—and nine dollars a barrel ten years later. This marketing inflation swallows up campaign treasuries too and puts an even higher premium on a candidate's ability to raise money.

Given the soaring costs, every commercial advertiser is haunted by the same question about the TV spots: Is anyone actually getting the message? The American audience is now overwhelmed by random bursts of advertising—300 messages a day for the average consumer, 9,000 a month, 109,500 a year. A TV spot may be shocking or funny or even visually beautiful, but it won't sell anything if the viewer cannot even remember the name of the sponsor. One survey found that 80 percent of viewers could not remember a commercial's content one day after seeing it. Some corporate sponsors are now using encephalograms to measure the brain waves of sample viewers in order to find out which commercials actually agitate the psyche; perhaps brain scans will be the next emerging technology in political campaigns as well.[4]

Politicians face the same dilemma as the beer industry: They are spending more and more money on messages that get weaker and weaker in terms of eliciting a reliable response from voters. That is the primary reason for the proliferation of negative ads in campaigns—the need to be heard, not the declining morals of candidates. Negative attacks are more exciting and, therefore, more memorable to viewers. They deliver provocative information that is more likely to stick in the minds of the audience—the buyer-voter who is besotted each evening with glossy appeals for his loyalty. Politics is merely following the negative trend in commercial advertising, where more and more companies are sponsoring their own "attack ads" on the competing products.

"Given the distaste most voters have for politicians," Democratic consultant Greg Schneider explained, "it is immeasurably easier to make your opponent unacceptable than to make yourself acceptable."

Exhortations to conscience from the press are not likely to reverse this trend. So long as political communication depends so singularly on expensive mass media, the competition for attention will drive the most high-minded candidates to explore the low road—because it promises a more efficient use of scarce advertising dollars. Republican campaign managers seem to understand this better than Democrats, especially during presidential campaigns.

As an organization, the Republican party shares many of the Democrats' problems: a client-based Washington establishment, a very weak party structure and the same preoccupation with political money. Republicans also lack connective tissue—people in communities who are reliably linked to the people in power. Paul Weyrich, a conservative reformer who is president of the Free Congress Research and Education Foundation, remarked: "The difficulty with the Republican party is that in large areas of the country, it doesn't exist."

But the Grand Old Party is more successful than the Democrats at raising political money and at deploying it. "The Republican National Committee has more influence than the Democratic Committee," said lobbyist Chuck Fishman, "because it puts together more money and assistance for campaigns. Industry gets calls. Then Republicans in Congress are invited to the industry dinners. You're getting the money and they're getting your vote and everybody's happy. That doesn't happen at the DNC."

The Republican party is less burdened than Democrats by the ethical implications of these money transactions. After all, it is the party of business enterprise. From Lincoln forward, it has always defended propertied wealth and corporations against the political claims of workers and others, so there is not the same tension of implicit betrayal when Republicans collect huge treasuries from business interests or wealthy individuals and institutions. Indeed, if the Republican party exists mainly to defend and enhance the monied interests, it has been a spectacularly effective political institution in recent years.

The more challenging question about the Republican party is how it manages to accomplish this—since the political results seem to pose a democratic contradiction. It wins national elections, often overwhelmingly, yet it is the party that most faithfully represents the minority, namely wealth holders. The Republican hegemony of the 1980s demonstrably benefited the few over the many—in private incomes and tax burdens, as well as in the distribution of public services. Yet its electoral success was undiminished, at least at the presidential level.

Nor can the contradiction be explained as public ignorance, since the public knows that the GOP is the party of money. In a *New York Times*/CBS survey, conducted in the midst of the 1988 presidential election, 64 percent of the electorate identified the Republican party as the party of the rich. Only 20 percent said it treats all classes equally; only 9 percent described Republicans as the party of the middle class. Furthermore, most people seem to have a roughly accurate sense of what Republican economic policy accomplished during the 1980s. They at least know their own tax burden grew while corporations and the wealthy enjoyed huge tax cuts.[5]

How does the GOP overcome this handicap? The Democratic party helped substantially by retreating from its own position as the party of labor and the "little guy." When there are no dramatic differences of substance between two candidates or two parties, the impact of the fantasy qualities concocted in TV ads grows even stronger. After all, one deodorant is pretty much like any other. The buyer who relies on sexy advertising images to choose his deodorant is not different from a voter who chooses a candidate on the same basis. Since the politicians all sound alike, he may as well vote for the guy with all the American flags.

Republicans have also succeeded through marketing themes that connect powerfully and positively with the deepest national values: patriotism; America's singular sense of itself in the world; our faith in individual work and enterprise; our abundant optimism. This success, however, still does not get at the heart of the explanation.

The party of money wins power in national elections mainly by posing as the party of the disaffected. From its polling and other research data, it concocts a rancid populism that is perfectly attuned to the age of political alienation—a message of antipower. "I think power is evil," said Lee Atwater, the Republican campaign manager who became national party chairman. The basic equation of Republican success, he explained in an interview shortly after the 1988 election, is: "us against them."

"Simply put," Atwater said, "there is constantly a war going on between the two parties for the populist vote. The populist vote is always the swing vote. It's been the swing vote in every election. The Democrats have always got to nail Republicans as the party of the fat cats, in effect, the party of the upper class and privilege. And the Democrats will maintain that they are the party of the little man, the common man. To the extent they're successful, Republicans are unsuccessful."[6]

The term "populism," so abused in modern usage, is now applied routinely to almost any idea or slogan that might actually appeal to ordinary people. In history, the Populists of the late nineteenth century constituted a specific citizens' movement that was rich in democratic promise and far-sighted ideas. Calling themselves the People's party, the farmers of the South and Middle West revolted against both major parties and the emerging dominance of corporate capitalism. They fell short of power themselves, but their far-sighted ideas lived and many were subsequently adopted in government. By that historical standard, there is very little in the trivial sentiments of modern politics that qualifies as genuinely "populist."[7]

When the term is used now, it usually means to convey not ideas, but a political mood—resentment against established power, distrust of major institutions and a sense of powerlessness. In this period of history, it is perhaps not an accident that so many of the effective political managers are southerners. The South understands alienation better than the rest of the nation. Feelings that were once peculiar to a single section of America—the defeated region within the nation—have now taken over the national mood. The winning strategies of modern Republicans owe more to George Wallace than to Barry Goldwater.

Uniting alienated voters into political coalition with the most powerful economic interests has a distinctly old-fashioned flavor of southern demagoguery, since the strategy requires the party to agitate the latent emotional resentments and turn them into marketable political traits. The raw materials for this are drawn from enduring social aggravations—wounds of race, class and religion, even sex.

The other party's candidate is not simply depicted as unworthy of public office, but is connected to alien forces within the society that threaten to overwhelm decent folk—libertine sexual behavior, communists, criminals, people of color demanding more than they deserve. The Republican party, thoroughly modern itself, poses as the bulwark against unsettling modernity. The TV political hucksters, utterly amoral themselves, promise to restore a lost moral order.

None of this is ever said very directly but is communicated superbly in the evocative images of TV commercials—pictures that do not need words. The method might seem overly coy to an earlier generation of racial demagogues, but the meaning does not elude an audience fully experienced at reading symbolic images on TV.

George Bush's "Willie Horton" became the topic at every dinner table in 1988, just as Atwater hoped, and was actually the most interesting event in the long, dreary presidential campaign. Is this an issue of prison furloughs for convicted murderers or is it really about black men raping white women? Two years later Senator Jesse Helms won re-election in North Carolina with a devastating commercial called "White Hands"—white hands replaced by black hands. Is this an argument about affirmative-action "quotas" or is it really about white people who resent uppity black people? No one can ever settle these arguments, any more than one can prove that the Budweiser commercials exploit adolescent sexual craving to sell beer.

These Republican messages build bridges across class lines. They give people who are not themselves well-to-do and do not share the economic interests of traditional Republicans a reason to join the party of money. The Republican party cannot win without them, as it well knows, so it must assemble a set of ideas that will attract millions of voters from the lower middle stratum of the economy—disaffected Democrats with conservative social and religious values—who are persuaded to see their old party as "them" and the GOP as "us."

The millions of Democrats drawn to the Republican ticket in the 1980s "are always looking for a reason to come home," Atwater explained. "If they could maintain that, well, you know, finally here's a Democrat, not a lot of difference between him and Bush, they could say: We get to vote Democratic again. So we felt like, if we didn't get out and draw the differences, we'd lose." The differences between Michael Dukakis and George Bush were the hot images constructed for the 1988 campaign—the "Harvard-boutique liberal" who was soft on Willie Horton and didn't even believe in the Pledge of Allegiance.

Race is only one of the bridges, though surely the most powerful. A generation ago, the alien force threatening American values was communism, and the GOP, led by Senator Joseph McCarthy, sought to expose the "traitors" lurking within the society—mostly, it seemed, within the Democratic party. In the turmoil of the 1960s, the bridge was expanded to include drugs and crime and the disturbances of cultural change. In the 1980s, all those themes endured and Democrats were portrayed, not simply as wrongheaded opponents, but as enemies of the American way of life.

"Now we have a way of dividing America," Representative Newt Gingrich of Georgia, the House Republican whip, told *The Washington Post*. He was referring to the "value-laden" issues of crime, drugs, education and corruption, which he attributed to the failures of Democratic liberals. "These people are sick," he told *The Wall Street Journal*. "They are destructive of the values we believe in."[8]

The basic problem with the Republican electoral strategy is that it does not have much to do with governing, especially at the federal level. American politics has always been rich in demagogic diversions and empty appeals to nativist emotions; both parties share that history. The modern Republican hegemony, however, is most striking in the divergence it fosters between elections and governing.

Millions of voters are persuaded to cross the bridge, but they do not get much in return on the other side. Once in power, the Republican government

serves the traditional Republican economic interests. The aggravations of
modernity, meanwhile, persist. The fears of crime and race and decaying
moral values do not abate. They merely accumulate for exploitation in the next
election.

Much of what agitates the disaffected voters is either beyond the reach of
the national government or contrary to the Republican purposes. The president, it is true, may introduce a "crime bill" or announce a "war on drugs"
or criticize a new civil rights measure designed to protect racial minorities. But
the governing responses to these public anxieties are mostly symbolic, like the
TV ads that stimulated the emotional connections in the first place. Politics
speaks to these social concerns endlessly, but it cannot deliver much that
would actually change things without intervening profoundly in the private
social fabric—which the Republican government has no intention of doing.

To act seriously would mean provoking a serious opposition among other
party constituencies—especially the young people who are voting Republican
in impressive numbers but have libertarian views on the social issues. Pornography cannot be banished without a change in the meaning of the First
Amendment; abortion cannot be fully prohibited without an amendment to the
Constitution. The first "war on drugs" was launched by Richard Nixon in the
early 1970s and lasted for several years; it petered out when law-enforcement
officers started arresting the children of prominent Republicans.

The Republican hegemony, therefore, depends upon a more subtle form of
betrayal. The party's method deliberately coaxes emotional responses from
people—teases their anxieties over values they hold important in their own
lives—but then walks away from the anger and proceeds to govern on its real
agenda, defending the upper-class interests of wealth and corporate power.
Government, as we have observed, is assumed to be rational and expert; the
raw emotions of people are unscientific and distrusted.

The Republican government, aside from empty gestures, has no serious
interest in resolving the anger it has aroused. After all, popular anger is the
political commodity that it uses, again and again. Everyone in Washington
understands this, Democrats and Republicans alike, and there is a professional
admiration for the way in which Republicans ignite bonfires of public passion,
then coolly walk away from them, without repercussions. George Bush ran
against the "Harvard-boutique liberals," then appointed Harvard people to six
Cabinet-level positions, plus many other second-rung government jobs. No
one really minds. Everyone knows it was just a slogan.

The reason the Republicans succeed at this may be that cynical citizens do
not expect much more from politics. Certainly, most voters who took the bait
do not express great surprise when a succession of Republican governments
fails to deliver meaningful responses to their discontent. Voters, as savvy TV
viewers, are perhaps wise enough to understand that the pictures that aroused

their emotions have no real connection with governing decisions, that nothing much will actually happen in Washington to deal with their fears or anger.

Possibly, people are entertained by Republican politics in the same way they are entertained by the mythological qualities that emanate from the commercial advertising. If all politicians are alike, corrupt and unreliable, you might as well vote for the one who got the patriotic music right, the one who at least talked about *your* anger, *your* fears.

People know elections, like television commercials, are not real. All that the campaign images provide them is an imagined moment of aroused feeling—a transient emotional bond with those who will hold power, a chance to identify with certain idealized qualities, but not an opportunity to connect with real governing power. If manipulated voters do not feel cheated, it is because the Republican party gives them a chance, as the perfume commercial says, to "share the fantasy."

"Ralph Nader and I rode on the same airplane recently and we talked at length and we agree about everything," said Paul Weyrich, a leading figure among the social conservatives in the Republican coalition. "Nader and I have the same contempt for officeholders and the process by which both parties get together and screw the public. Unlike most Washington-based people, we are in constant touch with the grassroots. Nader and I spend about half of our time on the road and, as a result, we know what the little guys are thinking.

"Both Nader's base of support and mine, though ideologically different, are the lower middle class. The difference is their perception of who's responsible for the mess. Nader's people would tend to blame big business and corporations. My people would tend to blame government and maybe labor unions. My view is they're all to blame."

Paul Weyrich, a conservative Catholic from Wisconsin, is one of those who helped build the bridges that led millions of working-class Democrats into the Republican party, and he now recognizes their growing sense of disenchantment. As founder of the Free Congress Foundation in the early 1970s, Weyrich mobilized both Catholics in northern cities and southern Protestants, evangelicals and fundamentalists, around conservative social issues—abortion, pornography, family and others.

"My father fired a boiler, shoveled coal in a Catholic hospital," Weyrich said. "He was a German immigrant. My relatives worked in foundries in Racine. I understand these people, I know the language they can understand. They felt invaded by societal forces—liberal forces, future shock. They felt threatened and threatened enough to become active and to switch parties."

The "populist" swing vote has been critical to the Republican hegemony. Lance Tarrance, a GOP pollster from Houston, studied the Republican electorates in the 1984 and 1988 presidential elections and described their ideological and social components: 67 percent were establishment conservatives with orthodox probusiness views, 26 percent populist, 7 percent libertarian.

But the Republican coalition is under strain from two sources: the disenchantment sown by nearly two decades of unfulfilled rhetoric on the social issues and the glaring divide of economic interests. Weyrich, among others on the right, thinks it is vulnerable to breakup.

"The country-club Republicans can't win without these people," Weyrich said, "but now, all of a sudden, the party is reverting to its old ways and they're heading for a real disaster, believe me. I just spoke to thirty-five clergy in San Diego and, boy, were they tough on the Republican party. 'They just use us. They trot us out every four years for presidential elections, but they don't include us in government. Well, if that's the way it is, we will take a walk.'

"You have the country-clubbers re-emerging to take over the party and to produce candidates who don't relate to working-class conservatives. This is much more than a single issue like abortion. It's really a class issue. . . . George Bush has been decent to me, but the party operatives in the states look upon Bush's victory as a restoration of the pre-Reagan Republican party. These are the very people who gave Republicans the name of the 'rich man's party' and go around babbling about capital gains and stuff like that. They make cultural conservatives feel unwanted."

Having exploited the antiabortion movement for fifteen years, Republican strategists began backing away from it in 1989 when they discovered that the electoral benefits of the issue were abruptly reversed. Once the new conservative majority on the Supreme Court actually threatened to recriminalize abortion (and Republican gubernatorial candidates in New Jersey and Virginia were torn up by the issue), the GOP rhetoric changed. The party that had for a decade imposed the antiabortion litmus test on both its candidates and all new federal judges suddenly announced that it was now a "big tent"—open to diverse views on the subject. Having teased racial resentments in 1988 with Willie Horton, George Bush ended up signing the new civil rights bill in 1991. The religious right, already weakened by internal problems, began to feel orphaned.

While the social issues evoke the strongest emotions, the unnatural nature of the Republican coalition is exposed most clearly on the economic questions of government. In the abstract, the social conservatives have the same ideological disposition toward unfettered business enterprise and smaller government that is espoused by orthodox Republicans. In the practical terms of their own class interests, however, these voters are often on the opposite side from the Republican orthodoxy.

They distrust big business more than government. Tarrance found, for instance, that 85 percent of the populist voters in the Republican presidential electorate supported the labor-backed measure on plant closings—a notification law that Democrats enacted over White House and business opposition. Among the Republican populists, 56 percent said they want more government loans for college students, not fewer. Paul Weyrich's legions come from more or less the same precincts in America as Lois Gibbs's grassroots environmentalists and they too are the victims of the unenforced federal laws on industrial safety or toxic pollution.

Notwithstanding their populist phrasemaking, most conservatives in Congress faithfully vote for the business position on these divisive issues and others. Republican politicians, for instance, talk endlessly about their devotion to protecting the family (and sometimes even describe Democrats as antifamily), but most of them voted against family rights and for corporate rights when the choice came down to that. The parental leave measure that Democrats pushed for working mothers and fathers was vetoed by Bush as an excessive intrusion on management practices; the profamily conservatives (including Paul Weyrich) limply went along with the business argument.

The deeper split in Republican ranks is about money. "Republicans didn't just suppress the conflict, they camouflaged it," political analyst Kevin Phillips said. "One of the great successes of Reaganomics was selling these things like tax cutting under a populist flag, as if everyone would benefit."

The character of Ronald Reagan—particularly his videogenic skills—was important in obscuring the corporate power in the GOP. "Reagan was critical," Weyrich said. "He did not strike social conservatives as being owned by those big business people. Reagan was 50 percent different from the old Republican party, he had elements of populism. Democrats never attacked Reagan on that. If I were them, I would have said, 'This guy may have come from a small town, but remember who owns him—General Electric and all that.'"

Democrats, if they had the will, could still break up the Republican coalition, Weyrich believes, by defining a stark opposition to Republican economics—in particular, on the trade issue and foreign competition, the continuing loss of American jobs and spreading foreign ownership of American real estate and companies. "Democrats can sound macho if they attack on that issue because it makes them sound like nationalists, but they don't seem to have it in them," Weyrich said.

The Democrats' reluctance is not simply a matter of will, of course, but of corporate political influence. In that regard, the Democratic elites and the Republican elites look very much alike. But the Republican party elites—lawyers, lobbyists, corporate managements, fundraisers—are even closer to the multinational corporations and foreign interests than the Democrats.

For that matter, social conservatives have themselves been quite timid about confronting the economic questions that matter greatly to their own people. Cultural conservatives have published various essays on the "social

function of property'' and endorsed the idea of increased health and safety
regulation, but the leaders have not directly challenged the corporate agenda
or its dominance of the Republican party.[9]

A profamily politics that is unwilling to challenge corporate politics is
never going to amount to much, since business practices and prerogatives
define so many elemental realities in everyday family life. The social conservatives have defined a cramped box for themselves: They are a faction that
cares intensely about sex, religion and family (domains that government will
always be loath to regulate), but they are unable to speak to the issues of
wages, working conditions and job security (family matters on which the
government does have the power to make a difference).

A conservative profamily critique of business, as Weyrich acknowledged,
is also partly inhibited by money—the funds that flow to right-wing organizations from corporate contributors. Notwithstanding its role as "populist'.'
spokesman, Weyrich's organization, for instance, has received grants from
Amoco, General Motors, Chase Manhattan Bank and right-wing foundations
like Olin and Bradley. Even the righteous voices of the right are constrained
by financial dependency.

"We have to coexist with these people [the Republican fundraisers] because if they put out the word that you're not reliable, your contributors will
go away," Weyrich said. "If those guys say Weyrich is a lunatic, they can cut
off a portion of your funds."

When Lee Atwater was dying in 1991, he undertook a self-accounting and
delivered a remarkable public report. "I committed myself to the Golden
Rule," he wrote in *Life* magazine, ". . . and that meant coming to terms with
some less than virtuous acts in my life." Atwater apologized to old adversaries, including Michael Dukakis, whom he had injured with his harshly negative style of politics. He expressed gratitude to old enemies, including the
Reverend Jesse Jackson, for the human comfort they extended in his hour of
crisis.

Atwater's most touching regret, however, was about the spirit of the
Republican era he had worked to create. "My illness helped me to see that
what was missing in society is what was missing in me: a little heart, a little
brotherhood," he wrote. "The '80s were about acquiring—acquiring wealth,
power, prestige. I know. I acquired more wealth, power and prestige than
most. But you can acquire all you want and still feel empty. . . .

"It took a deadly illness to put me eye to eye with that truth, but it is a
truth that the country, caught up in its ruthless ambitions and moral decay, can
learn on my dime. I don't know who will lead us through the '90s, but they
must be made to speak to this spiritual vacuum at the heart of American
society, this tumor of the soul."[10]

Vague misgivings about what the Republican hegemony has wrought were already spreading through circles of party activists before Atwater stated them so poignantly. Kevin Phillips produced a devastating delineation of who won and who lost from Republican economics in *The Politics of Rich and Poor*, a book that made the facts too clear to be easily denied.

The consequences of Republican rule seemed to be provoking a mild sense of guilt in the ruling party. The Heritage Foundation, source of so many right-wing legislative ideas, began to express an interest in designing social programs that might actually help people. Jack Kemp, former congressman and now HUD secretary, announced his department would conduct its own "war on poverty." Policy staffers at the White House took up an old New Left theme from the 1960s—"empowerment"—and promoted it as the new slogan of thinking conservatives. Empowerment for whom? For the people!

These Republican expressions of solicitude for the losers were touching in their cwn way, for they suggested a remarkable innocence about their own party and how it works. Despite a decade of contradictory evidence, many Republicans still liked to think of themselves as a party of ideas and ideology—the place where robust intellectual debate among conscientious conservatives hammered out the program for governing.

Their egotistical presumption was that, now that the Republican party had completed the main business of straightening out the American economy, it would generously turn its attention to mopping up the casualties. From the evidence of the 1980s, this faith in conservative ideas is most naive. While the Reagan era celebrated conservatism and wore its maxims like political armor, the way the GOP actually governed suggested a quite different understanding of what motivates the party.

The Republican party is not a party of conservative ideology. It is a party of conservative clients. Wherever possible, the ideology will be invoked as justification for taking care of the clients' needs. When the two are in conflict, the conservative principles are discarded and the clients are served.

The most fundamental ideological contradiction of the era was the extraordinary explosion of federal deficits and debt during the Reagan years and continuing under George Bush. Nothing else conflicts more profoundly with conservative beliefs about government, for the GOP was always the party of balanced budgets and fiscal responsibility (and indeed still limply claimed the mantle). Yet, twelve years after coming to power under Reagan, the supposedly conservative government produced an annual federal deficit of $390 billion.

When all of the fanciful economic argumentation is stripped away, the enormous deficits were provoked by the regressive tax cuts for business and wealthy individuals and by the rapid buildup in defense spending. Both of these actions served important clients in the Republican hierarchy, the defense industry and the wealth holders, and served them well.

Conservative anguish about the deficits was never sufficient to produce the painful action of actually reducing them, for that would have required the Republican White House to sacrifice its own clients. A third alternative—cutting Social Security and domestic social programs—was more appealing to Republicans, but Democrats were defending those clients and, as budget director David Stockman learned to his sorrow, Republicans were never very serious about this possibility anyway. "I have a new theory," Stockman declared bitterly in 1981. "There are no real conservatives in Congress."[11]

Conservative ideology opposes federal regulation of private enterprise, and the Reagan era advanced the cause of deregulation on many fronts—mostly by making irregular deals with specific industries that amounted to de facto decisions not to enforce the law. Nevertheless, in case after case, when industries pleaded for new federal regulation as a way of preempting meddlesome state governments, the conservative government swung around to the other side and decided in favor of federal regulation.

The true loyalties of the Republican regime were demonstrated most vividly in the continuing series of financial crises. When the small farm banks in the Midwest began to fail in greater numbers in the early 1980s, the Republican administrators articulated a laissez-faire response: Let the marketplace work its will, however painful. But when Continental Illinois, eighth-largest bank in the nation, failed in 1984, the same Republicans agreed that this bank was "too big to fail," and they came to its rescue with a multi-billion-dollar bailout. Subsequently, in case after case, the largest banks in Texas, Massachusetts, Washington, D.C., and elsewhere were saved from failure and their largest depositors were protected from loss, while smaller institutions were allowed to disappear.

When some of the largest commercial banks in the nation (fine old Republican names like Chase Manhattan and Citibank) were threatened with insolvency, George Bush's White House urged federal bank regulators to bend the rules, and its domestic agenda was preoccupied with enhancing the profitability of banks. When the big money is in trouble, the Republican party finds itself acting like a compassionate liberal.

The Republican governance, in sum, could not be described as conservative in any historical sense of the word. Taken all together, the Republican policies more nearly resembled a right-wing version of the New Deal—intervening massively on behalf of worthy clients. In practical affairs, the government functioned according to principles that were closer to the liberal government of Franklin Roosevelt than to conservative creeds espoused by Robert A. Taft or Barry Goldwater. The difference with FDR's New Deal was, of course, fundamental: The modern Republicans intervened, not on behalf of struggling labor unions or distressed sharecroppers or the destitute elderly, but in order to assist the most powerful enterprises in the economy.

To understand the Republican party (or the Democratic party, for that matter), it is most efficient to look directly at the clients—or as political scientist Thomas Ferguson would call them, "the major investors." On that level, the ideological contradictions are unimportant. Political parties do function as mediating institutions, only not for voters.

Ferguson, a University of Massachusetts professor, analyzes political parties by identifying the major sources of their financing—the individuals from finance and industry who naturally have the greatest stake in influencing government decisions. "The real market for political parties," Ferguson says, "is defined by major investors, who generally have good and clear reasons for investing to control the state. . . . Blocs of major investors define the core of political parties and are responsible for most of the signals the party sends to the electorate."[12]

Thus, in terms of governance, the most meaningful (and interesting) action of American politics is the continuing flow of rivalries and agreements among the contending power blocs in the private economy, not the shifting allegiances among groups of voters.

The Reagan-Bush governance, in Ferguson's portraiture, has been a running contest between two blocs of business interests with very different objectives in government policy. The "protectionists" are centered in old industries, textiles and steel for instance, that are traditionally Republican and anxious for help in the domestic markets. The "multinationals" are manufacturers and bankers as well as exporters, high-tech firms, oil companies, defense manufacturers—all interested in an aggressive global policy.

The list alone makes it clear which group has more girth and political power, but the Republican regime attempted to serve both blocs, when there was no irreconcilable conflict between them. "In effect," Ferguson wrote, "the Reagan economic coalition always had a huge seam running down its middle . . . the 'Reagan Revolution' was a giant banner under which two columns marched in different directions."[13]

For the Republican old guard in heavy industry, the party in power mainly provided temporary relief from long-standing aggravations—relief from imports, from organized labor, from government regulation and, of course, from federal taxes. The severe recession of the early Reagan years was devastating to manufacturing, but it also smashed labor unions and provided the opportunity for corporate restructurings, free of restraints from the workers. By 1985, the Reagan administration focused its diplomatic energies on driving down the dollar's foreign-exchange rate and, thus, launched an export boom for the domestic manufacturers—just in time for the 1988 election.

For the multinationals, from Boeing and Citibank to Exxon and General Electric, the political goals were much more substantial and even historic—maintaining America's role as manager (and occasionally enforcer) in the emerging global trading system anchored also in Japan and Germany. Dating from the New Deal era, multinational corporations and investment banks had once been aligned with the Democratic party, then the party of free trade. In Ferguson's telling, American politics got interesting in the 1970s when the multinationals shifted their allegiance to the GOP.

They have been well served by the new alliance. The U.S. buildup of armaments, which they had promoted, would be a significant token of leadership resolve to the competitor nations who were also allies (as well as an abundant source of contracts for the defense companies). The multinational financial institutions, banks and brokerages, benefited enormously from the rising dollar—and even from the accumulating deficits—because both produced expanded financial activity as the bankers recycled U.S. debt to Japanese lenders. The Third World debt crisis, though it threatened the overexposed banks, became an opportunity for the U.S. government to beat down the resistance in the developing countries to American ownership and deregulated economies.

While the Republican government extended trade protection to some of the old-line industrial sectors, its main energies were devoted to the multinationals—defending and extending their prerogatives in the global trading system. The close working relationships the Reagan and Bush administrations formed with Japan and Germany were integral to this objective—their governments wanted much the same outcome. But the U.S. strategy gradually turned into dependency, as America's financial position weakened and the nation became indebted to its economic competitors.

Quite apart from the economic injury done to individual classes of citizens, Republican governing—by and for the "major investors"—has not led to the general prosperity and economic stability described in the conservative rhetoric. On the contrary, while each influential sector gets what it wants, the economy overall has sunk deeper into debt and failures, dependency and competitive disadvantage.

In other words, what Lowi called "interest-group liberalism" has been transformed by Republicans into what might be called "interest-group conservatism." From labor law to financial regulation, conservatives use the governmental forms invented by liberal reformers to serve their own client interests. Liberals have difficulty coming to grips with this since the economic interventions on behalf of selected sectors or enterprises are consistent with their own governing philosophy.

The deleterious effects are visible for the nation as a whole. The short-run demands of elite interests do not add up to a workable scheme for governing the economy on behalf of the nation's long-term well-being. The powerful win their narrow victories; the country loses. So long as this system is the core of how the government decides the most important questions, ordinary citizens will find ample justification for their discontent.

Organized money versus organized people—the only way to break out of this governing system is, again, to imagine a democratic renewal that brings people back into the contest. Thomas Ferguson, though quite pessimistic about the prospects, described the outlines of the solution:

"To effectively control governments, ordinary voters require strong channels that directly facilitate mass deliberation and expression. That is, they must have available to them a resilient network of 'secondary' organizations capable of spreading costs and concentrating small contributions from several individuals to act politically, as well as an open system of formally organized political parties.

"Both the parties and the secondary organizations need to be 'independent,' i.e., themselves dominated by investor-voters (instead of, for example, donors of revokable outside funds). Entry barriers for both secondary organizations and political parties must be low, and the technology of political campaigning (e.g., cost of newspaper space, pamphlets, etc.) must be inexpensive in terms of the annual income of the average voter. Such conditions result in high information flows to the grassroots, engender lively debate and create conditions that make political deliberation and action part of everyday life."

Those "conditions" for effective citizen control of government are what is missing from both political parties and from American democracy. So long as citizens remain unorganized, they will be prey to clever manipulation by mass marketing. So long as people must rely on empty TV images for their connection to politics, then, as Ferguson concluded, nothing can "prevent a tiny minority of the population—major investors—from dominating the political system."

13

ANGLE OF VISION

If the political parties were real and functioned reliably on behalf of people, then the news media would matter much less in politics. But the distinctive quality of our contemporary political landscape, as everyone recognizes, is the rising influence of the press and television as principal gatekeepers for the dialogues of political debate. What matters to the press matters perforce to politicians. What the press ignores, the politicians may safely ignore too. What the newspapers tell people, whether it is true or false or cockeyed, is what everyone else must react to, since alternative channels of political information are now weak or nonexistent for most Americans.

The power of the press is another source of popular discontent, since these private corporate organizations seem to have an unchecked influence over the direction of public affairs. The glare of media can wrench politics this way or that, from trivial distractions to important exposés, but politicians and many citizens resent the arbitrariness of the choices. Who elected the reporters and editors? Why should they be able to set the political agenda according to their own peculiar tastes and interests?

That familiar complaint is not the heart of the matter, however. The press has always served American democracy as an important and controversial mediating voice for citizens, a corrective mechanism that both speaks to power and sometimes checks its abuses. What may really distress citizens in contemporary politics is that, for all the clamor of the news, the mechanism is not functioning, at least not for people distant from power.

Like the other primary political institutions, the press has lost viable connections to its own readers and grown more distant from them. Because of this, it speaks less reliably on their behalf. As an institution, the media have gravitated toward elite interests and converged with those powerful few who already dominate politics. People sense this about the news, even if they are unable to describe how it happened or why they feel so alienated from the newspapers that purport to speak for them.

This chapter sets out to explain the deeper economic and social forces that caused this to happen. The story is a kind of illustrated tour of how the rich, contentious variety of the free press has been transformed into a voice of dull sameness, a voice that speaks in narrow alignment with the governing authorities more often than it does in popular opposition. In its own way, the press has also failed its responsibility to democracy.

The city room of the *Cincinnati Post*, where I worked as a young reporter a generation ago, was a comfortably chaotic place, with the desks jammed together in clusters and stacked with piles of old newspapers. In some ways, it resembled an industrial space more than a business office, for pneumatic tubes and piping were exposed overhead and the wooden floors were swept and wet-mopped like a shop floor. People worked in shirtsleeves and the large windows along one wall were always open in summer since the building was not air-conditioned. The *Post*'s composing room was adjacent to the editorial department, a few steps away through an open portal, and the heat and hot-metal fumes from the printers' typecasting machinery sometimes drifted into the newsroom.

The reporters were mostly Irish, German Catholic or Jewish, Cincinnati's leading ethnic groups, with names like Halloran, Rawe, Hirtl, Feldman and Segal. There were also a few "country boys" from across the river in Kentucky. These reporters affected the wisecracking irreverence expected in newspapering (and a few were closet alcoholics), but most were churchgoing, family men.

They were smart and resourceful in their work and their quickness was regularly tested by the newspaper's relentless deadlines—eight editions each day, starting early in the morning and running until the "stocks/racing final" in late afternoon. A fire department bell in the corner sounded the fire alarms for the entire city and someone on the city desk would count the bells to determine the location.

Few of these reporters (or their editors, for that matter) had been to college; it was unnecessary for newspaper work in those days. They typically started as "copy boys" and relied on their own wit and common sense to become "journeymen." They also knew quite a lot about Cincinnati, Ohio. Most had grown up there and some remained in the neighborhoods and parishes of their childhood. There was no social distance between the newsroom employees and the *Post*'s printers and pressmen—they were all working class. Some printers and reporters drank together or went to the same churches. Some reporters and editors had cousins or brothers working in the back shop.

Two decades later, I was working in a very different newsroom on a much larger newspaper in a more important city. This city room was furnished with endless carpeting and sleek lines of color-coded desks, potted plants and glass-box offices, climate-controlled air and computers. The newsroom at *The Washington Post* might have passed for an insurance office or the trading room of a Wall Street brokerage. But it was different, above all, because it was staffed with a different class of people. The reporters and editors at *The Washington Post*, with few exceptions, were college graduates and many (like myself) had graduated from the most prestigious Ivy League universities— Harvard, Yale and even Princeton. Some held graduate degrees in law, economics or journalism.

Reporters at *The Washington Post* spoke—and could report and write— with a worldly sophistication that would have benumbed (and probably intimidated) the old hands I had known briefly at the *Cincinnati Post*. These educated reporters were "smarter," but only in the sense of knowing many more things about the world, more "serious" only in that chasing fires was no longer what mattered to newspapers. In culture and incomes, *The Washington Post* reporters were securely middle class and above, well read and well paid. They did not know any of the printers or pressmen who worked downstairs, much less socialize with them. Some had only the dimmest notion of how their own newspaper was produced each night.

The contrast I am making between these two experiences provides a metaphor for what happened generally to the press over the last thirty years. In the broad sweep of the last generation, educated young "journalists" displaced the quick-witted working-class kids who had merely been "reporters." A trade that had once been easily accessible to the talented people who lacked social status or higher education was converted into a profession. This did not happen only at top-rank newspapers like *The Washington Post*, but generally throughout the news media, even at the smallest small-town dailies. Journalism became a credentialed discipline that spawned its own educational system and categories of specialization and, eventually, its own celebrity.

What happened in newspaper city rooms—the upward mobility that transferred the work from one class to another—was not so different from what happened in some other fields over the last several decades, except that the political implications are more profound. The press is a commercial enterprise, but its function is integral to the political life of every community and, ultimately, to the nation's politics.

As a young reporter, without knowing it at the time, I was glimpsing the end of something important in American public life and the beginning of a broad social transformation, in which I would be a minor participant. Because I was personally involved, readers will recognize that it is especially difficult for me to be objective on the subject of the media. But I am describing the outlines of the transformation, not to indulge nostalgia for my own youthful experiences, but to try to explain what it is about the modern media that so regularly disappoints citizens—and to get at why the press, for all of its accumulated sophistication, falls short in its own responsibility to democracy.

The truth is that the *Cincinnati Post* of the 1950s was not a very good newspaper, especially by latter-day standards. In my youthful enthusiasm, I would have strenuously denied this at the time; I worked there two summers during college as a "vacation replacement" (before the loftier term, "intern," had been invented) and was enthralled by the place. As a newspaper, nonetheless, the *Post* was parochial and shallow, with a short attention span and a charming randomness in its coverage. Its front page was dominated by the "breaking news" of violent crimes or large calamities—industrial fires and plane crashes. It specialized in stories of impish surprise—little bits of human comedy that had no larger purpose than to startle or amuse or warm the heart. Except for war and major earthquakes, it did not care greatly about the rest of the world.

The *Post* was imbued with an uncritical hometown pride and obsessed with establishing a "local angle" to the news, however tenuous. When the *Andrea Doria* sank in the Atlantic Ocean in 1956, an enterprising rewrite man managed to interview several of the rescued survivors by ship-to-shore telephone (an amazing feat of technology, we thought then). Since these people were Cincinnatians, the *Post*'s banner headline smugly proclaimed that the sinking of the *Andrea Doria* was actually a Queen City story.

For all its shortcomings, the *Cincinnati Post* had one great redeeming quality. Like its reporters, the newspaper was frankly and relentlessly "of the people" and it practiced a journalism of honest indignation on behalf of their political grievances. Some of these were pedestrian complaints and some were quite shocking abuses of public office. But there was never any doubt in the tone and style of the *Cincinnati Post* that it meant to speak for a certain segment of Cincinnatians—mainly those who did not have much status or power themselves. When the *Post* took up their cause on some matter, it would hammer on it day after day, story after story, until someone in authority responded.

This focus came naturally to the Scripps-Howard newspaper chain. Along with Hearst, Pulitzer and a few others, E. W. Scripps had invented the format for the working people's newspaper at the turn of the century. The "penny press" was cheap and sensational but also served as an implacable civic troublemaker. The Scripps-Howard lighthouse insignia still proclaims a resonant credo for democracy: "Give light and the people will find their own way."

In Cincinnati, the *Post*'s daring investigative reporting early in the century broke up the old Republican machine. The newspaper has championed reforms of municipal government that endure. In a town that is naturally conservative and Republican, the *Post* was liberal-labor and mildly Democratic, though it mainly saw itself as a reform-minded watchdog. When one reporter nervily asked the managing editor about his own party affiliation, he replied: "I'm a Democrat when the Republicans are in and a Republican when the Democrats are in."

Like other institutions of that era, the newspaper reflected the sensibilities and biases of its audience. The *Post* spoke up for civil rights long before racial equality became a national cause, but there were no black reporters in the city room and there was not much coverage of the black community either. Women were mostly confined to the women's pages or took the role of "sob sister," writing syrupy prose about the bleeding-heart side of the news. The newspaper was seldom critical of the police because the reporters and photographers were very close to the police. It wasn't just that the cops fixed their parking tickets: In the larger scheme of things, policemen were on the same side as the reporters. They were working class too and some of the cops were relatives.

The *Cincinnati Post*'s various qualities made an especially strong impression on me, I suppose, because I came to its city room from the other side of town—the comfortable Republican suburbs of managers and professionals—where families invariably read the *Times-Star,* the Taft family newspaper, which was reliably Republican and conservative in its perspective. During my summers at the *Post,* I was given a brisk, egalitarian education in social reality—the human dimensions of a city that I hardly knew existed. Where I grew up, labor unions were the dull-witted behemoths who were destroying the American economy; now I was working among engaging, clever union people who routinely volunteered as generous instructors in their craft. As readers may infer, the *Cincinnati Post* taught me things as deep and lasting as what I learned during the school year at a prestigious eastern university.

As the city room's most junior reporter (still called a "cub" in that day), I was frequently sent out on the nastiest, least desirable assignments—bloody accidents or second-rate homicides—and, for the first time, I saw the grimmer precincts of the Queen City, white and black. My political education involved not only encountering the fetid slums and poverty, but also coming to terms with the passivity and powerlessness among the people who lived there. I was sent out to do stories on obscure neighborhoods with no other purpose than to demonstrate that the *Post* cared about them.

In other words, the *Cincinnati Post*, like many other similar newspapers in other cities, deliberately cast itself as a representative voice. In imperfect fashion, it functioned as an important strand in the community's web of political accountability, alongside political parties, unions and civic associations. It unabashedly identified with the people who were least likely to be heard on public issues and those citizens were invited to identify with it.

Most of those working people's newspapers are gone now, eliminated by the forces of a shrinking marketplace. The daily newspapers that were closed during the last thirty years were mostly afternoon papers, the ones tailored to blue-collar folks who went to work too early in the morning to read an A.M. newspaper. The afternoon papers that remain, like the *Cincinnati Post* and many other Scripps-Howard and Hearst papers, are mostly bland shadows of their former selves, shrinking and struggling. A once robust political voice has been reduced to a grumpily conservative sigh of resentment.

What was lost was the singular angle of vision. Newspapers do still take up for the underdog, of course, and investigate public abuses, but very few surviving papers will consciously assume a working-class voice and political perspective (the *Philadelphia Daily News* is an outstanding exception). The newspapers that have endured and flourished, often as monopolies, were mostly morning papers and they moved further upscale, both in their readership and in their content, responding to the demographics of the market. Their reporters all went to college.

It wasn't the college kids, of course, who did in the old newspapers but the revolution in communications technology, led by the brilliant glow of television, which decimated the loyalty of their readers. The revolution isn't over yet. Daily newspapers of every size and kind continue to struggle with the erosion of their audiences and many will continue to fail.

The consolidation of newspapers promoted blandness and social distance. As the shrinkage eliminated the peculiar and distinctive voices, the remaining papers naturally tried to incorporate abandoned readers into their own circulations. Cities that once read staunch Republican and Democratic newspapers and perhaps one or two others are now confined to one or two papers that politely try to speak for everyone.

Trying to hold the mass audience's loyalty, newspaper editors have retreated from identifying with any single part of their readership—especially the lower classes where reader attrition is greatest. This strategy has not been especially successful in halting their decline. But newspapers have adopted an angle of vision that presumes an idyllic class-free community—a city where everyone has more or less the same point of view on things.

The working people who made up the audience for old newspapers like the

Cincinnati Post—who felt represented by them—disappeared into the mass audience. Their own presence in the community (and in politics) became less distinct (and less powerful). Some argue conveniently that economic progress and social change simply eliminated the working-class perspective, even among union members. These people, it is supposed, all moved to the suburbs and became middle class and even Republican.

Many of them, it is true, did move to the suburbs, and the social forces that eroded the solidarity of labor unions or urban political machines also undercut the loyalties of newspaper readers. But, in stark economic terms, this class of citizens still exists, though socially fragmented. Their political grievances have not changed; their injuries, as we have seen, have grown larger. Yet they are now less visible to others and underrepresented in the public debate. Roughly speaking, they are the same people whom I have described at various places in this book as the politically orphaned.

If Hearst and E. W. Scripps invented the old newspaper format that is dying out, it is only slight exaggeration to suggest that Benjamin C. Bradlee, executive editor of *The Washington Post*, invented the new format that succeeded them. Other editors and other newspapers, of course, also found innovative ways to connect with the changing newspaper audience, but none more brilliantly and successfully than Bradlee at the *Post*. As it happened, I was also working in that city room when the most interesting changes occurred.

Television had stolen not only immediacy from newspapers but also the hot emotional content of the news. Newspaper reporters might still write melodramatic "sob sister" prose intended to evoke the pathos of violin music (I wrote many such stories myself), but nothing in print was ever going to match the TV camera's close-up of the grieving widow or the "film at eleven" of burning factories and dead bodies. Heartbreak and violence now belonged to video; the newspapers would have to find something else to sell.

Editors like Bradlee (and publishers like the *Post*'s Katharine Graham) perceived that the future belonged to quality—depth and national scope and intelligence—combined with provocative new forms of surprise. While many other papers were trimming back in the 1960s to cope with shrinking readership, *The Washington Post* went aggressively the other way, expanding and deepening its editorial staff, adding new categories of specialists and talented generalists. Publishers who made the same strategic choice—the Knight-Ridder newspapers, for example—generally survived the shrinkage and flourished.

The changing economics of newspaper audiences was a perfect fit with the coincident rise of the credentialed journalists. The first wave of the new generation, of which I was a part, was more escapist than political—well-educated, middle-class young people who were, somewhat irresponsibly, attracted to the fun of newspapers. At least that was my impression. Many of us were trying to elude the predictability of our own upbringing—the grayness of law school or business careers—and we escaped it in the luxurious variety and informality of newspaper life. In the conformity of the 1950s, the city room seemed a small retreat where minor eccentricities were still tolerated. A reporter would be poorly paid but, as I used to joke, you did not have to wear a hat or carry a briefcase.

Not so many years later, we realized with bemusement that we were now very well paid anyway—upwardly mobile in spite of ourselves—and some reporters even started carrying briefcases (though no one by then was wearing hats). The subsequent waves of well-educated young people coming into journalism seemed more purposeful and serious than we had been, even vaguely political in their intentions. By then, the unschooled Irish kids were mostly gone from newsrooms and bright, young graduates, even from the Ivy League, gravitated to careers in the news media. It seemed the place where one could "make a difference," as the more earnest ones explained.

By their nature, most of these new journalists were more liberal than those they had displaced, at least in social outlook. Certainly, they were more cosmopolitan and less religious, more tolerant of the unfamiliar and experimental. But they were not necessarily more skeptical of power than the reporters I had known in Cincinnati. They were probably more comfortable dealing with people in authority, given their own backgrounds, but not necessarily more critical. Nor were the new reporters necessarily more liberal on the bedrock economic questions of work and incomes than the working-class reporters they had replaced. Like most people, for better or worse, they innocently reflected the sensibilities and biases of their own origins.

This exchange of classes is reflected, inevitably, in the content of the news, and I have always thought it is a central element feeding the collective public resentment that surrounds the news media. People sense the difference, even if they cannot identify it. Conservative critics usually call it a "liberal bias" in the press, but I think it may be more accurately understood as social distance. The new reporters know much more about many things, but many of them do not grasp the social reality those old hands in Cincinnati understood.

Under Bradlee, *The Washington Post* succeeded simultaneously on two levels. It became celebrated and influential for its elite status as the provocative newspaper of the nation's capital. But the *Post* prospered in commercial terms because it also connected with its local audience more effectively than any other major newspaper. The *Post*'s daily circulation reaches 51 percent of the metropolitan area's households (70 percent on Sunday). If that does not sound very impressive, it is the highest penetration rate in the country among major metropolitan dailies. In part, this success is a function of the city's demographics: The Washington area has not only the highest average income in the country,

but also the highest level of educational attainment (even so, the *Post*'s penetration rate has also declined slightly, despite its virtual monopoly).

The *Post*'s strategy for developing loyal readers is as low-brow as the
huge quantity of comics it prints every morning and as urbane as the newspaper's Pulitzer Prize–winning dance critic. In effect, everyone gets something somewhere in the sprawling newspaper, something that will keep him or
her coming back. This balancing act is complicated by geography: The *Post*'s
readership area includes not just the predominantly black District of Columbia, but affluent suburbs in two states, Maryland and Virginia. On any given
day, white Virginia suburbanites grumble that the *Post* is preoccupied with
blacks in the inner city, while black people in D.C. neighborhoods complain
that their communities are ignored. The *Post* searches constantly for the center
ground, but there is no center that can bridge the deeper racial and economic
conflicts.

As a result, the newspaper never gets too close to anyone beyond the elite
circles connected to the federal government. This distance is reflected in many
dimensions, but most clearly in the sociological tone and perspective of the
reporting. When *The Washington Post* examines a matter of community distress, overcrowded prisons, drug violence or suburban overdevelopment, it
deploys impressive resources and its method of pursuit will be thorough and
cool. In college, its reporters studied sociology, political science and economics, and they are comfortable with academic techniques of inquiry.

The one thing they cannot do is express the honest outrage of a situation.
They cannot speak in a human voice that is identifiably "of the people" whom
they are writing about. With so many disparate audiences to serve, they are
implicitly prohibited from embracing anyone's complaint as their own. They
are very strong on digging out the facts, but weak on the intangible dimensions
of the human comedy. The *Post*'s angle of vision, reflected in its language and
style, resembles a hip social-science professor's—a fast-moving kind of pop
sociology that seems to look downward on its subject matter.

The distancing techniques that dull local coverage apply in a quite different way to the *Post*'s celebrated existence as a "national" newspaper. In the
1950s and before, the *Post* had been a predictably faithful tribune of the liberal
Democratic establishment and its causes (and a rather shoddy newspaper in
other respects). Starting in the mid-1960s, Bradlee instilled an educated sense
of irreverence toward power—an impish, occasionally reckless disregard for
the political establishment and its expectation of what properly belonged in the
capital's morning newspaper. Bradlee reinvented surprise, in a playfully sophisticated form.

The surprise became part of each morning's expectation: What rules of
news might the *Post* violate next? What powerful institution would it offend?
The paper could not match the authority of *The New York Times* or the

thoroughness of its coverage, but it could win attention by occasionally breaking eggs—cocking a thumb at some sacrosanct institution like the FBI director or the CIA, tweaking fraudulent celebrities or exposing the shadowy power brokers of Washington politics.

While the *Post* never abandoned the traditional formats of news and news writing, it regularly ignored them. The dull, repetitious voice of "objectivity" gave way occasionally to the evocative and reflective. The narrow agenda of orthodox news stories was frequently interrupted by stories of imaginative insight that cut across familiar subjects in deeper, more original ways. Power was examined, needled and sometimes accused with the brash authority claimed by the paper's well-educated reporters.

Bradlee's own personal chemistry was the primary inspiration, but it would have been out of character for him to articulate any grand principles. By birth and education, Bradlee held inherited status among the most prestigious elites. He was a Harvard classics major and a close friend of President John F. Kennedy. Yet, for whatever reason, he was also viscerally contemptuous of high-born pretensions and poseurs of official privilege. He talked, not like the son of a New England Brahmin, but in the blunt, profane language that had always been the masculine voice of the newsroom.

In that sense, Bradlee's approach—at least his crude delight in provoking self-important figures—kept alive the earthy skepticism of the old working-class city room. It also helped, of course, that during this period the nation itself was in turmoil—alive with political and cultural rebellion against the status quo. New voices of dissent were clamoring to be heard and the *Post* opened its pages to them.

For reporters, Bradlee's city room was an exhilarating (and occasionally harrowing) place to work, highly competitive and opportunistic, without many clear boundaries on what might be acceptable except the ancient rules of newspapers: Get it first, get it right. A French business sociologist who studied the place concluded that Bradlee's management technique was to encourage an "entrepreneurial mode of action," full of risk and adventure, the possibility of glory and also shame. The *Post*'s city room functioned, Jean G. Padioleau wrote, "closer to a free-jazz orchestra than to a military band." That is how I remember it too.[1]

The results were necessarily uneven, fluctuating between the silly and the profound, but the overall effect was a newspaper as exciting, in its own way, as a five-alarm fire. In time, we assumed, the brilliant qualities would drive out the embarrassing ones and the result would be a free-standing newspaper that was both more meaningful to readers and critically inquiring of the powerful. Some of us—the educated journalists—earnestly imagined that Bradlee, in his casual manner, was reinventing the meaning of "news."

The apogee of invention was, of course, Watergate, the scandal in which a newspaper brought down a president. The two young reporters, Bob Woodward and Carl Bernstein, perfectly reflected Bradlee's own contradictory sensibilities—the coarse, nervy side and the intellectual sophistication—and they acted out the combination brilliantly in their own reporting. Indeed, Woodward and Bernstein even embodied the two newspapering traditions: One was a Yale graduate from Republican suburbia, the other came from a labor family and started his career as a "copy boy."

Watergate, in addition to its other meanings, became a statement about political power: a thunder-and-lightning announcement that the news media had claimed a new place among the governing elites. The *Post*'s Watergate triumph (and Bradlee's other innovations) spawned a thousand imitators and changed political relationships everywhere. Watergate also, ironically, became the high-water mark for Bradlee's provocative form of newspapering—the beginning of the *Post*'s retreat to a safer tradition.

Institutions of every kind inevitably mature and level off, especially after bursts of invention and growth, and that was part of what happened to *The Washington Post*, a natural settling down after the excitement. But the Watergate episode accelerated the process because it conferred greater authority on the *Post*—people took it much more seriously after Watergate—and the newspaper responded, somewhat uneasily, to this new responsibility by taking itself more seriously.

The extreme highs and lows were gradually modulated. The engaging unpredictability of its front page gave way, in time, to a more earnest and orthodox catalogue of news stories, resembling the authoritative gradations that were made each day by the front page of *The New York Times*. The newspaper gradually became better managed and inevitably more bureaucratic—more thorough and deliberate in its coverage of important news, but also less adventurous and independent, less surprising and less profound.

After Watergate, the *Post*'s newly established political influence also came under intense attack from other power centers. Though the *Post* had never been as liberal as its reputation, especially on its editorial pages, a concerted campaign of propaganda and criticism was mounted from the right and corporate interests, portraying the newspaper and its reporters as the nerve center for left-wing manipulation of politics. The *Post,* it was said, was on the side of social unrest and disorder. Competing elements among the governing elites found opportunities to pay back the newspaper for past injuries.

In effect, *The Washington Post* became the most visible symbol of the media's new political power and the logical target for complaints about the arrogance and recklessness of unaccountable reporters. Starting with Spiro Agnew, the theme became a staple in politics, as politicians learned how to tap into public resentment of press and television. Since everyone sensed the media's new power, everyone enjoyed the role reversal.

The propaganda attacks alone might not have made much impact on the *Post*'s self-confidence—Bradlee, after all, lived for controversy—but a series of events seemed to confirm the thrust of the criticism. One was a tendentious multi-million-dollar libel suit brought by the president of Mobil Oil, who lost in the end but managed to damage the newspaper's name in the process—and force it to spend millions in legal bills. The prosperous *Washington Post* could shrug off that kind of expense, but the message to editors at large was intimidating: If you mess with major corporations and their executives, it may cost you millions of dollars, even when your facts are right.

A second event hit closer to home and was much more embarrassing to the *Post*—the discovery that one of its reporters had won the Pulitzer Prize based on a story that was totally fabricated. The episode could plausibly be traced to the "entrepreneurial mode of action" that Bradlee had fostered in the newsroom or, as outsiders said, to the *Post*'s hubris. In any case, the incident led to internal reform and stronger management controls over the news.

One other event pushed the *Post* further toward caution—the demise of its local competition. When the *Washington Star* folded in 1981, the *Post* became a virtual monopoly as a commercial venture. This is a commonplace occurrence in the newspaper business, but it was especially unsettling in the nation's capital. Like business monopolies in any other sector, a newspaper's monopoly both reduces the need for aggressiveness and increases the premium on agreeability. Any business that sits securely astride its marketplace, unthreatened by competitors, will naturally take fewer risks. A responsible newspaper, aware that there are no other voices to counter and contradict its own version of the truth, will usually lower its own voice.[2]

That is what happened to *The Washington Post* and, indeed, what has occurred generally through the press as more papers closed across the country. On many days now, the "free-jazz orchestra" sounds more like a "military band" that plays "ruffles and flourishes" to important personages and events. The newspaper's distinctiveness has waned. Its insightful forays and provocative examinations of governing institutions are quite rare. As a powerful institution, the *Post* became "responsible."

In effect, it made peace with power—the rival elites in both government and business. Both of those realms are occasionally still stirred to anger by something the newspaper does, but the *Post* has become a much more reliable partner in the governing constellation. Its reporters routinely defer to authority by accepting the official versions of what is true instead of always making trouble. If the government reports that financial disorders are a manageable problem, reporters do not question the assertion. If the government reports the economy is recovering smartly from recession and bankruptcies, that claim becomes the headline.

In the longer view of things, the pattern of consolidation and retreat at *The*

Washington Post is visible throughout the media and for roughly similar reasons. A monopoly enterprise typically uses its political clout, not to challenge authority, but to protect its monopoly. That is how the newspaper industry behaves as it faces the continuing erosion of readership and new competition for advertising revenue from high-tech alternatives. The press uses its political influence to maintain protective barriers. Its political alignments are compatible with its upscale readers and well-educated staff, but also with its own economic priorities.

The Washington Post's preeminent status is beyond challenge. The *Post* is a well-made and very profitable newspaper, rich in content for every segment of its audience. It prospers and exerts its political influence in conventional ways, not very different from other elite newspapers in other times. Ben Bradlee's inventive city room, which had seemed to promise something different, looked in hindsight like a brief, splendid aberration.

When a newly elected member of Congress comes to town, the first thing he or she discovers is that being a member of Congress is no big deal in Washington. There are 435 of them, plus 100 senators, and many will come and go without ever seeing their picture or their opinions in the major media that matter to the nation's capital. The ambitious ones quickly grasp that the power of the press is the power to make them visible in the crowd.

In the higher realms of politics, the media act as gatekeepers for the political debate. To some extent, this prerogative has always belonged to the press, but its power has been greatly magnified by the shrinkage of competing outlets, the modern mode of information-driven politics and the decline of other mediating voices. Everyone in politics turns to the press, if only to manipulate it or deflect it.

In this milieu, even second-string reporters and editors cannot escape feeling powerful because they are constantly approached, beseeched, inundated with appeals for their attention. The most conscientious reporters cannot possibly digest all of the story ideas and information dumped on them, much less write about them. So they are stuck with the burden of choosing.

In theory, this still ought to produce a rich diversity. Even after newspaper consolidation, there is still a multiplicity of potential outlets for ideas and opinions, both in press and in broadcasting. There is little diversity, however, among the most influential media, many of which rely on the same tired experts for analyses. The range of debate on foreign policy, for instance, often seems bounded by Henry Kissinger and Robert McNamara, two ostensibly divided "elder statesmen" who largely agree with each other on the big questions of war and peace. The cranky edge of dissent is missing.

A media watchdog group called FAIR analyzed the guest lists of authoritative figures invited to appear on ABC's *Nightline* and PBS's *MacNeil/*

Lehrer NewsHour and found the circle largely confined to white males of the credentialed establishment. Even supposed critics were usually drawn from within the safe bounds of elite opinion. A similar study of most newspaper editorial pages—or of the sources on whom most reporters rely—would likely produce similar results.[3]

In general, this is because the major media incline themselves toward power—the people and institutions that already hold power or at least seem to be connected to it. The media mainly rely on their judgment of what is important and relevant. Redundancy is much safer than throwing things open to a wild diversity of facts and opinions; it enhances the media's own standing within governing circles and protects them from disfavor.

The sponsored research at Washington think tanks has become a principal source for the ideas that reporters judge to be newsworthy and for the packaged opinions from "experts" that reporters dutifully quote on every current subject. David Ignatius, former editor of "Outlook," *The Washington Post*'s Sunday opinion section, wrote: "It often seems that these large and well-endowed organizations exist for the sole purpose of providing articles for opinion sections and op-ed pages." That, of course, is precisely why they exist.

"I will confess here to a dangerous vice," the *Post* editor declared. "I like think tanks, and mainly for one simple reason: their members know how to play the game, that is, they know how to be provocative, they can write quickly under deadline pressure and they don't mind being heavily edited." Ignatius mentioned as his favorite sources of opinion the Center for Strategic and International Studies, the Carnegie Endowment for International Peace, the Brookings Institution, the Heritage Foundation, the American Enterprise Institute. Except for Carnegie, all of these organizations are financed by major banks and corporations as their self-interested and tax-deductible contribution to the democratic debate.[4]

The influence of the think tanks is quite profound. Over time, they have shaped the very language and thought patterns of the media. "Special interests," a term that used to refer to concentrated economic power, utilities or railroads, the steel industry or banking, now refers to schoolteachers, women, racial minorities, homosexuals and similar groups. Frequent commentaries are devoted to describing the privileged position of those groups in American politics.

The sponsored scholars also connect comfortably with the reporters' own intellectual framework—the ostensible rationality and objectivity of disinterested statistics and abstract argumentation. The press reports everything from electoral politics to environmental protection in the garb of objective academic inquiry. The stories of real people, while often told in compelling detail, are treated as interesting "anecdotes" rather than hard evidence of political failure. When they wish to know what the public thinks, the media usually turn to opinion polling, a measuring device that is also distancing because it reduces public opinion to an impersonal commodity. When the results are in, various influentials are invited to debate what the polling statistics mean.

Modern organizational patterns have made the media less accountable to anyone. A reporter's accountability, to the extent it exists, is largely to his or her professional peers and employer, but also to the authorities who are the sources of news. Within that narrow framework, there is an intense and continuous competition to win the regard of one's rivals and one's sources. The goal is to be first in a very refined sense—to discover the new facts or ideas that will be the leading edge of changing opinion among the elite groups, to see the new "political trend" just before it becomes conventional wisdom. This competition is largely invisible and meaningless to the audience, but is a central motivation among Washington news people, for it gives them a palpable sense of their own power.

Being first confers a rewarding sense of influencing larger events. Being wrong threatens one's standing in the prestige circle. The news contest, thus, inhibits and ultimately limits diversity, because taking risks means accepting the likelihood of sometimes being different and sometimes being wrong. In the Washington milieu, a self-respecting reporter wishes to be first occasionally, but never to be alone for very long.

This reflex guarantees that most reporters (and editors) are always bunched closely together, searching for glory in small, incremental victories. It also explains why certain ideas and subjects suddenly become "hot" and sweep through the media—cover stories, special features, a blizzard of comment from the columnists—then disappear, as the conventional wisdom moves on to the next fashionable topic. Former Senator Eugene McCarthy once likened the Washington press to blackbirds on a telephone wire: One flies, they all fly.

As many citizens suspect, the Washington press operates in an incestuous climate that puts it much closer to power than to its audience—the numb, gray mass of people who are represented mainly through opinion polls. Given the celebrity that now attaches to some journalists, many justifiably regard themselves as social peers of the powerful figures whom they cover. The social intercourse, they will explain, is really work, an opportunity to learn valuable tidbits, but it is also quite flattering. The old hands I knew at the *Cincinnati Post* a generation ago would have been dumbfounded by the suggestion that they ought to have an after-hours drink with the mayor. The mayor would have been shocked too.

In Washington, symbiotic social relations are the routine, both formally and informally. Burt Solomon of the *National Journal* observed the coziness emanating from reporters and politicians at the annual banquet of the White House Correspondents Association and wrote afterward: "By evening's end, it wasn't clear whether Bush & Co. and the press considered themselves natural adversaries, who were pretending to be friends, or comrades in governing, who occasionally affected to be foes."[5]

Thomas L. Friedman, the *New York Times* correspondent who covers the State Department, played doubles with the secretary of state in Oman. Brit Hume, who covers the White House for ABC, played tennis with the president. Rita Beamish of the Associated Press jogged with him. The president and his wife stopped by a media dinner party at the home of Albert R. Hunt, bureau chief of *The Wall Street Journal*, and his wife, Judy Woodruff of *The MacNeil/Lehrer NewsHour*. Hunt videotaped the scene of his children greeting the chief executive at their doorway.

Andrea Mitchell, who covers Congress for NBC, is often seen in the presidential box at the Kennedy Center because she is—in the news gossip's euphemism—the "constant companion" of Alan Greenspan, chairman of the Federal Reserve Board. That is, she lives with him. At a Washington cocktail party, Mitchell got into a spat with White House budget director Richard Darman because it appeared that Darman was lobbying the NBC reporter in order to influence her mate, the Federal Reserve chairman. Mitchell rebuffed the budget director's attention. "If you want to send a signal," she snapped, "I suggest you pick up the phone and make a call."[6]

The media's sense of shared purpose with the political elites was formally expressed in 1989 when leading Washington reporters collaborated with prominent politicians in creating the Washington Center for Politics and Journalism. The founding members included Republican and Democratic party chairmen, prominent senators, representatives and professional campaign consultants— who were joined by "media heavies" from CBS, ABC, NBC, *Time* and *Newsweek*, *The Wall Street Journal*, *The Washington Post*, the *Chicago Tribune*, *The Boston Globe* and others. The purpose of the center is to educate young journalists on how to cover politics—thus replicating the incestuous perspectives that have helped to empty politics of its meaning.

Collaboration is not what the public wants from the news media. Barry Sussman, a public-opinion-polling consultant and the *Washington Post* editor who supervised Woodward and Bernstein during the Watergate affair, lamented the press's proximity to power in his book, *What Americans Really Think*. He cited a *Los Angeles Times* survey that found 67 percent of the public thinks the press doesn't do enough to keep the government honest. "Instead of seeing the major media as out to get the political establishment," Sussman reported, "most people, when asked, say that reporting on public figures is too soft and that the media are in bed with the leadership in Washington."[7]

In the early 1980s, the Gannett newspapers invented a bright new format for newspapering called *USA Today*, a paper composed of vivid pictures and graphics and short, easily digestible stories, all consciously designed to connect with the minds of television viewers. Though *USA Today* was a money loser as a commercial venture, other newspapers copied from it freely, searching nervously for the look that might reverse their own declining readership.

In many ways, *USA Today* was simply reviving the tone and folksy technique from that earlier era of newspapering—news with a human voice, stories about simple personal concerns, a newspaper imbued with civic pride and everyday cheerfulness. The new version also captured some of the mindlessness of the old "penny press." *USA Today* has a foreign editor but no foreign correspondents.

What was missing, however, was the singular political voice. Stories in *USA Today* speak of America in the optimistic "we" and are strong on national celebration—but nearly silent on authentic outrage. The newspaper, not unlike television, evokes a mythical nation that has a single, homogenized viewpoint, and the paper shies away from the difficult stories that would disrupt this sunny vision. As a political representative, *USA Today* is not just neutral but stripped of any awareness of class or economic conflicts. It is as if the cadaver of the old working-class newspaper had been exhumed from the grave and brought back to life, its cheeks rouged with gorgeous color photos—then lobotomized.

Newspapers everywhere will continue to experiment with the news—usually by degrading its quality in this manner—because they are continuing to lose the loyalty of their readers, especially among the young and less educated. None has yet found the magic talisman to secure their future and the long-term outlook is bleak. Newspapers are not going to disappear as a form of communication but they are likely to become far less important to the general public. Newspaper audiences will be confined more and more to elite readers with special tastes and attitudes and political opinions. As that occurs, the press's impact on democracy will likely become even more distorted.

There is one experiment that newspaper editors are unwilling to undertake—to take responsibility for their own readers. That is, to speak frankly in their behalf, to educate them as citizens, to create a space for them in the political debate and draw them into it. Many editors and reporters earnestly presume that they are already doing this or at least some of it. The erosion of democracy is the stark proof of their failure.[8]

From time to time, newspapers bemoan the ignorance of the general public—citizens who do not know the name of their own senator or hold grossly mistaken impressions about government—but newspapers would never blame themselves for the ignorance and inertia of their readers. The decline of voting and elections is the subject for regular sermonizing in the press, but newspapers would never accept that their own performance as mediating voices is perhaps implicated in the decay. Notwithstanding the usual civic bromides, newspapers, like other political institutions, run away from their own failure to communicate what matters to citizens, in a timely context that citizens might understand and act upon. How can the news industry congratulate itself with its annual prizes when, all around it, democracy is failing?

The suggestion that a newspaper ought to accept its own responsibility to democracy would be a radical proposition in any newsroom. Newspapers have learned to stand aloof from such questions, in order to protect their pretensions of objectivity. A newspaper that took responsibility for its own readers would assume some of the burden for what they know and understand (and what they don't know and understand). It would undertake to reconnect them with political power and to invent forms of accountability between citizens and those in power that people could use and believe in.

A newspaper trying to represent its readers would have to make some hard choices about what it believes to be true, about what it thinks is truly important in daily life and in political action. Among other things, it would start by recognizing that politics is anchored in government, not in campaigns. The politics of governing decisions, where citizens are weakest, is what matters most to people, not the partisan sweepstakes of winning or losing elections.

A responsible newspaper would try to bring people back into that governing arena or at least to warn them in a timely manner when they are about to be abused by it. A responsible newspaper would learn how to teach and listen and agitate. It would invent new formats that provide a tangible context in which people can understand power and also speak to it.

The media's failures, illustrated across many issues throughout this book, are rooted in this refusal to take responsibility. To cite an easy example, *The Washington Post*, if it chose, has the power to eliminate the exploitation of black and Hispanic janitors in the nation's capital (described in Chapter Eight) simply by focusing public outrage on their low wages and economic helplessness. To do so, the newspaper would have to confront prominent business and political interests in the capital (and also set aside its own hostility toward labor unions) on behalf of the exploited citizens. Such a crusade would be utterly out of character for the *Post* and for most American newspapers.

To cite a more complex example, the *Post* (or any other well-endowed newspaper) might take responsibility in a long-term and consistent way for focusing on the culture of lawlessness in the federal government—the permissiveness in regulatory law fostered by the capital's political commerce. If it were coherent, this attention could have enormous impact on the government, but it would also put the newspaper in conflict with the city's powerful sector of lawyers, lobbyists and corporate interests.

Or a responsible newspaper might grasp the great divide of political activity described in this book—irregular citizen politics versus the formal structure of government—and seek ways to redress the imbalance between the two.

People have fled from electoral politics and, one way or another, are trying to do politics out in the streets. The press at least might report on this other kind of politics with more respect and consistency.

No newspaper by itself can be expected to overcome the fundamental realities of power, not even *The Washington Post*, but a responsible newspaper would understand that all citizens are not equal in American politics. Some of them need help—both information and representation—in order to function as citizens in democracy.

Any editor or publisher will feel threatened by this proposition, but so will most reporters. To take responsibility would mean to rethink nearly everything they do, the presumptions of autonomy that protect them from criticism and the self-esteem that is based on prestigious feedback from elites. Reporters would have to reexamine their own methods for defining the content of news as well as their reliance on those in power. Editors would have to experiment and perhaps throw out some of the inherited rules for producing news—the conventions and formats invented by Hearst and E. W. Scripps and even Ben Bradlee—in order to overcome the political inertia of their readers.

What I am trying to describe is a newspaper that splits the difference, so to speak, between the old working-class papers like the *Cincinnati Post* and the college-educated sophistication of papers like *The Washington Post*. I imagine a newspaper that is both loyal and smart, that approaches daily reality from the perspective of its readers, then uses its new sophistication to examine power in their behalf. A newspaper with those qualities would not solve the democratic problem, but it could begin to rebuild the connective tissue that is missing.

Such a transformation would, of course, require editors with different kinds of skills (perhaps more like a political organizer's or a priest's) and reporters who were equipped to do a different kind of news—stories that began respectfully with what people needed to understand to function as citizens, not with the governing agenda of the higher authorities. What would such a newspaper sound like? How would it cope with the conflicting interests among its own segmented readers? How could it make itself sufficiently exciting— and needed—so that people would want to buy it every day? These are terribly difficult questions, even if newspapers wanted to ask them. The inertia of the news media more or less guarantees they will not be asked.

The news business, as Professor Robert M. Entman has pointed out, has no economic incentive to take responsibility for democracy—and faces economic risks if it tries. To embrace civic obligations that would alter the basic character of journalism might destabilize segments of the mass audience that media assemble for advertisers, the foundation of their commercial existence. Their readerships are already shrinking and news enterprises are not likely to invite more drastic losses by experimenting with their neutral political posture.

Only when they become small and enfeebled do struggling newspapers sometimes reach out, in desperation, and try to identify with their readers. By then, it is usually too late.[9]

In the end, the educated city room betrayed its promise. When the quick but unschooled working-class reporters were displaced and the well-educated took over the work, that social dislocation might have been justifiable if the news media were going to serve democracy more effectively, if the educated reporters were using their professional skills to enhance citizens' ability to cope with power in a more complicated world. The educated reporters instead secured a comfortable place for themselves among the other governing elites. The transformation looks more like a nasty episode of social usurpation, a power shift freighted with class privilege.

If the promise was not fulfilled, then what was the point of turning a craft into a profession? Aside from personal glory, what was really gained from all the journalists with college degrees, if they decline to use their skills to challenge power on behalf of their readers? Those of us who prospered from the transformation of the city room are burdened with those questions and naturally reluctant to face them. Educated journalists, it turns out, are strong on the facts and weak on the truth.

14

THE LOST
GENERATION

In the long-ago American past, politics was itself a principal form of entertainment, and people would travel many miles to hear the oratory and share in the spectacle of popular rallies. In the modern culture of mass-media communications, politics has been overwhelmed by entertainment. The many new channels of communication created by broadcasting and other technologies ought to have enriched democracy. In practice, the rise of mass media as the dominant venue for political dialogue completed the alienation of citizens from politics.

People are now lost in a bewildering display of sound and light, from the random anger of talk radio to the manipulative images of television commercials, from the celebrity culture fostered by mass media to the emotional directness of instant TV news. It is not that people are isolated from public affairs and utterly ignorant, as earlier generations of Americans were. Their problem is that they are inundated with messages—a raging river of information that is fake or true or alluring distraction. As a result, people are reduced to the role of sullen spectators, listening and watching without necessarily believing what they are told.

The paradox of modern media, as almost everyone senses, envelops contemporary politics and is central to the democratic problem. Television and other new technologies connect with people powerfully through vivid imme-

diacy. Yet, because they are centrally controlled, one-way channels of communication, they are also distancing. The media can be liberating for ordinary
people, carrying them into distant realms. Yet they also destroy the old social
connections that once held people together in community. Broadcasting is
inescapably populist in its quick accessibility yet also elitist in its organizational structure. The sound and light are exciting but, strangely enough, foster
a benumbed passivity in the general audience.

The mass-media culture has created one other paradox for democracy that
is seldom noted: It divided Americans into two distinct nations, two tribes of
citizens who see the world quite differently. They are the young and the old.
There are the people under forty-five years old who grew up entirely in the age
of television and were largely educated according to its definitions of reality.
Then there are the rest of us, the older citizens whose perceptions of politics
and everything else were shaped in childhood by more abstract sources of
information, books and newspapers and magazines.

This dividing lined defines another central dislocation in American democracy. The conventional view, usually expressed by the elders, describes
television as a mindlessly destructive force. The contrary view, which I share,
is that the new technologies of communication have truth-telling capacities
that, in time, can help restore democratic sensibilities to the political culture.

Has the mass-media culture destroyed any possibility for genuine democracy? Or is it perhaps a key to salvaging democracy's future? How one answers that question may determine whether one believes that democracy has a
future at all.

The formless anger and disconnectedness of mass media are played out every
afternoon in the darkened studio of KFI 640 radio in Los Angeles. Tom Leykis
stands under a single overhead spotlight, rocking on his heels, pacing back and
forth before the console, while he fumes at the city and stokes the anger of its
citizens.

"We're talking about the Department of Water and Power's ridiculous
attempts to get us to conserve water. While private industry is wasting water
all over Southern California! While Mayor Bradley wants to send the secret
water police around to see if we're washing the dog! What's going on? It's
ridiculous!"

Under the spotlight, Leykis looked like a solitary vaudevillian, performing
forlornly before an imaginary audience. Young and plump, with billowy long
hair floating on his shoulders, he was wearing dark glasses and a black satin
Kings jacket. His dramatic pauses and well-punctuated exclamations are familiar to legions of Los Angeles commuters. Leykis is KFI radio's drive-time
voice of populist outrage.

"Am I supposed to let my yard go brown while Dodger Stadium has a green outfield? What about Caltrans watering the freeways? Even when it's raining! It's a perfect example of how the little guy gets crushed while special interests and big business get more and more and more. The little guy gets to conserve and the big guys get whatever the hell they want.''

Larry from La Mirada was on the line, objecting. Water conservation is important, Larry said, and people should cooperate. Leykis listened for a moment, then blew him off with a tart put-down.

David from Rialto jumped in: ''It's just like the war on drugs, like the malathion they're spraying on us for the medfly. It's putting more and more regulations on the little guy and getting us used to more and more control over our lives.''

Craig, a first-time caller from Ventura, came on to argue for civic responsibility. ''Why don't you go down to your City Hall and demand that they pass laws that make big business conserve water too?'' Craig asked. Leykis pounced.

''Are you registered to vote, Craig? Are you?'' Craig said he wasn't. ''How did I guess?'' Leykis sneered. ''You don't give a crap. You don't even vote.''

''I'm an artist,'' Craig said meekly. ''I'm not up on all the issues.''

''Mister artiste,'' Leykis crooned. ''Isn't that wonderful. You hypocrite! Thank you, Craig, for making my point.''

Then there were Kevin from Corona and Richard from Ontario and Jim from Valencia and Chris on a car phone from Vista. All of them picked up the beat of Tom Leykis's accusation and amplified the outrage with personal anecdotes—industries they had observed wasting water flagrantly, while citizens like Richard got a ticket for washing his car.

''I tell you what I told the municipal guy who gave me the ticket,'' Richard said. ''You can take that ticket and stick it where the sun doesn't shine—unless you're willing to shut down those car-wash businesses too.''

''Good for you, good for you,'' Leykis said. ''What I'd like to see is more people flipping these guys the bird.''

When the broadcast concluded, Leykis was still bouncing around with nervous energy, his adrenaline pumped up by two hours of needling, exhorting and instructing the faceless voices who are his daily listeners. His mood level dropped precipitously, however, as he talked about these citizens.

''It's real easy for somebody to call in and whine,'' Leykis explained. ''But do they ever get off their ass and do something? They love the idea of punching on the touch tone and calling in and getting back at everybody. They get this vicarious thrill. But that's it. The people who call talk shows actually think they're doing something, but it's not the same as voting or going out and passing petitions. Then when things go bad and the air is brown, people call in and say, 'This is awful. How did this happen?' Then they say: 'Tom, you ought to do a campaign.' Great. Call Tom. It's like calling Domino's Pizza.''

Talk radio, it was supposed a few years ago, was becoming a new channel for democratic dialogue—a place where unorganized citizens could come together and speak directly to power. In the media age it might even be a device for assembling citizens in collective action. When dozens of talk radio hosts across the nation joined Ralph Nader in attacking the congressional pay raises in 1989, the resonating chorus of public anger traumatized Washington, at least briefly. In the end, Congress got its pay raise anyway.

As Leykis pointed out, several of the radio personalities who led that pay-raise crusade were subsequently fired, not for offending politicians, but because their ratings were down. "Some of the talk radio hosts are passionately political," he said, "and a lot of them are naive and believe that, just by going on the radio, they can make people care about an issue. Baloney. And some are just blatant opportunists looking for their next big gig.''

The electronic media—radio and television and, in the emerging future, personal computer networks—produce such contradictions. By their nature, these media empower ordinary citizens—providing access and information that did not previously exist for them, connecting them with distant events and authorities. But it is not clear, as yet, whether the new culture created by modern communications will someday lead to a revitalized democracy or simply debase the imperfect politics that already existed.

Tom Leykis engages the paradox every afternoon, from a liberal-libertarian perspective. In the mornings, KFI broadcasts the nation's most popular talk-radio host, Rush Limbaugh, who is a voice of populist outrage coming from the right. Despite their differences, Leykis and Limbaugh are essentially delivering the same message—flipping the bird at power—and they are speaking to the same audience, the vast sea of disaffected and impotent citizens.

"The one thing talk radio does that is positive," Leykis said, "is that it finds the rage bubbling underneath the surface and allows people to see that they're not the only ones who feel that way.''

Leykis is more idealistic than his corrosive opinions suggest and, on occasion, he has tried to mobilize his listeners in collective political action. When the California Department of Agriculture conducted aerial pesticide spraying of suburban L.A. neighborhoods to eradicate the medfly, Leykis rallied the protest movement. One evening, he broadcast from a parking lot in Irwindale, a community that was regularly sprayed with malathion. "We told people to bring surgical masks, we handed out umbrellas, we warned the department we were going to be there," he said. "But eight hundred listeners showed up in this parking lot, even though there was a risk they'd get sprayed. And they were. We were sprayed—live—on the air.''

The pesticide spraying was halted eventually, but Leykis did not claim victory. "It was public relations," he said. "They disarmed the entire protest movement with the announcement they were going to stop—then they went on spraying until they were finished with the job."

Tom Leykis holds a darkly pessimistic opinion of the electronic media's influence on democracy—the view that is widely shared in conventional politics. Broadcasting will not reinvigorate politics, he said, because it has fostered the very culture of shallowness and passive privacy that subverts political action.

"That pay raise issue was easy—a guy listens to the radio and hears that congressmen want a $35,000 raise," he said. "The savings and loan campaign on talk radio was a dismal failure, too complicated for the average person. We have a society that now, because of pop culture, the MTV–*Sesame Street* culture, has a short attention span. If you can't say it in twenty-five words or less, people don't want to be bothered. So everyone stays home, playing Nintendo.

"That's the essence of this country—convenience. As long as you've got the color TV and the VCR and the video games, why vote? It will take a crisis—a war, a great depression—to get people to vote. That's the only time we can get political movement in this country. The air is brown two or three days a week and apparently that's not a crisis. If there was a political movement that went into people's living rooms and dragged off their color TVs, then you'd see them voting."

Virtually all children in America, regardless of their family station, learn the same dispiriting lesson from television, and at a very early age. They discover that the television set sometimes lies to them. Typically, they learn this from the toy commercials. On screen, the robot performs miraculous feats or the little radio-controlled race car zooms around the track like the real thing or the doll baby coos and cries with lifelike charm. Every American child remembers the shock of recognition when the toy comes home from the store. It is just a toy, a piece of sculpted plastic and metal. Even if it works, the object delivers none of the magic qualities promised on television.

Every parent, likewise, remembers the awkward moment of having to deal with a child's disappointment. What does this experience teach small children about life? Does it make them wary of appearances and more astute? Or simply cynical and inured to deceitful manipulation? Parents feel helpless, sensing that they have lost control of their own children's education to this powerful teacher called television.

The medium makes children grow up faster, for discoveries and disillusionments that one used to first encounter in the adolescent years are now visited upon four-year-olds. When I asked my own daughter, who is now an adult, how she analyzed television's impact on her generation's political behavior, her first insight was about the toy commercials.

Everyone has some personal sense of the paradoxes of television but no one, including the experts, has a definite understanding of what the medium has done for the society and done to it. Parents and children, voters and politicians, church and state and business enterprise—everyone is still learning to live with it.

Some critics argue that the seductive culture spawned by television and related communications technologies has already obliterated, beyond repair, the very premises of democratic promise. Its directness disintegrated the old lines of loyalty and accountability and control in politics, from party organizations to representative newspapers. Its alluring images enabled politicians to manipulate the public with deceptive persuasion, an art form that each election season becomes more effective, more elusive. Its attractive surfaces destroyed the deeper content of political discourse.

This pessimistic view is widely shared, especially among older people, and supported by abundant evidence from everyday reality. Citizens, especially younger citizens, do seem dumber about politics. The people and political institutions trying to build strands of common interests among citizens are undercut by the competing glow of the tube. To critics, television seems like a primitive beast stumbling through the village and aimlessly wrecking political relations, education, values.[1]

On the other side, optimists are able to see the modern communications revolution as a great democratic leveler. They acknowledge that people and societies are still adjusting to its disorienting qualities, but the potential for democratic empowerment is enormous. Jacques Cousteau, the French marine biologist who, thanks to television, is known and loved by school children around the world, described the revolutionary implications of the medium:

"When people were illiterate, they had to elect the lawyer or the doctor or whoever had access to information and knowledge to represent them in government. But today the peasant has more information than the politicians, who lose their time in sterile partisan fighting. This kind of democracy is out of date."[2]

Cousteau, somewhat airily, imagines a politics without politicians. Citizens of the world, including peasants and school children, inform themselves and develop the consensus for public action, in spite of governments, in spite of vested political interests. This sense of media's power does not seem far-fetched when one considers the popular upheavals that destroyed the dictatorial regimes in eastern Europe. Radio and television from the western democracies seeped through the closed borders and delivered their subversive

messages; the revolutionary music in Czechoslovakia, East Germany and elsewhere was American rock 'n roll. Coming back the other way leading politicians in western Europe grumbled that on French and British television
Gorbachev got more air time than they did. In a free society, they are powerless to prevent it.

As readers might guess, I place myself among the optimists in this argument. My own impression, as a reporter who has traveled widely in the
country, is that Americans everywhere—especially in provincial backwaters—
are now more richly informed about public affairs because of television. The
polls and studies, I know, document an opposite conclusion, but I am regularly
struck by how much Americans know—how even people in the most remote
places seem to be talking about the same important items that preoccupy the
people at more exalted levels.

Television, at the very least, has unified the American population in new
ways, even if it also debased the content of the political dialogue. This unity
has been reflected in the outcomes of most of the presidential elections during
the last twenty years. Despite the elaborate electoral-vote strategies based on
America's regional differences, the nation is more or less voting in unison,
responding to the same themes and issues.

Still, in the absence of more intimate venues for communications, politics
is captured and confined by omnipresent television. Given the nature of TV
news, every important question is reduced to the "Dan Rather rule" of tax
politics. If it can't be explained in ten seconds, the public won't find out. That
trap, however, is created by the failure of other mediating institutions at least
as much as it can be blamed on TV.

My own optimism, in any case, rests partly on faith. If the pessimists (like
Tom Leykis) are right, then most of what I have explored in this book is beside
the point. If the mass-media culture has permanently robbed people of their
democratic capacities, then the deeper governing problems—or their remedies—will have no meaning to ordinary citizens. If people have been rendered
hopelessly inert, then these complicated questions will be left to the governing
circles that already control most outcomes. Obviously, I do not accept such a
fatalistic prognosis, about either the technology or the human spirit.

For a disconcerting glimpse of the contemporary culture, spend an evening
watching MTV and its marvelously facile storytelling. Or even watch for
fifteen minutes. The music-video channel is so fast moving—and essentially
repetitious—that even a brief encounter conveys its content: a promise of high
production values and trivial intellectual stimulus. The rock videos often play
out dramas with simple story lines, many with surprisingly wholesome messages (don't use drugs, don't cheat on your girlfriend), but the real appeal is

their visual-aural display. A few introduce strikingly original imagery, moody high-tech fantasies of light and color. Most of them borrow familiar visual clichés from movies and television.

The essence of MTV is expressed by one of its video logos—a high-speed flash of obscure images that are propelled at the viewer like a frenzied sight gag, too quick to understand. A butterfly dissolves into a pyramid, a human eye, a rush of disorganized color, a face like John Lennon's, an exploding flower that turns into what? Maybe it wasn't a flower, but an exploding butterfly that turned into John Lennon. It is all too quick—and pointless—for the mind to record.

For anyone who is older, anyone who grew up on books and newspapers before there was television, MTV is a disturbing experience. Is this what the minds of American youth are consuming? One envisions a nation of college dormitories nodding off on MTV's brainless trivia. One imagines decline and fall. Worst of all, one senses that there is a hip joke in these lightning images that old folks are not in on. The founder of MTV once said its programming is designed to drive everyone over fifty crazy.

The American electorate is astride an inescapable faultline that divides those who grew up on TV, fully acculturated by it, and those who didn't. Neither side fully understands the other or speaks the same language or sees quite the same reality in their perceptions of the world. The older half still generally controls things, including politics and government and the most important private institutions. But the younger half is inexorably replacing them, as the children raised by the TV culture grow older and the oldest of them now approach middle age themselves. The future of democracy—if it has a future—inevitably belongs to those who can watch MTV without feeling crazy.

The younger half learned to read from *Sesame Street*, a program widely applauded for its imaginative use of video for educational purposes. But what else did *Sesame Street* teach? That intellectual exercises are primarily visual and tactile experiences, rather than processes of abstraction. "*Sesame Street* is insidious because it implies that you can't learn your letters and numbers without colors and sounds," writer Linda Greider has observed. "Seeing the images for a minute and a half makes you feel like you've dealt with it. It makes you think: Now I know my letters. But what you really know are the marching colors. It's not reading anymore—it's TV."

Between MTV and *Sesame Street* and video games, the TV generation "knows" many things that older people do not know, but the accumulating evidence (mostly accumulated by the older people) emphasizes what is lost on them—the hard facts of political life and the daily action that is the important "news" to older citizens. Younger people know less about public affairs and they seem to care less. The children of TV, now the adults from eighteen to roughly forty-five years old, have more years of schooling than previous generations, a demographic fact that used to predict greater political involvement, but no longer does. Most citizens under forty-five have withdrawn from politics and, indeed, never entered that realm of American life.

They are the dropouts who are pulling down the formal meaning of electoral politics. It is their voting participation that has fallen most drastically during the last twenty years, not that of the people who are older than forty-five years. From 1972 to 1988, the voting level declined by more than one fourth among those who are eighteen to twenty-four years old. By 1988, only 36 percent of these young adults were voting. But voting has also declined among those who are twenty-five to forty-four years old. In 1972, 63 percent of them voted; by 1988, only 54 percent did.

Meanwhile, voting participation among older citizens held roughly constant—fluctuating around 70 percent. This divergence is explained by more than a question of settled maturity. The older voters were taught about democracy and the meaning of elections in the age before television; the younger people learned their civics from TV.

These statistics predict that the deterioration of electoral politics and voting participation is going to continue as the older citizens who still participate in elections die off and are replaced by the tuned-out citizens coming along behind them.[3]

The same divergence is visible in the "news" of public affairs that younger people tune out. The most memorable news event in the decade of the 1980s was the explosion of the *Challenger* space shuttle in 1986. Second was the San Francisco earthquake, third was the little girl in Texas who was rescued from a well. All were TV stories with terrific footage—riveting human dramas that appealed to everyone but especially to younger people. In contrast, the historic political upheavals of eastern Europe never absorbed the attention of more than 42 percent of people under thirty, even at the highly videogenic climax in the fall of 1989 when the Berlin Wall fell.

Only 11 percent of people under thirty followed President Bush's summit meeting with Gorbachev very closely. Only 9 percent were interested in the Japanese purchase of Rockefeller Center. Only 5 percent cared about the scandal that brought down Representative Jim Wright, the Speaker of the House of Representatives. They know Corazon Aquino (53 percent) because she plays a compelling role in a continuing TV soap opera about the Philippine government. They do not know House Speaker Thomas Foley (only 8 percent do) because he is merely the nice-looking man who sits in the background, next to Dan Quayle, when George Bush gives important speeches on TV.

These data are drawn from studies made by the Times Mirror Company's Center for The People & The Press, which monitors the attention span of news consumers. In a 1990 study, "The Age of Indifference," the center charted the gaps between the generations in attention and knowledge and concluded gloomily: "The ultimate irony . . . is that the Information Age has spawned such an uninformed and uninvolved population."[4]

By comparing Gallup Poll opinion surveys over five decades, the study identified a break-away point in the mid-1970s when the attention level of younger adults began to diminish—diverging from what the rest of the country knew and considered important. From the 1940s to the 1970s, the polls had found that young people knew as much about public affairs as their elders (and sometimes more) and that they followed major news events with approximately the same intensity. Starting in the years following the Watergate scandal and the war in Vietnam, the news attention of young people fell away sharply; so did their factual knowledge of political issues and personalities; so did their voting participation.

That decline could be attributed to the disillusionment fostered by those events, the cynicism bred by an era of political failures, except for this: The trend persisted throughout the 1980s, a time when Ronald Reagan restored political success to the presidency and was especially admired among the younger citizens. They liked Ronald Reagan, but his popularity did not persuade them to pay more attention or to vote.

A more likely explanation for the divergence is that in the 1970s, for the first time, the age group from eighteen to thirty consisted entirely of children who had been raised on TV. Those same people are now in their late thirties or early forties and, though they became somewhat more attentive and knowledgeable as they grew older, the age group from thirty to forty-five also now displays a deteriorating interest in the standard facts and events of politics.

Older people read *Time* or *Newsweek* to catch up on the week's news. Younger people, even well-educated ones, read *People* magazine as their idea of "hard news." Older citizens watch *60 Minutes* for its familiar format of methodical exposés of wrongdoing. Younger people watch *A Current Affair* or *Geraldo* or *Oprah* for their edgy sense of personal melodrama—an unabashed emotionalism that is not unlike the old working-class tabloids. Traditionalists shudder at the implications. Is television gradually producing a brain-dead citizenry, making it impossible to imagine a functioning democracy?

Or is it perhaps the opposite—that these younger viewers are able to see things through television that are not really visible to their elders? Possibly, they know something about politics that the rest of us were not taught when we were growing up, a reality that contradicts the comfortable civic faith instilled in us. Clearly, the system of political communication is malfunctioning when so many millions of citizens turn away from the continuing story of politics. But it may be the story itself or the storytelling system—not the audience—that is maladjusted.

What is it that the young and disaffected see in politics that leads them to switch channels? For one thing, they see a dispiriting sameness. It is not just the "talking heads" that, as every TV producer knows, make for boring television, but generally it is the same "talking heads" over and over again. Given the quickness that television values, a viewer will be bombarded with a succession of quick flashes—unfamiliar faces with tightly cropped opinions—that provide no context for understanding who is on which side or why they are being presented as glib authorities or what led them to their quickie opinions.

If one watches the evening news without much background understanding of public affairs, without regularly reading a daily newspaper (as most young people do not), much of the content is unfathomable, random sound bites and a boring blur that seems aimed at some other audience. For these sensibilities, the evening news may look as quick and mindless as MTV. Television politics—like *Sesame Street*—is experienced, not learned in an abstract mode. If the facts seem inconsistent with the images, the images will overwhelm the facts and refute them.

At least the rock videos tell a recognizable human story, however simple-minded. Many provide a vague sense of narrative—responding to the ancient human yearning for a story with a beginning, a middle and an ending—and deliver a passionate message that invites an emotional response (if not an intellectual one) from the audience. MTV invites its viewers to identify with its content. For that matter, so does *Sesame Street*.

Politics and political news, on the other hand, is a story about someone else, told in a not very coherent fashion. Politics on TV is a recurring blip of details about a fairly small group of people (mostly older people and some who seem ancient) who are off somewhere else doing important things. Without context, their words and actions will seem remote and meaningless to ordinary young viewers. The political events seem to be following a logic that is not revealed in the broadcast. People whom TV taught to be hip and wary and impatient naturally lose interest in what seems opaque and distant. The remoteness makes them feel passive, impotent.

The hottest public-affairs shows—frequently denounced as sleaze television—at least deliver a human drama (including even the possibility of a fistfight) and opinionmongers who seem recognizable since they are usually not politicians talking in the distant language of officialisms. Jim Bellows, former editor of the defunct *Washington Star* and now a television consultant, thinks shows like *A Current Affair* prosper because they deliver "a sense of outrage and passion. . . . The newspapers are much more dispassionate. . . . You don't have the alternative voices there that you used to have. Now, television, all of a sudden, is doing that. In some respects, the stuff is terrible, all that sleaze, but people want some kind of different voices and higher and lower emotional levels."[5]

TV portrays politics largely in the orthodox formats of "news," emulating the factuality and story lines originally fashioned for print, yet the sound and pictures frequently convey something else. Politicians frequently look like the salesmen who peddle kitchen gadgets on late-night TV. Their rhetorical exaggerations may remind one of deceptive toy commercials. If the words are not confirmed by the aural-visual imagery, the words lose their veracity. If the political story goes on and on repetitively, without any subsequent resolution or connection to real life, then it is just another TV concoction and not a very compelling one.

Beyond these questions of technique, there is a deeper explanation for why television deadens politics among the young: In its own way, television tells them the truth about politics, almost in spite of itself. For the generation that is fully attuned to the evocative contours of TV images, the medium delivers a most subversive message: The civic mythologies about politics and democracy that your parents believe are nonsense, since any viewer can see that the pictures tell a different story. The civic faith is not borne out by the political story told on television and, in fact, is regularly contradicted by it.

This truth-telling quality is partly the curse of intimacy that television inescapably promotes. When one can see the senator up close and personally witness his performance rather than read about it the next day in the newspaper, the senator inevitably becomes a less exalted figure, less magisterial and less mystifying, especially if he is yapping incoherently in a fifteen-second sound bite. Congress seemed a more noble deliberative body when people only read about it. Actually "experiencing" politics with the physical immediacy of TV makes it much harder to believe in the received truths about democracy that older people routinely accepted.

Now we can see democracy—live and in color—and it does not look much like what the civics textbooks taught. For older people, schooled to accept the civics abstractions, it is thrilling to watch the televised proceedings of the U.S. Senate on C-Span. For most younger people, the same broadcast simply seems boring and bizarre. After all, the U.S. Senate looks like an empty chamber lined with antique desks and a pretend "debate" to which no one seems to be listening.

"Television makes the events transparent, regardless of what it says about them," said Jann Wenner, editor and publisher of *Rolling Stone*, a mass-circulation magazine whose readers span the TV generation. "There is no real debate in politics. That's what younger people see on television and they're right. TV communicates that politics is controlled by a very few people and for everyone else it's meaningless. That's the message from TV and people got it. How many presidential elections do you have to watch before you conclude that the results don't make much difference? Things will go on the same. Why bother? That's an accurate message and TV conveys that message.

"Television is so unvarnished in the way it communicates—even aside from the manipulation in campaigns—that it has told the truth about government and politics so much better than ever before. That's why everyone is so dispirited about politics. They understand."

The question then is: Who sees the truth about American politics more clearly, the old or the young? Like Wenner and Jacques Cousteau, I would vote for the young. Like every generation, they are bound by their own illusions and vulnerable to deception and evasion in their own peculiar ways. But their basic perceptions, however shallow and out-of-focus, are not wrong. The democratic challenge, among its other aspects, lies in convincing the children of TV not only that politics matters, but that they matter in politics.

If television were to reinvent its storytelling techniques, it might be able to convey a more positive and supple sense of political action, bringing diverse human energies and aspirations into the story, breaking out of the claustrophobic definitions of "news" that TV inherited from print. But the underlying mood of disaffection is not likely to change much so long as the nature of politics does not change itself.

The lost generation of active citizens, in other words, may reasonably be blamed on the maladjusted communications engendered by the media revolution. But it should also be understood as the most threatening indictment of the American political system: American democracy is so deformed that it cannot convince its own young people that it's real.

What would bring them back? What would persuade these TV kids with their hip, laconic sense of things that political action is alive and meaningful, that it ought to engage their energies? Possibly, nothing. That is, nothing short of continuing revolution and upheaval in the way the American society communicates with itself. The late Lee Atwater expressed the view that the deep resentment and alienation that permeate modern American politics are connected to the communications revolution and he expected them to continue until the disorientations of communications work themselves out of the society.

If politics does not find a credible voice soon, then the next generation will be lost too. In the style of the video age, most younger people are more inward-looking in their lives, concentrating on the well-being of family and friends and themselves, convinced that nothing they do can have much effect on the larger problems, especially in politics. This is often denounced as self-centered and cynical, but the behavior also demonstrates a practical response to the political reality of impotent citizens.

In the meantime, until things change profoundly, there are still some old-fashioned political commodities that sell with young people: hope and idealism. Their responses to political life, however blurred and uninformed, consistently gravitate toward those people and events that convey those uplifting qualities. They followed Corazon Aquino attentively because she was an idealistic heroine and Nelson Mandela's struggle in South Africa for the same reason.

After twenty years of witnessing scandals and other sodden political events, young people recognized hope and idealism in Ronald Reagan—his uncomplicated sense of optimism about America, his rocklike faith in the country's virtue. One may argue (as I would) that they were deeply deceived by Reagan's sunny images (and by his mastery of video techniques), but that is hardly a new risk for self-government, since citizens were misled by skillful politicians long before television. Despite his advanced age, Reagan's hopeful politics resonated directly with the aspirations of the TV children (though it did not alter their declining participation in politics).

In 1988, when *Rolling Stone* magazine commissioned a broad opinion survey of people in the TV generation and their diverse opinions and attitudes, the most striking result was the choice of their most admired leaders. Contemporary politicians scored poorly. It was Martin Luther King, Jr., who led the list, followed by Robert F. Kennedy. Both men had been killed twenty years before, when many of these young people were infants or even before some of them were born.

King and Kennedy, however, both stand out in common memory for courageous statements of idealism and hope—a willingness to put themselves at risk on behalf of change, to make things better for people. It was a dreadful commentary on American politics: For younger citizens, the political heroes are dead and they do not see much on TV to remind them of what was lost.[6]

If politicians and corporate interests can steer public opinion through the art of mass-media images, why can't citizens? Since mass communication has become the dominant mode of civic discourse in America, some citizens have discovered how to use it too, even to address complex issues of government that are normally dominated by entrenched power. Even when the citizens win, however, the results may be less than fulfilling for democracy.

On February 26, 1989, CBS's *60 Minutes* broke the alarming story of Alar, a pesticide established as carcinogenic yet still authorized by EPA for agricultural use and sprayed on the apples that children eat every day. An EPA official admitted during the broadcast that, if Alar were a newly developed chemical submitted for regulatory approval, EPA would reject it. But since Alar was an old chemical already in use, EPA did not act to ban it.

The next day, actress Meryl Streep held a press conference in Washington, joined by the national president of the PTA and other distinguished citizens, and announced the formation of a new organization called "Mothers and Others for Pesticide Limits." They released a devastating research report from the Natural Resources Defense Council, describing the dangers to children in the food system caused by agricultural chemicals and EPA's weak efforts to regulate them. Streep also previewed a television commercial in which she appears, standing in a sunny kitchen while lunch is being prepared for the children, and warns other mothers of these risks.

Cover stories on Alar followed in *Time* and *Newsweek*, as well as feature stories in *Family Circle*, *Redbook*, *Woman's Day* and *People* magazine. The *Phil Donahue Show* took up the issue and so did all three of the TV networks' morning shows. Cast members from *L.A. Law* and *thirtysomething* came forward to reiterate Meryl Streep's concerns.

The entire thunderstorm of media attention, including *60 Minutes,* was cleverly orchestrated by a public-relations firm on behalf of the environmentalists—and Alar lost. The media techniques employed by the environmentalists were actually identical to those that major corporations and political parties routinely use to influence public opinion—the calculated repetition of an emotionally powerful message and the use of a trusted celebrity to deliver it.

The Washington Post and *The Wall Street Journal* countered the first Alar stories by reporting industry claims that Alar posed no significant risk to children, but the issue was already decided. Major school systems around the country began withdrawing apples from their lunchrooms and supermarkets cut back their normal orders. Apple sales plummeted, as the controversy stayed in the news day after day. A few weeks later, the manufacturer, Uniroyal, capitulated and Alar was withdrawn from the market.

Hill & Knowlton, the Washington public-relations firm hired by the apple growers, countered the onslaught of alarming stories by dispatching voluminous statistical data to the news media on the risk assessments of pesticide residues on apples. But to no avail. "On the first day," Frank Mankiewicz, the Hill & Knowlton account executive, recalled, "I said to myself: 'We're going to make a lot of money and we're going to lose. God, are we going to lose.' We got rolled in three days. The reason was that Meryl Streep sneaked on TV and said, 'This stuff will make your kids sick.' "

The apple growers and the chemical industry, seconded by EPA, insisted this wasn't quite so, but their complicated rebuttals entirely missed the point of public anxiety. The industry and EPA did not claim that Alar itself was safe to consume, only that the chances of one child consuming enough Alar on apples to contract cancer were remote. The public ignored these assurances, and for good reason: This was not an experiment parents were likely to undertake with their own children.[7]

Nor did the public believe EPA. The agency had itself prepared to take Alar off the market back in 1985, but backed off when its panel of scientific advisors objected. Seven of the eight EPA advisors, it was later revealed, had worked as consultants to the chemical industry, including one scientist who served on the EPA advisory panel on pesticides, then went to work for Uniroyal a few months later—representing it on the Alar issue. Such conflicts of interest are commonplace on government advisory boards, another reason for the public to distrust the government's science.[8]

"You could say the public banned Alar directly through the media," said David Fenton, whose public-relations firm designed the Alar campaign for the NRDC. "It was a case of direct self-government—no legislation involved, no government at all."

Fenton's adroit manipulation of the news media enraged the apple growers and the chemical industry as well as their conservative defenders in the press, but his strategy simply followed the basic principles of mass communications developed by business itself. "The corporate world is much more sophisticated about communications than public-interest groups and Republicans are much more sophisticated than Democrats," Fenton said. "Most of the big environmental groups have no budget for this sort of thing. Their idea of successful media is that an article appears in *The New York Times* and their peers see it. They have no sense of mass communications."

Fenton Communications, a firm that mostly represents left-liberal political causes, is used to operating on meager budgets (its Alar fee was $30,000 while Hill & Knowlton's was $200,000), so the Alar campaign relied almost entirely on orchestrating "free" space in the media—most of it arranged well before Alar became "news." Even the Meryl Streep TV commercials were slightly bogus since NRDC lacked the funds for television advertising. "This was a guerrilla action," Fenton said. "We made three TV spots but all we had for media time buying was $3,000, which wouldn't buy anything. We made the commercial and released it at a press conference and hoped the TV news shows would use it for free and they did. Then we bought ten spots on WJLA in Washington at very cheap hours, just so we could say that we did put it on the air."

Modern politics, Fenton argues, "is really a battle between lawyers and marketeers. Most of the environmentalists at the NRDC are lawyers and lawyers think issues will be settled by facts and arguments. Marketeers know this country doesn't work that way anymore, if it ever did.

"The media is setting the agenda for policymakers, but the media din is such noise that, if a story only appears for one day, it disappears. The government knows that a one-day story is on the air and then it's gone. People don't remember it, don't act on it. If a story appears a second day, they take notice. If it's in a third day, the government gets nervous. If the story goes any further, they appoint a task force.

"I recognized that, in order to get through the din, I would have to create repetition, so that this thing would hit with a bang and then keep appearing day after day for weeks. But that requires manipulation, doesn't it? Everybody who does PR in Washington understands that.''

Thus, on one level, the Alar episode opened new vistas for irregular citizen politics. It became a case study of how sophisticated public relations (and a rather small investment) could dramatically alter the political context for even a complex subject like federal pesticide regulation. The American public, almost overnight, was shocked and scared; the mass response overwhelmed the industry's influence on the government regulators.

George Bush used the image of Willie Horton, the black convict and rapist, to become president. The environmentalists used poisoned apples to banish Alar. Both are manipulating the mass media, but ultimately, they are also manipulating the mass audience.[9]

In a sense, it wasn't the people who banned Alar. It was Meryl Streep—because she was more believable than EPA and industry scientists. Frank Mankiewicz, whose PR firm represented the apple growers, remarked drolly on the use of celebrities to decide public-health policy:

"I was trying to make the point to reporters that Meryl Streep hasn't even played a nutritionist. At least when Robert Young talks about coffee on TV, we know we can believe him because Robert Young used to play a doctor.''

The dimensions of the modern media culture were aptly defined when *Publishers Weekly* issued its list of the twenty-five biggest best-selling books of the 1980s. People tend to buy books, like everything else, by brand names, only the brand names are those of celebrities who became famous for doing something other than writing books. The decade's nonfiction list was a hit parade of the household names made familiar by television or movies. Bill Cosby, Lee Iacocca and "Frugal Gourmet" Jeff Smith each had two books on it. Others hits were by or about Jane Fonda, Chuck Yeager, Donald Trump, Frank Sinatra, Elvis Presley. Even some of the most serious books on the list had the aura of celebrity: Carl Sagan and Stephen W. Hawking are about as famous as living scientists get. The rest of the bestsellers were mostly by famous diet and self-help experts.[10]

Celebrity itself is not a new phenomenon, of course, but the media age has pumped up the role of celebrity enormously (and further democratized access to that privileged realm). In the nineteenth century, Americans chose famous generals to be president and, since early in the twentieth century, movie stars have always seemed more interesting to people than most politicians. Movie stars who go into politics are especially interesting.

What is also different about contemporary celebrities is their power to assemble floating "communities" of like-minded followers—an identity that people can attach to and call their own. Celebrities are trusted, celebrities stand for certain things, the ideas and values to which followers can express political allegiance. In a fragmented society where people drift in isolation, this seems a weak (and sometimes pathetic) substitute for a genuine community, but people do the best they can with what they've got.

The TV preachers have been most successful and most methodical in assembling constituencies with multimedia technologies, then leading their adherents into the public arena. Their conservative political message eventually produced its own backlash (and scandal defrocked several of the pastors), but their imaginative enterprises are a model for how celebrity and television can organize a political presence for people who had none before.

James Dobson's daily radio program, *Focus on the Family,* airs on 1,250 stations (second only to Paul Harvey) and his California-based organization of the same name distributes books, films and pamphlets to millions. It is a ministry aimed at restoring conservative family values and influencing the political decisions on social questions. In early 1988, *Focus on the Family* flooded the congressional switchboards with a half million phone calls in a single day, all protesting the pending civil rights bill as "an incredible intrusion into religious liberties."[11]

On a somewhat different plane, rock 'n roll also recruits and educates citizens for political action. Sting, U2, Peter Gabriel, Bruce Springsteen and others have made "human rights" a household phrase among their young followers and around the world. They led the Amnesty International world concert tour in 1988 that played eighteen countries, including the Soviet bloc nations of eastern Europe, and a U.S. tour in 1986. Drawn by the music, fans went home with copies of the Universal Declaration of Human Rights (a document that was still suppressed in some of the countries). Some of the fans went home to organize their own Amnesty chapters and began writing letters on behalf of political prisoners.

"We played in front of a million real people and maybe a billion saw the movie, which is the concert with some politics," said John Healy, Amnesty's executive director. "Stars attract the people in, then we try to get them to do something actively. We have over two thousand high schools with organizations and teachers tell us that the most exciting thing in their schools is Amnesty. It turns out that the dictators don't know whether the letters are written by young people. All they know is they're getting lots of mail about political prisoners."

Furthermore, if one searched for an opposition critique to the conservative Republican regime of the 1980s, it was not to be found in the news media or the Democratic party, but in entertainment—the music and film celebrities who were willing to express themselves on large public issues, from the war against Nicaragua to environmental degradation to the maldistribution of wealth and incomes.

People evidently listened to them too. The opinion polling on how attentively young people follow the news found that eighteen- to thirty-year-olds were more interested than their elders in the news of Nelson Mandela's release from prison in South Africa. The rock stars had educated them on the subject.

But do the celebrities evoke a real political response or are the kids just coming out for a good concert that will include some righteous political rhetoric? Perhaps a bit of both. "Stars do it and they don't do it," Healy said. "The whole question is whether there's an edge in what they're saying. You take Bruce Springsteen, who says there is 'economic apartheid' in this country, which he said on the tour and in the movie. That's got an edge. That's different from some celebrity telling people to save the environment—build a house with old tires."

The debilitating political effects of the celebrity culture were brilliantly evoked in Michael Moore's film *Roger and Me,* a satirical journey through the devastation of Moore's hometown, Flint, Michigan, when General Motors collapsed its U.S. production in the early 1980s. Moore filmed a surreal parade of fading "stars" (Pat Boone, Anita Bryant, Bob Eubanks) who come to Flint to boost local spirits while the town itself sinks deeper into a kind of crazed denial of reality.[12]

But the most devastating element in the film is its mocking portrayal of Flint's passive victims. It invites the audience to laugh at the bizarre behavior of the unemployed auto workers—because the victims are laughing at themselves. No one gets angry because they are spectators too. They are watching their own demise and reacting as though it was a television game show, featuring Pat Boone, Anita Bryant and Bob Eubanks. When the last truck rolls off the line at the assembly plant, the workers cheer for the camera. "What are we cheering about?" one of them asks. "We just lost our jobs."

What Moore has captured is the fact that television creates an independent reality that people defer to and that separates them from the real political life where decisions are made. On camera, they become performers themselves, mimicking the idiomatic words and gestures they have seen and absorbed from the "stars." Off camera, they are sullen and passive, unable to imagine the connection that Moore illustrates between the indifference of General Motors executives and the destruction of their town.

The basic weakness in media-centered politics is that, whatever energy and presence it creates, it does not overcome these distancing qualities embedded in the medium itself. A rock star may exhort and educate, but it is still a one-way communication, floating in time and space, detached from any permanent place or institutional responsibility. The TV preachers develop an audience of citizens (and collect lots of money from them) but the fate of their political agenda hangs on the preacher, not the congregation. People feel empowered, but the effect is shallow and sometimes false. People become adherents, but they are still mainly spectators.

Ernie Cortes of the Texas IAF network, whose community organizations rely on the old-fashioned face-to-face dialogues, described what is missing from television politics:

"Television allows politicians to go directly to people and go into their living rooms. They go beyond the mediating institutions and make a mass appeal that doesn't differentiate about its audience. The TV preachers do the same. They are preachers who don't need churches. They communicate directly, but there is no permanent relationship being built."

This is the media problem that no one has yet solved: How might the power of this technology be adapted to developing genuine political relationships without also overwhelming them? The solution perhaps lies somewhere between the intimate interpersonal approach that the IAF groups rigorously pursue at the grassroots level and the glamorous mass appeals made by rock stars and TV preachers. One creates genuine connections among people, but cannot speak to the larger audience of citizens who are mainly listening to mass media. The other approach communicates high-volume messages to a vast audience but does not leave much behind in terms of human relationships.

Sooner or later, the optimists would say, someone somewhere will discover the media methods for doing both—developing and sustaining conversation with the listeners, activating the capacities of citizens without making them bit players in someone else's drama. The continuing emergence of wondrous new technologies—from desktop publishing to telecomputers—argues that human imagination will eventually find the links that can restore a sense of democratic vitality.

It requires invention, but it will also require a new sense of the institutional relationships. The media are not likely to bring people back into democracy so long as people have no control whatsoever over the media.

America's Funniest Home Videos may be dismissed as the kind of daffy (and irresistible) fluff that network television serves up, except for its revolutionary implications. The show is mostly devoted to ridiculous moments in everyday life—spontaneous, backyard sight gags captured by ordinary people with their own video cameras. But now and then the homemade videotapes reveal something more. Folks not only have their own TV cameras now, but many have learned the higher production values of television—the dramatic arts of staging and editing and narration that make the medium so effective. Given their store-bought equipment, these amateurs are now making quite skillful parodies of the professionals.

It is possible, in other words, to watch *Funniest Home Videos* and imagine America, someday soon, as a nation of TV producers. Citizens making their own messages for broadcast—that's power. Citizens everywhere covering the news for themselves—that's power too, as the Los Angeles policemen discovered when a home video recorded their brutal beating of a black motorist.

Possibly, some enterprising TV syndicate will eventually move beyond the sight gags and invite citizens to tell other kinds of stories about themselves—to send in videotapes that record deeper dramas from their lives or, who knows, even stories that express their own political ideas and aspirations. I can envision an entertaining and meaningful low-budget program that simply airs the most provocative works of America's TV guerrillas—citizen filmmakers who harness the outrage of talk radio to more purposeful content and with less manipulation by the on-air personality.

This sort of possibility is just the beginning of the next liberating revolution—and the new grounds for optimism about democratic possibilities. New technologies are coming into the marketplace that will give individuals more control over the nature of electronic communications. Once the means of creating the message are widely distributed in many hands, invention is sure to follow. The truly original ideas for using video—the techniques for adapting its power to democratic relationships—will not come from the corporate conglomerates that now control broadcasting and publishing. But they might come from someone's backyard.

George Gilder has sketched a most ambitious vision of democratic optimism, based on the emerging developments in microelectronics. Communications grids that decentralize the originating controls, telecomputers and personal data resources that will shift power away from institutions and to individuals—these technologies and others promise to empower citizens, Gilder explained. As this happens, people will be able to liberate themselves from mindless anonymity in the mass audience.

"The force of microelectronics will blow apart all of the monopolies, hierarchies, pyramids and power grids of established industrial society," Gilder declared. "It will undermine all totalitarian regimes. Police states cannot endure under the advance of the computer because it increases the powers of the people far faster than the powers of surveillance. All hierarchies will tend to become 'heterarchies'—systems in which each individual rules his own domain."[13]

Meanwhile, however, in the here-and-now, the pace of change is largely controlled by those corporations that own the equipment and existing franchises—and most of them, for obvious reasons, have a compelling interest in resisting change and preserving the status quo. Like George Gilder, one may assume that profound technological change sooner or later sweeps away the old order, regardless of its political power to resist. But the actual shape of the future still depends crucially on which economic and political forces get to design it.

The unmentionable political issue is who owns the media—unmentionable because neither media nor politicians will bring it up. Ben H. Bagdikian, former dean of journalism at the University of California at Berkeley, bravely explored the question and reached a frightening conclusion:

"The United States, along with other major democracies, is moving swiftly toward media control by a handful of gigantic multi-national corporations. The trend is unmistakable. Leaders in the trend are quite candid: they predict that in a few years a half-dozen corporations will control most of the public information available to Americans."[14]

If that sounds like an extreme forecast, consider the results of Bagdikian's research. When his book, *The Media Monopoly*, was first published in 1983, he counted fifty organizations that controlled most of the business in all major media—radio, television and its derivatives, newspapers, magazines and books. Five years later, when the second edition was published, he found the fifty organizations had shrunk to twenty-nine.

As Bagdikian demonstrated, the great promise of new communications technologies has been thwarted in the past by the commercial self-interest of those who owned them. Cable television, for instance, was heralded twenty years ago as the great liberating innovation that would foster diversity in broadcasting and reinvigorate the public dialogue—simply because cable grossly multiplied the number of available channels. On the whole, the promise has not been fulfilled. With rare exceptions, cable TV does not stray from the narrow commercial objectives of its owners—owners who are mostly the same companies that own newspapers, magazines, radio and television stations.

David Fenton, who orchestrated the Alar campaign, sees the problems of democracy rooted in the power of the media to set the agenda for public debate, however randomly they do so. "I agree with the right wing," Fenton said. "Here we have this powerful instrument for political opinion and solving social problems that is completely unaccountable and unwilling to examine itself and against letting itself be used to attack social problems. Citing the First Amendment is not an answer. Nobody wants to appoint politically corrupt bureaucrats to run the media, but maybe it's not so good to leave the media entirely in the hands of people who are only interested in private profit. If we want an environmentally sound economy, that little box can make it happen. Or do we have to leave it to little guerrilla operations like ours?"

The democratic imperative, therefore, is to develop new political and legal doctrine that will challenge the concentrated ownership of communications on behalf of democracy. As individual citizens develop their own communications skills and organize their own computer networks, they will be able to go around the mass media and talk to one another. But they will still be shut out of the mass-audience debate if the owners refuse them access. The proposals to allot free air time for political candidates in campaigns, for instance, are a useful but inadequate reform. The problem is also providing air time for citizens, not just for elections, but in every season.

To produce genuine change, media companies might, for instance, be prohibited from cross-ownership in different sectors of media or limited to some modest share of the overall national marketplace, as Bagdikian has suggested. Media owners usually hide behind the First Amendment when such questions are raised, but the practical effect of media concentration is actually to restrict the "free speech" of everyone else, the voiceless citizenry. Who gets to enter the debate? The choice belongs to reporters and editors and producers and, really, to the companies they work for. Sooner or later, this arbitrary restriction on democracy must be confronted.

Michael Kinsley of *The New Republic* has suggested, for instance, that companies that use their media ownership to promote their own products or political interests might find themselves restricted to the more limited First Amendment privileges accorded to "commercial speech." When NBC broadcasts an account of the success of the nuclear-power industry in France, is it informing the public or selling a product made by NBC's owner, General Electric? In 1990, the NBC *Nightly News* ran three segments, totaling fourteen minutes, on a new device to detect breast cancer without finding time to mention that the machine is manufactured by NBC's parent corporation. As the control of the major news media becomes still more concentrated, their supposed neutrality, in both commerce and politics, will become more and more suspect.[15]

To take another example of reform, cable franchises, originally envisioned as public utilities, could be broken up into multiple ownerships—commercial and noncommercial, political and nonpolitical. Public-access channels are available for free and inventive expression, but they have no institutional base from which to develop coherent programming and quality. Given the redundancies that now exist in the content of TV broadcasting, nothing would be lost if some channels or blocs of air time were assigned to responsible community institutions (churches or labor unions or even political parties) that are motivated, not by profit maximization, but by the desire to foster social connections.

Public accountability would require a diversity of voices and a rough sense of balance among the competing interests that are given control of the access. Ralph Nader has proposed, for example, an "audience network" in which citizens' groups, depending on their size, could be awarded an hour or so of air time to broadcast programming that originates with the public, not the media corporations. "Given the immense concentration of power and uniformity that characterizes the broadcasting industry,'' Nader wrote, ''leaving the dissemination and content of new information technology to myopic profit formulas runs counter to community sense and historical precedent.''[16]

At the very least, while we await the liberating possibilities of the next communications revolution, some new rules of equity need to be developed—rules that spread the costs of political speech among many in order to democratize its availability for everyone. Most individuals cannot undertake this for themselves. Without new institutional arrangements in communications, control of access inevitably will be held by the few.

The media corporations are busy concentrating their market shares and acquiring rivals. The politicians dare not challenge the structure of media ownership, for that would provoke severe retribution from press and television and their corporate owners. The power of corporate politics, as the next chapter makes clear, is the centerpiece in the institutional arrangements that dominate politics.

The debate about media power, therefore, has to come from the people—from the TV guerrillas who want to reach a larger audience with their original messages, from ordinary citizens who are able to envision a more robust democracy. If the people do not raise these questions, they will not be raised at all.

15

CITIZEN

GE

Corporations, by their nature, do not function as democratic organizations, yet it is they who have seized the political ground left vacant by citizens, the political parties and other mediating institutions. Business and finance stepped into the vacuum created by failed political institutions and took up the daily work of politics. Their tremendous financial resources, the diversity of their interests, the squads of talented professionals—all these assets and some others are now relentlessly focused on the politics of governing.

This new institutional reality is the centerpiece in the breakdown of contemporary democracy. Corporations exist to pursue their own profit maximization, not the collective aspirations of the society. They are commanded by a hierarchy of managers, not by democratic deliberation. Yet the modern corporation presumes to act like a mediating institution—speaking on behalf of others and for the larger public good. It is corporations that have taken the place of political parties, to the extent anyone has.

With varying degrees of sophistication and intensity, hundreds of these large corporate political organizations are now astride the democratic landscape, organizing the ideas and agendas, financing electoral politics and overwhelming the competing voices of other, less well-endowed organizations and citizens. They portray themselves as "good citizens," doing their part for public affairs.

For obvious reasons, this institutional arrangement is bound to disappoint democratic expectations. The contest of politics becomes mainly an indistinct competition among rival behemoths. The political space that once belonged to parties and other mediating institutions is usurped by narrow-minded economic interests. Citizens at large vaguely perceive that government is being steered by these forces and they naturally resent it.

The transformation occurred partly by default and partly by design. Corporate political organizations set out to seize the high ground, but they also simply learned how to do politics in the modern setting more inventively than anyone else. By necessity, they have adapted effectively to the new conditions of mass-media politics and the diffusion of government authority, while citizens and rival organizations have not.

Corporations, however, enjoy an anomalous status not available to anyone else: In the lawless government, corporate "citizens" are the leading outlaws. They may regularly violate the law without surrendering their political rights—committing felonious acts that would send people to prison and strip them of their citizenship. This contradiction is crucial to what has deformed democracy; the power relationships of politics cannot be brought into a more equitable balance until citizens confront the privileged legal status accorded to these political organizations.

In order to understand the power of corporations, it is not necessary to track the myriad political activities of hundreds of companies. The reality can be adequately demonstrated by describing the politics of one outstanding example among the many—an especially skillful and energetic political organization known as the General Electric Company. Like others, "Citizen GE" energetically promotes its own civic reputation while it tenaciously pursues its interests across an extraordinary range of matters. Like many other major companies, "Citizen GE" does its everyday politics despite its anomalous status as an ex-convict.

At forty-three, Benjamin Heineman, Jr., had the sort of political résumé that marked him as a future Cabinet officer, if the Democrats ever again won the White House. The son of a politically prominent Chicago industrialist, Heineman studied at Harvard, Yale and Oxford and became known in Washington for his quick and serious intelligence. He served as assistant secretary for planning at HEW in the Carter administration, then became managing partner in the Washington office of Sidley & Austin, one of Chicago's leading law firms. To some, it seemed a diversion from destiny when Heineman left the capital in 1987 to become general counsel of the General Electric Company in Fairfield, Connecticut.

Not at all, he explained to an interviewer. General Electric offered him the opportunity to influence public policy across an extraordinary front of governing issues, from the tax code to defense spending, from broadcasting to environmental regulation, from banking law to international trade, from Head Start to Star Wars. "GE is a mirror of the world economy," Heineman told the *American Lawyer*. "You have an opportunity to see everything."[1]

Philip A. Lacovara, a former Watergate prosecutor and the top litigator in another Washington law firm, joined GE for the same attraction—the chance, he said, to be "involved in major policy and issues." As GE's chief of litigation, Lacovara expected to write friend-of-the-court briefs on such diverse matters as the First Amendment and securities law, government contracts and corporate responsibility.

"American industry has been reticent," he explained. "GE recognizes that as a major economic entity it has the stature and responsibility to form opinions."

One of Lacovara's first projects at GE was to try to head off the new corporate-sentencing guidelines being prepared for the federal courts, guidelines intended to stiffen the consequences for corporations that break the law. General Electric has more than a theoretical interest in this policy question since the company itself has been convicted of a series of crimes in recent years, including defrauding the federal government. The legal standards for corporate criminality, Lacovara argued, "should be narrowed substantially."

Companies cannot be held responsible for the transgressions of far-flung employees, Lacovara explained in comments he filed with the U.S. Sentencing Commission. Instead of stiffer penalties for corporate violators, Lacovara suggested that federal prosecutors ought to offer special rewards to companies that cooperate with them—lenient fines and forgiveness—in order to encourage what he called the "good corporate citizen."

When the Justice Department endorsed a draft of the more severe sentencing guidelines in the spring of 1989, the GE lawyers took their complaints to the White House. An associate of Lacovara's warned the president's counsel that the proposed guidelines were "a corporate death sentence." George Bush's lawyer made some phone calls. The Justice Department backed off and withdrew its endorsement.[2]

As the episode suggested, there are no longer any distinct boundary lines between law, politics and corporate management. In the modern milieu of governing, these are all the same subject. General Electric recognizes this reality more astutely than most and, as Ben Heineman explained to the *American Lawyer,* was beefing up its legal department to take "an aggressive, offensive look at the problems of the company." GE's lawyers, he said, would track not just litigation, but also new legislation and regulation, alongside the company's lobbyists. "Preventing litigation is one thing," Heineman said. "But how do you calculate [the benefit] if you change a regulation or work something out with Congress?"

One of Heineman's new hires was a former colleague from Sidley & Austin, Stephen D. Ramsey, who had previously served as assistant attorney general for environmental enforcement in the Reagan administration. At the Justice Department, Ramsey had developed the liability rules for enforcing the Superfund law, the law that requires corporations to pay their share for cleaning up the thousands of dangerous toxic-waste dumps they created around the nation. At Sidley & Austin, Ramsey worked on how to stymie the Superfund law.

A legal memorandum prepared by Ramsey in 1986 provided a playbook for how corporate lawyers could confound the government's efforts to collect the billions owed by polluters. His Superfund memo was widely circulated among the law firms that defend corporations against Superfund claims because it spelled out the step-by-step tactics for hanging up the liability process in the tangle of court challenges. Ramsey, for example, advised fellow lawyers:

"Bear in mind that district courts, unlike courts of appeals, are generally unfamiliar with record review. This suggests opportunities to expand the record. . . . Use Freedom of Information Act, broadly and often, and challenge withholding of relevant documents. . . . There is an added appearance of arbitrariness and procedural sloppiness if the government refuses. . . . Artful use of the Book-of-the-Month-Club response ('If we do not hear from you, we assume you agree with us'). . . . Take full advantage of every opportunity to comment. . . . Force the government to respond to your comments. . . . And, document when they do not, to lay foundation for later challenge."[3]

EPA's chief of enforcement was sufficiently alarmed by Ramsey's memorandum that he issued an in-house warning to EPA legal and technical staff, urging them to "be prepared to handle challenges suggested by it."

General Electric is much in need of Stephen Ramsey's legal specialty. GE has been listed as a "potentially responsible party" at forty-seven Superfund sites—more than any other U.S. corporation. The forty-seven toxic-waste dumps are on EPA's priority cleanup list, sites where GE either was the operator or contributed significantly to the chemical wastes. Ramsey became the company's vice-president for corporate environmental programs. "I'll be ensuring that GE at a corporate and business level is doing everything they can to comply with existing laws and government regulations and to go beyond that," he declared.[4]

Heineman's imaginative recruiting spun the "revolving door" in other fields as well. A former Treasury Department legislative counsel from the Carter administration was hired to be GE's chief lawyer for tax planning and policy. A former energy counsel from the Ford administration was hired to be the top lawyer for GE's appliance division.

But Ben Heineman was simply applying to the legal department the same sophisticated political sensibilities that GE management has demonstrated for many years. The former chairman of the Joint Chiefs of Staff, retired Air Force General David C. Jones, is on GE's board of directors. So was Ronald Reagan's former attorney general, the late William French Smith.

But critics who focus on the career-ladder aspects of this phenomenon generally miss the larger meaning. The "revolving door" is not about personal opportunism, but about the organizational reality in American politics. A company naturally wishes to hire the best people to do its political work, since its bottom line depends directly on the political outcomes—not just now and then, but continuously every day, every year.

General Electric, like every other major corporation, is thoroughly engaged in the politics of governing—more intimately and extensively than any individual citizen would ever feel the need to participate, more aggressively than even hyperactive political activists could imagine. The company's practical politics is a function of economic necessity, not the ideology or civic sensibilities of its managers.

General Electric's wingspan is almost as broad as the government's. While it is too large and diverse to be considered typical, GE is an outstanding prototype of the modern corporation doing politics, since its product lines and corporate interests intersect with practically every dimension of the federal government's decision making. GE makes the things that government buys but also the things that government regulates and licenses: light bulbs and locomotives, jet engines and nuclear bombs, TV broadcasting and nuclear-power plants and financial services.

GE is the second-largest plastics manufacturer and, therefore, keenly interested in environmental law enforcement. But then it also manufactures pollution-control systems. Its medical-diagnostic equipment leads the world market—as do GE circuit breakers, industrial turbines, electric motors, aircraft engines. The company is intensely engaged in trade policy and the emerging global economy.

GE is a stockbroker, since it owns the Kidder Peabody brokerage. GE is also a major bank, since its financial subsidiary, GE Capital, has $91 billion in assets—equivalent in size to America's fourth-largest commercial bank. General Electric is also a media giant, since it owns the NBC network and NBC's seven local TV stations as well as footholds in television broadcasting in three other countries. It purchased Financial News Network and closed it down in order to eliminate competition for its own cable venture, the Consumer News/Business Channel.[5]

For all these reasons, General Electric is a conglomerate that, in addition to its productive, profit-making activities, also functions as a ubiquitous political organization. With great sophistication and tenacity, GE represents its own interests in the political arena, as one would expect. But that is not what makes it so influential.

General Electric also tries to act like a mediating institution—speaking on behalf of others. GE, like many other companies, assumes the burden of representing various groups of other citizens in politics—workers, consumers, shareholders, even other businesses and the well-being of Americans at large. GE has the resources to develop and promote new political ideas and to organize public opinion around its political agenda. It has the capacity to advise and intervene and sometimes veto. It has the power to punish political opponents. It also has the sophistication to lend its good name to worthy causes, such as the Urban League, only remotely related to the company's profits.

The permissive culture of the grand bazaar is especially well suited to the corporate style of politics. Corporations have both the money and the economic incentive to play politics on both levels—bargaining outcomes in obscure places that manipulate laws and mobilizing ideas and opinions to influence the visible public contest. To negotiate successfully in the grand bazaar, a political interest must have lots of lawyers, preferably with Washington connections. To influence the broad public debate, a political organization needs the status of "good corporate citizen," and GE has acquired that reputation too.

Other governing elites, including most elected politicians and the media, have found the corporate mode of politics congenial to their own interests. At least they have come to accept the corporate presence as the prevailing constant in how democracy now functions. Given the failure of other institutions to adapt and revitalize themselves, corporate politics has become the organizational core of the political process—the main connective tissue linking people to their government.

General Electric is a deeply Republican institution for obvious historical reasons. As the inheritor of inventor Thomas A. Edison, the company was one of the brilliant pioneers in the rise of America's industrial corporations early in the twentieth century and has always naturally aligned itself with the party of business. In the 1950s, it sponsored Ronald Reagan's TV career and launched him on the lecture circuit as a crusader against big government.

But the company's upper management is also now sprinkled with "country club Democrats" like Ben Heineman and, since New Deal days, the corporation has been active in designing social programs usually associated with liberal Democrats. For years, GE has been a faithful contributor to mainline civil rights organizations and to education projects for racial minorities.

General Electric's political director, so to speak, is Frank P. Doyle, an executive who bears the stylishly contemporary title of senior vice-president for "relations." A Democrat, Doyle ranks just below GE's CEO, John F. Welch, Jr., and alongside the senior vice-presidents for finance, research and development, executive management and legal counsel. Though he seldom appears as a public witness for company policy, Doyle is in and out of Washington regularly on myriad matters and he also spends a lot of time in Brussels, the capital of the European economic community.

His attention, it is said, is roughly divided between developing broader social issues such as education and job training, the consolidation of GE's position in Europe's emerging common market and the hardball politics of pursuing GE's specific lobbying agenda, from fighter planes to taxes.[6]

"Jack Welch has a sophisticated, modern vision of the corporate social role," said a congressional aide who has dealt frequently with GE on a spectrum of issues. "In politics, they are heavy-handed, big-stick players on their own issues, but they're not Dow Chemical. GE spends much more time on education, for instance, than other corporations. No one else is close. And they reap enormous benefits when they come around to collect their own nickels."

General Electric's political capacities depend upon an impressive infrastructure of different components—an elaborate team of lawyers and lobbyists, continuing financial investments in both charity and politics and programs of education and propaganda. These elements work together in both obvious and subtle ways as the institutional predicate for GE's political power.

In Washington, GE has a permanent team of two dozen lobbyists with a large support staff but, as the need arises, it regularly hires outside lawyers and lobbyists for targeted assignments.

Like other companies, GE finances the politicians in both parties. During the 1988 election cycle, GE PACs contributed $595,000 to congressional campaigns. One year, the company also paid $47,000 directly to senators and representatives to listen to them give speeches (the speakers, it turns out, were mostly members of the armed services and defense appropriations committees). The second-ranking lobbyist in GE's Washington office, Robert W. Barrie, is a leading "money guy" for congressional Democrats and always willing to get on the phone and canvass the lobbying community for money.[7]

GE is also a social philanthropist. Its tax-exempt foundations gave away $18.8 million in 1989, mostly to colleges and school systems, including major commitments to scholarships for the poor and racial minorities. Like any other good citizen, GE donates to United Way and other local community projects. Alongside the company's 1989 earnings of $3.9 billion, GE's sense of charity does not seem immoderate.

But the corporation's philanthropy also serves its own political objectives in direct ways. GE's tax-exempt contributions went, for instance, to lobbyist Charls Walker's American Council for Capital Formation (an "educational" front group that campaigns against the corporate income tax and for a national sales tax), the Institute for International Economics (a think tank that promotes the multinational corporate line on trade and economic policy), and Americans for Generational Equity (an issues front that campaigns for cuts in such entitlement programs as Social Security). GE gives substantially to the major policy think tanks that promote the conservative business perspective—Brookings and AEI—though not to zealously right-wing outfits, such as the Heritage Foundation.

GE is also directly active in political education and propaganda. It sponsors the *McLaughlin Group,* a right-wing TV talk show that is popular among political devotees for its quick, abusive style of discourse. GE is a leading member in the Business Roundtable, which disseminates the political agenda of Fortune 500 corporations. GE also enters dozens of trade associations and a continuous galaxy of temporary joint ventures like the Superfund Coalition formed to prepare public opinion for business objectives.

The Committee on the Present Danger, founded with defense-industry financing in 1976, created the propaganda base for the huge defense buildup of the 1980s. The Center for Economic Progress and Employment, despite its public-spirited title, is a front group formed by GE, Union Carbide, Ford and other manufacturers to weaken the product-liability laws. The center financed a lengthy study attacking liability lawsuits and, for added authority, arranged to have the Brookings Institution publish it.[8]

General Electric also fosters a positive political image directly through its own advertising—soft-focused TV spots that portray GE as an admirable citizen. According to INFACT, the Boston group leading a boycott of GE products, the company tripled its image advertising to $26.8 million a year after it came under attack in the mid-1980s as a producer of nuclear weapons. The increased self-promotion also coincided, however, with GE's embarrassing criminal indictment for cheating the government on defense contracts.

General Electric's commercials are more tasteful and entertaining than the hard-sell "issue" ads sponsored by some other companies. The TV spots usually tell compelling stories from GE's inventive past—the pioneering of jet engines, the development of lighting that ushered in night baseball. However, the contemporary GE is better known not for inventing new products, but for its hard-nosed corporate restructurings, buying and selling and taking apart whole companies.

One of GE's loveliest commercials depicts its role in helping to bring freedom to the people of Hungary. It is a gorgeous montage of Hungarian citizens joyously celebrating their liberation from communism, mixed with images of GE managers completing the purchase of Hungary's state-owned Tungsram Company, eastern Europe's major manufacturer of light bulbs. Like all effective propaganda, the commercial amplifies something that is true but strips away complicating facts that would conflict with the heartwarming message.

While GE was buying Tungsram for $150 million in late 1989, a flying squad of GE lawyers and lobbyists was blitzing the governments in Washington, Brussels and Budapest—wiring the deal against political risks. The U.S. Justice Department was quickly persuaded to waive antitrust questions, though GE was already the world's second-largest maker of light bulbs. The Overseas Private Investment Corporation, the federal insurance program for corporate overseas investments, was lobbied to insure the venture against political upheaval—the largest policy in the agency's history and its first in eastern Europe. GE used a former general counsel of OPIC to sell the deal. Simultaneously, GE lobbyists managed to defeat a crippling legislative amendment on the Senate floor.

Accomplished under tight deadlines, the multifront lobbying was a splendid example of GE's ambidextrous political capabilities. But GE's assistance to Hungarian freedom, as depicted in the TV commercial, might seem less noble and daring if the audience knew that the GE lobbyists had beforehand secured political protection for the venture.[9]

Anyone who watches television regularly knows that, in recent years, major corporations have significantly increased the millions they spend on both soft and hard propaganda—commercials designed to promote corporate images and political attitudes, not to sell specific products. According to annual surveys by *Public Relations Journal,* the volume of corporate-image advertising reached $941 million a year by 1987 in broadcasting and print media—enough money to finance four or five presidential campaigns.[10]

Americans are saturated in "feel good" messages about the largest business corporations. Dow Chemical, notwithstanding its notorious reputation as a polluter, portrays itself as an old friend of nature. AT&T saves eagles. IBM teaches children in the ghetto. Northrop, facing trial in Los Angeles for criminally defrauding the Air Force, began broadcasting commercials on Los Angeles TV that featured legendary test pilot Chuck Yeager extolling the high quality of Northrop's aircraft. The presiding federal judge was so upset he banned the ads on the grounds that Northrop was trying to influence potential jurors for its trial.[11]

What difference does all this propaganda make in terms of political action? Market research suggests that, while corporate propaganda may not do much to reduce the public's collective distrust of business, individual companies can significantly dilute the hostility toward themselves.

In California, for instance, Chevron targeted messages in its "People Do" ad campaign at the most hostile segment of citizens—the so-called "inner-directed" people with strong environmental values, who expressed heightened opposition to offshore oil drilling and low regard for Chevron. Two years later, the research director proudly reported, these people felt much better about Chevron and ranked it first among oil companies they trusted to protect the environment. They even bought more Chevron gasoline. They were still not, however, in favor of offshore drilling.[12]

General Electric's politics depends on all these various elements in its political infrastructure, but they are only preconditions for influencing political outcomes. In the public arena, what best advances GE's position is that, implicitly or explicitly, it is speaking on behalf of others.

GE accumulates power by pretending to serve as a mediating institution. The company lobbies expertly to enhance its own sales and profit, but General Electric routinely invokes millions of other citizens as the ultimate beneficiaries of its politics. When GE is threatened in Washington, it claims to be defending broader constituencies from injury. But when GE defines its policy objectives, it does not bother to consult the people it ostensibly represents. GE is a mediating institution that accepts no obligation to those for whom it claims to be speaking.

General Electric has 177 plants in the United States (plus 103 others in twenty-three foreign countries), which automatically provides a broad and varied platform of economic interests, including workers, whom it can plausibly represent. Some 243,000 Americans make their living working for GE. Approximately 506,000 Americans are stockholders. About 300 retailers, from Montgomery Ward to Levitz furniture, use credit-card systems run by GE Capital. The NBC network has 200 affiliate stations. GE's jet-engine assembly plants in Evendale, Ohio, and Lynn, Massachusetts, make the engines for two dozen different kinds of military aircraft.

In other words, the potential span of political interests that a corporation presumes to represent can be made to look much larger than the company itself. GE's political voice multiplies itself and intersects with millions of others—people who may or may not actually agree with its political objectives. GE mobilizes allies and its local cadres—workers, managers, customers, suppliers—when they do agree. If they don't, it simply invokes their names.

Frank Doyle, for instance, once protested to the Senate Foreign Relations Committee that, despite appearances, the Export-Import Bank's trade subsidies for such major corporations as GE and Boeing really help the little guys too, despite, as Doyle acknowledged, "a lingering perception that the bank is a big-company benefit." The smaller companies benefit, he insisted, because "they participate through us as sub-contractors."[13]

Defense issues, argued out in public on the esoteric plane of grand military strategy or weapons technology, are lobbied in private on an earthier stratum: How many jobs in my district or state are attached to this bomber or tank?

Though the Massachusetts delegation is as dovish as any in Congress, one congressional aide from the state said with only mild exaggeration: "Basically, the GE guy comes around and tells us which aircraft we are voting for because Lynn will make the engines for them."

Liberal members of Congress may be hostile to the bloated defense budget, but they love defense workers. "Yeah," Representative Barney Frank of Massachusetts acknowledged, "I guess I voted for the F-18 a couple of times because it has GE from Lynn. I'm sure I wouldn't have voted for it if the GE plant had been in Cleveland."

When General Electric speaks for its shareholders' interest in maximized profits, its approach necessarily becomes more oblique, since politicians are not likely to be terribly excited by the narrow goal of boosting stock values. The company's profit objective is, therefore, reformulated as a question of broad national economic policy—how to stimulate the economic growth from which the multitudes will presumably benefit.

According to GE, this goal can be achieved by cutting its taxes. Reginald H. Jones, Welch's predecessor as CEO, was a much more visible political player in Washington, relentlessly selling his arguments for corporate tax relief. Jones "seemed to spend his life at the Senate Finance Committee, lobbying for tax breaks and with some success," said Robert McIntyre of Citizens for Tax Justice. "Jones was literally at every single Finance Committee hearing I ever went to. His line was the same old bullshit about how we have to increase American competitiveness and all you need to do to increase American competitiveness is reduce GE's taxes."

Phillips S. Peter, head of GE's Washington office, was simultaneously acting as a principal in the Carlton Group, the permanent caucus of corporate tax lobbyists who basically wrote the business provisions for the watershed tax-cutting legislation of 1981. As is now well known, the companies were well rewarded for their political energies. Hundreds of them—including General Electric—wound up paying no taxes at all for several years.

On such matters, economic blackmail is a standard tactic of corporate politics. On the eve of the 1981 tax vote, members of Congress were inundated with telegrams and personal visits from corporate CEOs, warning them in the most explicit terms that their districts would lose jobs if the business tax reductions failed to pass. Even a politician who dismissed these threats as specious was forewarned that his next opponent could accuse him of voting against jobs—a charge that would be corroborated by the Fortune 500.

As it turned out, General Electric was possibly the biggest single winner in Ronald Reagan's celebrated tax cuts. It had corporate profits of $6.5 billion during 1981–1983 and, astonishingly, received a tax rebate of $283 million from the federal government. Its tax burden went from $330 million a year to minus $90 million a year—money the government now owed GE. By rough estimate, the 1981 tax legislation yielded as much as $1.3 billion for General Electric over several years and probably much more in the long run.

GE's windfall did not, however, create any new jobs for Americans. On the contrary, the company was in the process of drastically shrinking its U.S. workforce—eliminating nearly fifty thousand people from its payroll through layoffs, attrition and the sell-off of subsidiaries. The tax windfall, however, did help GE finance its aggressive campaign of corporate acquisitions, as it bought such important companies as Utah Construction, RCA and NBC.[14]

The same pattern was general in American business. After the generous tax cuts of 1981, capital investment by American corporations accelerated, but not in the United States. The new investments were primarily made in foreign countries. American taxpayers, in other words, were unwittingly subsidizing the globalization of their own industrial structure.[15]

As Congress struggled in subsequent years to recover some of the lost tax revenue from 1981, GE sometimes went its own way—splitting from the corporate coalition on some crucial tax questions and skillfully protecting its own balance sheet. One of the most egregious loopholes created in 1981 effectively allowed companies to swap tax shelters with each other by leasing equipment instead of purchasing it. Since GE Capital was already a major leasing enterprise, this provision helped the parent corporation erase tens of millions in taxes. But, given all the new competition that the loophole was attracting into the leasing business, GE decided it would be better off with repeal.

On this issue, GE sang with the reformers and against its former political allies in business. Winning on its own terms, however, required the adroit use of GE's political connections. At the final hour in the 1982 debate, Bob Barrie, the GE lobbyist who is a valued fundraiser for Democrats, called in his chits with the House Democratic leaders. As Thomas B. Edsall of *The Washington Post* described the episode, Barrie made a nifty end run around the phalanx of corporate lobbyists who were on the other side of the tax-leasing issue.

"Barrie was able to get with Rostenkowski, with the Speaker, with the entire Democratic leadership to explain what was a horribly complex issue," an allied lobbyist told Edsall. "And he got them on board. From GE's point of view, it was quite a coup."[16]

General Electric does not always win, however, and eventually it was compelled to start paying taxes again. CEO John Welch bitterly opposed the 1986 tax reform measure, which set a minimum corporate tax and repealed the investment tax credit, but corporations lost in the end. Wealthy taxpayers, on the other hand, won with drastic reductions in individual tax rates.

By 1989, GE was paying $1.1 billion in federal taxes—an effective tax rate of about 23 percent, still well below the statutory rate of 34 percent. GE, meanwhile, carries on its books $3.5 billion in legally deferred tax liabilities—money it owes the government but, thanks to various loopholes provided for defense contractors, doesn't have to pay until sometime in the future. Overall, corporate tax revenue has consistently fallen $20 billion to $30 billion a year below what the 1986 reforms had predicted.[17]

Beyond their individual objectives, GE and the other corporate organizations also act in concert as important gatekeepers for the political debate—guarding the public agenda with more purpose and consistency than the news media. When consensus develops among the major players of business and banking, ideas that were thought to be dormant or impossible suddenly turn into active issues in the political arena.

Universal health-care reform is the latest example. For decades, the American public expressed its support for national health insurance and such groups as organized labor actively campaigned for it. Nothing happened. Now major corporate leaders—the CEOs of Chrysler, American Airlines, Ford and many others—have declared support for basic reform for their own purposes, because the soaring cost of the private health-insurance system is devouring corporate balance sheets too.

The political community, therefore, is at last stirring on the subject. A goal that was routinely dismissed as "socialist" or too expensive has abruptly found a place on the agenda. High-level negotiations are underway between labor and the major corporations (including General Electric) on how to define the health-care solution. When the political solutions are proposed, they may be shaped as much by the cost-saving imperatives of major corporations as by the popular distress expressed by citizens.[18]

The distinctive quality in General Electric's politics is not, however, its behind-the-scenes deal making or the skillful ways in which it amplifies its own interests by invoking the interests of workers, small business or consumers. These are the standard approaches employed by corporate political organizations of every kind.

What sets GE apart from most other companies is the seriousness with which it represents people in the society whose lives are not connected to the fate of General Electric—especially society's losers. These include children and poor people, disadvantaged racial minorities and even ex-workers, the tens of thousands who lost their jobs at General Electric during the 1980s. In various ways, as GE's leaders have figured out, this is good for the company.

Frank Doyle has testified eloquently, for instance, on behalf of greater federal funding for Head Start and early childhood education programs, invoking an economic rationale for the company's social concern. "A competitive America—let alone a compassionate America—will need every trained mind and every pair of skilled hands," Doyle declared. "But the appalling fact is that one in five of our teenage children and younger live in poverty."[19]

GE cares about these children, Doyle explained, because if they are not trained for high-skill work in the global economy, they will become future costs to the society in terms of welfare and crime. The company has also been an ardent advocate of government job-training and retraining programs for the workers displaced by economic change. With grants from the Labor Department, GE operates such programs for its own former employees.

"When the GEs and GMs and AT&Ts and USXs of America no longer have low-skill, low-value-added jobs—because they have adjusted to a high-skill, high-value-added global competitive world—those left out will be locked out of the great American middle class," Doyle warned. "And every time that happens, it is a tragedy for America."

While the rhetoric sounds public-spirited and compassionate—even dangerously bleeding-heart for tough-minded businessmen—General Electric's social concern serves its own long-term political interests. It provides a shield against hostile political action and deflects political attention from the company's own controversial behavior in the American economy. Above all, it defines the economic debate in the terms that are most congenial to GE's own future.

Like other major multinational corporations, GE wants maximum freedom to do as it chooses in the global economy—shifting production and jobs wherever seems most efficient. And it wants minimal responsibility for the economic consequences that follow for the U.S. workforce—the steady loss of high-wage industrial jobs. The company's "social concern" is, thus, quite shallow: It cares about educating little children, but accepts no responsibility for what economic dislocation does to adult workers and their communities.

GE and other important corporate voices, including the Business Roundtable, instead promote the argument that the remedy for job losses and the downward mobility of industrial workers is simply more education and better training. This analysis conveniently shifts the blame from corporations to the educational system and the workers themselves. But it requires the corporations to make a highly dubious claim: that America is facing a shortage of skilled workers.

"Our industrial economy," Doyle asserted, "is generating more jobs than we have people with skills to fill them." Many recent college graduates learned otherwise when they went out to begin their careers and were compelled to take work below their educational levels. The shortage they encountered was not one of well-trained workers, but of good jobs.

Labor economists from the Economic Policy Institute examined the corporate claim of an impending "skills shortage" and declared it a hoax. The corporate political objective, they concluded, is to divert attention from the real wage problems—the proliferation of low-wage jobs and the declining value of industrial wages generally.[20]

Doyle's assertion of skilled-labor shortages, in fact, comes from a company that abandoned fifty American plants and shrank its overall workforce, foreign and domestic, by roughly one fourth during the last decade. The forty-six thousand American workers let go by GE since 1981 were not mainly janitors or unskilled general laborers or low-level clerks. They were people with premium wages—machinists and electricians, engineers and white-collar managers.

Union leaders bitterly dubbed GE's CEO "Neutron Jack" because, like the so-called neutron bomb, Jack Welch eliminates the people and leaves the buildings standing. During the 1980s, GE bought more than three hundred businesses and sold off more than two hundred others, searching for the right mix of domestic and foreign products to lead in world markets. GE transformed itself from a company that was two thirds manufacturing and one third services to one that is the reverse.

Welch's strategy, widely admired in business and financial circles, is to create what he calls "a boundaryless company"—a corporation that "will recognize no distinctions between 'domestic' and 'foreign' operations." In practice, his restructurings compelled GE unions to negotiate wage contracts that were really job-shrinking agreements with provisions for severance pay and early retirement.

For white-collar management, Welch also virtually eliminated the old, unwritten assurances of mutual loyalty and trust that used to prevail in companies like GE. "Loyalty to a company, it's nonsense," Jack Welch told *The Wall Street Journal.* Frank Doyle told *Business Week:* "We now want to create an environment where employees are 'ready to go and eager to stay.' " *Business Week* concluded that at General Electric the old social contract between employer and employees has been nullified.[21]

Throughout this transformation, however, Doyle and other GE spokesmen have reiterated their sympathy for the losers—and encouraged them to improve their skills while they look for other jobs. "I'm not advocating a crude, vote-with-our-feet ethic or asking displaced workers and their families to crisscross the country reading the want ads," Doyle told the Congressional Competitiveness Caucus. "What I am advocating is the basic premise that people will change jobs, upgrade skills and switch industries, not once but several times in their careers."[22]

What Doyle and General Electric never adequately explained is where all these new, high-skilled jobs are going to come from—when major companies like GE are busy eliminating them. It requires a mighty leap of faith to imagine that everyone will somehow climb up the "skill ladder," as Doyle called it, and become computer technicians. For the last twenty years, the American experience with industrial globalization has produced the opposite result for American workers.

The deterioration of wages and incomes and the structure of the job market is the central economic question facing American families, but corporate political organizations have succeeded in deflecting the issue from serious scrutiny. GE favors federal aid for the unemployed, but it is opposed to any political measure aimed at the behavior of employers in the global economy (the subject explored directly in Chapter Seventeen). Politicians debate trade policy and bash Japan, but they do not scrutinize the loyalty of America's own global companies. Frank Doyle's most impressive political achievement is the debate that never occurs on the nature of the multinational corporations.

The politicians who attempt to stand and defend workers against these forces are ridiculed by elite opinion—labeled irresponsible and reactionary or perhaps punished in other ways as well. "Let's be certain," Doyle warned the congressional caucus, "that those who should provide positive leadership don't seek retrogressive, fear-driven solutions."

Thus, the underlying political tension lies in the question of who really speaks for the best interests of Americans and their future. GE's rhetoric stresses "we"—the warm-spirited Americanism of its TV commercials—but its vision of itself as a "boundaryless" company does not really depend upon the general well-being of Americans, any more than it depends on loyalty to its own employees. In fundamental ways, GE's own long-term political interests are in conflict with the interests of many of the people it presumes to speak for—workers and communities and poor people, but also the general prosperity. Corporate politics, though it may intimidate politicians, cannot be expected to function as a trustworthy mediator for others. This connective strand only runs one way.

Given its girth and skill and other attributes, a politically active corporation like General Electric acts like a modern version of the "political machine," with some of the same qualities of the old political machines that used to dominate American cities. In form and behavior, the modern corporation has the same cohesion and sustaining purpose that made the old urban organizations so influential in politics. Its stubborn permanence is a force that others must contend with. Its supple sense of strategy permits temporary alliances with old enemies and occasional betrayal of friends. Except, of course, there is not just one corporate "machine" operating in American politics, but hundreds of them.

Like the old big-city organizations, the corporate "machines" can be maddeningly parochial but also occasionally farsighted. Fiercely loyal to its own interests and civic values, a corporation may be arrogantly dismissive of larger public concerns. And, like the old urban machines, the corporate political organizations often display a tolerance for corrupt behavior, so long as the corruption enhances the organizations' own well-being.

Unlike a party organization, however, a company like GE does not develop its political agenda by consulting its cadres or the constituencies for whom it speaks, not even the shareholders. Most of the old local party organizations, notwithstanding their negative qualities, did give ordinary people a connecting point to government and sometimes a genuine venue for speaking to power. Political decisions are closely held in the corporate machine, not unlike the worst of the big-city bosses. The dependent constituencies are reduced to a passive role resembling that of ward heelers, with not much choice except to follow the dictates of the organization.

The corporation has acquired many of the same political skills that party organizations are supposed to have—it teaches and organizes, it agitates and leads. But it has no need to listen to its adherents or assume responsibility for them. For these political machines, there are no elections.

This organizational reality is a central element in what deforms and confuses modern democracy. The new political machines, like the old ones, dot the political landscape like free-floating baronies, independent and self-sustaining and unaccountable. They have similar interests and frequently merge their power in coordinated strategies, just as the big-city machines used to do. But they are also often in conflict with one another and it is those contests among competing client groups that usually define the largest issues and frequently stalemate them. If the government in Washington is unable to govern, it is stymied, not by reckless public opinion, but by the conflicting demands of the corporate machines.

The implications of this structure of power are obviously antidemocratic. Yet, as a political system, it "works." That is, it works in the narrow sense that it takes care of the everyday chores of politics. The corporations, together and separately, finance the parties and politicians. They sponsor the public-policy development needed to shape the governing debate. They mobilize public opinion around political agendas. In their own self-interested manner, they even hold elected officials accountable for failure to perform.

Above all, the formidable, ubiquitous presence of corporate political organizations persuades many citizens to retreat from the contest. That may be the gravest damage of all. Faced with this assembled power, many people accept their own impotence and defer. They assume that the hard work of democracy—debating public issues, contesting elections, helping to organize their own lives—is work that belongs to others.

The price for this default is enormous in terms of what the government decides. When the corporate perspective defines the outlines of debate, it shrinks the nation's political values to the amoral arithmetic of the bottom line.

The rich and complicated fabric of American life—and the infinite political imagination of its citizens—is reduced to sterile calculations of cost-benefit analysis. Competing political aspirations, whether for equitable taxation or environmental protection or affordable housing, are judged according to a narrow question: Is it good for the machine?

All these facts add up to a daunting challenge for democracy—how to come to terms with the institutional reality of corporate power without disrupting anyone's elementary rights. The guarantees of free speech and open debate, after all, extend to agents of concentrated economic power as much as to anyone else. The solution does not lie in curtailing democratic rights for certain parties. It involves applying the obligations of citizenship to corporations as forcefully as they are applied to individuals.

The great project of corporate lawyers, extending over generations, has been to establish full citizenship for their business organizations. They argue that their companies are entitled to the same political rights, save voting, that the Constitution guarantees to people. In 1886 the Supreme Court declared, without hearing arguments, that corporations would henceforth be considered "persons" for purposes of the Fourteenth Amendment—the "due process" amendment that was established to protect the newly emancipated black slaves after the Civil War. Fifty years later, Justice Hugo Black reviewed the Supreme Court's many decisions applying the Fourteenth Amendment and observed that less than one half of one percent invoked it in protection of the Negro race, and more than 50 percent asked that its benefits be extended to corporations.

In the New Deal era, the Supreme Court finally curtailed the corporations' use of "due process" to thwart state and federal governments in the regulation of business. But, during the last twenty years, the corporate lawyers have staged a comeback. In the modern era of regulation, they are invoking the Bill of Rights to protect their organizations from federal laws. Professor Carl J. Mayer of Hofstra University described their victories:

"Consider, for example, the following recent Supreme Court decisions: a textile corporation successfully invoked the Fifth Amendment double-jeopardy clause to avoid retrial in a criminal anti-trust action. A consortium of major corporations, including the First National Bank of Boston, joined in a First Amendment lawsuit that overturned state restrictions on corporate spending for political referendums. An electrical and plumbing concern invoked the Fourth Amendment to thwart federal inspections conducted under OSHA. A California public utility relied on the First Amendment to overturn state regulations designed to lower utility rates. Twenty years ago, the corporation had not deployed any of these Bill of Rights provisions successfully."[23]

Corporations, in other words, claim to be "citizens" of the Republic, not simply for propaganda or good public relations, but in the actual legal sense of claiming constitutional rights and protections. Whatever the Supreme Court may say on the matter, everyone knows a corporation is a legal-financial artifice, not a living person. Whatever legal theories may eventually develop around this question, the political implications are profound. If corporations are citizens, then other citizens—the living, breathing kind—necessarily become less important to the processes of self-government.

A corporation, because it is an "artificial legal person," has inherent capacities that mortal citizens do not possess. For one thing, it can live forever. For another, a corporation, unlike people, can exist in many places at once. Or it can alter its identity—chop off its arms or legs and transform itself into an utterly different "person." Or it can sell itself to new owners, including owners who are not themselves Americans. Are these foreigners now empowered as U.S. "citizens" by virtue of owning an "American corporation"?

Above all, a corporation by its nature possesses political resources that very few individual citizens can ever hope to accumulate—the wealth and motivation to influence political outcomes directly and continuously. Thus, if corporations are to be regarded as citizens, they are equipped to hold the front rank in American politics and nearly everyone else will inevitably become citizens of the second class.

But the corporate claim to citizenship raises a crucial contradiction: When corporations commit crimes, they do not wish to be treated as people, but as "artificial legal entities" that cannot be held personally accountable for their misdeeds. If an individual citizen is convicted of a felony, he automatically loses his political rights—the right to vote, the right to hold office—and sometimes his personal freedom as well. More broadly, ex-convicts are not normally invited to testify before congressional hearings or to advise the White House on important policies.

When corporations are convicted of crimes, they lose none of their diverse abilities to act in politics. Corporations are "citizens" who regularly offend the law—both in the criminal sense and in the civil terms of flouting regulatory statutes. Yet their formidable influence on political decisions goes forward undiminished, as well as the substantial financial rewards they harvest from government.

This contradiction is not a narrow complaint against a handful of corporate rogues. It applies generally to many (though not all) of the nation's leading corporations—Fortune 500 names that are regularly listed as "defendants" for criminal activity or civil complaints. Reforming the permissiveness and non-enforcement of modern laws cannot possibly be accomplished without addressing the ambiguous terms by which corporations presume to be citizens.

General Electric, for instance, is certainly not the worst "corporate citizen'' in the land, but the company has accumulated an impressive rap sheet in recent years. GE, understandably, does not depict this side of its character in the engaging corporate-image commercials.

After a fourteen-week trial in 1990, a jury in Philadelphia convicted GE of criminal fraud for cheating the Army on a $254 million contract for battlefield computers. Rather than appeal, GE paid $16.1 million in criminal and civil fines, including $11.7 million to settle government complaints that it had padded its bids on two hundred other military and space contracts. In Cincinnati, GE agreed to pay the government $3.5 million to settle five civil lawsuits alleging contractor fraud at the Evendale, Ohio, jet-engine plant. A machinist at Evendale had come forward to accuse the company managers of altering nine thousand daily labor vouchers to inflate its Pentagon billings for military jet engines.

GE paid $900,000 to settle allegations that it overcharged the Army for electronic adapters used in the M-1 tank and Bradley fighting vehicles. It settled a similar complaint for cheating the Navy on components for guided missile frigates. It pleaded guilty to 108 charges of making false claims to the Air Force on a contract for the Minuteman intercontinental missile. In that case, the chief engineer of GE's space systems division was convicted of perjury; the company paid a fine of $1 million.[24]

Given this record, one begins to grasp why GE wants the best lawyers it can find, especially lawyers familiar with Washington. It has cheated the Army, Navy and Air Force. A defense contractor like GE is sometimes ''suspended'' from doing business with the Pentagon but, in GE's case, the disbarment is always lifted in time for the next round of contracts.

GE has offended the law in other areas as well. It was convicted in 1981 on charges of creating a $1.25 million slush fund with which to bribe a Puerto Rican official on a $92 million power-plant contract. Three GE executives went to prison in that case. Kidder Peabody, GE's stock brokerage, paid $25.3 million to settle the Securities and Exchange Commission's complaint of insider trading. GE Capital paid $275,000 in civil penalties in 1989 for discriminating against low-income consumers, the largest fine collected under the Equal Credit Opportunity Act. The corporation itself settled an employment discrimination complaint in 1978 for $32 million in compensation to women and minorities. About the same time, GE's Canadian subsidiary was being convicted (with Westinghouse and other companies) of conspiracy to fix prices on light bulbs. And so on.[25]

GE's corporate headquarters typically expresses surprise when the wrongdoing is revealed and protests its own innocence. These incidents, it explains, are the transgressions of individual employees, not of company policy. Sometimes it fires the employees, other times it pays for their defense attorneys. Philip Lacovara compared a corporation's employees to the population of a midsized city and no city, he observed, is free of crime. "It is entirely unrealistic to attribute every act of a miscreant employee to the corporation's directors and officers on the theory that they 'should have known' what was happening," Lacovara told the U.S. Sentencing Commission.

This line of defense seems especially disingenuous for a corporation that, during the last decade, introduced the high-pressure management culture of "Neutron Jack" Welch. GE first turns up the heat on its line managers by creating a climate of purposeful insecurity—everyone's job is at risk if his or her division's profit performance lags. Then, when division managers in the field are caught in false billings and other forms of profiteering, GE piously disavows them as "miscreant employees."

To reassure the public after its Pentagon fraud cases, General Electric announced a companywide "initiative" to teach ethics to its workforce. The training was evidently insufficient because, in August 1991, GE was again accused of defrauding the federal government—this time for $30 million. The Justice Department filed civil fraud charges that accused the company of collaborating with Israeli military officials on false billings between 1985 and 1988 for jet engines built at Evendale for Israel but paid for by the Pentagon. GE's top management once again expressed its innocence and fired the international sales manager.[26]

If one sets aside the contentious issues of corporate criminality, the character of Citizen GE is still delineated clearly enough in more routine matters of noncriminal offenses, especially its offenses against the environment. The economists' narrow conception of "efficiency" encourages such behavior. By saving money for itself, a corporation throws off huge costs on somebody else, usually the general public.

General Electric is implicated in a harrowing list of places ruined by pollution. Four of GE's factories were on EPA's list of the most dangerous industrial sources of toxic air pollution. The company has been identified as responsible for contributing to the damage at forty-seven Superfund sites.

For nearly twenty years, ending in 1964, GE was the principal operator at the government's Hanford nuclear reservation in Washington—the bomb-making plant that is now notorious for the epic contamination of surrounding land and ground water with both radioactive and toxic substances. Restoration, if it is possible at all, will cost billions; GE is being sued and has made no comment on its responsibility for the devastation.

For thirty-four years, GE has also operated the Pinellas plant near St. Petersburg, Florida, where it makes the nuclear "trigger" for the hydrogen bomb. Toxic and radioactive wastes have been discovered in the Pinellas County sewage system and nearby Boca Ciega Bay. The plant was described by the St. Petersburg Times as an "environmental mess." GE announced in 1991 that it was getting out of Pinellas because new contracting rules from the

Department of Energy "would have exposed the company to increased legal and financial risks."[27]

In Alabama, General Electric (and Monsanto) settled out of court when the state sued it for dumping PCBs in the Coosa River. In New York, a forty-mile stretch of the Hudson River above Albany was polluted in the same way; GE has been arguing with state officials for fifteen years over the multi-million-dollar cleanup for the river. Meanwhile, GE agreed with New York authorities to spend $20 million restoring the ground water at its Waterford, New York, plant contaminated with benzene, trichloroethylene, vinyl chloride and other toxics. In New Hampshire and Massachusetts, GE and forty-eight other companies settled for $33.1 million for illegally dumping toxics at four sites. In Ohio, GE was part of a $13.5 million cleanup agreement for a chemical dump site in the Cincinnati suburbs. And so on.[28]

In fairness to General Electric, its antisocial profile is distinctive in part because of the company's size and diversity. But its behavior is not unusual. Anyone who reads *The Wall Street Journal* faithfully can collect a similar assortment of florid headlines about other famous American corporations. Indeed, the story of corporate crime or coverups is so routine, it is losing its shock value.

Mobil Oil: A federal jury awards $1.4 million to a former Mobil employee who said he was fired for refusing to conceal environmental problems. Northrop: Caught bribing foreign governments in the 1970s, the company is caught again in 1990, accused of funneling $6.2 million in illegal payments to South Korea. Waste Management: The nation's largest waste-disposal company has paid more than $50 million in fines and settlements for environmental violations, including disconnecting the monitoring devices at its waste-disposal sites. Eastern Airlines: The company was indicted with nine of its managers for falsifying airplane maintenance records. Hughes Aircraft: The fifth-largest defense contractor and a General Motors subsidiary, Hughes pleads guilty to obtaining bootleg copies of classified Pentagon documents, a plot that involved four other major defense contractors.[29]

Professor Amitai Etzioni of George Washington University found that 62 percent of the Fortune 500 corporations were involved in one or more "significant illegalities" in the decade from 1975 to 1984. Nearly half of them—42 percent—were identified in two or more episodes of corrupt behavior. Fifteen percent of them—seventy-five major corporations—were involved in five or more cases.[30]

The basic question is: What exactly produces this repetition of injurious or illegal behavior by corporations? It is not properly blamed on the ethical failings of company managers, who, as a group, are presumably as moral as anyone else in the society. The core cause is the corporation's own values—an ethic of efficiency that creates the cost-cutting imperative driving every manager's behavior. A plant manager can never escape from this imperative, regardless of his personal values or the ethics courses that business schools offer to MBA students.

The power of this cost-cutting imperative was dramatically illustrated in a case in which General Electric was accused of concealing design flaws in a giant nuclear-containment vessel it sold to the Washington Public Power Supply Systems. WPPSS was forced to spend hundreds of millions on repairs to make the plant safe and it sued GE for contract fraud. The presiding judge described the testimony by GE personnel as "forced, sometimes forlorn and sometimes incredible."

In particular, the judge cited internal company documents that made it clear GE had identified the potential dangers early on, but chose to do nothing. "General Electric knew these problems should be examined but decided to adopt only an analytical approach," Judge Alan A. McDonald declared, "because the full-scale tests required . . . would be—I am quoting from the documents—'very expensive.' "[31]

General Electric's own lawyer, Philip Lacovara, obliquely acknowledged the connection between a company's bottom line and its attitude toward the law in his comments to the U.S. Sentencing Commission. "In the absence of substantial credit for voluntary disclosure, it is not in the organization's economic self-interest to search for and disclose offenses that management has been unable to prevent," Lacovara wrote. ". . . The economic disadvantages of voluntarily disclosing suspected misconduct may well discourage corporations from reporting their suspicions or assessments to agency regulators and law-enforcement personnel."[32]

Concealing the truth in order to save money is not, of course, peculiar to General Electric. When the Conference Board, a business-sponsored research center, surveyed three hundred corporate managers on business ethics, it asked what they would do if they were told about public-health risks caused by their companies' toxic emissions. One in five said they would do nothing—even though a responsible company official brought the danger to their attention. If the employee alerted the public anyway, half of the three hundred managers would fire him. Another fourth of them would reassign him to a different job. Only 6 percent of the managers said the company should immediately change its manufacturing process to reduce the dangerous emissions.[33]

How might American corporations be compelled to accept their obligations to law and society in a more reliable manner? And why is it that corporations, while regularly abusing public law and trust, are allowed to continue functioning as the preeminent citizens in American politics? For ordinary citizens, the law has elaborated thorough answers to those questions—people who are criminals are barred from formal politics. For corporate criminals, the law is more forgiving.

The two questions could be answered together if meaningful sanctions and penalties are developed that will punish lawless corporations in the only language that an "artificial legal person" understands: profit and loss. The corporation must know that repeatedly offending the law puts it at risk of losing real value—the financial privileges of government contracts or tax preferences, but also the political privileges of appearing in the public arena as an advocate for itself and others.

The new sentencing guidelines being prepared for the federal courts are a modest step toward this kind of discipline, though not a fundamental departure from the status quo. Fines and other penalties will be stiffened. In extreme circumstances, courts may be able to impose terms of probation on corporate managements, a kind of conservatorship that monitors corrective action. California, likewise, has enacted tough new standards for corporate criminal liability, partly in frustration with the federal government's weak enforcement against industrial violators of environmental and occupational safety laws.[34]

Criminal prosecution of companies, though somewhat increased in recent years, is still quite rare—especially for major corporations that have the legal capacity to negotiate away their troubles with the law. In 1988, for instance, there were only 475 federal criminal cases brought against companies—and 85 percent of those involved very small businesses, with fewer than fifty employees and sales of less than $1 million. Criminal prosecution of individuals can be therapeutic, especially in pollution cases, but sending the managers to jail will not necessarily change the behavior of a recidivist corporation.[35]

In the interest of equity, law and legal doctrine must fashion methods for altering corporate behavior: sanctions that reverse the incentives inside corporations by raising the bottom line cost of lawlessness. Any company, to be sure, may on rare occasions be unwittingly implicated in an offense. For the repeat offender, however, a system of graduated penalties ought to extract real losses. Because it is not a real person, a corporation cannot be sent to prison, but its freedom as an enterprise could be restricted in other ways.

A recidivist, as Ralph Nader has proposed, should be barred for a specified time from selling things to the government—banishment prescribed in law, not at the Pentagon's discretion. To avoid economic disruption, a company could be required to divest a subsidiary that has a record of defrauding the government or committing other offenses. The forced sale of a division would cost the offending company dearly, but the factories and jobs would continue to operate under new ownership. Like ordinary criminals, a corporation with a well-documented rap sheet ought to be ineligible to hold government licenses for television stations or other lucrative franchises. GE's growing media empire, for instance, would be put at risk by its continued cheating at the Pentagon.

Corporations might also forfeit their political rights, just as citizens do.

Lawful standards could establish a felonious status for "corporate citizens" that bars a lawless company from political activity for a fixed period of time. A convicted company, for instance, would be prohibited from financing political candidates or lobbying Congress directly or appearing before regulatory hearings or pressuring the regulators in private. The suspension of corporate political rights would be equivalent to what happens to people when they are convicted felons. The corporate ex-convicts would have to learn how to live for a time without their Washington lobbyists.

This basic principle of accountability could be incorporated in many different kinds of statutes—especially the tax code—with evidentiary thresholds that are less demanding than criminal law. A company that accumulates repeated civil offenses against the environment or public health could be treated in law as an antisocial organization that has lost its usual privileges. The tax code, for instance, provides a long list of allowances, exceptions and preferences that feed tens of billions into corporate balance sheets. When Congress enacts such tax benefits, it could stipulate that no corporation will be eligible for the money if it has violated laws and regulations during the preceding years.

This would be harsh medicine indeed, guaranteed to make corporate executives concentrate on the "miscreant" behavior within their own organizations. But why should law-abiding taxpayers subsidize the lawless ones? The ethical choices facing business managers would be set in a new framework that makes it easier for them to do the right thing—protecting the company's profits by obeying the law.

Addressing the legal obligations of corporations leads to broader questions about their social obligations. Why, for example, should companies receive tax credits for their research and development when they are simultaneously shrinking their U.S. employment? Why should government pick up the tab for cleaning up social problems that were generated by private employers who failed to observe minimal social obligations to their workers and communities? The questions lead in the direction of establishing in law a social context for corporations—legal obligations like parental leave and other worker benefits that involve using the government's authority rather than spending the taxpayers' money. As it stands now, in the name of fostering prosperity, Americans are helping to finance enterprises that do not reciprocate the loyalty.

PART FOUR

TRIUMPH AND LOSS

16

CRACKPOT REALISM

The end of the Cold War represents a rare opening for democratic possibilities, but it is also the source of new political crisis. This new epoch suddenly revives questions about the nature of American self-government that have been successfully evaded for two generations. Ready or not, American politics must change, for the world has changed around it.

The country has reached a satisfying end to a struggle that for four decades dominated our national priorities and permeated every corner of the political culture. The Cold War was the central engine driving the government's management of the economy. Fear was the political idea that unified national life for two generations. Now it is abruptly over. America has won; the Soviet Union has disintegrated as a global power.

Yet American politics has also been destabilized by the victory. The mobilizing fear has evaporated, but the institutional structure of government and politics remains on a permanent war footing. Massive armaments and American troops are deployed around the globe; $30 billion a year is devoted to spying and other intelligence activities. The industrial base is still propped up by defense spending; the routines of secrecy and political control developed by the national-security state are still the operating norm. It will not be easy to find a new purpose in the world that justifies these abnormalities as efficiently as communism did.

Nor will it be so easy to rationalize the grave damage the Cold War has done to democracy. The permanent mobilization has altered the democratic relationships profoundly, concentrating power in remote and unaccountable places, institutionalizing secrecy, fostering gross public deception and hypocrisy. It violated law in ways that have become habitual. It assigned great questions of national purpose to a militarized policy elite. It centralized political power in the presidency at the expense of every other democratic institution. The question is: Now that the enemy has vanished, is it possible that democratic order can be restored?

In addition to all the daunting obstacles and deformities enumerated in this book, the democratic problem is now compounded by these large questions about America's place in the world. The post–Cold War reality is actually eclipsed by an even larger force threatening national well-being—the global economy. While governing elites struggled obsessively against communism, the world changed in other ways that now threaten the nation with continuing economic loss and political impotence. The system of globalized enterprise, as the next chapter explains, directly undermines the widely shared prosperity that has been a prerequisite for America's political stability. But the global economy also steadily erodes the nation's sovereign control over its destiny.

Ready or not, Americans are now confronted with some unprecedented questions about self-government and whether the concept will continue to have meaning in the world.

Hardly anyone took note when Senator Daniel Patrick Moynihan introduced his grandly titled legislation—the End of the Cold War Act of 1991—because six days earlier the United States had gone to war again. The senator proposed to abolish the Central Intelligence Agency, the institutional agent and symbol of the Cold War, and fold the CIA's secret activities into the State Department and the Pentagon, where they might be more accountable to political oversight. His legislation set out to prohibit various irregular practices tolerated in government for four decades and to restore a sense of lawful legitimacy to foreign policy.

"The law of nations," Moynihan intoned. "Somewhere that got lost in the fog of the Cold War. It just got lost. We have become a national-security state, a country mobilized for war on a permanent basis, and we got into the business of saying everything is secret. Can we recover the memory of what we were before we became what we are now? Can we rediscover a sense of proportion in the national-security state? The task of purging the Cold War from our institutions is enormous. It will require a sustained and determined effort."[1]

The senator's timing was oblivious to the national mood. At that very moment, the nation was gathered before its TV sets, watching night flashes from the American bombing of Baghdad and the gunsight footage of "smart bombs" finding their Iraqi targets. Six weeks later, America was celebrating victory—a splendid little war in which only a few hundred Americans died. The nation's military prowess was demonstrated for the world; its virtuous intentions were confirmed in the scenes from Kuwait of liberation and home-coming.

In that context, Senator Moynihan's questions seemed eccentric. The Cold War might be over, but now suddenly there was a new struggle to replace it. America is committed, the president announced unilaterally, to establishing and defending a "New World Order." The concept was scarcely defined, but popular support for the American military surged, as did popular support for the president.

Moynihan's questions, however, will return to haunt the country. Saddam Hussein, notwithstanding the barbarity of his regime, proved to be an inade-quate substitute for the Cold War. When the Iraqi dictator seized neighboring Kuwait, George Bush invoked the specter of Hitler, a metaphor that resonated with the start of the Cold War forty years earlier. World War II was America's finest moment in world affairs and nostalgic memories of it powered the long struggle against Soviet communism on countless fronts. Now, President Bush explained, a new dictator was threatening the integrity of nations and must be confronted in the same spirit.

Events, however, failed to sustain the metaphor. For one thing, Hussein was defeated much too quickly and easily. He was also allowed to remain in power, an outcome impossible to reconcile with the president's histrionic rhetoric on the march to war. If Saddam was Hitler, why was he not killed or conquered and put on trial for crimes against humanity?

Other complicating facts developed in the aftermath: The Kuwaiti ruling family, whom we had fought to rescue, demonstrated again that it was itself a despotic feudal regime, contemptuous of the individual rights associated with democracy. The defeat of Iraq produced internal rebellions that eventu-ally mired the United States in the awkward role of a neocolonial warden.

Above all, the war produced this contradiction: In the first year of the post–Cold War era, while the Soviet military apparatus was being withdrawn and dismantled, U.S. defense spending actually increased. The bloated de-fense budget would shrink eventually, as even the Pentagon leaders accepted, but not while the country was waging another war.[2]

Furthermore, neither the end of the Cold War nor U.S. victory in the Persian Gulf could obscure the nation's deteriorating financial strength. The defense buildup of the 1980s had been financed largely on deficit spending— money the federal government borrowed from the allied nations (Japan and Germany, principally) that the United States was defending, more or less for free. If America was now the world's only superpower, it was stuck in a most anomalous predicament. Wall Street financier George Soros described the contradiction: "There are many examples in history where military power was sustained by exacting tributes, but there is no precedent for maintaining military hegemony on borrowed money."[3]

The excitement of an occasional war is, in fact, one of the few remaining opportunities for alienated citizens to feel connected again with their nation's higher politics. So long as the wars are relatively quick and painless, they provide a rallying point for ordinary citizens, a momentary illusion of shared national purpose. The war making offers a fantasy of power for those who are, in fact, powerless. When the euphoria dissipates, as it always does, people resume their distance and disenchantment.

In the aftermath of the Gulf War, Americans did not rally around the "New World Order" proposed by the president. Nor did public opinion embrace the notion that U.S. firepower must police the world. On the contrary, people overwhelmingly expressed the opinion (85 percent to 11 percent in one survey) that military initiatives against global disorders should be led by the United Nations rather than the United States. Their own government, Americans said, should turn its attention to the problems at home. The national-security threat that most troubled ordinary citizens was America's deteriorating position in the global economy.[4]

In the 1950s, when the Cold War temperament was enveloping the thought and language of American politics, the sociologist C. Wright Mills derided what he called "the crackpot realism of the higher authorities and opinion-makers." Absurdities were cloaked in technocratic jargon and passed off to the public as brilliant insight or the fruits of sophisticated intelligence.

The ability of national-security experts to describe reality in arcane ways that ordinary citizens could not easily test for themselves, much less challenge, was a central element of power in the Cold War era and one of its most debilitating influences on democracy. "Crackpot realism" consumed trillions of dollars and built enough nuclear bombs to destroy life on the planet.

Huge, secret bureaucracies were created in government to discover the hidden "facts" about the dangerous world around us, especially the machinations of the Soviet empire, and to shape national-security policy accordingly. Much of this knowledge was considered too sensitive to share with the public, but provocative details were regularly communicated in the form of warnings about new "threats" that had emerged—deadly new missiles pointed at America or revolutionary stirrings in Third World countries said to be inspired by Moscow. The history of the Cold War is a series of such alarums, based on espionage and classified documentation, and of the subsequent events that refuted them.

Given the insular nature of American society, most citizens had little real knowledge of distant nations and no independent way to evaluate the government's description of reality. In the absence of clear contradictory evidence, people generally were prisoners of what the government authorities told them about the world. They accepted what the spies and analysts had discovered about the enemy, at least until the war in Vietnam devastated the government's authority. The alternative—questioning the president while the nation was at war—seemed unpatriotic.

"Crackpot realism" has flourished right up to the present time and the Central Intelligence Agency was a principal source for it. As late as 1989, as Moynihan observed, the CIA reported that the economy of communist East Germany was slightly larger than the economy of West Germany—an intelligence estimate ludicrously debunked a few months later when the East German regime collapsed and its citizens streamed westward in search of jobs, consumer goods and food. The following year, the CIA corrected the record by abruptly shrinking the threatening dimensions of East Germany by more than one third.

The same gross exaggeration was repeated, year after year, when the CIA made its estimates of the Soviet Union's awesome capabilities. The 1989 analysis claimed that the growth rate of the Soviet bloc exceeded western Europe's. But then the CIA had solemnly reported for four decades that the Soviet economy was growing faster than the U.S. economy—almost half again faster. The result, it said, was a formidable industrial power—second-largest in the world and much larger than Japan, according to the CIA.

If that were true, this nation was an adversary rightly to be feared, since it had the economic capacity, not only to match the U.S. arsenal, weapon for weapon, but to achieve something the experts called "superiority." Hundreds of billions of America's dollars, even trillions, were devoted to forestalling that dread possibility.[5]

Of course, it was not true. It was not true in the 1950s and it was especially not true in the late 1970s and early 1980s when America launched another massive arms buildup. Some journalists and scholars had been making this point about the Soviet economy for many years, pointing out the decay and malfunctioning that was visible despite the Soviet censors. But U.S. official authority and propaganda always succeeded in maintaining the enemy's strength.

When Gorbachev opened the Soviet society to full inspection, what western experts saw more nearly resembled a Third World country than a major industrial power. Its economy was a crude joke compared to the high-tech industrial systems of Japan, West Germany and the United States. The Soviet Union, aside from its size, was not second strongest in the world or third, probably not even fourth or fifth.

Americans, in other words, were propagandized by their own government for forty years. Were citizens deliberately deceived or were the CIA spies so befogged by their own ideological biases that they missed the reality themselves? This is one of the questions that a post–Cold War debate might take up for closer examination.

Senator Moynihan, though he raised the embarrassing facts, preferred to believe that everyone had acted in good faith. The senator had served himself as vice-chairman of the Senate Intelligence Committee and, like most politicians, had believed fully in the Soviet threat right until the end. He had been a consistent and eloquent champion of the Cold War arms buildup and had disparaged anyone who questioned the need to keep enlarging the U.S. arsenal. Now, Moynihan disparaged the CIA, with the sharpness of one whose trusting nature has been betrayed.

"It would be pretty obvious," the senator said, "to cut their budget in half so they wouldn't pass around these silly reports."

The government's persistent inflation of the enemy made plausible many other versions of "crackpot realism" that emanated from intelligence experts and somberly ruled the political debate on national defense. A "missile gap" discovered by these experts in 1960 was eventually acknowledged to be illusory, but only after the Kennedy administration had launched a program to double America's nuclear missile force. A theoretical "window of vulnerability" that defense authorities identified in the late 1970s became the pretext for the trillion-dollar defense modernization of the Reagan presidency. Yet the Reagan administration's cornucopia of new weaponry never attempted to close the supposedly dangerous "window."

In the early 1980s, American intelligence discovered Cubans constructing a large airport on the Caribbean island of Grenada and concluded that it was to be a future launching pad for Soviet bombers aimed at America. After the U.S. invasion and conquest of that tiny country, the American government finished building the airport so it could be used for jumbo-jet tourist traffic, the purpose Grenada had always claimed for it. The most enthusiastic advocates of the U.S. surrogate war against Nicaragua, including President Reagan, described a "domino theory" of nations in which Nicaragua, Honduras, Guatemala and Mexico would one by one fall to the Communists. If America did not defeat the Sandinistas, the Red armies would someday be massed on the border, poised to attack Harlingen, Texas.

For four decades, NATO defense policy was premised on a latter-day version of blitzkrieg—a vision of the Soviet armies launching a surprise attack that sweeps across the plains of central Europe and swiftly arrives at the English Channel, just like Hitler. The allied generals earnestly prepared to fight World War II in Europe all over again, a burden that consumed nearly half of the U.S. defense budget.

Of course, the scenario was absurd, as the U.S. intelligence community itself belatedly acknowledged in November 1989 when the "threat" analysis was abruptly changed. Half of the Soviet divisions poised to strike from eastern Europe, it turns out, were actually manned at token levels—5 percent to 25 percent of their fighting strength. In order to attack the West, the Soviets would have had to transport 150,000 troops from the Soviet Union and activate 800,000 reservists in the Warsaw Pact nations. Nevertheless, President Bush was still insisting on the scenario (and proposing new and highly dangerous battlefield nuclear weapons for western Europe) only a few months before the Berlin Wall fell.[6]

The point of reciting such examples of exaggeration is not to reargue the Cold War, now that it is over, but to demonstrate what an overpowering idea the Cold War was. People believed and accepted the most threatening possibilities and the government acted on them. It was not that the dubious alarums were never questioned. But the concept of vigilance against an awesome enemy swept away critical opposition and, often, rationality.

American politics created a mythology and then was ruled by it. A senator or representative might safely challenge the Cold War on subordinate issues— does America really need more aircraft carriers?—but any politician would be vulnerable to defeat if his argument was not safely couched in the context of mortal struggle against a malevolent adversary. Political contests deteriorated into manly arguments over who was "hard" and who was "soft" toward this enemy. Mere citizens were mostly excluded from the dense technical esoterica of the defense debate, except on those crude terms. Most citizens, not surprisingly, preferred political leaders who seemed "hard."

From the beginning, the Cold War put citizens in the same weak defensive posture that characterized their position on large domestic issues. But the people did sometimes block the government's most outrageous plans. When the Reagan regime prepared for another war of intervention against Nicaragua, public opposition stood in the way and the government was compelled to mount a surrogate war, which it quaintly referred to as a "covert operation." Preventing a U.S. invasion constituted a victory of sorts for the citizens.

Still, as in Nicaragua, the Cold War's institutional apparatus produced an inevitable series of extralegal activities in the government, offending both domestic and international law. This was not simply the occasional misadventures of "rogue" intelligence officers who "went too far," as authorities always explained when the CIA was implicated in assassination plots or other covert actions that violated law and morality. In many ways, the institutional arrangements were created in order to allow the president to operate outside the law.

Some conservative Republicans recognized this danger at the outset and they were principled opponents to the legislation that in 1947 created the CIA (designed and promoted by liberal Democrats). In congressional debate, a handful of conservatives argued that the CIA, with its secret budget and cloaked activities, would give the chief executive enormous new powers to make foreign policy in secret—and indeed to wage secret wars—without submitting his decisions to the due processes of open political debate, authorization and appropriate and formal declarations by Congress.

The conservatives were right, of course, but then that was the idea of the CIA—to empower the president by circumventing democratic processes. Conservatives have since embraced the all-powerful chief executive as the ideal, while many liberals have learned to question it, especially after the liberal debacle in Vietnam.

The illegal consequences of creating a secret government did not remain very secret, despite the popular lore of spies and their stealthful routines. The CIA helped engineer changes of government, sometimes violently, in Iran, Guatemala, Brazil, Chile and a long list of other nations. It was implicated in the counterrevolutionary massacres in Indonesia and the successful assassinations of at least three foreign leaders as well as other murder plots that failed. It managed a secret army in Laos and its agents laid the groundwork for the war in Vietnam, where, among other functions, the CIA supervised an infamous program of targeting and killing suspect citizens, without benefit of trial. The CIA ran the not-so-covert war against Nicaragua. It assembled an army and invaded Cuba with disastrous results.

At home, the CIA penetrated universities, private business corporations and other government agencies, especially the State Department, partly to obtain cover for its intelligence officers, partly to gather proprietary information and partly to compromise others. When asked to by various presidents, the agency spied on American citizens who were political dissidents, in the name of protecting the nation against subversion. It created scores of dummy corporate organizations to transact its business, so as to conceal the fact that an agency of government was illegally laundering money or transporting arms to overseas conflicts or doing deals with the Mafia. It infiltrated domestic political associations and tax-exempt foundations in order to advance the propaganda war against communism.

Abuses by the national-security state have continued right up to the present. In 1982, the FBI conducted a secret subversion investigation of Physicians for Social Responsibility because the group opposed Reagan's nuclear weapons policy. PSR and its worldwide affiliates later won the Nobel Peace Prize. In 1986, the FBI fired an agent who refused to conduct a "domestic security/terrorism" investigation of two citizen groups opposing Reagan's policy in Central America. During the 1980s, the FBI delivered data from its investigations of domestic political opposition to the White House.[7]

These are a sampling of the scandalous matters that are known and documented; some would insist there is a far darker portrait of the CIA to be drawn from outlaw behavior that is less well authenticated. The point of reciting the history, in any case, is to demonstrate the fundamental irregularity of this institution and its capabilities. When the nation is at war, unlawful measures are often accepted as necessary to national survival. Lincoln suspended habeas corpus during the Civil War; Roosevelt interned Japanese-American citizens in World War II. In the Cold War, however, it was the irregular institutional arrangement itself that committed the offenses, while it functioned to keep the nation at war.

Despite recurring scandals (always followed by appropriate "reforms"), the Central Intelligence Agency and allied components remain intact outside the normal structure of democratic accountability. It is available to any president who feels the need for extralegal activities of almost any kind. The president need only issue a secret executive order authorizing the venture; a handful of congressional leaders will be informed, but only upon their agreement to keep the facts from the public.

As president, Ronald Reagan issued 298 National Security Decision Directives—secret edicts that are accorded the force of law. By private writ, the president is able to mobilize government resources for subversion or order surveillance of private citizens or launch aggressive wars against other nations, all without public debate or even public knowledge.[8]

The fundamental conflict is not about the need for intelligence gathering, but about respect for law, both domestic and international law. And the problem is not rooted in the CIA's peculiar charter, but in the White House and the nature of modern executive power. In the end, it was the presidents who authorized the lawlessness and who benefited politically from the corruption of regular democratic process. If the "New World Order" means the U.S. government is going to use its power around the globe to uphold law and promote democracy, it might usefully start at home.

If Iraq violated the "law of nations," as it did, then so has the United States. The invasion of Grenada, for example, "was the clearest possible violation of Article 18 of the Charter of the Organization of American States, a document as much of our drafting as was the Charter of the United Nations," Senator Moynihan wrote. "It was a violation of the latter also."[9]

American officials always claimed virtuous motives for their invasions of foreign countries and argued that there were justifying provocations, but the American interventions were always made unilaterally, decided by the chief executive alone, oblivious to the formal procedures by which such actions are sanctioned under international law or by the U.S. Constitution. When presidents authorized a covert aggression against another nation, the government did not even bother with public justifications, but pretended instead, with a broad wink, to official innocence.

American citizens cannot escape the consequences of a government that ignores the law. Twice in the last decade alone, the U.S. president was caught out in engagements that demonstrably violated either international law or U.S. law or both. Each event caused a political stir, but the president remained aloof.

In 1983, during the covert war against Nicaragua, CIA agents mined the harbors of that country, an action that is defined in international law as a direct act of aggression against a sovereign state. Clearly prohibited by international treaties, the mining also raised the constitutional question of who in the American government had authorized an act of war. When distressed senators complained, the CIA blandly promised not to do it again.

When Nicaragua prepared to take a formal complaint to the International Court of Justice in The Hague, the Reagan administration announced peremptorily that it would no longer accept the World Court's jurisdiction over "disputes with any Central American state or arising out of or related to events in Central America." The United States thus set aside temporarily a treaty obligation it had accepted, by Senate ratification, in 1946.

The World Court heard Nicaragua's case, nonetheless, and ruled in 1986 that the United States had violated "general principles of humanitarian law" in numerous ways—mining harbors, bombing oil installations, arming the Contras and distributing guerrilla-warfare manuals that encouraged the violent intimidation of Nicaraguan citizens. This was the first time in American history, Senator Moynihan noted, that an international tribunal had ever found the United States in violation of law. Yet the World Court's decision received only brief, passing notice within the United States.

The other episode of presidential lawlessness was more celebrated—the Iran-Contra affair in which the Reagan White House ignored the legislative prohibition against providing further aid to the Contra army it had created in Nicaragua. Among the many complicated illegalities generated by the White House in that matter, one pointed unambiguously at the president's own failure to faithfully execute the law. Reagan personally authorized Cabinet officers to raise funds from foreign governments for the war, despite the congressional prohibition of U.S. involvement. "The plain fact," Moynihan wrote, "is that the president did invite and almost certainly deserved impeachment."

Actually, a resolution of impeachment was filed against President Reagan by Representative Henry Gonzalez, the Texas Democrat who compares the unbridled power of modern American presidents to that of the Roman Caesars. Americans, Gonzalez said, no longer have a republic in the original meaning; presidential power has trampled it beyond recognition. Gonzalez's complaint was ignored. Ronald Reagan continued in office and retired with honor, an affable Caesar who was much loved by the people.

When President Bush went to war in the Persian Gulf, Gonzalez filed another impeachment resolution against him. Gonzalez charged that Bush had violated law and constitutional process, first by unilaterally committing five hundred thousand troops to a foreign combat zone in violation of the terms of the War Powers Act, then by bribing foreign nations to accede to his strategy. A $7 billion loan to Egypt was forgiven without congressional approval. Zaire was promised military aid and partial debt forgiveness. Turkey was given a larger import quota for its textiles. China was assured of favorable trade terms if it did not veto the U.S. initiative in the UN Security Council. The Soviet Union was promised billions in aid so it would cooperate too. In the glow of victory, everyone assumed the president had the power to do these things— that he is free to do whatever he wants in wartime.[10]

This overbearing nature of the modern presidency is what has most crippled democracy. But the permanent Cold War mobilization made the accumulation of power seem "normal," and over two generations the public memory of a presidency accountable to the Constitution has been nearly lost. The idea that democracy ought to function in any other way now seems eccentric.

The Cold War president became a mythological figure—a warrior president surrounded by warriors, preoccupied with questions of global conflict above all others. As the Cold War cliché goes, "all our lives are in his hands," and, in those circumstances, people assigned mystical qualities to the warriors who were running things. Military officers became commonplace in the uppermost reaches of government. A general served as secretary of state; an admiral led the CIA. A CIA director became president.

The office of the president has many valuable qualities—particularly the ability to educate and unify the nation—but the institution cannot possibly carry the full burdens of democracy. It is too narrow and singular and, above all, too private in its actions, notwithstanding the TV images of presidential comings and goings that are provided daily. The centralized political power has encouraged the evasion and hollowness that permeate the domestic dimensions of government.

The White House has become a convenient "safe house" for governing without any of the messy obligations required by a genuine democracy—a sanctuary where things finally get decided privately and without public debate. This retreat encourages others in the political community to avoid hard decisions by passing on the toughest questions to the White House where the president can settle them in the protected reserve of the Oval Office.

The rich diversity of democratic dialogue has been collapsed into a single, opaque institution. Self-government has been reduced to a single mind and heartbeat. Dismantling the Cold War, restoring a democratic order, means cutting the presidency down to appropriate size.

* * *

From the beginning, the Cold War fulfilled an ironic purpose in domestic politics: It allowed all patriots to embrace a twisted, back-door version of socialism. The federal government claimed a rationale for intervening massively in the private economy, but without the usual debate over free enterprise and limited government. Washington stimulated economic demand with contracts and subsidies; it directed private investment through industrial planning and capital allocation. It created millions of jobs for workers. It built and owned scores of factories for private enterprises to operate.

Conservatives could ride along free on this arrangement without blemishing their ideological purity and, in time, conservatives became its most enthusiastic advocates. No one had to justify government-owned industrial plants and vast research laboratories and government-financed industrial development (including the occasional bailout of failing companies). It was all done in the name of defending the nation.

If the Cold War has truly ended and no great unifying cause can be found to replace it, then conservatives have lost their cover and the government has lost its rationale for steering the private economy through the federal budget. This economic reality will likely lead to a continuing political crisis, as many Americans discover how much their own economic well-being was dependent on the permanent mobilization and as political leaders search for saleable substitutes.

The modern defense budget, it is true, now consumes less than 5 percent of the gross national product, so it is often argued that even a major shrinkage in defense spending can be absorbed by the overall economy without great pain. That assumption misunderstands the socialist relationship.

For better or worse, the Pentagon is like a big rock propping up American manufacturing. Roughly one fifth of U.S. manufacturing output is purchased by the federal government via defense contracts. In 1985, for instance, the military spent $165 billion buying goods from a broad spectrum of 215 industries—21 percent of the manufacturing gross national product. Defense-related work employs one in ten of America's manufacturing workers.

The military allocates $38 billion a year for research and development and supports at least one in every four U.S. scientists. Defense pays for roughly 50 percent of the university research on computer science and electrical engineering. It provides 96 percent of the income for American shipbuilding. It accounts for about one fifth of the nation's modernizing capital investment.[11]

In other words, a forty-year addiction to socialist-style intervention is now threatened by cold-turkey therapy. If the defense budget shrinks drastically, it is going to leave a big hole in the American economy—especially in the crucial realm of long-term development and investment. Who will buy the state-of-the-art machine tools? Who will pay for the basic science? The government will have to invent other rationales and methods for force-feeding private research and investment or else retreat to laissez-faire principle and hope that private enterprise somehow makes up the difference.

That is one dimension of the crisis that demobilization is bound to engender. Another dimension is the fierce politics of lost contracts and employment. Depending on how rapidly the defense budget shrinks, the shutdown of weapons production could eliminate more than five hundred thousand jobs for both skilled industrial workers and the technical professions.

These are the "good jobs" in the American economy—premium-wage manufacturing jobs held by machinists, electricians, engineers and others. These workers will not easily find comparable positions in an economy in which heavy industry has been shrinking its employment base for the past decade. The overall effect could resemble another round of the deindustrialization and downward mobility that workers in steel, autos and other sectors have already experienced.

Given these harsh facts, the political response has largely been like an unreformed alcoholic's—denial and avoidance. The president traveled now and then to defense plants where he congratulated the defense workers on the high quality of their work and assured them he personally wanted to keep buying their tanks or airplanes. This put him on the smart side of the short-run politics: When the defense contracts were canceled and the factories closed, George Bush would be able to say it was not his idea.

In Congress, roughly the same political strategy played out much more messily—state by state, district by district—as liberals and conservatives alike fought to keep open their factories and their military bases at the expense of someone else's. Long Island mobilized to keep alive Grumman's F-14, while the Pentagon kept trying to kill it. St. Louis mourned the loss of McDonnell Douglas's A-12. Newport News, Virginia, sued the Navy to save Tenneco's Seawolf submarine contract. General Dynamics announced, for obvious political effect, that nearly one third of its ninety thousand workers would be laid off, perhaps forever.

These dislocations and others were just the beginning, and the next round promised to be more severe. The Defense Department was planning a modest five-year reduction in the Cold War mobilization—a 25 percent cut in the uniformed forces and a $15 billion decline in its budget authority. But that would still leave the defense budget around $280 billion—still gigantic for a nation in debt, unable to finance a long list of competing domestic priorities and unable to identify a credible enemy beyond a few tinpot dictators. If the U.S. defense budget were cut in half, it would still be four or five times larger than that of the next-strongest nation.[12]

The dramatic cancellations of weapons systems occasionally reported in the news were mostly projects the country couldn't afford in the first place, even when the Cold War was flourishing. As defense budgets soared during the 1980s, each of the three services signed up for a dizzying wish list of new toys—commitments so ambitious that, as one defense expert said, the Pentagon was trying to buy $400 billion worth of firepower on a $300 billion budget. This dilemma was well understood by defense experts (and politicians) for years and they responded to it by ordering procurement stretch-outs—buying fewer of each weapon every year so they would not have to cancel anybody's favorite. This approach naturally raised the per-unit cost of procurement and made defense production even more inefficient.

The Bush administration belatedly struggled to eliminate this "bubble" of false expectations from defense-budget projections. The next round of demobilization would be for real: bringing home troops that had been stationed abroad since the 1950s, closing scores of domestic military bases, shuttering more factories.

Aside from the president's vague talk about the "New World Order," neither political party offered a coherent strategy for how the nation might cope with this economic transformation. A few liberals introduced "conversion" bills that did little more than encourage communities and industries to plan for their post–Cold War future. Conservative thinkers concentrated, meanwhile, on trying to devise substitute "threats"—Third World terrorism or nuclear proliferation—that might justify continuing the nation's permanent war footing.

The Pentagon, ironically, was one of the few places where arguments over the economic implications had hesitantly begun, perhaps because the military itself would suffer the consequences first and most severely. As the defense budget shrinks, companies will fail or get out of the weapons business and the defense industrial base will shrink too. Thus, the unit cost of acquiring new weapons—already grossly inflated—is expected to spiral still higher. Without much hyperbole, the military planners envision a juncture where they will be buying fewer and fewer tanks and airplanes for higher and higher prices—unable to maintain their force levels, even if their global mission is defined in less grandiose terms.

The transformation of high-technology production in the global economy, meanwhile, promises to make the United States more dependent on foreign producers for crucial weapons components, especially in the advanced technologies. If nothing else changes, one can predict a not-distant future when the world's only superpower is borrowing money from its allies to buy the high-tech weapons components they manufacture—so the supposed superpower will be able to protect these allies from worldly harm. In a minor way, this was already the case.

The American public, if it ever caught on, would not be terribly enthusiastic about arming America with made-in-Japan electronics. Indeed, anxious members of Congress were already calling for a "Buy America" doctrine in defense procurement. Pentagon officials had to explain that "Buy America" would mean tanks or airplanes that were missing key parts.

For all these reasons, as well as their obvious self-interest, some of the conservative leaders of the defense community were beginning to flirt with a radically different economic doctrine—government engagement in the private economy that would merge defense-production requirements with the broader objective of improving America's competitive position in commercial markets. Even Defense Secretary Richard Cheney, a conservative ideologue in most other matters, made an implicit pitch for some sort of industrial policy. "The United States," Cheney declared, "cannot persist in its current laissez-faire approach to the competition in advanced technologies without incurring major economic and security problems of its own in the future."[13]

Jacques S. Gansler, an authority on the defense industry and chairman of the Defense Science Board's study on the advanced technology crisis, has argued for a radical restructuring in which defense manufacture and commercial production are fully integrated with each other—both to preserve the defense industrial base and to foster the modernization of U.S. manufacturing.

Essentially what Gansler and others have proposed is that the government set aside some of the notorious fictions of the Cold War era and frankly acknowledge that it manipulates the private economy through defense spending but that it has been doing so in ways that are wasteful and ineffective, partly because the money was spent without regard to the nation's overall economic condition.

Some of the cold warriors of the Pentagon, a few at least, are hesitantly beginning to recognize that, while they were devoting the nation's capital to Cold War weaponry, another, more ominous threat to the national security was emerging from America's loss of economic power.[14] Pentagon reform—harnessing defense procurement to economic competitiveness—would at least lead to a more honest version of socialism or, more politely, a deliberate "industrial policy" that is more like those of Japan and the other allies who are America's global competitors.

But this approach contains large perils for democracy and for ordinary citizens—the possibility of corporate socialism for entrenched economic interests. Given the deformed structure of political power that now exists, an industrial policy of any kind, especially one supervised by the Pentagon, might swiftly deteriorate into an extravagant program for taking care of the same old crowd, in the name of "competitiveness." In the global economy, furthermore, there is the more complicated question of which companies are really "American." Why should American taxpayers underwrite the development of advanced technologies for multinational corporations if those companies are free to transfer the processes to their foreign plants and low-wage foreign workers?

An American industrial policy, in other words, is not a plausible solution in democratic terms unless politics has also confronted the questions about corporate loyalty. If American companies are not made to accept a stronger sense of national obligation—the kind of commitment that Japanese or German companies routinely accept in their societies—a new industrial policy might simply subsidize the continuing erosion of the American wage structure, using taxpayer dollars to finance corporate globalization.

The post–Cold War political question is: How can the nation begin to restore a peaceable economic balance and evolve toward a society that is not so relentlessly organized around the machinery of war? To put it another way, how might America begin to domesticate its military-industrial complex?

One way to accomplish the transition might be to encourage civic action by the military—the assignment of domestic functions that could provide a practical justification for maintaining so many men and women in uniform, but would also take advantage of the military's natural assets. The armed services, aside from war-making capabilities, have many valuable qualities, including skills and experience and organizational cohesion that could be effectively applied to political problems at home.

The U.S. military, for one thing, is probably the nation's largest educational institution and its training methodologies are well tested and reliable. The military manages vast real estate at home and abroad. It knows how to build things, from roads and dams to hospitals and housing, on a mass-production scale. It knows how to take raw recruits, often ill-educated young men and women, and prepare them to perform complicated tasks in a disciplined manner. It is the nation's most successful equal-opportunity employer and a crucial ladder of upward mobility for children of poverty.

These are assets that might all be usefully mobilized on the home front. The armed services, for instance, might be assigned a leading role in job training or drug therapy or as a manager of emergency employment. It could operate a civic-action corps that builds useful structures while it upgrades the skills and disciplines of recruits. It might, for instance, oversee a workforce, in or out of uniform, that tackles the massive backlog of damaged sites that need environmental cleanup, including the sites the military itself polluted.

If the nation does decide to change its priorities, there is much work to be done. The armed services have functioning infrastructures that already exist and might even reduce the costs of undertaking these new priorities. The military, likewise, enjoys political standing that might make it easier to sell these domestic undertakings. In turn, the military would benefit from a positive role in solving large, unattended public problems.

This approach, of course, has its obvious perils too. Commanders who are trained to fight wars regard civic action as a diversion from their real mission. Domestic political interests, meanwhile, fear the military as unwanted competition or, worse than that, an enveloping influence that might militarize peacetime endeavors. These are real risks, certainly, but so is the national dilemma of this moment in history. The dimensions of that dilemma are so profound that prevailing political prejudices may have to be set aside before the country can think clearly about its future.

The military institution exists, a huge and expensive reality that permeates the national political life. After four decades in place, the national-security state is not going to go away any time soon. The daunting question is how its components might be reintegrated—in productive ways—with the concerns and institutions of a regular democratic order.

Otherwise, if nothing much changes, there will be a continuing political imperative to seek out new conflicts that justify the existence of the national-security state. The CIA, if it remains independent and secretive, will keep churning out its inflated assessments of new "threats." The armed services, if not restructured and reduced in size, will inevitably be dispatched to fight again on dubious battlefields. The presidency, if its warrior prerogatives are not rescinded, will be free to continue the Cold War under some other name.

The triumph of World War II created a dynamic and satisfying parable for Americans, a story that described the nation as both strong and good. America was, therefore, obliged to take action on behalf of others, just as it had done against Hitler. The parable became the central vision behind the Cold War and motivated political action across two generations. It was shared by nearly everyone in the society, from top to bottom, and still dominates political imagination.

But the old parable, comforting as it was, is breaking up in visible ways, as other complications press in. It no longer resonates accurately with surrounding realities, as people are beginning to sense. Since early 1988, opinion polls have found that the American public now identifies Japan as the principal threat to the United States. The Soviet Union was far down the list of public anxieties—long before the Berlin Wall fell and long before political leaders were willing to adjust their thinking.

In the Cold War, while the United States was preoccupied with military power and spent its treasure on the defense of allies, the allies were tending to other business—the development of modernized industrial economies. Indeed, the old adversaries of World War II are now the leading challengers to American hegemony in the world. They are also the leading lenders propping up American indebtedness. The parable has led the United States into a dangerous cul de sac.

Yet political elites were so successful adhering to the old story line, they are reluctant to abandon it. They are as yet unable to imagine a new parable for America that would match the new realities in the world. The transient euphoria generated by occasional war and parades does not change the fact that the United States has drifted into a dependent and vulnerable condition. With bad luck, this new condition is going to teach Americans some harsh lessons about economics and the real nature of global power in the post–Cold War world.

The stakes have thus been raised for American democracy, partly by events beyond anyone's control, partly by the long period of evasion when the economic realities were masked by Cold War propaganda. The nation's margin of error is now much smaller, its general abundance less secure. In addition to all the other burdens enumerated for conscientious citizens in this book, the task of restoring a vital democracy starts now from much greater disadvantages.

The spirit of the American parable—a country that is at once great and good and active in the world—can be carried forward in powerful new terms, but only if people recognize the full outlines of the democratic problem. It is not only the decay of domestic political institutions, the permissive legal culture, the privileges of concentrated power and the other pathologies that have subverted democracy.

In inexorable ways, as the next chapter reveals, American democracy is gradually being dismantled by the dynamics of global economics now astride the world at large. To salvage democracy at home, Americans must begin to think of themselves in much larger terms. They must learn how to act like democratic citizens of the world.

17
THE CLOSET
DICTATOR

$\mathbf{T}$he ultimate democratic dilemma that confronts contemporary citizens is unlike any other in the nation's past, for it lies beyond the nation's borders. If Americans wish to repair their own decayed democracy, they must also make themselves into large-minded citizens of the world. To protect their own economic interests, they will have to develop an interest in the economic conditions of people elsewhere. To defend the sovereignty of American law, citizens will have to confront political power that is global.

With the end of the Cold War burdens, Americans were understandably inclined to turn inward and attend to the many neglected priorities at home. But American democracy is now imprisoned by new circumstances—the dynamics of the global economy—and this has produced a daunting paradox: Restoring the domestic political order will require a new version of internationalism.

The rise of transnational enterprises and production systems, the easy mobility of capital investment and jobs from one country to another, has obvious benefits as a modernizing influence on the world. It searches out lower costs and cheaper prices. But its exploitative effects on both rich and poor nations remain unchecked.

As a political system, the global economy is running downhill—a system that searches the world for the lowest common denominator in terms of national standards for wages, taxes and corporate obligations to health, the environment and stable communities. Left unchallenged, the global system will continue to undermine America's widely shared prosperity, but it also subverts the nation's ability to set its own political standards, the laws that uphold the shared values of society.

The economic consequences of globalized production have already been experienced by the millions of U.S. industrial workers who, during the last two decades, were displaced when their high-wage jobs were transferred to cheaper labor in foreign countries. This transformation, more than anything else, is what has led to the declining real wages in the United States and the weakening manufacturing base. The deleterious impact on American wages is likely to continue for at least another generation.

But the economic effects are inseparable from the political consequences. The global competition for cost advantage effectively weakens the sovereignty of every nation by promoting a fierce contest among countries for lower public standards. If one nation's environmental laws are too strict or its taxes seem too burdensome, the factory will be closed and the jobs moved elsewhere—to some other nation whose standards are lax, whose government is more compliant.

This reality constitutes the largest challenge confronting American democracy, one that underlies every other aspect of the democratic problem. The global economy has the practical power to check almost every effort Americans may undertake to reform their own political system—unless people learn how to confront the global system too. Elite political opinion holds that such resistance is undesirable and, in any case, impossible.

For ordinary Americans, traditionally independent and insular, the challenge requires them to think anew their place in the world. The only plausible way that citizens can defend themselves and their nation against the forces of globalization is to link their own interests cooperatively with the interests of other peoples in other nations—that is, with the foreigners who are competitors for the jobs and production but who are also victimized by the system. Americans will have to create new democratic alliances across national borders with the less prosperous people caught in the same dilemma. Together, they have to impose new political standards on multinational enterprises and on their own governments.

The challenge, in other words, involves taking the meaning of democracy to a higher plane—a plateau of political consciousness the world has never before reached. This awesome task does not begin by examining Americans' own complaints about the global system. It begins by grasping what happens to the people at the other end—the foreigners who inherit the American jobs.

*   *   *

On the outskirts of Ciudad Juarez, across the river from El Paso, Texas, the sere hillsides are a vast spectacle of human congestion. A canopy of crude huts and cabins, made from industrial scraps, is spread across the landscape, jammed together like a junkyard for abandoned shipping crates. The houses are not much more than large boxes, with walls of cardboard and floors made from factory pallets or Styrofoam packing cases. The tarpaper roofs are held in place by loose bricks; an old blanket or sheet of blue plastic is wrapped around the outhouse in the yard. Very few homes have running water and many lack electricity. Streets are unpaved and gullied. There are no sewer systems. For mile after mile, these dwellings are visible across the countryside—dusty, treeless subdivisions of industrial poverty.

The *colonias* of Ciudad Juarez are like a demented caricature of suburban life in America, because the people who live in Lucio Blanco or Zarogoza or the other squatter villages actually work for some of America's premier companies—General Electric, Ford, GM, GTE Sylvania, RCA, Westinghouse, Honeywell and many others. They are paid as little as fifty-five cents an hour. No one can live on such wages, not even in Mexico. With the noblesse oblige of the feudal padrone, some U.S. companies dole out occasional *despensa* for their struggling employees—rations of flour, beans, rice, oil, sugar, salt—in lieu of a living wage.

In addition to the cheap labor, the U.S. companies who have moved production facilities to the Mexican border's *maquiladora* zone enjoy the privilege of paying no property taxes on their factories. As a result, Ciudad Juarez has been overwhelmed by a burgeoning population and is unable to keep up with the need for new roads, water and sewer lines and housing. The migrants who came from the Mexican interior in search of "American" jobs become resourceful squatters, scavenging materials to build shelters on the fast-developing hillsides. In time, some of these disappointed workers decide to slip across the border in the hope of becoming real Americans.

"A family cannot depend on the *maquila* wage," explained Professor Gueramina Valdes-Villalva of the Colegio de la Frontera Norte in Juarez, an experienced critic who aided workers at the Center for Working Women. "If you evaluate what these wages translate into in purchasing power, you see a steady deterioration in what those wages provide. They can't buy housing because there is a housing shortage. When they go into the squatter situation, they can't invest in public services. We have a shortage of water, sewers, electricity, streets. The city is pressed heavily by the two sectors who do not pay taxes—the *maquiladora* companies and the minimum-wage workers.

"The saddest thing about it is, not only does the city become unbearably unlivable, but then the city becomes unproductive too. As the city deteriorates, it becomes more expensive for companies to locate here. For the first time last year, we had negative growth in Juarez. Some of the employers are leaving. We can see the companies looking at their other options. Eastern Europe has become very attractive to them.

"The companies are periodically confronted with these complaints and they usually deny that there is any negative effect. At the same time, their answer is that this is a worldwide process and they cannot do anything to change it."[1]

If Americans wish to visualize the abstraction called the global economy, they need only drive across the U.S. border into Mexico and see the human consequences for themselves, from Matamoros and Juarez to Nogales and Tijuana. A vast industrial belt of thirteen hundred plants has grown up along the border during the last twenty years, encouraged by special duty-free provisions but fueled primarily by low wages and the neglect of corporate social obligations.

By moving jobs to Mexico, companies not only escape higher industrial wages, but also U.S. laws and taxes, the legal standards for business conduct on health and safety and social commitments that were established through many years of political reform in America. Mexico has such laws but it dare not enforce them too energetically, for fear of driving the companies elsewhere.

The *maquiladora* factories, notwithstanding their handsome stucco facades and landscaped parking lots, are the modern equivalent of the "sweatshops" that once scandalized American cities. The employers are driven by the same economic incentives and the Mexican workers in Ciudad Juarez are just as defenseless. The Juarez slums reminded me of the squalid "coal camps" I saw years before in the mountains of Eastern Kentucky. Those still-lingering "pockets of poverty" were first created in the late nineteenth century by the coal and steel industries and they employed the very same industrial practices—low wages, neglect of public investment, dangerous working conditions, degradation of the surrounding environment, the use of child labor.

The well-being of Americans is intertwined with this new exploitation, not simply for moral reasons or because most of the Mexican plants are owned by American companies, but because this is the other end of the transmission belt eroding the structure of work and incomes in the United States. Jobs that paid ten dollars or eleven dollars an hour in Ohio or Illinois will cost companies less than a tenth of that in Ciudad Juarez. The assembly work turns out TV sets, seatbelt harnesses, electrical switches and transformers, computer keyboards, disposable surgical garments, luggage locks, battery packs and a long list of other products.

There are more than 240 *maquila* plants in Juarez (second most after

Tijuana), employing one hundred thousand people. Most of the workers are very young—teenagers—and the majority are girls.

Juarez, of course, is but a snapshot of the much larger reality around the world. Corporate apologists often point out that if the American jobs did not migrate to Mexico, they would go somewhere else—Singapore or Brazil, Thailand or now perhaps eastern Europe—where the consequences would be less easily observed by Americans. This is true. The easy mobility of capital is the core element in the modern global economy. It is made possible by invention, brilliant planning and the new technologies that connect corporate managers with far-flung factories and markets and allow them to relocate production almost anywhere in the world.

Given the fierce price competition generated by global production, any single manufacturing company is vulnerable if it does not respond to the trend of seeking out lower labor costs and tax-free havens. In the long run, it is not only Japan and Germany that threaten American prosperity, but the cheap labor of China and Indonesia and Thailand, even Sri Lanka and Bangladesh.

To confront the effects of the global system, Americans must educate themselves about the world—to understand not only their own losses but also what is happening to others. Ciudad Juarez (or any other border city) is an excellent place to start, mainly because it starkly refutes so many of the common assumptions surrounding globalization. Aside from profit, the justifying and widely accepted rationale for global dispersion of production is the benefit to the poor, struggling masses. Their economies, it is said, will move up to a higher stage of development and incomes will rise accordingly. The auto workers in Ohio will lose, certainly, but the new auto workers in Juarez will become middle-class consumers who can afford to buy other products made in America. Thus, in time, everyone is supposed to benefit.

On the streets of Juarez, the workers tell a different story: Their incomes are not rising, not in terms of purchasing power. They have been falling drastically for years. These workers cannot buy American cars or computers. They can barely buy the basic necessities of life.

Fernando Rosales had just quit his job at Chrysler, where he assembled safety harnesses, because it paid the peso equivalent of only $4.20 a day. While he builds a squatter house in Lucio Blanco, Rosales searches for work as an auto mechanic, away from the *maquila* plants.

"I came here six years ago, thinking I would better myself, but I won't be able to do that," Rosales said. "It's been very difficult. The only benefits I had were transportation—they sent a bus for us—and one meal a day. Maybe for the government, it's okay. But for the people it really is shameful that American companies pay such low wages."

"The wages are very low, that's just the way it is," said Daniel Fortino Maltos, twenty-one years old and married with a baby. He works for General

Electric at a plant making capacitors, as does his wife. "Young people generally leave after a few months or a year because the salary is so low, they can't make it," he explained.

Outside Productos Electricos Internacionales, another GE plant, a group of teenage workers on their lunch break described the same conditions. "The turnover is roughly every three months," said Fernando Rubio. "They just bring new ones in. There is such a big demand for workers, people can leave and go elsewhere." General Electric operated eight plants in Juarez, more than any other company.

Many of the workers blame the Mexican government for their condition, not the American employers. An older woman, Laura Chavez, who just quit her job at Delmex, a General Motors plant, expected to find another easily because of the extraordinarily high turnover in the *maquila* factories. "Look, it's not enough," she said. "If you're going to be living off that salary, it's not enough. I don't blame the companies. I blame the Mexican government because the wages are whatever the government requires."

In Mexico, the federal government does periodically raise the legal minimum-wage level but, for the last decade, the increases have lagged further and further behind the rising cost of living—thus providing cheaper and cheaper labor for the American employers.

Indeed, the *maquiladora* industry boasts of this attraction in the glossy publication it distributes to prospective companies. In 1981, the industry association reported, the labor cost for a *maquila* worker was $1.12 an hour. By the end of 1989, the real cost had fallen to 56 cents an hour.[2]

What these workers have surmised is correct: Their own government is exploiting them too. Mired in debt to American banks since the early 1980s, Mexico has been desperate to raise more foreign-currency income to keep up with its foreign-debt payments. Aside from oil, the *maquiladora* industry provides the country with its largest influx of U.S. dollars, and the Mexican government has attracted more U.S. enterprise by steadily depressing the wages of the workers. If it had not, Mexico might have lost the jobs to its principal low-wage competitors (Singapore or Taiwan or South Korea) and lost the precious foreign-currency income it needed to pay its bankers.

Wages for workers are, thus, falling on both ends of this global transmission belt. The people who lost their premium manufacturing jobs in the United Sates are compelled to settle for lower incomes. But so are the Mexican peasants who inherited the jobs. On both sides of the border, workers are caught in a vicious competition with one another that richly benefits the employers.

Most labor unions in Mexico did not try to stand in the way of the wage exploitation and those that did were easily brushed aside. In Matamoros, militant unions initially attempted to organize the *maquiladora* workers but, for fifteen years, the companies simply ignored Matamoros and located their plants in other border cities—until the Matamoros labor organization relented. In the United States, of course, industrial unions were drastically weakened as well, as they struggled against the shrinking employment and falling wages imposed by the global system.

The wage depression in Mexico is an extreme case, but not at all unique in the world. In many of the other countries attracting global production, similar exchanges occur that victimize workers and their communities and often benefit the country's established oligopoly of wealth and political power. The CEO of an American clothing company was asked if his company's imported goods from China might, in fact, have been manufactured with slave labor. "Everybody is a slave laborer," he replied. "The wage is so cheap."[3]

Most impoverished nations are understandably desperate to participate in this development. The denial of basic human rights is accepted as a temporary blemish; the long-term vision is that someday, when their people have become experienced industrial workers, they will become the next South Korea or Taiwan.

Mexico bought that vision twenty-five years ago when the duty-free rules for the *maquiladora* zone were first established, but the present reality of Ciudad Juarez and the other border cities denies the promise. The factories exist, it is true, but the capital investments are still easily portable, if attractive options appear elsewhere, and that threat hovers over every *maquiladora* factory. Meanwhile, the border cities deteriorate further and any attempt to improve them through higher taxes elicits rebukes from the companies.

"The government of Mexico in 1988 suggested a 5 percent tax on salaries that would be dedicated to urban infrastructure," Professor Valdes-Villalva recalled. "The suggestion was up in the air for about ten days before it was knocked down by the companies. The companies were saying they will have to leave if the tax is imposed. The association that represents them shot it down. The government dropped the idea."

Instead of an experienced workforce, the *maquiladora* zone has created a bewildering stream of young people tumbling randomly from one job to another.

"We have begun to see more fourteen-year-olds in the plants—children fourteen to sixteen years old," Valdes-Villalva said. "The *maquila* workers are very young on the whole, we're talking sixteen to twenty-one years old. Usually, the companies are careful to see that the youngest girls and boys get permission slips from their parents.

"Workers do not age in this industry—they leave. Because of the intensive work it entails, there's constant burnout. If they've been there three or four years, workers lose efficiency. They begin to have problems with eyesight. They begin to have allergies and kidney problems. They are less productive."

By maintaining a young and impermanent workforce, the companies are able to cut down on their labor costs because, under Mexican law, a worker who is fired gets severance pay and is compensated for every year of seniority. If a company plans to leave someday, it does not want a large experienced workforce that will be entitled to severance when the plant is moved to some other country.

The workers themselves matter-of-factly describe the reality of children who have left school for these jobs. "Quite a lot say they are sixteen but I know they are probably thirteen or fourteen or fifteen years old," said Sylvia Facoln at the GE plant. "I know of people who are less than fourteen years old and I myself brought one of them to work here. It's very common in all the *maquilas*."

The scandal of major American corporations employing adolescent children to do the industrial work that once belonged to American adults has been documented in many settings, yet it provokes no political response in either Washington or Mexico City. The *Arizona Republic* of Phoenix ran a prize-winning series on the *maquiladora* across from Nogales, Arizona, where, among other things, the reporter found thirteen-year-old Miriam Borquez working the night shift for General Electric (the same company that cares deeply about educating disadvantaged minorities at home).

The girl quit school to take the job, she explained, because her family needed the money. They were living in a nine-by-sixteen tin hut. The *Arizona Republic*'s conservative editorial page lamented: "Has greed so consumed some businessmen that human lives in Mexico are less valuable than the next saxophone shipped to the U.S. from Sonora?"[4]

Maquiladora officials always protest their innocence in this matter. Mexican labor law permits them to hire fourteen-year-olds if their parents grant permission. These laws are faithfully observed, the officials explain, but companies cannot always verify the true age of young job applicants and children sometimes forge permission slips from parents or use someone else's documents. This is sometimes true, according to Ignacio Escandon, an El Paso businessman familiar with the Juarez labor market, but the excuse hardly relieves the corporations of their moral burden. "The companies don't ask many questions," Escandon said. "The demand for labor is constant."

There is a general lack of political scrutiny. Beyond anecdotes, no one knows the real dimensions of the exploitation. The use of child labor is one of the many aspects of the Mexican *maquiladora* that has never been authoritatively investigated, since neither government has much interest in exposing the truth.

Environmental damage from the *maquiladora* plants, likewise, has never been squarely examined by federal authorities though gross violations have been cited in numerous reports and accusations from private citizens and some state agencies. The National Toxics Campaign described the U.S.-Mexican border as already so polluted with dangerous chemicals that it may become "a two-thousand-mile Love Canal."

From twenty-three tests, the grassroots environmental organization found seventeen *maquiladora* sites with significant discharges of toxics in groundwater or streams and eight sites with severe pollution. A University of Texas study found heightened levels of gall bladder and liver cancer in thirty-three Texas counties along the Rio Grande. In Nogales, where the streams (and sewage) flow north into Arizona, Arizona state officials detected a chemical plume of tetrachloroethylene that had crossed the border too. This is but a sampling of the evidence.[5]

In Ciudad Juarez, an official of the *maquiladora* industry association actually admitted to the *El Paso Times* that 40 percent or more of the hazardous wastes generated by the Juarez plants was probably dumped illegally. "Now I can't say for sure those *maquiladoras* are dumping their toxic wastes in the city's sewer system or landfill," Lino Morales told the newspaper, "but where else would they be disposing of it?"[6]

For years, Professor Valdes-Villalva and her associates have tried to track down what the companies do with the toxic chemicals that are brought into the Mexican plants. Mexican law requires that imported hazardous materials must be shipped back to the United States but the researchers could only find customs documents covering less than 5 percent of the volume. They suspect—but can't prove—that the bulk is trucked to illegal dumps in the interior, future Superfund sites waiting to be discovered by Mexican authorities.

"For ten years," Valdes-Villalva said, "they told us they handled no toxic wastes. I was attacked by the plants as an alarmist. Now, they are beginning to admit that they do handle toxic wastes but, unless we can find out what they do with the wastes, there's no way to stop them."

The health consequences that frightened American citizens when they first encountered the casual disposal of toxic wastes in their own communities now worry Mexican citizens too. Like the Americans before them, the concerned Mexicans are confronted by official denial and a lack of reliable information to confirm or refute their fears.

"What most concerns me is the health within the plants," Valdes-Villalva said. "This is where we are lacking. We have no money for research, but we hear these complaints from workers. We find high levels of lead in blood samples. We have situations in which we find a tremendous amount of manic depressives, which does not follow the usual amount in the population. So what I'm beginning to think is that this is a central nervous system disorder, physical not psychological. It could be solvents. It's heavily concentrated in the electronics industry. There's also a tremendous number of Down's syndrome children. Other disorders you find in high incidence are cleft palates and other deformities."

Her description of working conditions is echoed in sidewalk conversations with young workers. The group outside the GE electrical assembly plant talked about the skin problems that some coworkers develop from working with fibers—sometimes severe enough to send them to the hospital. Daniel Fortino described similar problems. "I use zinc and the only protection I've been given are glasses," he said. "Among some of the workers, I know they get all kinds of rashes on their arms and they've been told it's the materials they are using."

Like the American citizens who have formed thousands of grassroots political organizations to combat industrial pollution, Mexican citizens who summon the courage to protest are utterly on their own—aligned against both industry and government, without the resources to challenge the official explanations or the political influence to force the government to act. But, of course, the Mexican citizens are in a much weaker position to undertake such political struggles. Their communities are impoverished. Their national economy depends crucially on these factories. Their own democratic institutions are weak and underdeveloped or corrupted.

The situation seems overwhelming, but not entirely hopeless. Along the border and elsewhere, some people of both nationalities are beginning to grasp the fact that citizens of neither nation can hope to change their own conditions without the support of the other. Mexicans cannot hope to stand up to General Motors or GE from the *colonias* of Ciudad Juarez. Nor can Americans expect to defend their own jobs or their own social standards without addressing the hopes and prospects and afflictions of their impoverished neighbors.

Genuine reform will require a new and unprecedented form of cross-border politics in which citizens develop continuing dialogues across national boundaries and learn to speak for their common values. Only by acting together can they hope to end the exploitation, not just in Mexico but elsewhere across the global production system.

This kind of sophisticated internationalism has not been characteristic among Americans, to put it mildly. It raises the stakes enormously for anyone who envisions a revitalized democracy for it means that, in addition to everything else, the restoration of American democracy will depend upon Americans' thinking and acting with a larger perspective on the world. Most Americans, aside from what they are told about the Cold War rivalry and occasional military conflicts, have been educated into ignorance about the world at large.

That is the daunting nature of the global political dilemma. People like Valdes-Villalva have already seen it clearly and so do some Americans. A Coalition for Justice in the *Maquiladoras* was formed in 1991 by more than sixty American environmental, religious, community and labor organizations, including the AFL-CIO, in order to speak out against the injustices and confront the multinational corporations with demands for civilized conduct. Leaders from the Mexican *maquiladora* communities are being brought to the United States to spread the word to Americans on the true nature of the global economic system.[7]

"Moral behavior knows no borders," Sister Susan Mika, president of the coalition, declared. "What would be wrong in the United States is wrong in Mexico too."

Valdes-Villalva described the new democratic imperative:

"In order for workers to protect themselves, they have to see that they are tied to workers worldwide," she said. "It is the transnational economy that is undermining labor. A new union has to emerge that crosses national borders and makes a closer relationship among workers—a new kind of union that cooperates worldwide. Companies can make agreements among themselves about markets and production. The only competition in the global economy is between the workers."

Wolfgang Sachs, the German social critic, offered a mordant metaphor to describe the antidemocratic qualities of the global economy. The global marketplace, he said, has become the world's new "closet dictator."

"The fear of falling behind in international competition has become the predominant organizing principle of politics, North and South, East and West," Sachs wrote. "Both enterprises and entire states see themselves trapped in a situation of relentless competition, where each participant is dependent on the decisions of all other players. What falls by the wayside in this hurly-burly is the possibility for self-determination."[8]

Others have expressed similar perceptions, albeit less dramatically. Jacques Attali, the French economist, noted: "We already know they [the global economic changes] demand that politicians and statesmen accept the unpopular abandonment of sovereignty." W. Michael Blumenthal, chairman of Unisys: "I wouldn't say the nation-state is dead, but the sovereignty has been greatly circumscribed . . . even for a country as large as the U.S."[9]

For Americans, this is a new experience, profoundly at odds with national history and democratic legacy. We are now, suddenly, a nation whose citizens can no longer decide their own destiny. The implications offend the optimism and self-reliance of the American character, eclipsing our typical disregard for the rest of the world. Citizens of most foreign nations—smaller, less powerful and more dependent on others—have had considerable practical experience with the limitations and frustrations of global interdependency. Americans have not. They are just beginning to discover what global economics means for their own politics.

ACORN, the grassroots citizens' organization, discovered, for instance, that the prospect for financing low-income housing—a major priority for its members—had been seriously damaged by a new banking regulation that assigns an extremely high risk rating to bank lending for multifamily housing projects. "This will be a disaster for poor people unless Congress intervenes immediately," Jane Uebelhoer of ACORN testified. "This is outright government red-lining and it will be the end of low-income home ownership in Detroit, in Chicago, in New York and elsewhere."[10]

But the new credit regulation did not flow out of any legislation enacted by Congress and the president. It was a small detail in an international agreement forged among the central bankers from a dozen industrial countries, including the United States. The central bankers met periodically in Basel, Switzerland, for several years as the Committee on Banking Regulations and Supervisory Practices, trying to reconcile the different banking laws of competing nations and create a "level playing field" that would standardize the capital requirements for banks.

America's representative (and the leading promoter of the agreement) was the Federal Reserve, the nonelected central bank that enjoys formal insulation from political accountability. While America's most important multinational banks were consulted beforehand, no consumer representatives were included in the Federal Reserve's deliberations nor were any of the groups that speak for low-income home buyers.[11]

By the time ACORN and other community organizations saw the implications, the Federal Reserve had already issued the implementing regulations. Unfavorable terms were thus set for low-income housing and decided in an obscure venue far distant from the affected citizens or even from their elected representatives. Community housing advocates pleaded with Congress (to no avail) to undo the deal fashioned in Switzerland. They asked the Federal Reserve and other bank regulatory agencies to reconsider (also to no avail).

"When we talk to the federal regulators," Chris Lewis, an ACORN lobbyist, complained, "they say to us: 'Oh, that's an international treaty, we can't possibly do anything about that.' So now we have housing policy determined by central bankers with no accountability whatsoever."

American politics, in other words, is moving offshore. The nature of the global economy pushes every important political debate in that direction— further and further away from the citizens. As companies become multinational, able to coordinate production from many places and unify markets across national boundaries, they are taking the governing issues with them. From arcane regulatory provisions to large questions of national priorities, the corporations, not governments, become the connecting strand in offshore politics, since they are the only organizations active in every place and coping with all the world's many differences.

Arguments that were once decided, up or down, in the public forums of democratic debate are now floating off into the murk of international diplomacy and deal making. They are to be decided in settings where neither American citizens nor their elected representatives can be heard, where no institutional rules exist to guarantee democratic access and accountability.

Environmental activists discovered, for instance, that U.S. proposals for the current round of international trade negotiations would effectively vitiate domestic laws on food safety by assigning the question of standards to an obscure UN-sponsored commission in Rome. If the nation (or a state government) enacts laws on pesticides or food additives that exceed the health standards set by the Codex Alimentarius Commission in Rome, then other nations can declare that the environmental standards are artificial "trade barriers" designed to block foreign products and, therefore, subject to penalties or retaliation.

The goal proclaimed by Bush's trade negotiators is to "harmonize" environmental laws across the boundaries of individual nations to encourage freer trade. But that objective, inevitably, means lowering U.S. standards. Indeed, that is the objective for major components of American agribusiness, including the multinational chemical manufacturers who are enthusiastic supporters of what is blandly called "harmonization."

Agriculture Secretary Clayton Yeutter (later named national Republican chairman) declared: "If the rest of the world can agree what the standard ought to be on a given product, maybe the U.S. or the European Community will have to admit they are wrong when their standards differ."[12]

Thus, laws and regulation that go beyond the status-quo consensus of the global economy are depicted as obstacles to prosperity. When California voters ratified their strict new food-labeling law by referendum in 1986, Yeutter accused California of "going off on a tangent" by writing its own rules. "How can we get international harmonization when we can't get it here at home?" he complained. When the European Community proposed a ban on imported beef treated with artificial growth hormones (that is, U.S. beef), Yeutter objected that the European regulation would "contravene our mutual objective of achieving international harmonization in this sensitive area of food safety."

Yeutter's real target, as his remarks made clear, was the domestic political opposition from American environmentalists who are themselves pushing for more stringent food regulations. The European ban, he complained, will simply "add fuel to the fires for those who wish to have public policy decisions made on the basis of emotion and political pressure."[13]

The scientific experts whom Yeutter claims will make rational decisions, free of "emotion and political pressure," are not free of corporate influence, however. The Codex is an obscure agency utterly unknown to ordinary citizens, but the multinational companies that help devise its standards are well aware of its significance. At a recent session of the commission, the American delegation included executives from three major chemical companies—Du Pont, Monsanto and Hercules—serving alongside U.S. government officials. Among other things, the Codex standard permits DDT residues on fruit and vegetables that are thirty-three to fifty times higher than U.S. law allows.[14]

As environmentalists and some allied farm groups have argued, the current round of high-level treaty negotiations known as GATT (for General Agreement on Tariffs and Trade) is actually aimed at fostering a new generation of deregulation for business—without the inconvenience of domestic political debate.

"The U.S. proposals (for GATT) represent a radical attempt to preempt the authority of its own citizens and the citizenry of other countries to regulate commerce in the pursuit of environmental and social ends," David Morris of the Institute for Local Self-Reliance in St. Paul, Minnesota, declared. "It is an attempt to impose a laissez-faire philosophy on a worldwide basis, to allow the global corporations unfettered ability to transfer capital, goods, services and raw materials across national boundaries."

Other citizen groups and interests, from sugar growers to insurance companies to state governments, have also discovered that global politics is encroaching on their domains. Japan protests that state-set limits on U.S. timber harvesting constitute a GATT violation. European trade officials complain that the state of Maine's new law on throwaway bottles is an artificial trade barrier that the federal government should preempt in accordance with the international trade agreement.

The centrifugal diversity of the American federalist system, in which states can legislate and experiment independent of the national government, is thus headed for collision with the leveling, homogenizing force of the global marketplace. One or the other will have to yield power and prerogatives.[15]

American democracy is ill equipped to cope with offshore politics, both in its institutional arrangements and in its customary responses to foreign affairs. Treaty making and diplomacy belong traditionally to the presidency, even though the U.S. Senate must ratify the results, and there is a time-honored tendency to defer to the chief executive in negotiating foreign relations so that the nation may speak with one voice.

Congress, for instance, has ceded its lawmaking authority to the president across vast areas by authorizing the so-called "fast track" status for trade negotiations like GATT or the proposed trade agreement with Mexico. "Fast track" means that, when the agreement is completed, Congress will take only a single up-or-down vote on approving the entire package, with no chance to amend or reject particular sections. Naturally, this strengthens the president's bargaining position in the international arena, but it also cuts out the democratic process.

Since the trade agreements will repeal or alter numerous sections of existing domestic law, the members of Congress have put themselves in a very weak position to legislate. The only way to resist these changes in law will be to vote "no" on the finished trade agreement and thus undercut the president in global affairs. This would also incur the wrath of corporate interests and the other sectors who are beneficiaries.

The "fast track" approach is another form of political cover for cowardly legislators—a way for them to accomplish unpopular results while pleading that their hands are tied by the president. In 1991, both organized labor and a broad front of environmental groups joined forces to mount an energetic campaign against the "fast track" status for the Mexican trade negotiations. They cited the *maquiladora* experience as evidence of what will follow in terms of lost jobs, environmental damage and exploitation of Mexican workers. They lost—a measure of how strongly the corporate political organizations (and conventional wisdom) are pulling in the opposite direction.[16]

The overall political effect of globalization is to further enhance the power of the presidency—just as the Cold War did—at the expense of representative forums, public debate and accountability. Once an issue has become part of high-level diplomatic exchanges, all of the details naturally become murkier, since negotiators do not wish to talk too freely about their negotiating strategies. The discussions often literally move offshore and behind closed doors— more irregular deal making that will have the force of law.

When international deals are being struck, it matters enormously who is doing the bargaining and who is in the room offering expert advice. The so-called G-7, for instance, meets regularly to "coordinate" economic policies among the major industrial nations (including fiscal policy, a realm the Constitution assigns to Congress). Yet there is no visible procedure—much less legislated agenda—by which the Treasury secretary or the Federal Reserve chairman is empowered to make international economic policy for the nation. Those two officers, by their nature, represent a very narrow spectrum of American interests—mainly banks and the financial system—and they cannot be expected to reflect the full, rich diversity of American perspectives on economic issues. Bankers are well represented, but who speaks for the home builders or the auto industry or machine tools or the farmers?

Substantial institutional reforms are needed, obviously, to prevent global politics from gradually eclipsing the substance of democratic debate and action. At the very least, that would mean democratizing reforms to ventilate the U.S. negotiating routines in a systematic way so that everyone can follow the action. It might also require refusal to participate in any international forum or agency that lacks democratic access to the information and decision making. If the chemical companies can lobby the Codex in Rome for weaker health standards, then surely any other American citizen should be able to sit at the table too. When central bankers meet in Basel to decide U.S. housing policy, then housing advocates should also be in the room.

The first, overriding imperative, however, is to defend the nation's power to govern its own affairs. If democracy is to retain any meaning, Americans will need to draw a hard line in defense of their own national sovereignty. This is not just about protecting American jobs, but also about protecting the very core of self-government—laws that are fashioned in open debate by representatives who are directly accountable to the people. Among other things, this challenge requires Congress to confront the presidency and restrain it—to refuse to grant the chief executive the power to bargain away American laws in the name of free trade or competitiveness or any other slogan.

Offshore politics threatens the ability of free people to decide the terms of their own social relations; it allows the closet dictator to decide things according to the narrow interest of "efficiency." The "harmonizing" process begins with the regulatory laws that business interests consider meddlesome and too expensive, but the attack will lead eventually to the nation's largest social guarantees, welfare or Social Security or health, since those programs also add to the cost of production and thus interfere with the free-flowing commerce among boundaryless companies.

Who will decide what is equitable and just for American society? A closed meeting of finance ministers in Geneva? An obscure group of experts in Rome coached by corporate lobbyists? Such questions have already penetrated the fabric of self-government. Americans, in addition to their other democratic burdens, need to get educated on the answers.

Other nations, with more experience at global interdependence, are caught in the same pressures, but many of them understand, much better than Americans do, how to protect their own social values and institutions against the closet dictator's hand. Japan is the leading example of a nation that espouses free trade but ignores the principle whenever it needs to defend its domestic institutions against foreign intrusion. Japan does not do this only for economic advantage, as Americans suppose, but often to satisfy domestic political values. Japan shelters its rice growers from cheap imports (that is, American rice) because the island nation feels strongly about self-sufficient food production. It protects small retail outlets against the intrusion of giant retailing corporations because the tradition of small shops and shop owners is valued.

Japan breaks the "rules" in countless ways when its own prerogatives are threatened by global economics, but so do many others. The nations of western Europe have resisted more successfully than the American government has, even as they move toward an integrated European economic community. For that matter, many developing nations impose protective rules as the entry price for foreign investment, rules the multinational companies cheerfully accept. Some countries, such as South Korea, virtually seal their borders to foreign products that might undermine domestic development. Only in America are these governmental actions regarded as forbidden.[17]

The political problem this issue poses in America, aside from the ignorance and powerlessness of citizens, is that the elite groups that govern are mobilized on the other side. The elites of media, business, academia and politics have already made up their minds on these questions. They are committed to promoting the global economic system—and to defending it against the occasional attacks from angry, injured citizens.

To speak for national sovereignty, to speak on behalf of American jobs or political values, is to be labeled reactionary by the dominant political culture. The corporate political organizations, with their overwhelming resources, are able to depict any dissenting voice as a backward protectionist, standing in the way of modernizing enterprise. The gross injustices of global commerce are concealed behind the high-minded platitudes about free trade.

The governing elites face one large impediment, however, in their campaign for unfettered globalization: The American public, on the whole, doesn't buy it. As virtually every opinion poll demonstrates, the public wants the national government to defend American jobs and economic independence more aggressively, especially against trading partners like Japan or West Germany. The public envisions the U.S. government leading the world toward stronger public standards on the environment and other issues, not promoting the leveling process that pulls American laws down to the lowest common denominator. Americans, it is true, may be unfamiliar with the complexities of global politics, but their gut suspicion—that valuable assets are being lost—is not misguided.

The tension on this subject between the people at large and the powerful interests that dominate politics and government is emerging as the most serious, fundamental conflict in the decayed American democracy. The politics of the global economy, more profoundly than any other issue, puts the self-interest of the governing elites in conflict with the common ambitions of the governed. The governing elites have the power to advance their own narrow interests. For the public at large, however, their actions carry disturbing implications of disloyalty and betrayal.

The concept of the "boundaryless company" has now become commonplace among executives of major multinational corporations. They are American companies—sort of but not really, only now and then when it suits them. IBM, the flagship of American industrial enterprise, is composed of 40 percent foreign employees. Whirlpool is mostly not Americans. GE puts its logo on microwaves made by Samsung in South Korea.[18] Chrysler buys cars from Mitsubishi and sells them as its own. America's most important banks operate legally authorized "foreign facilities" right in Manhattan for the benefit of depositors who wish to keep their money "offshore."

The question of what is foreign and what is American has become wildly scrambled by global commerce. The multinational enterprises, unlike Americans generally, are already securing alliances in this fierce world of global competition—networks of joint ventures, coproduction and shared ownership with their ostensible rivals in the world, including state-owned enterprises in foreign nations. Every U.S. auto company has become partners one way or another with its competitors, the Japanese car companies. Producers of electronic equipment, computers, even aircraft have melded their American citizenship in similar arrangements.

Multinational executives work to enhance the company, not the country. The president of NCR Corporation told *The New York Times*: "I was asked the other day about United States competitiveness and I replied that I don't think about it at all." A vice-president of Colgate-Palmolive observed: "The United States does not have an automatic call on our resources. There is no mindset that puts this country first." And the head of GE Taiwan, where so many U.S. industrial jobs have migrated, explained: "The U.S. trade deficit is not the most important thing in my life . . . running an effective business is."[19]

John Reed, CEO of Citibank, America's largest troubled bank, has said he is actively scouting options for moving the corporation headquarters to a foreign country in order to escape U.S. banking laws. "The United States is the wrong country for an international bank to be based," Reed declared. Meanwhile, his bank's deposits are protected by the U.S. taxpayers and his lobbyists in Washington actively promote a multi-billion-dollar government bailout to save large commercial banks like Citibank from insolvency.[20]

These men are merely expressing the prevailing values of the "stateless corporation," as *Business Week* called it. This creature operates most successfully when it discards sentimental attachments like patriotism and analyzes global opportunities with a cold, clear eye. Some of these same corporations, it is true, wave the flag vigorously when bidding for defense contracts or beseeching the U.S. government for tax subsidies, but their exuberant Americanism dissipates rapidly when the subject is wages or the burden of supporting public institutions.

Their weak national loyalty has profound implications for the nation's politics because these men, on the whole, are also influential voices in shaping the outlines (and often the close details) of national economic policy—not just for trade policy, but for taxation and government spending priorities. Politicians in both parties (especially the Republican party) defer to their worldly experience. Most economists and political commentators have embraced their argument that America's future prosperity will be best served by a laissez-faire regime in which governments get out of the way and let the marketplace develop its global structure.

But here is the blunt question: Can these people really be trusted to speak for the rest of us? How can they faithfully define America's best interest when their own business strategies are designed to escape the bounds of national loyalty? What is good for IBM or General Electric may or may not be reliable advice for the country as a whole and for most of its citizens.

The impressive fact about ordinary Americans is that, despite years of education and propaganda, they still cling stubbornly to their skepticism about the global economy. With the usual condescension, elite commentators dismiss the popular expressions of concern as uninformed and nativist, the misplaced fears of people ill equipped to grasp the larger dimensions of economics.

Ordinary citizens generally form their economic opinions and perceptions, not from distant abstractions or even from the endless tides of propaganda, but from their own commonsense values and their own firsthand experiences. What they have seen of the global economy in the last two decades tells them to be wary and even hostile. In a functioning democracy, these popular insights, though not derived from sophisticated techniques of analysis, would be respected as the baseline for political debate and decision making.

Common sense tells people that it cannot be good for America's long-term prosperity to lose millions of high-wage manufacturing jobs. Even if this hasn't affected their own employment, it means that middle-class families are losing the wherewithal to be viable consumers, and sooner or later, that has to hurt the overall economy. Workers know this; so do merchants.

While most citizens do not sit down and try to calculate exactly what "declining real wages" have meant to their own incomes, they do know something bad is happening to them. They are working longer hours, but their paychecks don't seem to buy the same things they used to buy. When they go to look for a new car or a home, they discover that their idea of where they stood financially was mistaken—their expectations are now beyond the reach of their incomes. This widely shared anxiety is expressed in opinion polls as a preoccupation with the "cost of living" and, when analyzed by political elites, is interpreted as a complaint about rising prices and inflation.

Actually, as pollster Stanley Greenberg discovered in his focus groups with voters, the personal fears about the "cost of living" are really grounded in shrinking wages. The common perceptions are quite accurate. In 1979, for instance, an American worker earning average wages had to work twenty-three weeks to earn enough to buy an average-priced car. A decade later, he or she had to work thirty-two weeks to buy the same car. As the president of Chrysler put it: "We're looking at the pooring of America."

At this stage, people are not much beyond a general quandary about why this is happening to them. If pressed for explanations, they will blame various things, from welfare and affirmative action to crooked politicians. But the principal explanation expressed in public opinion is foreign competition. Industrial workers, who have now had two decades of close experience with the global marketplace, are more knowledgeable than others. They can explain the effects of internationalized labor and pricing in rich, detailed analysis based on the circumstances in their own workplaces. Americans are gradually being educated about the world through their own painful encounters with it.

People generally do not have coherent ideas about how the wage deterioration might be reversed—except that the government ought to be fighting aggressively on that front. Virtually no one in the top ranks of American politics—with the exception of the Reverend Jesse Jackson—speaks for this unorthodox point of view. To take it seriously would require politicians to debate the nature of the "stateless corporations" and entertain legislation aimed at their unfettered conduct.

The erosion of U.S. wages has proceeded unevenly since the early 1970s and will not soon be reversed. An average weekly paycheck worth $270 in 1981, if measured in constant purchasing power, declined to $254 by 1991 and is heading still lower. This average loss was, of course, not spread uniformly through the society, since some gained enormously while many others lost much more than the average.[21]

In fact, many orthodox economists routinely assume that the American wage decline must continue for at least another generation. The subject came up occasionally during interviews I conducted with various economists at Wall Street brokerages in the mid-1980s and the Wall Street economists, without exception, predicted further erosion for the next twenty to twenty-five years. Unfortunate but inevitable, they said. The trend is driven, they explained, by the deep and ineluctable process in which worldwide wage patterns are moving toward equilibrium—a "harmonization" of labor costs among nations, just as some officials wish to "harmonize" the environmental laws.

American workers will not descend to the poverty levels of Indonesia or Bangladesh, the economists assured me, but their standard of living must decline further until the relative costs and advantages of production locations in the world system have found a balancing point. American workers, once the best paid in the world, have naturally suffered the consequences first but, over time, others will feel it too. U.S. industrial wages have already fallen behind those of Germany and some other European nations, even though American productivity remains the highest in the world.

Apostles of the global economy constantly preach to American workers that, if they want to maintain their incomes, they must increase their productivity. But the evidence of the 1980s contradicts those sermons. The productivity of U.S. workers overall increased cumulatively by more than 12 percent during the decade, while their hourly wage rates increased by only 2 percent. For manufacturing workers, the disparity was much greater: Their output per hour increased most dramatically during the industrial realignments of the 1980s, but they were not compensated for it.[22]

The dismal forecast for American wages is a predicate for explosive politics in America, but the Wall Street economists did not anticipate any great rebellion. Wages have been falling for nearly two decades, they noted, and so far the American people have accepted it with patience and maturity. Indeed, American voters keep electing conservative governments that are committed to unfettered globalization.

The trend, however, has a flavor of betrayal that could ignite political upheaval, as it becomes clearer to people. The globalization process is generating great prosperity for the upper stratum of the society, the best-educated and least vulnerable citizens. Roughly speaking, if one is securely connected to one of the emerging global enterprises, whether American or foreign-owned, the future looks bright. Indeed, the last decade has been an extraordinary time of expanding incomes and wealth for those who are managers or professionals or investors attached to the international commerce.

The fissuring of common interests—and the power relationship behind it—is expressed most vividly in what has happened to executive compensation. The people at the top are literally leaving everyone else behind. Between 1977 and 1990, the period when average wages were stagnating, compensation for top corporate executives rose by 220 percent (this was, of course, also when the people in the top income brackets were winning their dramatic tax cuts). In 1960, the average pay for chief executives at the largest American corporations, after taxes, was twelve times greater than the average wage for factory workers. By 1990, it was seventy times greater.[23]

In fact, the upper stratum of citizens and their global enterprises benefit enormously from the very things that injure the other classes of workers—the depression of wages and the dismantling of national sovereignty. National interest is fracturing into two distinct and opposing poles. The new global elites are gradually "seceding" from their responsibilities to the general well-being of the nation, as Robert B. Reich has put it. The process could accurately be described in harsher terms—as betrayal—except that probably no one sets out deliberately to accomplish that. It is simply a matter of the people with power taking care of themselves, while leaving the nation mired in an awesome backlog of economic and social problems.

The diverging political interest explains much of what has happened in government in recent years and it shows up regularly in different forms on the governing agenda. The Bush administration's bank reform proposal, for instance, was based on the German and Japanese model of concentrated banking power and designed to create a handful of U.S. global banks, freed of regulatory restriction and able to dominate American industry as well as finance (though still sheltered from loss by the "full faith and credit" of the American taxpayers).

In education, the so-called "school choice" issue is also an effort of elites to separate themselves from the mass. Stripped of reformer rhetoric, "school choice" is really a scheme to divert taxpayer financing to private schools and thus foster a two-tiered educational system—an elite, selective school system that trains the professional talent needed by global enterprise and an underfinanced public school system for everyone else. The Business Roundtable and leading multinational companies are promoting the cause as their own—in the name of competitiveness.

The elites' abandonment of national loyalty is also reflected in the political commerce of Washington. It is now commonplace for top operatives in both parties to use the skills and influence they acquired from government service on behalf of foreign interests. The Center for Public Integrity checked the career paths of fifty-three senior officials who had left the office of U.S. trade representative over fifteen years and found that 47 percent of them went to work for the other side—registered as foreign agents.

"Japan is running an ongoing political campaign in America as if it were a third major political party," economist Pat Choate wrote in his book *Agents of Influence*, which described the awesome dimensions of how the Japanese interests manipulate U.S. policy through their hired American agents.[24]

Focusing on the influential Americans who work as Japanese agents misses the fundamental point, however, and wrongly demonizes that country. The Japanese are simply emulating—albeit with lots of money—the methodology of American corporate politics. They have adapted efficiently to Washington's techniques for mock democracy: Hire squads of well-connected lobbyists and lawyers from both political parties, contribute generously to think tanks and other ostensibly civic organizations, finance research and propaganda on behalf of your position. "A big part of the problem," said Karel van Wolferen, the Dutch journalist who is an authority on Japanese politics, "is that Americans can be bought so easily."

The more fundamental point, however, is that the Japanese line in American politics is not essentially different from the line of America's own multinational corporations and banks. The two interests even merge in such places as the Institute for International Economics, where they speak as one voice. Japanese and American multinationals compete with one another for market shares in global commerce, but both want roughly the same things from the U.S. government—the same policies on trade, on taxes, on managing the American economy.

The unpleasant truth is that, on the largest political issues, the views of

America's global corporations are much closer to those of their Japanese economic rivals than they are to those of the majority of American citizens. For that matter, the managers and technicians active everywhere in global commerce are closer to their counterparts in other nations than to their fellow citizens. They have a common political perspective, regardless of their citizenship, which they promote in the politics of Europe, Asia and the United States. In America, a bewildered and intimidated political system can no longer even figure out what the "American position" is.

The majority of Americans are not wrong in their unsophisticated skepticism. The new reality of global competition generates a vicious economic trap for worldwide prosperity: a permanent condition of overcapacity in production that insures destructive economic consequences. Simply put, the world's existing structure of manufacturing facilities, constantly being expanded on cheap labor and new technologies, can now turn out far more goods than the world's consumers can afford to buy. That is, more cars, computers, aircraft, appliances, steel and so forth are made than the marketplace can possibly absorb.

The auto industry is an uncomplicated example: Auto factories worldwide have the capacity to produce 45 million cars annually for a market that, in the best years, will buy no more than 35 million cars. "We have too many cars chasing too few drivers," a Chrysler executive remarked. The economic consequences are obvious: Somebody has to close his auto factory and stop producing. This marketplace imbalance in supply and demand is the larger reality that underlies the fierce competition for advantage among companies and among nations—the awesome force driving everyone toward the lowest common denominator.

Whose factory must be closed to bring the worldwide supply into balance with the worldwide demand? Whose workers will be laid off? The older, less modern factories are closed first, of course, but also the plants that pay the highest wages and the ones where government provides less generous tax subsidies to the employer. American workers in steel and autos and other industries have had a lot of experience watching this process at work—seeing factories they knew were viable and productive suddenly declared obsolete. But so will workers in the less abundant nations. This process closed Ohio factories and someday it will close Mexico's. So long as global productive capacity exceeds global demand by such extravagant margins, somebody somewhere in the world has to keep closing factories, old and new.

The companies have no choice. They must keep moving their production, keep seeking the lowest possible costs and most favorable political conditions, in order to defend their market shares. Eventually, as economist Jeff Faux has written, South Korea will be losing jobs to cheap labor in Thailand and even

China may someday lose factories to Bangladesh. The popular notion among struggling nations that they can someday become the next South Korea—as the reward for a generation or so of the degradation of their workers—is fatally at odds with the logic of permanent overcapacity. The Mexican *maquiladora* cities thought they were going to become the next South Korea, but instead they may be the next Detroit.[25]

In fundamental economic terms, the globalization process produces three interlocking economic consequences that together are deleterious to everyone's well-being. First, it destroys capital on a large scale by rendering productive investments useless to the marketplace. That is the meaning of closing viable factories that can no longer meet the price competition: The invested capital is lost, the idle factories are written off as tax losses. Modernizing production with new technologies always produces this destruction, of course, but the global dispersion of production lives on it—like a game of checkers in which advantage goes to the player who made the last jump.

Second, the overcapacity permanently depresses wage levels worldwide, since no workers anywhere can organize and bargain very successfully against the threat of a closed factory, whether they are well-paid Americans or impoverished peasants working somewhere in the Third World.

Finally, these two effects—the instability of capital investment and the depression of wages—combine to guarantee that global demand can never catch up with global supply. New consumers for the world's output, to be sure, emerge with new development, but other existing consumers are lost, as their jobs are lost or their wages decline in real terms. So long as the process is allowed to run its course, the flight will continue downhill—too many factories making too many goods for a marketplace where too many families lack the wherewithal to buy them.

The way out of this economic trap is a grand political strategy for growth that focuses on workers and wages worldwide. The global economy can proceed to develop, without the destructive qualities, if an economic order of accelerated global growth is designed to generate rising incomes for ordinary citizens and, thus, greater consumer capacity for what the world is able to produce. A strategy that fosters higher wage levels would gradually unwind the condition of enormous overcapacity, while it also discourages the desperate edge of capital flight.

This approach would require, of course, a great reversal in the conservative economic doctrines that now dominate most governments in the industrial world. It would also require convincing guarantees to the citizens of impoverished nations who long for jobs—guarantees that they will not be shut out of the rising prosperity. The economic policies for accomplishing such a strategy are plausible enough. What is not plausible at this moment in history is the politics.[26]

*   *   *

It does not require great political imagination to see that the world system is heading toward a further dispersion of governing power so the closet dictator of the marketplace can command things more efficiently, from everywhere and nowhere. The historic paradox is breathtaking: At the very moment when western democracies and capitalism have triumphed over the communist alternative, their own systems of self-government are being gradually unraveled by the market system.

To cope with this complicated new world, every government naturally seeks to centralize its command of policy and thus become more hierarchical, less democratic. Societies like Japan have a natural advantage because they already practice a feudal form of state-administered capitalism, dominated by a one-party monopoly in politics, managed through government-assisted cartels and insulated from popular resistance. Some elites in the United States, though they do not say so directly, would like to emulate the efficiency of the Japanese political structure—equipping the chief executive with even more authority and putting citizens at even greater distance from government.

For many years, a wishful presumption has existed that, in time, the hegemony of global corporations would lead the way to the construction of a new international political order—world institutions that have the representative capacity to govern equitably across national borders. That prospect is not at hand in our time.

On the contrary, what is emerging for now is a power system that more nearly resembles a kind of global feudalism—a system in which the private economic enterprises function like rival dukes and barons, warring for territories across the world and oblivious to local interests, since none of the local centers are strong enough to govern them. Like feudal lords, the stateless corporations will make alliances with one another or launch raids against one another's stake. They will play weakening national governments off against each other and select obscure offshore meeting places to decide the terms of law governing their competition. National armies, including especially America's, will exist mainly to keep the contest free of interference.

In that event, the vast throngs of citizens are reduced to a political position resembling that of the serfs or small landholders who followed church or nobility in the feudal system. They will be utterly dependent on the fortunes of the corporate regimes, the dukes and barons flying their national flag. But citizens will have nothing much to say about the governing of these global institutions, for those questions will have moved beyond their own government. If national laws are rendered impotent, then so are a nation's citizens.

A different vision of the future requires great political imagination—a new democratic sensibility in which people in many places manage simultaneously to overcome their sense of helplessness. Americans, given their heritage, are as well positioned as anyone in the world to take up the challenge and begin to develop a different script, one that is grounded in democratic principle and action. As its starting point, ironically, this requires a wise, purposeful kind of nationalism—in which Americans confront the global system and defend their own political values against it.

A single nation is not helpless before these forces, despite what conventional wisdom teaches, and the United States especially is not helpless. Citizens have enormous potential leverage over the global economy if they decide to use it through their own national governing system. A corporation's behavior abroad is not separable from its home country because it enjoys so many special benefits at home.

In the United States, a multinational corporation that wishes to be treated as an American citizen for the purposes of the law and government benefits can be made to play by America's rules, just as Japan's are, or else surrender all the tax subsidies, government contracts and other considerations, including national defense, that American taxpayers provide.

Why should Americans, for instance, provide research and development tax subsidies for corporations that intend to export their new production and to violate common standards of decency by exploiting the weak? Why should American military forces be deployed to protect companies that do not reciprocate the national loyalty?

These are among the many contradictions created by the global system that only nationalism can reconcile. American law cannot police the world and need not try, but it can police what is American. To take the starkest example, no U.S. company should be treated as a lawful entity, entitled to all the usual privileges, if its production is found to exploit child labor in other countries. The same approach applies across the range of corporate behavior, from environmental degradation to ignoring tax laws.

The American political system also has enormous leverage over the behavior of foreign-owned multinational enterprises—access to the largest, richest marketplace in the world. Because of that asset, the United States could lead the way to new international standards of conduct by first asserting its own values unilaterally. If trade depends upon price advantages derived mainly from poverty wages for children or defenseless workers prohibited from organizing their own unions or factories that cause great environmental destruction, this trade cannot truly be called free.

The purpose of asserting America's political power through its own marketplace would be to create the incentive for a new international system of global standards, one which all the trading nations would negotiate and accept. For a start, the United States ought to reject any new trade agreements that do not include a meaningful social contract—rules that establish baseline standards for health, labor law, working conditions, the environment, wages. The

U.S. government might also prohibit the familiar tax-dodging practices of companies that exploit communities as the price for new jobs. Indeed, companies ought to post community bonds when they relocate—guaranteeing that they will not run away from their obligations to develop roads and schools and the other public investments.[27]

Fundamentally, it is not just the exploited workers in the United States who need a higher minimum-wage law. The world economy needs a global minimum-wage law—one that establishes a rising floor under the most impoverished workers in industrial employment. A global minimum-wage law would recognize, of course, the wide gaps that exist between rich and poor, but it could establish flexible ratios aimed at gradually reducing the differences and prohibiting raw exploitation like that in the *maquiladora* zone in Mexico. No one imagines that world incomes will be equalized, not in our time certainly. But, as nations move toward equilibrium, they ought to be governed by a global economic system that pushes the bottom up rather than pulling the top down.

The democratic imperative is nothing less than that: to refashion the global economy so that it runs uphill for everyone, so that it enhances democracy rather than crippling it, so that the economic returns are distributed widely among all classes instead of narrowly at the top. This is the daunting outline of the next frontier for citizens who still believe in the idea of democracy. It will be as difficult as any barrier to democracy that Americans have faced previously in their history.

Despite our insularity, Americans are equipped in special ways to lead the next march toward democracy. After all, we have come from almost everywhere else in the world. Many of us still speak the languages of home countries and still know the cultures and political contexts of other places. Furthermore, the American popular culture travels before us everywhere in the world, expressing the nation's joyful sense of invention and optimism and individualism—the American qualities others wish to share.

The American people, however, also have a peculiar handicap to overcome. It is their own source of shame. While the American system is the world's beacon, speaking to the universal thirst for democratic possibilities, the reality of democracy is quite different at home, as Americans know. However brave and resourceful they may be, Americans cannot teach democracy to the world until they restore their own.

Conclusion:
The American Moment

My earliest political memory was the death of Lincoln when I cried inconsolably. I was four or five years old at the time and my mother read to me from one of those picture books with exemplary messages. The story of Lincoln's life unfolded in simple black-and-white etchings, from the humble origins in a frontier cabin to the White House. Young Abe learning to read by the light of the hearth, honest Abe the store clerk who walked many miles to return a customer's change, President Lincoln who freed the slaves and preserved the Union. Then, at the moment of triumph, the cruel assassination. The pictures ended in black bunting, a tragedy I found inexplicable.

My mother, who has romantic sensibilities, did not attempt to explain away the contradiction. Life is strange, life is wonderful, she often mused. The best and the worst, she meant, are frequently side by side in human experience. I came away, I suppose, with her melodramatic sense of things.

Lincoln, I believed as a child, was the actual fulfillment of America's democratic faith. He embodied the possibility that sovereign citizens, regardless of birth or status, could collectively decide their own destiny and somehow become greater than themselves. Yet the potential for tragic disappointment was also always present.

As an adult, I read deeper histories and learned the mature facts about Lincoln, the devious politician, the elusive and uncertain commander, but none of this contradicted what I had learned as a child. In fact, the full portrait made Lincoln seem even larger because, fully human and fallible, he could encompass every paradox about the nation's character—the crass and cunning side alongside its virtuous principles, the blind willfulness and also America's capacity to defy history.

He was still Lincoln. He still stood for an idea of democracy that I think is now widely dismissed as mystical—the belief that only from the many can this nation fulfill its larger qualities. My impression is that many Americans, perhaps most of them, no longer really believe this. Or they are sullenly resigned to the assumption that, given modern complexities, a genuine, full-throated democracy is no longer practical in America. Given the realities of power, it no longer seems plausible to them. Possibly, they are correct. If so, America will come to be identified, like other nations before it, by its grosser parts—mere geography defined by muscle and appetites and national eccentricities.

I choose to believe otherwise: The American saga always was and still remains a difficult search for democratic meaning. This nation, more than most, is driven by a transcendental imperative, an idea never fully realized, often blunted and even suppressed, but central to the society's energies. Genuine democracy, as Vaclav Havel has said, is like a distant horizon that no human society has yet reached or perhaps ever will reach. But that does not end the story and, in some ways, the search in America may be only just beginning.

At this moment of history, Americans are in the awkward position of receiving congratulations from around the world for upholding the democratic example when they know, if they are honest, that this adulation is directed at a political system that is not functioning in good faith with its own ideals and principles. No one can contemplate American democracy in the late twentieth century without experiencing the dissonance between the idea and the reality. Some citizens, the energetic minority who still believe, struggle to resolve these contradictions.

In a cynical era, a childhood reverie on Lincoln may seem ludicrously romantic. Reflections on democratic faith are dismissed as "unrealistic," like the tired boilerplate of campaign speeches. My conviction, however, is that an active faith in democratic possibilities dwells at the very center of the American experience. The first step toward renewal is to free ourselves of the cynical expectations of these times and to reassert that faith without hesitation or apology—to declare stubbornly that what we were all taught in childhood is still true, or can be true, if we decide to make it so.

The burden of this book has been critical, an attempt to explain the antidemocratic conditions that deform American politics. A clear-eyed understanding of these circumstances may be necessary in order to change things, but it is not a guarantee that things will change. Certainly, history provides abundant evidence of human societies that were well aware of their own contradictions and simply chose to evade them. Americans have the capacity for evasion too, as the nation's history amply demonstrates.

But the United States is still quite young as nations go and still a country capable of new departures, with the potential to surprise the world and even surprise itself. In the nature of things, this capacity is mainly a matter of faith.

After thirty years of working as a reporter, I am steeped in disappointing facts about self-government. Having observed politics from the small-town court-house to the loftiest reaches of the federal establishment, I know quite a lot about duplicitous politicians and feckless bureaucracies, about gullible voters and citizens who are mean-spirited cranks. These experiences, strangely enough, have not undermined my childhood faith in democratic possibilities, but rather tended to confirm it.

Reporting for newspapers (or magazines or broadcasting) is not a reflective occupation, but the work has one wonderful, redeeming quality to it. Reporters have a license to go almost everywhere in the society and talk to almost anyone, from U.S. senators and corporate managers to bus drivers and schoolteachers and poor people on welfare. In a random, roving manner, a reporter may experience this country firsthand—from top to bottom—with a variety of encounters not accessible to most other citizens. What I learned about America deepened my faith in the democratic possibilities.

Among other things, I have seen up close the frailties of power. At the pinnacles of political command, whenever I have been able to peer behind the veil of platitudes, I have usually glimpsed a scene of confusion and often chaos—the trial and error, folly and misapprehensions of people in charge trying to decide what to do. The randomness of human endeavor exists at the top too; history confirms that this is nearly always the reality of power.

For several generations, however, Americans have been systematically taught to defer to authority and expertise in a complicated world. The modern political culture, transmitted by schools and universities and the news media, teaches implicitly that those chosen to hold power have access to special knowledge and intelligence not available to others and, therefore, their delib-erations and actions are supposedly grounded in a firmer reality. My own experience, on the contrary, has corroborated again and again the native American skepticism of elites. I believe that, if the real inside story were known, every statesman and politician would prove to be as recklessly human as the rest of us.

This fallibility should not be held against them; the same qualities exist in authority figures of every kind, from corporate executives to church prelates. There is a "reassuring anarchy," as I once called it, in the most exalted realms of power and this encourages my conviction that rigid arrangements of power are much more vulnerable to intrusion and change than the experts and authorities wish people to believe. If citizens could grasp, sympathetically, the human dimension of the political failures that are periodically revealed in high places, they might recognize a greater capacity in themselves for influencing and even commanding the larger outcomes of the society.

The people who are running things are especially prone to error when they are isolated from the shared ideas and instincts of the larger community. Indeed, that is the pragmatic argument for democracy: A governing system that is well grounded in the common reality of the society at large is likely to produce sounder decisions, connected to real facts and conditions. The hard work of democracy involves constructing and sustaining those connections.

My encounters as a reporter with ordinary citizens have also led to optimism about the potential for democratic renewal. America has its full quota of fools and scoundrels, but this is a nation of people who are mostly smart and capable and, on the whole, generously disposed. If one is open to it, the wild variety of American life is endlessly strange and entrancing. As one gets to know these different people in their own peculiar circumstances, it seems extraordinary that we are all Americans, living in the same vast nation and with more or less the same civic values, and yet we are.

As a younger reporter, I spent many years getting on airplanes, flying around the country and dropping down into the lives of strangers, often at their worst moments, when a local crisis or conflict had become newsworthy. Nearly always, I came away refreshed by these encounters and even awed by the people and their stories, their openness and level-headed sense of things, the raw eloquence and inventive humor and sometimes their courage. Some of those citizens have appeared in this book.

Even in the most benighted corners of this country, in burned-out slums or on desolate Indian reservations, I have always met some whose forceful intelligence shone through the barriers of language and education and class. I frequently came away thinking to myself: Those people would be running things if they had been born with a bit more luck. If they spoke in formal English and dressed in blue pinstripes, they could pass for U.S. senators or bank presidents. I recognized, of course, that my insubstantial sympathies did not answer their complaints. Their anger would be satisfied only when it could speak for itself.

This is difficult, I know, for the well born and well educated to believe about the ordinary run of Americans (and perhaps threatening to some) for it suggests there is a vast pool of unrealized ability dwelling in the American population—people with important things to say who are not heard. America, it is true, would be a very different place if all of those unheard ideas and aspirations were given a full voice in politics. Democracy disrupts power.

Ordinary people, as this book has illustrated, do assert themselves despite the obstacles. Indeed, if there is one constant in all my years of observing politics, it is the single, shocking fact that the most far-reaching developments in my memory did not emanate from Washington or anywhere else in the elected structure of politics but came instead from obscure, unpredictable places where unanointed citizens found a way to express themselves. The civil rights movement is, of course, the most compelling example. It changed the fabric of American life more profoundly than anything else in my lifetime, save World War II.

I remember, in particular, interviewing the aging black leaders of Summerton, South Carolina, nearly two decades after they had filed one of the initial lawsuits that led to the Supreme Court's historic school-desegregation decision. These were yeoman farmers and laborers, a school principal, a minister, a café owner. Many of them had paid a terrible personal price for challenging the status quo. Men and women were fired from jobs, small businesses were ruined. Some had been driven out of the county permanently.

Looking back, they spoke with the pride of people who knew they had helped to move the national history but also with self-conscious precision, like witnesses wanting to set down the true facts, not inflated afterthoughts. Their struggle had begun over a pitifully small matter, they explained, when they asked the white school board to supply coal to heat the black children's one-room country schoolhouse. When the school board refused, their anger deepened. Some of these men had just come home from World War II and the contradictions of the racial caste system mocked their patriotic sacrifice.

So they raised their demands further. They also wanted school buses for the black kids and no more hand-me-down textbooks, and decent buildings with indoor plumbing. Politics failed and the dispute became a lawsuit. When the civil rights lawyer came down from New York (he was Thurgood Marshall, later a Supreme Court justice), he told them that, since they were in this fight, they might as well go all the way and challenge the caste system itself. The idea was frightening and some hesitated. These people were already enduring reprisals and the intimate hostilities that are part of life in a small town. They agreed to go forward, however. Their legal cause was expanded to challenge the law of racial segregation itself and eventually their suit became a companion in the decision known as *Brown* v. *Board of Education*.

Long years later, I am still awed by their elemental courage. "Courage" is another word not often used now in politics, along with "loyalty" and "trust," but these humble citizens were putting themselves at risk in terms much more stark than losing an election and for a far larger public purpose.

They did not presume to reach for power for themselves and certainly not to change the social order. They embarked on a quite modest plea for justice and, improbably, found themselves perfecting its meaning. Years later, in fact, the underlying social order of Summerton itself had not changed that much, even though their struggle had helped to change the nation. Life is strange, as my mother said. These people balanced their political disappointments with the intangible rewards of self-realization. In addition to changing America, they discovered that they had also changed themselves and this achievement was permanent.

If there is a mystical chord in democracy, it probably revolves around that notion—that unexpected music can resonate from politics when people are pursuing questions larger than self. As a reporter, I have seen that ennobling effect in people many, many times—expressed by those who found themselves engaged in genuine acts of democratic expression, who claimed their right to help define the larger destiny of their community, their nation. Power can accumulate in mysterious ways, if citizens believe they possess this right. Their power atrophies when they no longer believe in it. This book is for the believers.

Rehabilitating democracy will require citizens to devote themselves first to challenging the status quo, disrupting the existing contours of power and opening the way for renewal. The ultimate task, however, is even more difficult than that: building something new that creates the institutional basis for politics as a shared enterprise. The search for democratic meaning is necessarily a path of hard conflict, but the distant horizon is reconciliation. Americans coming to terms with themselves—that is the high purpose politics was meant to serve.

This renewal, if it occurs, will not come from books. A democratic insurgency does not begin with ideas, as intellectuals presume, or even with great political leaders who seize the moment. It originates among the ordinary people who find the will to engage themselves with their surrounding reality and to question the conflict between what they are told and what they see and experience. My modest ambition for this book is that it will assist some citizens to enter into "democratic conversations" with one another, asking the questions that may lead them to action.[1]

The random anger visibly accumulating in so many sectors of the society can be therapeutic, but only in a limited sense. The democratic problem requires hard work from citizens who have been taught to be passive consumers in politics. It means people must learn once again to come together and develop their own understanding of events, free of the slogans and propaganda. It requires them to take the daring step of assuming some personal responsibility for self-government.

The task of learning is naturally intimidating. This book has set out many of the complicated conditions that history has dealt to the present—the political circumstances that confine citizens to cramped roles and warp the lines of accountability and control. I have also suggested various new ways that people might think about how to reform the political order. But there are no easy and simple ways around these barriers. In my estimate, the status quo is much more vulnerable to purposeful challenges organized by citizens than conventional wisdom supposes. But I do not presume to know exactly how or where the insurgency begins.

Democratic solutions will emerge only from the trial-and-error of active citizens who learn for themselves how to do politics, who discover the methods and principles that work because people have tried and occasionally failed. It requires of people the patience to accumulate social understandings that they have tested against reality and then to pass on their knowledge freely to others.

Strange as it may seem to an era governed by mass-market politics, democracy begins in human conversation. The simplest, least threatening investment any citizen may make in democratic renewal is to begin talking with other people about these questions, as though the answers matter to them. Harmless talk around a kitchen table or in a church basement will not affect anyone but themselves, unless they decide that it ought to. When the circle is enlarged to include others, they will be embarking on the fertile terrain of politics that now seems so barren.

A democratic conversation does not require elaborate rules of procedure or utopian notions of perfect consensus. What it does require is a spirit of mutual respect—people conversing critically with one another in an atmosphere of honesty and shared regard. Those with specialized expertise serve as teachers, not commanders, and will learn themselves from listening to the experience of others. The respect must extend even to hostile adversaries, since the democratic objective is not to destroy them but to reach eventual understanding. At its core, the idea of democracy is as simple as that—a society based on mutual respect.

This obvious human quality, seemingly available to all, is what's missing from American politics, drenched as it is in mass manipulation and deception and sour resentments. Indeed, mutual respect, above and beyond the usual social and economic distinctions, is missing from the general fabric of American life. A society that regularly proclaims democratic pieties also devotes extraordinary energy and wealth to establishing the symbols and trappings of hierarchy, the material markings that delineate who is better than whom.

The search for honest conversation, like other aspects of the democratic experience, can be its own reward, whether or not it leads to the fulfillment of power. It opens a path to self-realization grounded in social relationships— knowing others on terms that are reliable and enduring. Americans are already searching for "relationships," almost frantically it seems, on a close personal level. What many of them fail to grasp is that politics, in its original sense, also offers a practical means for mending the damaged social relations that afflict American life.

Building a politics grounded in intimate human terms seems so remote from the present that many will regard it as an impossible task. The organizational barriers are obvious and formidable, reflecting the inequalities of private status and the fractured nature of the society itself. Certainly, it is work for years or decades, not seasons.

But ordinary citizens, as this book has demonstrated, have their own inherent advantages in this enterprise, including their ability to see the reality more clearly sometimes than those who hold power. In some scattered places, the democratic ideal is already in motion, often among humble citizens who lack any personal advantages. These are people who still believe, as the Ohio auto worker said, that "the ultimate power is in their hands." They regularly find their faith confirmed in actual experiences.

When incumbent officeholders begin to perceive a real threat developing to their power, that is the moment when electoral politics can begin to become serious and interesting again. A genuine democratic dialogue can follow, one that promises accountability and also trust between the governed and their government. When the organized presence of citizens can deprive others of power, all the deeper power relationships surrounding government will be put at risk too.

The cynical cannot grasp this possibility, but the believers know that it is the actual history of American democracy. At the most creative moments in the American past, the nation found its true source of political energy and ideas among those citizens in unexpected quarters who took it upon themselves to renew the search.

As a nation, Americans are coming to the hard part of the saga, I believe, the time when things become less easy and the true character of the nation is revealed. In my romantic optimism, I have come to imagine that this may be the moment of testing that history was preparing for us all along. After two hundred years of fabulous invention, adventure and abundance, we are on new ground: awesomely powerful yet insecure and dependent, a democratic beacon for others yet profoundly troubled in our own social reality.

Americans are about to learn whether the American experiment was truly unique—capable of defying history—or simply another chapter in the rise and fall of muscular nation-states. Until now, the national experience seemed to unfold without boundaries, either geographical or material or psychological. The transcendental expectations were regularly fulfilled and the promise of future fulfillment was kept alive for almost everyone. But the space of that promise has shrunk visibly and the nation is bumping up against some harsh new obstacles to its power. National reputation and the military might of empire do not necessarily prevail over the new economic forces at work in the world. Citizens are told to temper their ambitions and appetites; the new realities are said to be beyond our control.

If the idea of America as specially positioned in history was nothing more than legend, then the future seems fairly clear and is commonly described as decline. Nothing in history guarantees, after all, that the richest, most energetic and inventive place on earth will remain so forever. The usual story of great powers is that sooner or later, when the glory faded, they sank into social decay and bitterness. That is the usual ending for a political system that persistently ignores reality, and for a people who become alienated from their own values.

My own optimism insists that this new crucible can yield a different outcome. But this is the hard part: The only way I can imagine this may happen is through the restoration of the civic faith. The American moment cannot be about accumulating more wealth or weaponry or territory; the facts will not allow it. It must involve a more difficult and introspective search for social invention—politics that takes the democratic idea to its next plateau in human history.

The present generation and the next, in other words, must find tangible ways to reinvigorate the social faith in the promise of democracy. The nation's sense of its own continuing search for something better is endangered and, without that civic faith, this nation is in deep trouble. If democratic character is lost, America has the potential to deteriorate into a rather brutish place, ruled by naked power and random social aggression. Innocent faith is what makes America work.

That faith does not imply impossible notions of perfection, but it does require convincing forward motion toward a social contract that most everyone will understand and accept—mutual understandings that promise equitable and shared objectives. To achieve this in the contemporary circumstances, the present generation of Americans may have to face some of the Republic's oldest contradictions, contradictions that were always successfully evaded in the past.

Boundless prosperity and adventure, throwing off new wealth and dispersing it widely, allowed the political system to avoid confronting questions of hierarchy and class and race, the inequalities of poverty and plenty, the privileges embedded in the political order. Endless expansion ignored the accumulating damage to the natural environment. General abundance made it easier to accept a political system that had become steadily more distant from popular control. Now we are up against those questions again.

These matters have been evaded for good reason; they are the most difficult to resolve and no society anywhere that calls itself a democracy has succeeded in facing them. Americans, however, have much more at stake because this nation depends crucially upon sustaining the idea of a democratic society. It is the essential strand that binds diverse peoples together and enables the society to see itself as a functioning whole.

Americans need a new parable for themselves—a story of national purpose that faces the present realities maturely but does not sacrifice the country's youthful idealism and inventiveness and self-confidence. If Americans set out to rehabilitate their own democracy, they may discover new democratic vistas for others. It is a chance to organize the future—to lead the world to ground where no one has ever been before.

Despite the centuries of struggle and advance, democracy is still a radical proposition. "This is an unsanctioned idea," historian Lawrence Goodwyn observed, "but this is the democratic idea: that the people will participate in the process by which their lives are organized."

New possibilities are opened for any society that takes that idea seriously. The oldest questions of human existence remain unanswered by modern societies, despite the gloss of technology and wealth. The complexities of modern life have ensnared people in new forms of subservience. Why do millions still starve when the world is awash in surplus food? How can the modern economic system be transformed so that growth and prosperity do not depend so centrally on waste and despoliation? What are the outlines of a democratic system in which workers and owners and communities would truly share a voice in organizing their own lives? None of these matters remains unresolved because of physical constraints. They are political questions, waiting on democratic answers.

Americans should not suppose that they are the only people who need to ask such questions or are equipped to find the answers. While American democracy has decayed, people in the most unlikely nations have become the new inventors of democratic possibilities—toppling the most rigid forms of power with the force of organized people.

Their experiments, even their failures, have provided a tonic for small-d democrats everywhere in the world. They have restored, above all, honest language—the capacity to speak about democracy with clarity and sincerity, as if the idea of self-governing people is fresh and alive and still practical. They have further restored an understanding that, as Vaclav Havel said, democracy is the unfinished story of human aspirations.

"Man must in some way come to his senses," Havel wrote from his prison cell. "He must extricate himself from this terrible involvement in both the obvious and hidden mechanisms of totality, from consumption to repression, from advertising to manipulation through television. He must rebel against his role as a helpless cog in the gigantic and enormous machinery hurtling God knows where. He must discover again, within himself, a deeper sense of responsibility toward the world, which means responsibility toward something higher than himself."[2]

The American beacon helped to teach people everywhere to aspire to self-realization and to rebel against powerlessness. Now, it seems, the former students must re-educate Americans in the meaning of their own faith. Perhaps that is when the American moment will begin: when Americans find the courage to speak honestly again in the language of democracy.

Notes

<small>Introduction</small>: Mutual Contempt

1. The human yearning for democracy is profound and universal, as the upheavals in Communist nations have most recently confirmed. It is driven fundamentally by the impulse for individual self-realization, a desire to discover and establish one's one worth in the collective context of the surrounding world. The struggle to achieve this is so difficult that the search has proceeded fitfully even in the most congenial settings, such as the United States.

The history of nations has reflected this search over the last four or five hundred years as different societies sought to discover democratic meaning and establish its terms. Some places have advanced not at all; some created the forms of democracy but without the substance. Other places—most notably the United States—embraced the idea in their national character and have worked fairly steadily toward improving upon it. Democracy is a presumption, not that the majority of the voters will always be right, but that real choices will be put before them.

2. Alexander Hamilton defined the paternalistic skepticism of popular rule that is still reflected in the modern elites of both political parties. Quoted in John F. Manley, "The American Dream," *Nature, Society and Thought,* Fall 1988.

3. *The New York Times* published a four-part series in March 1990, called "The Trouble with Politics, Running vs. Governing," which concluded: "Politicians in both parties say government is being crippled by a new superstructure of politics that makes ideas harder to discuss and exalts public opinion over leadership."

4. Ernesto Cortes, Jr., "Powerlessness also corrupts," Speech to Farm Crisis Workers Conference, published in *Texas Observer,* July 11, 1986.

5. The voting decline of 20 percent was calculated by Curtis Gans of the Committee for the Study of the American Electorate. Dissatisfaction with the 1990 elections was described in "The People, the Press & Politics 1990," Times Mirror Company, November 16, 1990.

6. The poll was taken by Stanley Greenberg and Celinda Lake and reported in *The Commonwealth Report,* April 1989.

7. Polls on public perceptions of who controls government have shown increasing alienation for nearly thirty years with a brief reversal in the early 1980s when Ronald Reagan took office. Data from the Center for Political Studies, University

of Michigan, were cited, for instance, by Herbert Gans, *Middle American Individualism: The Future of Liberal Democracy,* Free Press, 1988.

8. Lewis H. Lapham, ''Inspectors General,'' *Harper's,* July 1989.

9. Senator D'Amato was quoted in *The Wall Street Journal,* January 30, 1990.

10. Inventories of the powerful are generally compiled by eccentric scholars of the left and right and their work often inspires a kind of brittle paranoia—the image of a few influentials meeting somewhere in some dark room. Power in American politics is too diffuse—and sometimes chaotic—for such facile definitions. The sociologist C. Wright Mills came much closer a generation ago when he defined the ''power elite'' as five generic subcategories: the upper classes and wealthy; corporate executives and owners; the political directorate at the top of government, including lawyer-statesmen; the military managers and their industrial partners; and that vague status system known as celebrity. See C. Wright Mills, *The Power Elite,* Oxford University Press, 1956.

ONE: Mock Democracy

1. An analysis by Common Cause determined that 239 practitioners of leveraged buyouts, their wives and children contributed $3.5 million, including $1.2 million in so-called ''soft money'' for George Bush. *Washington Post,* October 22, 1989.

2. The internal details of how the Superfund Coalition was organized were provided in memorandums made public by the Natural Resources Defense Council and other protesting environmental organizations.

3. I have no evidence to indicate that the *New York Times* story by Peter Passell on September 1, 1991, was directly linked to the Superfund Coalition, but it relied prominently on experts from General Electric and Clean Sites, an industry-sponsored organization that deals with toxic cleanup projects.

The major polluters were also active on the legal front in their efforts to stymie Superfund enforcement and force Congress to rewrite the law. The corporations launched a flurry of liability lawsuits against municipalities and small businesses—even pizza parlors—arguing that these enterprises had also contributed toxic wastes and should share in the cleanup costs, even if their liability was minuscule compared to that of the large manufacturers and insurance companies. This effort was designed to stimulate a political backlash against Superfund and persuade Congress to back off the original legislation. See *Wall Street Journal,* April 2, 1991.

4. Tommy Boggs was quoted in the *National Journal,* June 13, 1990.

5. The sampling of AEI's corporate patrons is from 1987, reported by James T. Bennett, *Patterns of Corporate Philanthropy: Ideas, Advocacy and the Corporation,* Capital Research Center, 1989.

6. Some details on how business set out to mobilize in Washington are drawn from David Vogel, *Fluctuating Fortunes: The Political Power of Business in America,* Basic Books, 1989.

7. The Commerce Department per-capita income rankings are for 1987, *Washington Post,* March 1, 1990.

8. The rise of high incomes and the decline of low-income families in the

Washington area are from *Market Trends*, Greater Washington Research Center, November 1988.

9. Business's growing share of interest organizations is from Michael D. Reagan, *Regulation: The Politics of Policy*, Little, Brown, 1987. The Senate Government Affairs Committee study of citizen participation was done in 1979 in an effort to rally support for government grants to citizen representation groups, a brief experiment that had its own flaws but, in any case, was killed during the Reagan years. The data were cited in Gary C. Bryner, *Bureaucratic Discretion: Law and Policy in Federal Regulatory Agencies*, Pergamon Press, 1987.

10. Anthony Downs, an economist at the Brookings Institution, is better known in contemporary Washington as an authority on real estate and urban development. His thesis in political philosophy challenged the civic smugness promoted by the mainstream political scientists extolling the virtues of pluralism. Anthony Downs, *An Economic Theory of Democracy*, Harper & Row, 1957.

11. Politicians in tax-exempt activities, *National Journal*, December 9, 1989.

12. The New York Academy of Sciences reported, for instance, that the cancer death rate among men, excluding lung cancer, which is often attributable to smoking, has increased by 9 percent since 1950 in industrial nations. The report, compiled by twenty-six scientists in thirteen countries, adjusted for such factors as aging populations—the explanation often offered for the rising cancer rates. *Washington Post*, December 10, 1990; also the Natural Resources Defense Council's report in *Cancer Statistics Review, 1973–1986*, National Cancer Institute, May 1989.

13. The study of scientific bias was cited by Gary C. Bryner in *Bureaucratic Discretion*, previously cited.

14. An exhaustive academic literature exists on the vagaries of cost-benefit analysis, most of it written by policy thinkers who deplore the weaknesses and inconsistencies, but still regard it as a useful tool for decisions of resource allocation. They do not, by and large, acknowledge the broader moral context in which they are operating and they seem unaware that public decisions made by government rely on a different kind of authority than the cost-benefit decisions made by private business.

The examples of life value arguments are drawn from several sources: Michael D. Reagan, *Regulation*, previously cited; V. Kerry Smith, editor, *Environmental Policy under Reagan's Executive Order: The Role of Benefit-Cost Analysis*, University of North Carolina Press, 1984; Martin J. Bailey, *Reducing Risks to Life: Measurements of the Benefits*, American Enterprise Institute, 1980; and an interview with David Vladeck of Public Citizen.

15. Charles E. Lindblom described democracy as "imprisoned" by markets. See "The Market as Prison," in Thomas Ferguson and Joel Rogers, editors, *The Political Economy: Readings in the Politics and Economics of American Public Policy*, M. E. Sharpe, 1984. Lindblom's argument was elaborated more fully in his own book, *Politics and Markets: The World's Political-Economic Systems*, Basic Books, 1977.

Two: Well-Kept Secrets

1. The frayed principles of liberals on the House Banking Committee were displayed in raw form when some of them in late 1989 tried to depose Henry Gonzalez as chairman. Their complaint was that he had failed to consult them on committee business and was insufficiently partisan. The reality is that Gonzalez is an independent-minded critic of the cozy relations between banking and the federal regulatory apparatus. Gonzalez, furthermore, had embarrassed his own party by holding a series of investigative hearings on Charles Keating and other S&L moguls who had manipulated various Democratic politicians with campaign money. For years, the liberals were silent when their committee was chaired by a corrupt finagler. When an honest politician became chairman, they rebelled. In any case, Gonzalez prevailed, by a vote of 163–89, in the House Democratic caucus.

2. I described the financial and economic consequences of the 1980 financial deregulation in *Secrets of the Temple: How the Federal Reserve Runs the Country*, Simon & Schuster, 1987, and also in *The Trouble with Money*, Whittle Direct Books, 1989. The most deft description of how deregulation doomed the savings and loan industry came from Albert M. Wojnilower, chief economist of First Boston Corporation. "Freeing the thrift and mortgage markets from government subsidy and guarantee," he wrote, "is like freeing the family pets by abandoning them in the jungle."

3. Senators Garn and Proxmire were quoted by the Associated Press, July 26, 1985. The Treasury secretary's testimony was before a Senate banking subcommittee on June 13, 1985.

4. Alan Greenspan, as private consultant, wrote to federal regulators and asked them to give Lincoln Savings and Loan an exemption from the regulation limiting direct real-estate investment. He described Lincoln's management as "seasoned and expert in making direct investments"—the very opposite of what subsequent events proved about Charles Keating's management. The Federal Reserve chairman, when asked later about his intervention in behalf of Keating, replied, "Of course I'm embarrassed." *New York Times*, November 20, 1989.

5. See my article, "The Growing Crisis in Our S&L Industry," *Rolling Stone*, August 11, 1988, which quoted Robert Dugger and other bank lobbyists on how they intended to do the taxpayer bailout right after the election.

6. The separation of electoral politics from governing politics is deeply ingrained in the culture that shapes and limits corporate journalism. After the 1988 election, with some embarrassment, political reporters recognized that they had missed the savings and loan story, but they pursued it in the same narrow terms—which party might suffer more from this scandal at the next election? Political reporters are averse to the "substance" of such issues and often quite ignorant about them. In general, despite their embarrassment with the savings and loan debacle, the media repeated the same opacity as the crisis of failing commercial banks grew larger.

7. Theodore J. Lowi, a Cornell political scientist, wrote: "The people are shut out at the most creative phase of policy making—where the problem is defined." See "The New Public Philosophy: Interest-Group Liberalism," in Thomas Fer-

guson and Joel Rogers, editors, *The Political Economy: Readings in the Politics and Economics of American Public Policy,* M. E. Sharpe, 1984.

8. General Electric purchased the apartment complexes with a promise that one third of the units would be available to low-income families. Robert Bass, the wealthy Texas investor, was among others who acquired defaulted properties under the program that reformers had enacted. See Leslie Wayne in *The New York Times,* June 27, 1991.

9. As one who participated in discussions of the Financial Democracy Campaign's proposals, I witnessed up close the dilemma of citizen groups that try to penetrate the special-interest circle surrounding legislative issues. At meeting after meeting, the participants in the coalition fell into the same argument among themselves: whether to push genuinely fundamental reforms that went far beyond the conventional terms of debate or to advance modest proposals on the margins that had at least some chance of acceptance.

Generally, the old hands from Washington-based groups tended to favor the moderate strategy since they had considerable experience in the frustrating task of lobbying for large ideas that no one in Congress would listen to. People who have spent years establishing working relationships with a handful of sympathetic members of Congress are not anxious to sacrifice their connections by pushing them to sponsor ideas bound to lose.

The other side, including myself, argued that nothing fundamental was likely to happen in Washington anyway until the general public became aroused and much better educated about their stake in the contest. The process of political education could only begin if the reformers pushed the larger ideas, regardless of whether Congress was ready to listen.

In the end, the campaign did a bit of both but its legislative efforts inevitably gravitated toward the narrower focus of modest amendments that seemed doable, given existing political realities. In this manner, even groups that wish to change the political agenda are co-opted by the status quo.

THREE: Bait and Switch

1. The shift in tax burdens was described in "The Decline in Progressivity and the Decline in Revenue," Citizens for Tax Justice, February 23, 1990.

2. Kevin P. Phillips described the shift of tax burdens with brilliant documentation in *The Politics of Rich and Poor,* Random House, 1990. But Phillips concluded by predicting that old cycles of American politics would correct the injustices—Democrats would rediscover the working class and return to power to make things right. My argument is that the cyclical swings in which Phillips puts his faith are another of the self-correcting mechanisms that no longer seem to work. Democrats were principal coauthors of the vast shift in taxation and, unless there is a dramatic turnover within that party, Democrats will be reluctant to undo what they helped to create.

3. The imbalance of financial wealth was reported in the Federal Reserve Board's "Survey of Consumer Finances, 1983," *Federal Reserve Bulletin,* September and December 1984.

4. For more details on how elite opinion rallied around an austerity agenda during the presidential campaign, see my articles in *Rolling Stone*, "The Shadow Debate on the American Economy" and "The Real Election in America This Year," July 14 and August 25, 1988.

5. Alan Greenspan's statement on the need to curtail domestic consumption was in response to a written question submitted by Senator William Proxmire at a Senate Banking Committee hearing, February 24, 1988.

6. "Opinion leaders respond very differently from the general public when asked about potential new revenue sources to cut the deficit," the Gallup survey reported. "While much of the public would support a new tax on gasoline only as a last resort, opinion leaders overwhelmingly favor (74 percent) such a tax. . . . A majority of corporate leaders (54 percent) and about half of financial leaders (48 percent) favor the establishment of a national sales tax. . . . Slightly over half of the financial leaders surveyed (52 percent) favor taxing Social Security at the same rate as ordinary income." See "The Press, People & Economics," Times Mirror Company, May 1989.

7. The Gallup and IRS surveys as well as much other data on the public's opposition to the regressive trend in taxation are described by Barry Sussman in *What Americans Really Think: And Why Our Politicians Pay No Attention*, Pantheon, 1988.

8. Details on tax collection can be found in "Income Tax Compliance Research, Gross Tax Gap Estimates and Projections for 1973–1992," IRS; statement of Representative J. J. Pickle, oversight chairman, House Ways and Means Committee, February 20, 1990; speech by Charles A. Bowsher, comptroller general, "An Emergency Crisis: The Disinvestment of Government," December 2, 1988; and "Facts on the Federal Income Tax System—1989," National Treasury Employees Union.

9. The shifting income shares were described by Joseph A. Pechman of the Brookings Institution in "The Future of the Income Tax," a paper distributed December 22, 1990.

10. Darman was referring approvingly to the 1986 tax legislation that sharply reduced tax rates for the upper-income brackets, *Washington Post*, February 26, 1989.

11. Anthony Downs, in *An Economic Theory of Democracy*, described democracy's theoretical inclination to favor the many over the few. "The equality of franchise in a democratic society," Downs wrote, "creates a tendency for government action to equalize incomes by redistributing them from a few wealthy persons to many less wealthy ones."

12. Mellon's celebrated dictum was quoted in "Less Taxing Alternatives," *Democracy Project Reports*, March 1984. For an authoritative account of the intellectual combat surrounding the progressive income tax, see Ronald Frederick Key, "From Redistributive to Hegemonic Logic: The Transformation of American Tax Politics, 1894–1963," *Policy & Society*, 1983.

13. "Put the jam on the lower shelf" has been attributed to Ralph Yarborough by those who heard him campaign in the 1950s. I first heard the slogan in Kentucky

politics in the early 1960s, employed by a Republican state senator from a rural district.

14. Darman's remarks were in a speech at the National Press Club, July 20, 1989.

15. Thomas B. Edsall, *The New Politics of Inequality,* W. W. Norton, 1984.

16. David Stockman was quoted by the author in *The Education of David Stockman and Other Americans,* New American Library, 1986.

17. The *Wall Street Journal* poll found that people with incomes over $50,000 favor a higher tax rate on unearned income, 61 percent to 19 percent. *Wall Street Journal,* October 26, 1990.

18. John D. Raffaelli was quoted in "Zap! You're Taxed," *National Journal,* February 3, 1990.

19. The White House argument that persuaded Reagan to endorse the Social Security tax increase was related by Richard E. Neustadt and Ernest R. May, *Thinking in Time: The Uses of History for Decision-Makers,* The Free Press, 1986.

20. Survey data on the 1983 Social Security legislation are from Barry Sussman, *What Americans Really Think.* Neustadt and May, professors at Harvard's Kennedy School, offered the Social Security episode as one of several case studies of wise political management in their book, *Thinking in Time.*

21. The statistics on the revenue shifts are from a statement by Senator Daniel Patrick Moynihan, January 14, 1991.

22. See Barry Sussman, *What Americans Really Think,* for an insightful discussion of the public's skepticism toward tax reform. Burns Roper testified before the Joint Economic Committee, quoted in my article, "Break Dancing," *Rolling Stone,* October 1986. The windfall tax cuts in the 1986 legislation are drawn from data from the Joint Committee on Taxation. Other wealthy individuals were, of course, forced to pay more taxes since they were losing the benefit of various loopholes. Overall, however, all people with incomes above $200,000 enjoyed an average tax cut of $2,856 each—compared to a $200 tax cut for middle-income families. Sponsors argued the income-tax legislation was marginally progressive, but that claim was meaningless since it left out the rising burden imposed on most families by Social Security taxes.

23. Rostenkowski disparaged Moynihan's proposal in a speech before the Futures Industry Association convention in Boca Raton, Florida, March 9, 1990, where he promised to protect the brokers against federal taxes on their transactions. The evasion of Representative Richard Gephardt, House majority leader, was described by Fred Barnes, "Leaders to Follow," *New Republic,* May 14, 1990.

24. See *The Wall Street Journal,* March 14, 1990, and *Washington Post,* March 11, 1990, for details of Rostenkowski's plan.

25. For an insightful discussion of the Democrats' collaboration with Republicans on taxes and other matters, see Robert Kuttner, "Congress Without Cohabitation," *American Prospect,* Winter 1991.

26. *The Wall Street Journal,* because it rigorously and unsentimentally covers business's interface with government, is the best available source for news of the governing politics that I have described in this book. *Journal* reporters usually go

right to the bottom line: Who won and who lost and how much? Three of its reporters, Jeffrey H. Birnbaum, David Wessel and Jackie Calmes, undoubtedly contributed to the 1990 rank-and-file revolt in Congress by describing the implications of the bipartisan budget agreement with such inescapable clarity. *Wall Street Journal,* October 2 and 3, 1990.

27. Reporters Donald L. Bartlett and James B. Steele found that a provision limiting personal exemptions for the well-to-do, which was billed as raising $10.8 billion from the wealthy, would actually yield no more than $2 billion or $3 billion—and that money would come from upper-middle-income families, not the rich. The same measure was proffered by congressional tax writers as proof of their even-handedness back in 1986 when it was first enacted. See *Philadelphia Inquirer,* November 4, 1990.

28. The Lipsey-Kravis study also challenged the conventional argument that the U.S. saving and investment rate lags far below its competitors' and that this explains disappointing economic growth. The different savings rates, they concluded, are really in large part differences in economic definitions of what counts as capital formation and in the cultural preferences of different nations. Robert E. Lipsey and Irving B. Kravis, *Saving and Economic Growth: Is the United States Really Falling Behind?* The Conference Board, 1987.

FOUR: The Grand Bazaar

1. Robert B. Reich's regulatory community included 12,000 lawyers in law firms representing business before courts and agencies, 9,000 lobbyists in firms specializing in lobbying, 42,000 trade association lobbyists and employees, 9,300 public-relations and public-affairs specialists, 1,200 trade journalists, 3,500 consultants advising government agencies and 15,500 lawyers and lobbyists from large corporations and federal agencies. Reich, "Regulation by Confrontation or Negotiation," *Harvard Business Review,* May–June 1981, cited by Bryner in *Bureaucratic Discretion.*

2. I can testify from personal experience on the enormous difficulty of covering regulatory politics in a manner that matches the demands of a daily newspaper. As assistant managing editor for national news at *The Washington Post,* I made several attempts to do so and all failed. In 1981, under my supervision, the *Post* initiated the "Federal Page," devoted each day to large and small stories from the regulatory government. For a year or so, the expanded coverage of regulation seemed engaging and occasionally significant, but in time the effort lost its energy and focus.

To cover the full range of complex regulatory battles with any depth would require a substantial number of reasonably sophisticated reporters and lots of patience—an investment of resources that very few news organizations are able or willing to make. As a result, the coverage of regulatory issues is almost totally dependent on the sporadic alarums sounded by interested parties. A news story may be generated, for instance, by an environmental organization that exposes malign behavior in an agency's decisions. But otherwise reporters keep their distance from the process and are usually quite ignorant of who is winning or losing.

3. The growth of regulatory laws was cited by Bryner, *Bureaucratic Discretion*.

4. The unifying effect of modern regulation on business political action is described by Carl J. Mayer in "Personalizing the Impersonal: Corporations and the Bill of Rights," *Hastings Law Journal,* March 1990.

5. Theodore J. Lowi is the most penetrating critic of the governing system he calls "interest-group liberalism." See *The End of Liberalism: The Second Republic of the United States,* W. W. Norton, 1979.

6. The environmentalists' record of winning 68 percent of those challenges to EPA that were decided by judges was between 1970 and 1980, cited in Bryner, *Bureaucratic Discretion.*

7. The "grand bazaar" metaphor I am using in this chapter is borrowed from an essay I wrote on the same subject fifteen years ago on the eve of Jimmy Carter's inauguration. This ought to establish at least that my own analysis of lawless government did not result from the scandals in the Reagan years. See *Washington Post,* January 20, 1977.

8. The Nixon-Ford-Iacocca dialogue lasted only thirty-five minutes on the morning of April 27, 1971. The ill-focused quality of their conversation is a jarring contrast with the conventional claim that regulatory matters of health and safety should be decided with scientific precision. The tangled history of airbag regulation was recounted by Joan Claybrook, president of Public Citizen and highway-safety administrator under Jimmy Carter, in a speech, "Influencing Agency Decision-Making," August 1, 1983.

9. The delayed enforcement of the ban on red dyes was reported by Bryner, *Bureaucratic Discretion.*

10. Nuclear accidents and fines were analyzed by Ken Bossong, leader of Critical Mass, Ralph Nader's watchdog organization on nuclear power.

11. The fraud cases involving defense manufacturers covered seven years before 1990, *New York Times,* November 12, 1990.

12. On EPA's lax enforcement, see Michael Reagan, *Regulation: The Politics of Policy,* Little, Brown, 1987, and the testimony of John C. Martin, EPA inspector general, before Senator John Glenn of Ohio in "Serious Management Problems in the U.S. Government," Senate Government Affairs Committee, September 28, 1989.

13. Frederick Malek's manual on how to politicize the civil service was revealed during the Watergate investigations into the Nixon administration. The text was published in *Federal Times,* December 18, 1974. Malek himself became campaign manager for George Bush's 1992 re-election campaign.

14. Data on federal regulatory personnel are from Michael Reagan, *Regulation: The Politics of Policy.* Details on how the Reagan administration cut back enforcement are from David Vogel, *Fluctuating Fortunes.*

15. Gregg Easterbrook, "Radio Free Watkins and the Crisis at Energy," *Washington Post Magazine,* February 18, 1990.

16. Senator Pryor was quoted by Kirk Victor, "Farming It Out," *National Journal,* December 16, 1989.

17. Elite leaders, led by Lloyd Cutler and former Federal Reserve Chairman Paul Volcker, began a campaign in the late 1980s to reverse the decline of government management. The National Commission on the Public Service, chaired by Volcker, warned of a "quiet crisis" in the senior ranks of the civil service. The campaign produced some progress on salaries for senior executives, but it also collided with the antigovernment attitudes that conservative business interests had spent two decades encouraging. It seemed out of character for a think tank like the American Enterprise Institute to begin worrying about the quality of government employees, when AEI had devoted so much scholarship over the years to demeaning their efforts.

18. *The New York Times's* dramatic and repetitious coverage of this scandal actually drew some reproach from other news organizations, which seemed to consider it untoward for a major newspaper to "crusade" on public matters. In an earlier time, repetition and dramatic emphasis were the standard techniques that newspapers used to force political attention to neglected issues. See *Washington Post,* January 8, 1989.

19. Exhaustive congressional hearings as well as press investigations have focused on pollution by federal agencies, particularly the Energy and Defense departments. These few examples are from among scores cited in the following sources: "Review of Hazardous Waste Disposal Practices at Federal Facilities," August 15, 1983, and "Hazardous Waste Problems at Department of Defense Facilities," November 5, 1987, House Government Operations Committee; "Environmental Compliance by Federal Agencies," April 28, 1987, and "Cleanup at Federal Facilities," March 3, 1988, House Commerce Committee. See also: Howard Kohn, "America's Worst Polluter," *Rolling Stone,* May 3, 1990.

20. The issues surrounding EPA's ability to enforce the law against other federal departments were explored in "Environmental Compliance by Federal Agencies," House Commerce Committee, April 28, 1987.

21. Data on OSHA prosecutions is from Raymond Maria, Labor Department inspector general, in "Serious Management Problems in the U.S. Government," Senate Government Affairs Committee, September 28, 1989. The National Safe Workplace Institute in Chicago has published a series of shocking reports on OSHA's weak enforcement, including "Unintended Consequences: The Failure of OSHA's Megafine Strategy," June 25, 1989.

22. Construction industry data are from "Construction: The Most Hazardous Industry in the Nation," Laborers' National Health and Safety Fund, 1990.

23. EPA also responded to the Lordstown workers' complaints and fined General Motors $1.5 million for toxic air pollution from the plant. Union and company officials again dismissed the action, claiming that GM had already complied with the law. *Youngstown Vindicator,* March 7, 1991.

FIVE: Hollow Laws

1. Mary Johnson's account of the Americans with Disabilities Act, *Nation,* October 23, 1989.

2. The academic studies on the failure of modern regulation, some of which have

been cited here, generally focus on the managerial questions, not the larger democratic principles enunciated by Theodore Lowi. Many critical scholars start from a conservative probusiness position that assumes these laws were ill advised in the first place and attempted to deliver impossible goals that would not truly benefit the society. Others tend to focus on the techniques by which the laws are frustrated and propose various managerial reforms, but without examining the larger framework of power.

3. The EPA data on high-risk industrial facilities were released by Representative Henry Waxman, chairman of the House subcommittee on health and the environment, January 12, 1990. EPA placed a cautionary disclaimer on the data, which, it said, were calculated for purposes of relative comparisons and rankings of pollution sources but could not be relied upon as a plant-by-plant measure of health risks. Waxman acknowledged that the ratings were based on simplified assumptions but should nevertheless "raise a red warning flag in communities where these facilities are locating—and spur prompt action to investigate the plants further."

4. Senator Moynihan sarcastically announced his own more modest goal for the year 2000—that by then the nation would at least understand that the political system is not serious about improving education. See his speech, "Goals for the Year 2000," March 12, 1990.

5. The surveys of public opinion on environmental trade-offs were reported in *The Wall Street Journal*, April 20, 1990, and *The New York Times*, April 17, 1990.

6. Robert W. Crandell, "The Political Economy of Clean Air: Practical Constraints on White House Review," in V. Kerry Smith, editor, *Environmental Policy Under Reagan's Executive Order*, University of North Carolina Press, 1984. Some environmentalists predict that the modest progress on clean air will be reversed during the 1990s as the number of vehicles continues to multiply without offsetting improvements in emission controls.

7. The leisurely development of RCRA regulations in the Carter administration was described by Marc K. Landy, Marc J. Roberts and Stephen R. Thomas, *The Environmental Protection Agency: Asking the Wrong Questions*, Oxford University Press, 1990. The frustrations that led to development of the "hammer" provisions in the 1984 legislation are recounted by Richard C. Fortuna and David J. Lennett, *Hazardous Waste Regulation: The New Era*, McGraw-Hill, 1987.

8. The corporate intention to abandon deep-well injection in favor of higher treatment was reported in *Pollution Prevention News*, published by EPA, August 1990.

9. The intense discussions between EPA and industry lobbyists conducted between the proposed rule and the final rule are partially revealed in the administrative record—meeting notes that agency officials are required to maintain on their contacts with regulated industries. This record does not disclose, however, any of the informal political conversations at the White House or EPA that may have accompanied the decision making.

SIX: The Fixers

1. Many details on the Bush task force are from my article, "When Big Business Needs a Favor, George Bush Gets the Call," *Rolling Stone,* April 12, 1984.

2. Invoking global competition as an argument against sterner environmental regulation is particularly specious because the main industrial competitors in Europe and Japan have much better performance in this area. The leading foreign producers generate 50 percent to 80 percent less industrial waste than American companies—efficiency that gives them a significant cost advantage in their production. See Warren Brookes, *Washington Times,* January 9, 1990. Vice-President Quayle's intervention was disclosed in *The Washington Post,* December 20, 1990.

3. When regulators, members of Congress and public-interest advocates became increasingly alarmed at Quayle's tampering in behalf of business, OMB Watch and Public Citizen's Congress Watch issued a joint report, "All the Vice President's Men: How the Quayle Council on Competitiveness Secretly Undermines Health, Safety and Environmental Programs," September 1991.

4. In 1986, Congress threatened to rein in OMB's powers by cutting off funding for the Office of Information and Regulatory Affairs, but settled for an informal letter of agreement by which OMB promised to make public after the fact its communications with agencies and private interests. In practice, the reporting requirement has produced a grossly inadequate record of what transpired. The studies on OMB's impact on regulation in the Reagan and Bush terms were reported in the OMB Watch newsletter, *OMB Watcher,* September 30, 1990, and in testimony by Gary D. Bass before the Senate Governmental Affairs Committee, February 21, 1990.

5. Douglas Costle is quoted in Landy, Roberts and Thomas, *The Environmental Protection Agency: Asking the Wrong Questions.*

6. The analysis of desk officers at OMB's Office of Information and Regulatory Affairs was reported in "Playing the Numbers: OMB and Paperwork Reduction," OMB Watch, October 1989.

7. The anonymous policy analyst is quoted in Landy, Roberts and Thomas, *The Environmental Protection Agency: Asking the Wrong Questions.*

8. The examples of inconsistency in Regulatory Impact Analyses are from W. Norton Grubb, Dale Whittington and Michael Humphries, "The Ambiguities of Benefit-Cost Analysis: An Evaluation of Regulatory Impact Analysis under Executive Order 12291," in *Environmental Policy Under Reagan's Executive Order,* V. Kerry Smith, editor.

9. The examples of OMB intervention are from *OMB Watcher,* the newsletter of OMB Watch, and congressional testimony from Gary D. Bass, executive director of OMB Watch.

10. Patricia M. Wald, "The Sizzling Sleeper: The Use of Legislative History in Construing Statutes in the 1988–89 Term of the U.S. Supreme Court," *American University Law Review,* Winter 1990.

11. Robert Bork's complaint was in a review of Jeremy Rabkin's book *Judicial*

Compulsions: How Public Law Distorts Public Policy, which makes similar arguments, *Wall Street Journal,* October 13, 1989.

12. Judge Laurence H. Silberman, *"Chevron*—The Intersection of Law and Policy," *George Washington Law Review,* 1990.

13. For a parallel argument about democracy and the confusion over government authority, see James A. Morone, *The Democratic Wish: Popular Participation and the Limits of American Government,* Basic Books, 1990.

14. Data on what the poor receive in federal assistance are from "Receipt of Selected Non-Cash Benefits: 1987," Bureau of the Census. Among 11.9 million designated as poor, 7.6 million received no cash stipends from welfare or Social Security. And 4.6 million received neither cash nor noncash benefits. The nonrecipients are typically screened out by the complex eligibility requirements of different programs, but the Reagan administration also conducted a visible campaign to drive poor people out of programs by challenging their applications and tightening the rules. The lives of the poor were one of the few areas of government activity that Reagan conservatives did not try to deregulate.

15. For further discussion of preventative protection for the environment, see Bruce Piasecki and Peter Asmus, *In Search of Environmental Excellence: Moving Beyond Blame,* Touchstone, 1990, and Barry Commoner, *Making Peace with the Planet,* Pantheon, 1990. How the tax code favors exploitation of virgin materials is described in "Facing America's Trash: What Next for Municipal Solid Waste?" Office of Technology Assessment, Congress, 1989.

16. Examples of state initiatives are from Margaret E. Kriz, "Ahead of the Feds," *National Journal,* December 9, 1989, and "Building an Environmentally Sustainable Economy," Center for Policy Alternatives, December 15, 1990.

SEVEN: The Politics of "Rude and Crude"

1. The Citizen's Clearinghouse estimate of seven thousand grassroots environmental groups seems excessive on its face, since it would mean an average of 140 such organizations in each of the fifty states. On the other hand, some states where environmental degradation has become a principal public issue have several hundred of these community organizations. Because the groups come and go or merge with others, it is difficult to find a precise answer to the question of their number.

2. The examples of successful protest tactics are taken from *Everyone's Backyard,* December 1990, monthly newsletter of the Citizen's Clearinghouse for Hazardous Wastes. Literally hundreds, perhaps thousands of such encounters occur every year and provoke local controversy but seldom rise to the level of national news events.

3. The Union Carbide memo was written by C. E. Greenert, director of corporate contributions, public issues and administration, November 24, 1989. A letter of apology from Ronald S. Wishart, Union Carbide's vice-president for public affairs, said: "I'm sorry that Mr. Greenert's (purloined) internal memorandum implies that the founder of CCHW has communist leanings, which was his short-

hand for a concern about the political directions some environmental activism seems to be taking.''

4. EPA research, reported in the *Archives of Environmental Health,* March 1989, found excessive deaths from various kinds of cancers in Superfund counties in different regions of the country compared with counties that had no major hazardous-waste dumps. The patterns of increased disease, the EPA researchers noted, might be attributable to other causes, such as direct pollution from local industries, not exactly a comforting explanation for local citizens. A summary of the findings was reported in *Rachel's Hazardous Waste News,* May 2, 1989.

5. William Ruckelshaus was named CEO of Browning-Ferris Industries in 1988 to improve the company's environmental image, but BFI's hazardous-waste division, a small part of its overall operations, continued to face expensive controversies. New York State rejected its application for a new hazardous-waste site in Niagara Falls. In Ohio, BFI paid $3.5 million in fines and civil damages for past pollution at a dump outside Cincinnati. In Louisiana, it paid $1.5 million to settle allegations of violating hazardous-waste rules. *Wall Street Journal,* April 6, 1990.

6. The survey on political sophistication was cited by Herbert J. Gans, *Middle American Individualism: The Future of Liberal Democracy,* The Free Press, 1988. For an insightful essay on the strengths and weaknesses of citizen activism, see Karen Paget, ''Citizen Organizing: Many Movements, No Majority,'' *The American Prospect,* Summer 1990.

7. *The Washington Post*'s 1983 survey on environmental issues was cited by Barry Sussman, *What Americans Really Think.* Next to environmentalists, people most trusted local governments (55 percent favorable; 30 percent unfavorable), then the EPA (46 percent to 36 percent). President Reagan scored almost as poorly as business leaders (36 percent favorable; 45 percent unfavorable).

8. The StarKist boycott and others were described in *The Wall Street Journal,* ''Facing a Boycott, Many Companies Bend,'' November 8, 1990.

9. Gillette, Dow Chemical, Sara Lee, and Sears Roebuck are among the companies that modified products in order to comply with California's ''Prop 65'' requirement of warning labels. In the political debates, of course, this is the sort of remedial action that corporations usually insist is impossible. See ''California Spurs Reformulated Products,'' *Wall Street Journal,* November 1, 1990.

10. The Los Angeles survey was cited by Ken Hoover, ''On the Take,'' *Golden State Report,* March 1990.

11. Tax-cutting measures were rejected in Massachusetts, Colorado, Nebraska and Utah, among other places, in 1990. California entertainment celebrities campaigned for ''Big Green,'' the omnibus environmental initiative, but the chemical and agriculture industries countered with a trustworthy celebrity of their own, former Surgeon General C. Everett Koop, who advised voters that the proposed bans on carcinogenic chemicals would not benefit the health of children. For a survey of initiatives, see *The Wall Street Journal,* November 8, 1990.

12. Mervin Field's analysis of referendum voters was in ''Falling Turnout—A Nonvoting Majority,'' *Public Affairs Report,* Institute of Governmental Studies, University of California at Berkeley, March 1990.

13. The plastics industry's alarm and Larry Thomas's letter were reported in *Everyone's Backyard,* Citizen's Clearinghouse for Hazardous Wastes, March 1990.

14. Robert O. Aders's remarks to Produce Marketing Association are from an unpublished text, October 17, 1989.

15. I am indebted to the *National Journal* for its excellent coverage of regulatory politics and, in particular, its continuing reports on the power struggles between the states and the federal government and the cross-pressures generated by business interests and citizen reform groups. See, for instance, W. John Moore, "Stopping the States," July 21, 1990; Margaret E. Kriz, "Ahead of the Feds," December 9, 1989; and Julie Kosterlitz, "The Food Lobby's Menu," September 29, 1990.

16. The industry petition to the Federal Trade Commission was reported in *The New York Times,* February 15, 1991.

17. The Advocacy Institute and Congress Watch declaration was cited by W. John Moore, "Stopping the States," *National Journal.*

18. Enactment of federal preemptions for business regulation and health and safety laws increased from 65 in the 1970s to 72 in the 1980s. The data from the Advisory Commission on Intergovernmental Relations were reported by W. John Moore in "Stopping the States," *National Journal.* The agency counted a total of 350 federal preemptions, 127 for business regulation and 134 for health and safety regulations. In two other areas, civil rights and financial regulation, the number of new preemptions declined during the decade.

EIGHT: Political Orphans

1. The leaflet was quoted by Jon Cohen, "Down and Dirty," *City Paper,* May 19, 1989.

2. AEI's complete catalog of books, Fall 1989, lists the minimum-wage literature it has sponsored.

3. Richard Thompson was quoted in *City Paper,* May 19, 1989.

4. Details on the NLRB are from David Vogel, *Fluctuating Fortunes: The Political Power of Business in America,* Basic Books, 1989.

5. For a compelling account of how law has helped to collapse the labor movement, see Thomas Geoghegan, *Which Side Are You On? Trying to Be for Labor When It's Flat on Its Back,* Farrar Straus Giroux, 1991.

6. Michael Merrill, "Why There Will Be a Labor Party by the Year 2000," *Social Policy,* Spring 1990. See also my article, "Down but Not Out: Labor Struggles to Find Its Voice," *Rolling Stone,* October 17, 1991.

7. The D.C. minimum wage, like that of many states, was higher than the level set by federal law and would have been pushed upward if Congress had enacted a sufficiently large increase. The D.C. wage board subsequently adopted a $7.25 minimum for clerical workers (though not janitors), but the city council reduced this to $5.25 under pressure from local businesses.

8. The Progressive Policy Institute's report was entitled "Work and Poverty: A Progressive View of the Minimum Wage and the Earned Income Tax Credit," June 1989.

9. The survival "cheating" on federal benefits by the working poor is described by Christopher Jencks and Kathryn Edin in "The Real Welfare Problem," *American Prospect,* Spring 1990.

10. The late Joseph A. Pechman of the Brookings Institution, leading expert on tax equity, described the perverse effect of improving welfare benefits when the income-tax structure was no longer progressive: "The tax system has been getting less progressive in the last two decades, while the ratio of transfers to income has been increasing. In other words, the recent increases in transfer payments in the United States have been financed by the low and middle-income groups, while the rich have been getting tax cuts." Pechman, "The Future of the Income Tax," *Brookings,* December 22, 1989.

11. The charity event was a fund-raising gala for the Jewish Community Center of metropolitan Washington, and the Charles E. Smith Company changed its labor policies after several rabbis in the Washington area expressed their support for the demands made by "Justice for Janitors." *Jewish Week,* the community newspaper, also published a sympathetic account of why the janitors had staged their demonstration at the community center's banquet.

NINE: Class Conflict

1. For an enthralling history of Martin Luther King, Jr., and the politics of the civil rights movement, see Taylor Branch, *Parting the Waters,* Simon & Schuster, 1988.

2. This insight was elaborated by J. Hunter O'Dell in his essay, "Notes on the Movement, Then, Now and Tomorrow," *Southern Exposure,* Spring 1981.

3. Michael Waldman is director of Public Citizen's Congress Watch. See his book, *Who Robbed America? A Citizen's Guide to the Savings & Loan Scandal,* Random House, 1990.

4. The contours of "political avoidance" are described by Herbert J. Gans, *Middle American Individualism,* The Free Press, 1988.

5. *Outside* magazine, September 1990. The magazine's lowest regard— "Milquetoast"—was for the National Wildlife Federation and the Nature Conservancy.

6. Lois Gibbs's remark on poor people is from Ana Radelat, "Avenging Angel," *Public Citizen,* September 1990.

7. The community leaders were invited to subsequent conferences at the behest of Tufts University, a cosponsor, according to a letter from Lois Gibbs to Nancy Newman, league president, October 21, 1986.

8. Grassroots activists dubbed the private meeting between Reilly, Waste Management's Dean Buntrock and Jay Hair, president of the Wildlife Federation, "Reillygate." Details are from the EPA investigative record into charges that Reilly's meeting was in violation of agency rules. The administrator was cleared and the controversy never achieved visibility in the national press but was covered aggressively by some local newspapers where citizen groups are aroused on toxic-waste issues. See the *Winston-Salem Journal,* April 21, 1989.

9. Samuel P. Huntington was among the academics who originally expressed

alarm at the upsurge of citizen politics, fearing that reformers were immobilizing government. In the 1970s, he described these challenges as "an excess of democracy" but moderated his views subsequently when it became clear that neither government nor business interests were in danger of losing their power. Samuel P. Huntington, *American Politics: The Promise of Disharmony*, Harvard University Press, 1981.

10. My account of class conflicts in the environmental movement has been enriched by Eric Mann, "Environmentalism in the Corporate Climate," and Robert Gottlieb, "Earth Day Revisited," both in *Tikkun*, March 1990. Penny Newman was quoted in Mann's essay.

11. Details on corporate gifts to environmental groups are from *Everyone's Backyard*, October 1990.

12. The study of philanthropists was based mainly on individuals, and the portrait is less apt for some of the larger, long-established foundations such as Ford or Carnegie or Mellon that are now distant from the family wealth that created them. On the other hand, the new generation of corporate foundations provides grants that are usually intimately connected to the political self-interest of the companies that provided the money. See Teresa Odendahl, *Charity Begins at Home: Generosity and Self-Interest Among the Philanthropic Elite*, Basic Books, 1990.

TEN: Democratic Promise

1. Father Leo J. Penta, "Organizing and Public Philosophy: Fifty Years of the Industrial Areas Foundation," *IAF Reflects*, August 1990.

2. The story of Alinsky's career and political philosophy is told by Sanford D. Horwitt, *Let Them Call Me Rebel: Saul Alinsky, His Life and Legacy*, Alfred A. Knopf, 1989.

3. Edward Chambers was quoted by Geoffrey Rips, "A Democratic Conversation," *Texas Observer*, November 22, 1990. The *Observer* issue included two other valuable articles on IAF: Mary Beth Rogers, "Gospel Values and Secular Politics," excerpted from her book, *Cold Anger: A Story of Faith and Power Politics*, University of North Texas Press, and Linda Rocawich, "Interview: Ernesto Cortes Jr."

4. Cortes's remark about the "conjugal" nature of power and love is from his speech to the Farm Crisis Workers Conference, *Texas Observer*, July 11, 1986.

5. The IAF Texas network conducts a running series of seminars for its organizers and senior community leaders on a vast range of subjects. As the author of a book about the Federal Reserve and the money and credit system, I was invited to teach at one of these sessions and was deeply impressed by their seriousness.

6. Andres Sarabia's remark on anger was in the *San Antonio Light*, November 26, 1990.

7. Cortes's remark on "bullying" is from Linda Rocawich, "Interview: Ernesto Cortes Jr.," *Texas Observer*.

8. Alinsky's acknowledgment is from Sanford D. Horwitt, *Let Them Call Me Rebel: Saul Alinsky, His Life and Legacy*.

ELEVEN: Who Owns the Democrats?

1. Thomas Jefferson's letter to President Washington is a wonderfully evocative political document, even if it does not quite say what modern Democrats suppose. Jefferson described the political divisions—North and South, agrarian and rural—developing around Washington. He lamented that the Federalist financial interests, led by his rival Alexander Hamilton, were steadily corrupting the Congress. Once they succeeded in seizing control, Jefferson warned, they would install a monarchial form of government centered in the presidency and the people's right to govern themselves would be effectively extinguished. His letter is found in *The Papers of Thomas Jefferson,* Volume 23, Charles T. Cullen, editor, Princeton University Press, 1990.

2. Michael McCurry, a former aide to Senator Daniel Patrick Moynihan and Arizona Governor Bruce Babbitt during his brief campaign for president, left his DNC post in late 1990 to work in a political public-relations firm. His candid remarks on the party's condition were made to me, however, while he was still working for the DNC.

3. The National Association of Manufacturers, like other business groups, lobbied to defeat the toxics-labeling legislation, but Eizenstat says he merely addressed its "significant flaws." Among other things, he urged Congress to give certain employers immunity from damage suits and to keep the identity of notified workers confidential so they could not be readily recruited for lawsuits. *Daily Labor Report,* Bureau of National Affairs, February 16, 1988.

4. When PSI Holdings, Inc., added Eizenstat to its board, it also added Kenneth M. Duberstein, a Republican lobbyist who had served as chief of staff in Ronald Reagan's White House. *Indianapolis Business Journal,* January 29, 1990.

5. Tommy Boggs was quoted in the *National Journal,* January 13, 1990.

6. Williams and Jensen's lobbying for Pittston was reported in *Legal Times,* October 16, 1989. Its role in financing a study by the Employee Benefit Research Institute was reported in *Pensions & Investment Age,* April 2, 1990. Williams's jocular remark on arguing the "merits" was quoted in *Legal Times,* May 23, 1988.

7. Details on O'Connor and Hannan's work for ARENA and the Minneapolis City Council's reaction are from the *Bulletin of Municipal Foreign Policy,* Winter 1989–1990.

8. Among other tax-issue clients, Akin, Gump represented the Distilled Spirits Council of the United States and the Mutual Fairness Taxation Association, formed by mutual insurance companies. The lobbying of the NEC by his firm's clients was described in *Legal Times,* November 7, 1988.

9. Akin, Gump's Fujitsu account was reported in the *Financial Times,* February 19, 1990. The lobbying on trade by prominent Democrats was described by John B. Judis, "K Street's Rise to Power of Special Interest to U.S.," *In These Times,* November 1, 1989. Judis wrote: "The denizens of K Street constitute a new mandarin class in America. Unlike the Chinese bureaucrats of old, however, the lawyer-lobbyist-pollsters of K Street are beholden not to a higher wisdom but to the highest bidder."

10. Frank Lorenzo's assembling of influential Democrats to represent him was described in *Legal Times*, May 16, 1988, and the *American Lawyer*, July 1988. The $12.7 million in legal bills for the bankrupt airline was described in *The Wall Street Journal*, May 21, 1990.

11. The *Legal Times* estimate of law firms with PACs was reported in the *National Journal*, December 16, 1989. The Common Cause estimate is from *The New York Times*, December 29, 1989. Charles Babcock provided a systematic analysis of campaign money in *The Washington Post*, September 30, 1991.

12. Kirk O'Donnell was quoted in *Legal Times*, June 26, 1989.

13. The DLC's corporate sponsors were described in *The Washington Post*, March 29, 1990. See also Robert Kuttner, "What's the Beef?" *The New Republic*, April 2, 1990.

TWELVE: Rancid Populism

1. Karen Olshan and Paula Drillman were quoted by Bernice Kanner of *New York* magazine in "Mind Games," *Best of Business Quarterly*, Winter 1990.

2. Lee Atwater was quoted in *The New York Times*, March 19, 1990, and Douglas Bailey in *The Washington Post*, April 20, 1990.

3. Douglas Bailey spoke at a seminar on the Republican presidential coalition sponsored by the Progressive Policy Institute, February 26, 1990.

4. The data on advertising costs and proliferation are from *The Wall Street Journal*, March 22, 1991.

5. The *New York Times*/CBS poll was cited by William A. Galston, "Rebuilding a Presidential Majority," unpublished paper, March 1989.

6. Lee Atwater's description of the "populist swing vote" is from my interview, *Rolling Stone*, January 12, 1989. "Power is evil" is from Marjorie Williams, "The New Lee Atwater Lies Low," *Washington Post Magazine*, November 19, 1989.

7. If readers wish to glimpse the outlines of a genuine democratic experience in American history, they will find it in the powerful narrative of the original Populist movement, recounted by Lawrence Goodwyn, *The Populist Movement: A Short History of the Agrarian Revolt in America*, Oxford University Press, 1978.

8. Representative Newt Gingrich was quoted in *The Washington Post*, February 26, 1989, and *The Wall Street Journal*, May 20, 1988.

9. An example of social conservatives trying to develop a broader perspective that would let them address economic issues is an essay published by an affiliate of the Free Congress Foundation. See William S. Lind and William H. Marshner, *Cultural Conservatism: Toward a New National Agenda*, Institute for Cultural Conservatism, 1987.

10. Lee Atwater's account of his illness and self-discovery was entitled "Lee Atwater's Last Campaign," *Life*, February 1991.

11. David Stockman's remark is from my book, *The Education of David Stockman and Other Americans*.

12. For an exposition of Thomas Ferguson's theory, see "Party Realignment and American Industrial Structure: The Investment Theory of Political Parties in His-

torical Perspective," *Research in Political Economy,* Volume 6, JAI Press, 1983.
13. For a more precise version of Thomas Ferguson's analysis of the Republican party, see his article, "Who Bought Bush, and Why," *International Economy,* January 1989. His analysis of the major investors dominating the Democratic party—investment banking, major real-estate developers, high-tech manufacturers and others—was reported in "Private Money and Public Policy," *International Economy,* September 1988.

THIRTEEN: Angle of Vision
1. Jean G. Padioleau spent some months in the *Post* newsroom as part of a comparative organizational study in which he concluded that *The Washington Post,* notwithstanding its corporate hierarchy, had elements of freedom and innovation that were stronger than those at *Le Monde,* a newspaper ostensibly controlled by its own staff members. The insights quoted here are from an unpublished essay Padioleau prepared on the *Post's* newsroom management. See also Jean G. Padioleau, *Le Monde et le Washington Post,* Presses Universitaires de France, 1985.
2. *The Washington Post's* monopoly was complicated slightly by the founding of the *Washington Times,* a staunchly conservative daily financed by the Unification Church. The *Times* produces a lively contrast to the *Post,* but is utterly unthreatening to it, as an alternative for either readers or advertisers. Despite many millions invested by its right-wing sponsors, the *Washington Times* remains small and unprofitable.
3. The studies of *Nightline* and *MacNeil/Lehrer* were reported in FAIR's newsletter, *Extra!,* Winter 1990.
4. David Ignatius described think tanks in "Fishing for a Few Good Ideas," *Washington Post,* March 11, 1990.
5. Burt Solomon's reflections were in "Bush Cultivates the Press Corps . . . Hoping for a Harvest of Goodwill," *National Journal,* May 5, 1990.
6. The social intimacies between the media and government are so commonplace that dozens of other examples could be cited. The participants are utterly oblivious to the implications and indeed offended by the suggestion that their closeness to power has compromised their rugged independence. Some of these details have been drawn from the *National Journal,* May 5, 1990; *Washington Post,* January 20, 1989; and *The Wall Street Journal,* December 28, 1989.
7. Barry Sussman discusses public criticism of the media in *What Americans Really Think: And Why Our Politicians Pay No Attention,* Pantheon, 1988.
8. For an excellent academic analysis of how the media fail democracy, see Robert M. Entman, *Democracy Without Citizens: Media and the Decay of American Politics,* Oxford University Press, 1989.
9. The Times Mirror Company, publisher of the *Los Angeles Times, Newsday* and other high-quality newspapers, has at least begun to explore this terrain—the distance between orthodox news and the public—by commissioning a series of polls that measure the interest levels and inattention of readers to the stories that editors and reporters regard as important. Thus far, however, the focus of these

studies has been on the readers' responses, not on the production values of the news media.

FOURTEEN: The Lost Generation

1. Among the critics, one of the most insightful pessimists is Neil Postman, a professor of communications at New York University and author of many books. See, for instance, *Conscientious Objections,* Alfred A. Knopf, 1988.

2. Jacques Cousteau was quoted by columnist Jim Hoagland as Hoagland pondered the political implications of his own young daughter and her school friends' taking responsibility for protecting the global environment. See *Washington Post,* July 10, 1990.

3. The voting data are based on surveys by the U.S. Census Bureau in which people are asked whether they voted in the last election. This approach usually inflates the numbers slightly, since some people are always reluctant to admit they did not vote. In the census data, voting participation fell from 50 percent to 36 percent among eighteen- to twenty-four-year-olds, from 1972 to 1988. It fell from 63 percent to 54 percent among those who are twenty-five to forty-four years old during the same period. Voting levels were virtually unchanged among those forty-five to sixty-four years old (68 percent in 1988) and actually increased modestly among those who are sixty-five and older (69 percent in 1988, up from 64 percent in 1972). See "The Age of Indifference: A Study of Young Americans and How They View the News," Times Mirror Center for The People & The Press, June 28, 1990.

4. The Times Mirror Center has taken month-by-month surveys of what in the news captures the most interest of the audience. See especially "The Age of Indifference," among its other periodic reports.

5. Jim Bellows was quoted in *The Washington Post,* January 9, 1989.

6. The *Rolling Stone* survey, conducted by Peter Hart, covered a broad group of people, ranging in age from eighteen to forty-four, and demonstrated that, notwithstanding all the generalizations about younger people, they are as diverse in their attitudes as any other generation of Americans. My discussion in this chapter of political behavior and perspectives has relied substantially on the findings. See my article, "The *Rolling Stone* Survey," *Rolling Stone,* April 7, 1988.

7. The scientific dispute over Alar centered on samplings that tested how much residue was found on apples in the marketplace and whether that constituted a risk to humans. The NRDC research argued that government standards were too lax because they did not take into account the smaller body weight of young children and the large amount of fruit that they consume.

8. The details on EPA's advisory panel on pesticides are from *The Washington Post,* May 26, 1989.

9. The apple growers subsequently sued the NRDC for damages, but Alar remained off the market and the NRDC had performed a public service by exposing EPA's lack of enforcement. The product was first linked to cancer in 1973 and nothing had happened for more than fifteen years, according to Adrian de Wind, NRDC chairman. The NRDC report found that Alar in apple products created

cancer risks at least 240 times greater than EPA said were safe. See *New York Times,* July 9, 1991, and a letter from de Wind, *New York Times,* July 30, 1991.

10. The *Publishers Weekly* list was printed in *The Wall Street Journal,* January 16, 1990.

11. James Dobson's "profamily" politics and organization were described in *The Wall Street Journal,* October 17, 1988.

12. I am indebted to Frank Mankiewicz for this insight about the deeper content of Michael Moore's film, which, Mankiewicz said, "captures the strange new terms in which the victims are laughing at themselves. Everyone is standing at the center of the debate, watching the show. There's nobody saying: those bastards."

13. George Gilder describes his vision of the coming revolution in *Life After Television: The Coming Transformation of Media and American Life,* Whittle Direct Books, 1990.

14. See Ben H. Bagdikian, *The Media Monopoly,* Beacon Press, 1983.

15. Michael Kinsley wrote: "Media companies in the U.S. enjoy the First Amendment rights of all American citizens. But like other major corporations they are 'artificial persons,' legal fictions; and if they begin to abuse their editorial prerogatives through systematic in-house cross-promotions, government may restrict them to a more limited set of First Amendment privileges." See *New Republic,* May 7, 1990. The NBC stories promoting GE products were reported by FAIR in its newsletter, *Extra!,* January 1991.

16. Among his many projects, Ralph Nader has created the Audience Network Coalition in Washington in an attempt to generate support for fundamental reform of the federal communications laws.

FIFTEEN: Citizen GE

1. This account of why Benjamin Heineman, Jr., and other Washington lawyers joined General Electric relies mainly on reporting in the *American Lawyer,* September 1989, and D. M. Osborne, "The Sidley-Heineman Connection," May 1990, as well as the *National Journal,* April 7, 1990.

2. Philip Lacovara filed "Preliminary Comments of General Electric Company on the U.S. Sentencing Commission's Proposed Organizational Sanctions," September 11, 1989. The brief was cosigned by Victoria Toensing, a former deputy assistant attorney general in the Reagan administration who as a Washington lawyer was hired by GE to fight the corporate-crime sentencing guidelines. It was Toensing who lobbied the White House and persuaded the president's counsel, C. Boyden Gray, to intervene at the Justice Department. She was representing GE, Martin Marietta, ITT and other firms, according to *The Washington Post,* April 28, 1990.

3. The Sidley & Austin memorandum on Superfund litigation was circulated by Stephen Ramsey at an American Bar Association teleconference on hazardous waste, according to David T. Buente, chief of EPA's environmental enforcement section. Buente in turn distributed it to EPA lawyers with a warning memo on June 4, 1986.

4. The description of General Electric's potential Superfund liability is from

"Nuclear Power Development and Related Energy Issues: General Electric Co.,"
Proxy Issues Report, Investor Responsibility Research Center, March 30, 1990.
Ramsey was quoted in the *American Lawyer,* May 1990.

5. Details on GE's scope are drawn from the company's 1989 *Annual Report* and
the 1989 *GE Foundations Annual Report;* Stratford P. Sherman, "The Mind of
Jack Welch," *Fortune,* March 27, 1989; Russell Mitchell and Judith H. Dobrzyn-
ski, "Jack Welch Reinvents GE," *Business Week,* December 14, 1987; and Doug
Henwood, "NBC: The GE Broadcasting Co.," *Extra!,* May 1989.

6. General Electric, as bespeaks its power, declined to cooperate with my examination of its political operations. Frank P. Doyle turned down my request for
an interview. The public-affairs officer for GE's Washington office acknowledged
that there is a company named General Electric, but declined to provide additional
details.

7. Common Cause, which calculated GE's political contributions, filed a share-
holder's resolution challenging the practice, *Wall Street Journal,* January 9, 1989.
The GE honoraria were for 1985 and reported in "INFACT Brights GE to Light,"
INFACT, 1988. Robert W. Barrie's role in raising money for Democrats was
described by Thomas B. Edsall, "Bringing Good Things to GE," *Washington
Post,* April 13, 1985.

8. The corporate lobbying on product-liability legislation was described by Gary
Lee in *The Washington Post,* July 29, 1991.

9. GE's lobbying blitz to protect its venture in Hungary against what it called
"the inherent uncertainties" was described by the *National Journal,* February 10,
1990.

10. Obviously, corporate-image advertising is often intended to produce a commercial benefit as well as political protection, but the propaganda effect is the
same, regardless of intent. In the survey of nonproduct corporate advertising for
1987, General Electric was the ninth-largest spender. Dow Chemical was the
fourth-largest spender with the commercials attempting to overcome its reputation
as a polluter. See Amy J. Barnes, "Top Heavy: The 17th Annual Review of
Corporate Advertising Expenditures," *Public Relations Journal,* September 1988.

11. The Northrop episode was reported in *The Wall Street Journal,* February 20,
1990.

12. The Chevron campaign was reported by its director of research in public
affairs, Lewis C. Winters, "Does It Pay to Advertise to Hostile Audiences with
Corporate Advertising?" *Journal of Advertising Research,* June 1988.

13. Frank Doyle testified before the Senate Foreign Relations Committee subcommittee on European affairs, March 28, 1990.

14. Details on the taxation of GE and other corporations are drawn from Citizens
for Tax Justice's "Annual Survey of Corporate Taxpayers and Corporate Free-
loaders," October 1989.

15. In 1990, for instance, overseas investment by American companies grew by
16 percent while capital spending in the United States increased by a tepid 6.7
percent. See Robert B. Reich, *The Work of Nations: Preparing Ourselves for 21st
Century Capitalism,* Alfred A. Knopf, 1991.

16. Bob Barrie's lobbying on tax leasing was described by Thomas Edsall in "Bringing Good Things to GE," *Washington Post,* April 13, 1985.

17. GE's 1989 tax rate was calculated from its *Annual Report.* Details on the shortfall in corporate tax revenue are from *The Wall Street Journal,* February 8, 1990, and *The New York Times,* March 6, 1990.

18. Though the process has received little attention from the press, the real political action on universal health care is located in the high-level negotiations that have been convened as the "National Leadership Coalition for Health Care Reform." The discussions include an extraordinary list of major corporations and labor unions and a few health groups, but not the hospitals, doctors and insurance companies that are the main supporters of the status quo. See Frank Swoboda, "Devising a Cure for High Costs of Health Care," *Washington Post,* February 12, 1991.

19. Frank Doyle testified for increased Head Start funding before the Senate Labor Committee, March 1, 1990.

20. The so-called "skills shortage" was refuted by Lawrence Mishel and Ruy A. Teixeira, "The Myth of the Coming Labor Shortage: Jobs, Skills, and Incomes of America's Workforce 2000," Economic Policy Institute, July 1991.

21. John Welch was quoted on loyalty in *The Wall Street Journal,* August 4, 1988, and Frank Doyle on "ready to go" employees in *Business Week,* December 14, 1987. The loss of loyalty evidently extends fairly high up the management ladder. According to the *Journal* account, top-level managers transferred to GE's consumer electronics division, based on Welch's expressed interest in revitalizing it. They were stunned when Welch sold the entire product line a few months later.

22. Frank Doyle described GE's global premises for the company and for America before the Congressional Economic Leadership Institute with the Congressional Competitiveness Caucus, July 30, 1987.

23. The history and legal arguments surrounding corporate use of constitutional rights are recounted by Carl Mayer in their political context: Corporations had to invent new strategies for countering the more intrusive noneconomic regulation for the environment or health and safety that developed in the modern era. See Carl J. Mayer, "Personalizing the Impersonal: Corporations and the Bill of Rights," *Hastings Law Journal,* March 1990.

24. The facts on GE's legal offenses are all drawn from regular news accounts. The company's dossier is rarely, if ever, examined in full by the news media, so each new episode of corporate misbehavior is reported as if it were a shocking aberration. See these dispatches: Army battlefield computers, Associated Press, Philadelphia, February 3, 1990, and *The New York Times,* July 27, 1990; military jet engines, AP, Cincinnati, February 24, 1989; Army M-1 tanks, *Wall Street Journal,* October 13, 1989; Navy missile frigates, *Wall Street Journal,* February 10, 1988; and Air Force Minuteman, AP, March 24 and July 26, 1985.

25. For the assortment of GE offenses, see these news reports: Puerto Rican bribery, Associated Press, Trenton, February 11 and June 23, 1981; Kidder Peabody insider trading, AP, New York, June 4, 1987; GE Capital consumer discrimination, AP, Washington, October 3, 1989; GE job discrimination, AP,

Washington, June 15, 1978; and price-fixing in Canada, *Wall Street Journal,* April 14, 1977.

26. General Electric's latest case of fraud was reported in *The New York Times,* August 15, 1991.

27. General Electric's role in nuclear-bomb manufacture and attendant environmental problems are described in "INFACT Brings GE to Light," *INFACT,* 1988. GE's plan to discontinue its management of the Pinellas nuclear plant, confirmed by the company, was reported in *Everyone's Backyard,* Citizen's Clearinghouse for Hazardous Wastes, February 1991.

28. For GE pollution cases, see these news reports: Coosa River pollution, Associated Press, Birmingham, November 14, 1979; Hudson River contamination, *Christian Science Monitor,* June 12, 1990; Waterford, New York, settlement, AP, Albany, September 3, 1987; New Hampshire and Massachusetts toxic dumping, AP, Boston, August 4, 1988; and Ohio dump settlement, AP, Washington, December 20, 1989.

29. A General Electric subsidiary, RCA, was also involved in the defense-industry scandal of companies' obtaining classified Pentagon documents to enhance their bidding on contracts. However, the criminal events occurred before RCA was acquired by GE (which later sold off the company, except NBC). RCA pleaded guilty and paid a $2.5 million fine, Associated Press, Fairfield, Connecticut, February 5, 1990. For other corporate cases, see these news reports: Mobil Oil, *Washington Post,* November 22, 1990; Northrop, *Wall Street Journal,* September 20, 1990; Waste Management, *Wall Street Journal,* May 1, 1991; Eastern Airlines, *New York Times,* July 26, 1990; and Hughes Aircraft, *Wall Street Journal,* July 6, 1990.

30. Professor Amitai Etzioni's findings were reported to the U.S. Sentencing Commission. See also his book *Capital Corruption: The New Attack on American Democracy,* Transaction Books, 1988.

31. The judge's criticism of GE was reported in *The Wall Street Journal,* September 27, 1990.

32. Philip Lacovara proposed "substantial mitigation" for companies that cooperate in disclosing criminal conduct. He suggested that prosecutors regard corporate managements as "partners" and reward them with "an explicit, corresponding adjustment in any penal sanction." Even so, he added, "it is important to recognize that corporations cannot necessarily cooperate to the extent prosecutors would prefer." See "Preliminary Comments of General Electric Company," U.S. Sentencing Commission, September 11, 1989.

33. The survey of corporate managers on ethical dilemmas was conducted in the late 1980s and reported in "Corporate Ethics," the Conference Board, *Research Report No. 900,* undated.

34. In 1990, the California legislature passed a tough new law called the Corporate Criminal Liability Act, which, among other things, puts companies and their managers at risk of criminal prosecution if they fail to report internal health-and-safety dangers promptly. Another new measure, setting up five-year probation status for environmental offenders, was enacted by the California legislature but

vetoed by the governor. See Jaye Scholl, "Giving Business the Business," *Barron's,* March 25, 1991.

35. The statistics on 1988 prosecutions are from a study done for the U.S. Sentencing Commission by Mark A. Cohen, "Corporate Crime and Punishment: An Update on Sentencing Practice in the Federal Courts, 1988–90."

SIXTEEN: Crackpot Realism

1. Senator Moynihan's argument for restoring respect for international law in American foreign policy is elaborated in his book, *On the Law of Nations: A Historical and Personal Account of the Role of International Law in Foreign Policy,* Harvard University Press, 1990.

2. The costs of the Persian Gulf War were shared by allied contributions but, even so, the U.S. share offset the modest reduction in defense spending that had been in place for 1991. See Robert L. Borosage, "How Bush Kept the Guns from Turning into Butter," *Rolling Stone,* February 21, 1991.

3. George Soros, "A Great Light in the East?" *Geopolitique,* No. 26, 1989.

4. The postwar opinion survey was conducted jointly by Market Strategies, a firm that specializes in research for Republicans, and Greenberg/Lake, a Democratic firm. See "Americans Talk Issues," Survey No. 15, April 1991.

5. Details on the CIA's exaggeration of Soviet power are drawn from an interview with Senator Moynihan as well as his book, *On the Law of Nations,* and his article in *The Washington Post,* July 11, 1990.

6. The revised "threat" assessment in Europe was made jointly by the CIA, the Defense Intelligence Agency and the Joint Chiefs of Staff and reported by Patrick Tyler in *The Washington Post,* November 29, 1989.

7. A full account of the government's actions against domestic political opponents in the 1980s was produced by Jonathan Dann of the Center for Investigative Reporting in San Francisco and published in the *Los Angeles Reader,* June 10, 1988.

8. All but about 50 of Reagan's 298 national-security directives remained secret. The outlines of the secret "lawmaking" process at the National Security Council were described by Angus Mackenzie and Eve Pell of the Freedom of Information Project at the Center for Investigative Reporting, *Albuquerque Journal,* October 16, 1988.

9. Moynihan's statement is from his book, *On the Law of Nations.*

10. The foreign minister of Iraq, surveying the nations allied against his country, observed: "A lot of money, billions of dollars, was spent to create that coalition." The full facts of the Bush administration's actions are not known, of course. Representative Henry Gonzalez outlined his accusations in the *Congressional Record,* January 16, 1991. See also *The Wall Street Journal,* January 14, 1991.

11. The defense share of manufacturing is from "Bolstering Defense Industrial Competitiveness," *Report of the Under Secretary of Defense for Acquisition,* July 1988. Other estimates of defense-driven spending and investment are from Jacques S. Gansler, a former deputy assistant secretary of defense and chairman of Defense Science Board's 1990 study on technology and the defense industry.

12. For detailed accounts of the defense-budget politics, see David C. Morrison, "End of the Line," *National Journal*, June 8, 1991, and "Schizophrenic Budget," *National Journal*, February 9, 1991.

13. Secretary Cheney's declaration is from the 1989 edition of "Soviet Military Power," quoted by Jacques S. Gansler in testimony before the Senate Banking Committee, March 1, 1990.

14. Jacques S. Gansler's argument for integration of defense and commercial manufacturing was made in his testimony before the Senate Banking Committee, March 1, 1990.

SEVENTEEN: The Closet Dictator

1. Professor Gueramina Valdes-Villalva, whom I interviewed in July 1990, worked for many years to aid the exploited *maquiladora* workers and to challenge the practices of the companies. She died in a plane crash in Texas on February 13, 1991. My guides and translators in Ciudad Juarez were two Americans, Sister Maribeth Larkin, an organizer with EPISO, the IAF organization in El Paso, and Ignacio Escandon, a businessman who is active in EPISO.

2. The statistics on falling labor costs are from *Twin Plant News: The Magazine of the Maquiladora Industry*, May 1990.

3. The "slave labor" remark was quoted by Lane Kirkland, president of the AFL-CIO, speech to the American International Club of Geneva, June 24, 1991.

4. The *Arizona Republic* and reporters Jerry Kammer and Sandy Tolan of Desert West News Service won the Robert F. Kennedy journalism award for their series on the Nogales industries, published in April 1989. *The Wall Street Journal* published a harrowing account of a twelve-year-old working in a Mexican shoe factory and described child labor as general throughout the country—exploiting five to ten million underage workers. See Matt Moffett, "Working Children: Underage Laborers Fill Mexican Factories," *Wall Street Journal*, April 8, 1991.

5. This is a small sample of the complaints about environmental damage from the *maquiladora*. Details were reported in *In These Times*, May 22, 1991, and "Border Trouble: Rivers in Peril," National Toxics Campaign, May 1991, as well as the *Arizona Republic* series.

6. The Juarez official was quoted by Guadalupe Silva, "Twin Plant Toxics May Reach Water Table," *El Paso Times*, May 21, 1989.

7. Formation of the Coalition for Justice in the *Maquiladoras* was reported in the newsletter of the Federation for Industrial Retention and Renewal, Spring 1991. Coalition members include FIRR, the National Toxics Campaign, the Interfaith Center for Corporate Responsibility, the AFL-CIO and a variety of others.

Some major labor unions such as the food and commercial workers' are beginning to develop their own strategies for cross-border politics with similar unions in Europe, Asia and Latin America, having discovered that they are up against the same companies and similar labor practices, regardless of their own nation.

8. Wolfgang Sachs, of the Essen Institute for Advanced Studies, wrote in *New Perspectives Quarterly*, Spring 1990.

9. Jacques Attali, former advisor to President Mitterrand, wrote in the *New*

Perspectives Quarterly, Spring 1990. W. Michael Blumenthal was quoted in "The Stateless Corporation," *Business Week,* May 14, 1990.

10. Jane Uebelhoer of ACORN testified before the Senate Banking Committee, April 4, 1990.

11. The international agreement signed by the Federal Reserve and other central banks created a system of risk-based capital ratios for banking—capital requirements geared to the level of risk in each bank's portfolio. Housing suffered because the Federal Reserve assigned a 100 percent risk ratio for multifamily projects—a rating identical to the most speculative business loans—which would raise the cost of such lending for banks. The central bank, in effect, had promulgated a credit-allocation policy that would discourage investment in low-income housing—when the nation faced an obvious shortage. Federal regulators claimed that they were bound by international agreement, but the fact is that other nations' central banks were prepared to assign a more favorable risk rating to housing than was the Federal Reserve.

12. Clayton Yeutter was quoted by Mark Ritchie, "Trading Away Our Environment: GATT and Global Harmonization," *Journal of Pesticide Reform,* Fall 1990.

13. Clayton Yeutter's remarks on California's "Prop 65" food-safety law were quoted by David Morris, "Trading Our Future: Talking Back to GATT," Institute for Local Self-Reliance, St. Paul, Minnesota, undated. His comments on the European ban of beef growth hormones are from Mark Ritchie, "Trading Away Our Environment."

14. Details on Codex standards and the influence of American chemical companies are from Eric Christensen, "Food Fight: How GATT Undermines Food Safety Regulations," *Multinational Monitor,* November 1990. The GATT negotiations reached an impasse in early 1991 on other economic issues but presumably will resume.

15. Examples of GATT objections to U.S. state laws were recounted by Bruce Stokes, "State Rules and World Business," *National Journal,* October 27, 1990.

16. The Bush administration, responding to attacks on the "fast track" approach, issued various promises to address the problems of environmental damage and working conditions in the trade negotiations with Mexico, but these were no more than expressions of good intent. The overall effect of the agreement will be to extend the *maquiladora* preferences to all of Mexico—and thus set off another round of U.S. job losses as well as other consequences. In economic terms, the Mexican government expects to gain the U.S. currency income to deal with its foreign debt—a powerful incentive to ignore the ancillary effects on its citizens. In the end, the flight of U.S. jobs to Mexico will directly benefit the U.S. banks— the major banks that loaned tens of billions to Mexico in the first place and would now have some chance of being paid back. Given the timing, the Mexican agreement will probably not reach completion and political debate until sometime after the 1992 election.

17. The mythologies of "free trade" and national sovereignty are examined in a devastating critique by David Morris, "Free Trade: The Great Destroyer," Institute for Local Self-Reliance, January 16, 1988.

In western Europe, where organized labor has a much stronger political position, unions are encountering the same threatening effects of multinational politics that undermined American labor and many of its hard-won protections. In response, European unions have proposed a "social charter" for the European Economic Community that would establish minimum legal requirements on working conditions, social guarantees and other matters for the entire community of nations. The effort has been weakened, however, by political deadlock led by Britain's conservative government, and the new social charter may or may not become a reality.

18. Details on IBM, Whirlpool and GE microwaves are from Robert B. Reich, *The Work of Nations: Preparing Ourselves for 21st Century Capitalism,* Alfred A. Knopf, 1991.

19. The three corporate executives from NCR, Colgate-Palmolive and GE were quoted by David Morris, "Trading Our Future."

20. John Reed's efforts to relocate Citicorp in a foreign country were described as his "pet project" by *The Wall Street Journal,* August 9, 1991. Lloyd Cutler, whose Washington law firm represents Citibank, has proposed a vast recapitalization of commercial banks by the Federal Reserve.

21. The weekly wage average is from *Economic Indicators,* Joint Economics Committee, May 1991. Many families, it is true, manage to make up for the shortfall in various ways, usually by someone else in the family going to work. This exchange of time for money may maintain their financial status for a time, but it also erodes family life.

22. The productivity-wage gap for all employees in business is from *Economic Indicators,* May 1991, Joint Economics Committee. Conservative columnist Warren Brookes has described a much starker disparity for manufacturing workers: Their productivity increased more than 35 percent during the 1980s but their real wages rose only 2.7 percent. This is in contrast to the 1960s, when manufacturing productivity increased by 32 percent and wages rose by 22 percent. See Warren Brookes, *Washington Times,* March 20, 1991.

23. The compensation data are from Robert B. Reich, *The Work of Nations: Preparing Ourselves for 21st Century Capitalism.* Reich described global webs of what he calls "symbolic analysts" linked in common enterprise.

24. The office of U.S. trade representative as a trade school for foreign lobbyists is described in "America's Frontline Trade Officials," Center for Public Integrity, December 1990. Pat Choate detailed Japanese influence in *Agents of Influence: How Japan's Lobbyists in the United States Manipulate America's Political and Economic System,* Alfred A. Knopf, 1990. Karel van Wolferen is quoted by Choate.

25. The contours of the global process were described by the Economic Policy Institute's director, Jeff Faux, "Labor in the New Global Economy," *Dissent,* Summer 1990.

26. The outlines of a global growth strategy based on rising wages and incomes have been described in many places, including my own book, *Secrets of the Temple.* Walter Russell Mead's book, *Mortal Splendor,* and his various essays in

the *World Policy Journal* provide perhaps the most comprehensive and plausible description of the new economic order that the world needs.

27. Lane Kirkland, president of the AFL-CIO, spoke for this idea in terms of labor rights: "A trade policy that encourages or tolerates the spectacle of corporations roaming the world in search of the cheapest and most repressed labor is more perversely protectionist than any tariff or quota, and serves in the last analysis to restrict and undermine markets and lower standards the world over. In the interest of basic fairness and the continued elevation of the human condition, the denial of workers' rights should be clearly defined internationally as the unfair trading practice it is, through the incorporation of a social clause in the General Agreement on Tariffs and Trade." Speech to American International Club of Geneva, June 24, 1991.

CONCLUSION: The American Moment

1. The origin of political movements and the painstaking effort they require of people are explained by Lawrence Goodwyn in his authoritative history of the Populist movement and also in *Breaking the Barrier: The Rise of Solidarity in Poland,* Oxford University Press, 1991. The kind of political development that produces fundamental change requires many years, even decades, to achieve power and is so difficult that throughout history it has regularly failed. For a portrait of contemporary Americans trying to recreate their own politics, see also Harry C. Boyte, *Commonwealth: A Return to Citizen Politics,* The Free Press, 1989.

2. The statement is from Vaclav Havel, *Disturbing the Peace,* Alfred A. Knopf, 1990.

Acknowledgments

Many wise teachers prepared me to write this book, too many to name, but I wish to thank them all. They include active politicians, critical editors and thousands of engaged citizens whom I encountered along the way during three decades as a reporter. My own education in politics was formed not from theory, but mainly from their experiences and insights and the hard questions they asked. This book borrowed freely from them.

I owe a special debt, as should be evident from the text, to the influence of three professional teachers—Lawrence Goodwyn, Theodore Lowi and Thomas Ferguson. Courageous scholars are rarer than courageous politicians, but each of these thinkers has opened important new understandings of American politics by standing outside the confines of conventional academic thinking. The language of "democratic promise" is Goodwyn's. The resonant phrase "How may the people speak to power?" is borrowed from Lowi. My economic analysis of political institutions was enriched by what Tom Ferguson taught me.

Larry Goodwyn, in particular, served as a wise teacher and generous friend in his critical reading of the manuscript. An extended "democratic conversation" ensued between us on the ideas contained in this book, many of which were inspired by Goodwyn's own work on the neglected subject of democratic development. His patient questions and moral support amounted to a great gift from a brilliant teacher. Readers who intend to explore further into the meaning of democracy ought to begin with Goodwyn's engrossing accounts of people in democratic action—*The Populist Moment* and *Breaking the Barrier: The Rise of Solidarity in Poland*.

I am also indebted to my editors at Simon & Schuster, Alice Mayhew and George Hodgman, who brought their own critical talents to this project and, like Larry Goodwyn, challenged my excesses and pushed to make the argument as coherent and direct as possible. I thank as well all of the other people at Simon & Schuster, including especially Marcia Peterson, Sean Devlin, and Stephen Messina for excellent copyediting, and also my agent, Lynn Nesbit, for her support and counsel.

The sum of everything I know about human relationships, how they are nurtured and sustained, I learned from my family—my parents, Harold and Gladys Greider, and Linda Furry Greider, my wife, and my children, Cameron and Katharine, to whom this book is dedicated. The qualities that are missing in politics—loyalty and trust, integrity and courage, honesty and responsibility—I have found in my family. Learning from our children has been the most exalting experience of our lives; it continues in interesting new directions. The relationships they have formed as adults—Katharine with David Ullman Andrews, Cameron with Lalou Lambelet Dammond—enlarge the dimensions of our optimism for the future.

Index